✥✥ Forbes

TRAVEL GUIDE

Formerly Mobil Travel Guide

SOUTH

ACKNOWLEDGMENTS

We gratefully acknowledge the help of our representatives for their efficient and perceptive inspections of the lodgings listed. Forbes Travel Guide is also grateful to the talented writers who contributed to this book.

Some of the information contained herein is derived from a variety of third-party sources. Although every effort has been made to verify the information obtained from such sources, the publisher assumes no responsibility for inconsistencies or inaccuracies in the data or liability for any damages of any type arising from errors or omissions.

Neither the editors nor the publisher assume responsibility for the services provided by any business listed in this guide or for any loss, damage or disruption in your travel for any reason.

SOUTH ★★★★★

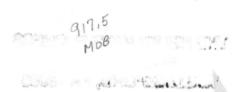

ISBN: 9-780841-61424-6   Manufactured in the USA

10 9 8 7 6 5 4 3 2 1

TABLE OF CONTENTS

SOUTH
★★★★

STAR ATTRACTIONS

If you've been a reader of Mobil Travel Guide, you will have heard that this historic brand partnered with another storied media name, Forbes, in 2009 to create a new entity, Forbes Travel Guide. For more than 50 years, Mobil Travel Guide assisted travelers in making smart decisions about where to stay and dine when traveling. With this new partnership, our mission has not changed: We're committed to the same rigorous inspections of hotels, restaurants and spas—the most comprehensive in the industry with more than 500 standards tested at each property we visit—to help you cut through the clutter and make easy and informed decisions on where to spend your time and travel budget. Our team of anonymous inspectors are constantly on the road, sleeping in hotels, eating in restaurants and making spa appointments, evaluating those exacting standards to determine a property's rating.

What kind of standards are we looking for when we visit a proprety? We're looking for more than just high-thread count sheets, pristine spa treatment rooms and white linen-topped tables. We look for service that's attentive, individualized and unforgettable. We note how long it takes to be greeted when you sit down at your table, or to be served when you order room service, or whether the hotel staff can confidently help you when you've forgotten that one essential item that will make or break your trip. Unlike other travel ratings entities, we visit the places we rate, testing hundreds of attributes to compile our ratings, and our ratings cannot be bought or influenced. The Forbes Five Star rating is the most prestigious achievement in hospitality—while we rate more than 8,000 properties in the U.S., Canada, Hong Kong, Macau and Beijing, for 2010, we have awarded Five Star designations to only 53 hotels, 21 restaurants and 18 spas. When you travel with Forbes, you can travel with confidence, knowing that you'll get the very best experience, no matter who you are.

We understand the importance of making the most of your time. That's why the most trusted name in travel is now Forbes Travel Guide.

STAR RATED HOTELS

Whether you're looking for the ultimate in luxury or the best value for your travel budget, we have a hotel recommendation for you. To help you pinpoint properties that meet your needs, Forbes Travel Guide classifies each lodging by type according to the following characteristics:

★★★★★These exceptional properties provide a memorable experience through virtually flawless service and the finest of amenities. Staff are intuitive, engaging and passionate, and eagerly deliver service above and beyond the guests' expectations. The hotel was designed with the guest's comfort in mind, with particular attention paid to craftsmanship and quality of product. A Five Star property is a destination unto itself.

★★★★These properties provide a distinctive setting, and a guest will find many interesting and inviting elements to enjoy throughout the property. Attention to detail is prominent throughout the property, from design concept to quality of products provided. Staff are accommodating and take pride in catering to the guest's specific needs throughout their stay.

★★★These well-appointed establishments have enhanced amenities that provide travelers with a strong sense of location, whether for style or function. They may have a distinguishing style and ambience in both the public spaces and guest rooms; or they may be more focused on functionality, providing guests with easy access to local events, meetings or tourism highlights.

★★The Two Star hotel is considered a clean, comfortable and reliable establishment that has expanded amenities, such as a full-service restaurant.

★The One Star lodging is a limited-service hotel or inn that is considered a clean, comfortable and reliable establishment.

For every property, we also provide pricing information. All prices quoted are accurate at the time of publication; however, prices cannot be guaranteed.

STAR RATED RESTAURANTS

Every restaurant in this book comes highly recommended as an outstanding dining experience.

★★★★★Forbes Five Star restaurants deliver a truly unique and distinctive dining experience. A Five Star restaurant consistently provides exceptional food, superlative service and elegant décor. An emphasis is placed on originality and personalized, attentive and discreet service. Every detail that surrounds the experience is attended to by a warm and gracious dining room team.

★★★★These are exciting restaurants with often well-known chefs that feature creative and complex foods and emphasize various culinary techniques and a focus on seasonality. A highly-trained dining room staff provides refined personal service and attention.

★★★Three Star restaurants offer skillfully-prepared food with a focus on a specific style or cuisine. The dining room staff provides warm and professional service in a comfortable atmosphere. The décor is well-coordinated with quality fixtures and decorative items, and promotes a comfortable ambience.

★★The Two Star restaurant serves fresh food in a clean setting with efficient service. Value is considered in this category, as is family friendliness.

★The One Star restaurant provides a distinctive experience through culinary specialty, local flair or individual atmosphere.

Because menu prices can fluctuate, we list a pricing range rather than specific prices. The pricing ranges are per diner, and assume that you order an appetizer or dessert, an entrée and one drink.

STAR RATED SPAS

Forbes Travel Guide's spa ratings are based on objective evaluations of more than 450 attributes. About half of these criteria assess basic expectations, such as staff courtesy, the technical proficiency and skill of the employees and whether the facility is clean and maintained properly. Several standards address issues that impact a guest's physical comfort and convenience, as well as the staff's ability to impart a sense of personalized service. Additional criteria measure the spa's ability to create a completely calming ambience.

★★★★★Stepping foot in a Five Star spa will result in an exceptional experience with no detail overlooked. These properties wow their guests with extraordinary design and facilities, and uncompromising service. Expert staff cater to your every whim and pamper you with the most advanced treatments and skin care lines available. These spas often offer exclusive treatments and may emphasize local elements.

★★★★Four Star spas provide a wonderful experience in an inviting and serene environment. A sense of personalized service is evident from the moment you check in and receive your robe and slippers. The guest's comfort is always of utmost concern to the well-trained staff.

★★★These spas offer well-appointed facilities with a full complement of staff to ensure that guests' needs are met. The spa facilities include clean and appealing treatment rooms, changing areas and a welcoming reception desk.

ALABAMA

IF YOU'VE NEVER BEEN TO ALABAMA, YOU'RE IN FOR A SURPRISE. IT IS A SCENIC, VERSATILE place marked by sophisticated cities, diverse geography and Southern charm. From postcard-perfect beaches to the gentle Appalachians, Alabama offers plenty of space for visitors to play outdoors, and its cities and towns chronicle the state's fascinating—if sometimes turbulent—history. Alabama's cultural offerings are as rich as anywhere else in the South: the state lays claim to the famed Alabama Shakespeare Festival, one of the nation's finest year-round theaters; the National Civil Rights Museum, the country's first comprehensive museum dedicated to civil rights history; and countless art museums, musical venues and performing arts groups.

Alabama has the dubious honor of being the birthplace of both the Civil War and the Civil Rights Movement, separated by about 100 years. The order to fire on Fort Sumter—the first shots of the War Between the States—came in April 1861 from Confederate General P.G.T. Beauregard in Montgomery. Alabama contributed between 65,000 and 100,000 troops to the South's efforts. (The white male population at the time was about 500,000.) The state did not see much fighting, and by the late 19th century, it was regaining its economic strength.

Nearly a century after the Civil War, a black seamstress named Rosa Parks refused to give up her bus seat to a white man, thereby sparking the Montgomery Bus Boycott that ignited the civil-rights movement, much of which played out on Alabama soil. Dr. Martin Luther King Jr. preached his first messages of nonviolence in a church in Montgomery, and wrote his "Letter from Birmingham Jail," explaining the importance of street demonstrations to the movement.

Alabama preserves and tells its history with candor and compassion, but its historical legacy stretches beyond these events to quieter stories that bear telling. Helen Keller was born and raised in Tuscumbia, and visitors can see the water pump where her teacher, Anne Sullivan, finally broke through Keller's dark world and taught her how to communicate despite her inability to see, speak or hear. And W.C. Handy, a.k.a. "Father of the Blues," grew up here, giving the South a powerful musical legacy.

Another of the state's important—and obvious—legacies is its link to sports. Bo Jackson, Hank Aaron, Willie Mays, Jesse Owens, Bobby Allison and many more sports icons perfected their swings, sprints and sacks in Alabama. Birmingham's Alabama Sports Hall of Fame celebrates stars from many different games, but football is king here, fueled by a healthy rivalry between Auburn University's Tigers and the University of Alabama's Crimson Tide. Certainly their annual clashes attract many visitors, but even after the season ends, the state has another unique sports draw: the Robert Trent Jones Trail, the largest golf construction project ever undertaken. The project provides 378 holes stretching over more than 100 miles of golf.

So no matter what your pleasure, chances are you'll find it in the Heart of Dixie. History, culture, gorgeous scenery and plenty of places to play—it's all here.

ALEXANDER CITY

See also Montgomery

Know as "Alex City" to the locals, this community—southeast of Birmingham, northeast of Montgomery—is the perfect spot to indulge your inner Gilligan. Lake Martin on the Tallapoosa River is one of the South's finest inland recreation areas.

WHAT TO SEE
WIND CREEK STATE PARK

4325 Highway 128, Alexander City, 256-329-0845; www.dcnr.state.al.us

This 1,445-acre park along Lake Martin's shores offers a prime spot for swimming, boating, camping or just relaxing on the beach. Bathhouses, a marina and ramps, hiking and bike paths, picnic areas, campsites and an observation tower are all at the park. Daily.

WHERE TO STAY
★BEST WESTERN HORSESHOE INN

3146 Highway 280, Alexander City, 256-234-6311, 800-780-7234; www.bestwestern.com

90 rooms. Bar. Complimentary breakfast. Pool. $61-150

★JAMESON INN ALEXANDER CITY

4335 Highway 280, Alexander City, 256-234-7099, 800-526-3766; www.jamesoninns.com

60 rooms. Complimentary breakfast. Fitness center. Pool. $61-150

WHERE TO EAT
★CECIL'S PUBLIC HOUSE

243 Green St., Alexander City, 256-329-0732

Set in a restored turn-of-the-century home, this local favorite offers country staples such as chicken-fried steak and an array of sandwiches. Feeling indulgent? Opt for the chicken margaux or lobster ravioli.
American. Lunch, dinner. $15 and under.

ANNISTON

See also Birmingham

Built on the edge of the Appalachian foothills, Anniston was founded by Samuel Noble, an Englishman who headed the ironworks in Rome, Georgia, and Daniel Tyler, a Connecticut capitalist. They established textile mills and blast furnaces to help launch the South into the Industrial Revolution after the devastation of the Civil War. Today, residents work hard to preserve the town's past by refurbishing storefront façades and historic homes. Stop by for a little small town Southern charm, only 90 miles from Atlanta.

WHAT TO SEE
ANNISTON MUSEUM OF NATIONAL HISTORY

Lagarde Park, 800 Museum Drive, Anniston, 256-237-6766; www.annistonmuseum.org

Where else can you find full-scale models of an Albertosaurus and a meteorite mere feet from Egyptian mummies and a 9-foot-tall termite mound? Located on the 185-acre John B. Lagarde Environmental Interpretative Park, the museum offers nature trails, open-air exhibits and picnic facilities.

Admission: adults $4.50, seniors $4, children 4-17 $3.50, children under 4 free. Tuesday-Saturday, 10 a.m.-5 p.m., Sunday 1-5 p.m.

BERMAN MUSEUM
Lagarde Park, 840 Museum Drive, Anniston, 205-237-6261; www.bermanmuseum.org
Need your James Bond fix? Check out these unique artifacts, collected by a real spy from his treks all over the world. The museum features paintings by European and American artists, historical documents, art from Asia and treasures from the American West and World War II eras, including a Royal Persian Scimitar encrusted with 1,295 rose-cut diamonds, 60 carats of rubies and a single 40-carat emerald set in three pounds of gold.
Admission: adults $5, seniors $4.50, children 4-17 $4, children under 4 free. September-May, Tuesday-Saturday 10 a.m.-5 p.m., Sunday 1-5 p.m.; June-August, Monday-Saturday 10 a.m.-5 p.m., Sunday 1-5 p.m.

CHURCH OF ST. MICHAEL AND ALL ANGELS
1000 W. 18th St. and Cobb Avenue, Anniston, 256-237-4011; www.stmaaa.org
Celebrated for its architectural beauty and historical significance, St. Michael's boasts, among other wonders, a 95-foot bell tower and a 12-foot Carrara marble altar, imported in the late 1800s from England and Italy.
Daily 8 a.m.-4 p.m.

COLDWATER COVERED BRIDGE
Coldwater, three miles south via Highway 431, five miles West on Highway 78 at Oxford Lake and Civic Center
Built before 1850, this bridge is one of 13 restored covered bridges in Alabama.

WHERE TO STAY
★★AMERICA'S BEST VALUE INN-RIVERSIDE/PELL CITY
11900 Highway 78, Riverside, 205-338-3381; www.americasbestvalueinn.com
70 rooms. Restaurant. Pool. $61-150

★BAYMONT INN AND SUITES OXFORD
1600 Highway 21 S., Oxford, 256-835-1492, 877-229-6668;www.baymontinns.com
129 rooms. Complimentary breakfast. Business center. Fitness center. Pool. $61-150

★★★THE VICTORIA COUNTRY INN
1604 Quintard Ave., Anniston, 256-236-0503, 800-260-8781; www.thevictoria.com
Built in 1888, this beautifully restored country inn is a wonderful example of early Victorian architecture. Enjoy comfortable rooms, fine dining and a piano lounge.
60 rooms. Restaurant. $61-150

WHERE TO EAT
★BETTY'S BAR-B-Q
401 S. Quintard Ave., Anniston, 256-237-1411
American. Lunch, dinner. Closed Sunday. $15 and under.

★★THE VICTORIA
1604 Quintard Ave., Anniston, 256-236-0503; www.thevictoria.com
American. Dinner. Closed Sunday. $36-85

AUBURN
See also Tuskegee
Home to Auburn University and its 23,000 students from across the globe, Auburn is a quintessential college town. School spirit is practically a religion here, especially during football season. The rest of the year, public parks, golf courses and a historic downtown shopping district offer plenty of fun to keep residents and visitors entertained. Keep an eye out for the town's rich architectural history on display, including examples of Greek Revival, Victorian and early 20th-century buildings.

WHAT TO SEE
AUBURN UNIVERSITY
202 Mary Martin Hall, Auburn, 334-844-4000; www.auburn.edu
Alabama's first four-year institution to admit women on an equal basis with men, Auburn is a university steeped in campus traditions and lore. One example: local legend suggests that the school's famous "War Eagle" battle cry dates back to 1892—the first time Auburn and the University of Georgia met on the football field. According to the legend, a Civil War veteran brought his pet eagle to the game; all of a sudden, the eagle broke free and circled the field, just about the time Auburn began its steady push toward the end zone. A thrilled crowd began yelling "War Eagle" to cheer on its team. Daily.

CHEWACLA STATE PARK
124 Shell Toomer Parkway, Auburn, 800-252-7275; 334-887-5621; www.alapark.com
The 696-acre park offers a little something for every kind of nature enthusiast. Water lover? Rent a boat and fish in Chewacla Lake. Landlubber? Opt for a hike on the trails and a picnic. Facilities include bathhouses, a playground, concessions, campgrounds and newly renovated cabins. Daily.

JOHN B. LOVELACE MUSEUM
Donahue Drive and Stamboard Avenue, Auburn, 334-844-0764; www.lovelacemuseum. com
This orange and blue shrine pays homage to famous Auburn University athletes, such as Bo Jackson and Charles Barkley. Interactive exhibits change frequently.
Monday-Friday 8 a.m.-4.30 p.m., Saturday 9 a.m.-4 p.m.

WHERE TO STAY
★★LEXINGTON HOTEL UNIVERSITY CONVENTION CENTER
1577 S. College St., Auburn, 800-282-8763; www.lexingtonhotels.com
100 rooms. Restaurant, bar. Complimentary breakfast. Fitness center. Pool. $61-150

★★★THE HOTEL AT AUBURN UNIVERSITY
241 S. College St., Auburn, 334-821-8200, 800-228-2876; www.auhcc.com
Located near the university and downtown Auburn, this hotel and conference

center offers elegant Southern hospitality. Guest rooms have been newly renovated and include granite vanities, plasma TVs and plush bedding. Golfers should take advantage of the hotel's privileges at the private Auburn University Golf Club.

248 rooms. Restaurant, bar. Fitness center. Pool. $61-150

BESSEMER

See also Birmingham, Tuscaloosa

Founded in 1887 and named for a scientist who invented the steel-making process, Bessemer has a long history of manufacturing iron and steel, explosives and building materials. Today, this town of about 30,000 residents is a growing suburb of Birmingham. Its downtown core is listed on the National Register of Historic Districts.

WHAT TO SEE
ALABAMA ADVENTURE THEME PARK

4599 Alabama Adventure Parkway, Bessemer, 205-481-4750; www.alabamaadventure. com

Satisfy your inner wild child with a ride on Rampage, one of the nation's oldest and fastest wooden roller coasters in the park's Magic City USA. Or cool off on the slides at Splash Beach, the adjacent water park. The summer concert series features famous Alabama natives.

Admission: adults $34.99, seniors and children 2-18 $24.99, children under 2 free. May-September, hours vary.

HALL OF HISTORY MUSEUM

1905 Alabama Ave., Bessemer, 205-426-1633; www.bessemerhallofhistory.com

Housed in a former train terminal (Southern Railway Depot), the museum tells the story of Bessemer's triumphs and trials. Exhibits are updated throughout the year.

Tuesday-Saturday 9 a.m.-noon, 1-4 p.m.

TANNEHILL IRONWORKS STATE HISTORICAL PARK

12632 Confederate Parkway, McCalla, 205-477-5711; www.tannehill.org

If you've ever wondered what life might have been like in the height of Alabama's 19th-century iron boom, visit Tannehill to find out. In addition to the park's 1,500 acres for hiking and camping, the restored pioneer cabins house artisans. From fall to spring, you can catch the blacksmith and miller hard at work. The park features bathhouses, fishing, nature trails, picnicking, concessions and camp grounds. Daily.

WHERE TO EAT
★BOB SYKES BAR-B-Q

1724 9th Ave. N., Bessemer, 205-426-1400; www.bobsykes.com

Barbecue. Lunch, dinner. Closed Sunday. $15 and under.

BIRMINGHAM

See also Bessemer, Cullman, Talladega

Alabama's largest city, Birmingham has found a way to preserve its history and still give off an air of urban sophistication—a combination that appeals to visitors and residents alike. Beautiful city streets, stylish boutiques and restaurants and diverse cultural attractions make Birmingham a must-see stop on any trek through central Alabama.

Founded in 1871 and named for a British industrial city, Birmingham started out as a center of steel production. The late 19th century brought disease and a nationwide financial panic that almost ruined Birmingham, but the city boomed in the early years of the 20th century. Just as Birmingham was enjoying a streak of prosperity after the end of World War I, a secret white supremacist group, the Ku Klux Klan, garnered power, leading to violence against African-American citizens that lasted for decades.

Not surprisingly, Birmingham served as the setting for many battles during the Civil Rights Movement, including of course, Dr. Martin Luther King Jr.'s "Letter from Birmingham Jail," written April 16, 1963. In it, King explains why the demonstrations in the streets of Birmingham and other Southern cities were crucial to the fight for civil rights for African-Americans. Several months later, on September 15, 1963, a member of the Ku Klux Klan bombed Birmingham's 16th Street Baptist Church, killing four girls. The emotional response to the bombing galvanized the movement and helped lead to the passage of the 1964 Civil Rights Act.

By the 1970s, Birmingham was booming again, and in 1979, its citizens elected the city's first black mayor, Dr. Richard Arrington Jr. Today, Birmingham is not only a rich historic area, it is also home to the University of Alabama Medical Center, which attracts patients from all over the world and beefs up the local economy.

By day, soak up Birmingham's history, and by night, swing by Five Points South, Birmingham's entertainment district, where you'll find great people-watching, fine dining and clubs to satisfy even the pickiest music aficionados.

WHAT TO SEE
ALABAMA SPORTS HALL OF FAME MUSEUM
2150 Richard Arrington Jr. Blvd. N., Birmingham, 205-323-6665; www.ashof.org
The museum celebrates sports heroes from the Heart of Dixie, including Willie Mays, Carl Lewis and Jesse Owens. See vintage equipment and uniforms, awards and photographs, and interactive kiosks and life-sized sculptures.
Admission: adults $5, seniors $4, students $3. Monday-Saturday 9 a.m.-5 p.m., Sunday 1-5 p.m.

ARLINGTON ANTEBELLUM HOME AND GARDENS
331 Cotton Ave. S.W., Birmingham, 205-780-5656; www.birminghamal.gov
Visit Birmingham's last remaining antebellum house in the Greek Revival style, built circa 1850 on a sloping hill in Elyton. The oak and magnolia trees that surround the house suggest that Rhett Butler might stroll by any minute.
Admission: adults $5, students $3. Tuesday-Saturday 10 a.m.-4 p.m., Sunday 1-4 p.m.

DOWNTOWN BIRMINGHAM

Birmingham, home of the Civil Rights Institute, offers a powerful lesson about African-American history and culture.

Start at the Historical Fourth Avenue Visitor Center (319 17th St. N., 205-328-1850), where you can pick up a map or take a guided tour of the historic African-American business district.

Across the street from the visitor center is the Alabama Jazz Hall of Fame, located within the historic Carver Theater (1631 Fourth Ave. N., 205-254-2731). Exhibits cover the history of jazz and celebrate such artists as Dinah Washington, Nat King Cole, Duke Ellington and W.C. Handy, among others. The theater also hosts live performances. On the other side of the visitor center, the Alabama Theater (1817 3rd Ave. N.) has been restored to its 1920s splendor and is now a cinema.

Head west along Third Avenue one block to La Vase (328 16th St. N., 205-801-5165), a restaurant that serves hearty home-style soul food. After your meal, trek north up 16th Street three blocks to Kelly Ingram Park, the scene of civil-rights clashes in the 1950s and 1960s.

The Birmingham Civil Rights Institute (520 16th St., 205-328-9696), across the street from the park, is the city's premier attraction. A short film introduces the city's history, and vintage footage illustrates the Jim Crow era and the development of the civil-rights movement. Exhibits emphasize Birmingham's role—positive and negative—in the Civil Rights Movement, and the bookshop has a good selection of African-American history and heritage titles.

Cross Sixth Avenue to reach the 16th Street Baptist Church (1530 6th Ave. N., 205-251-9402), where four girls were killed when a Ku Klux Klan member bombed the church in 1963. The rebuilt church hosts tens of thousands of visitors each year.

BIRMINGHAM BOTANICAL GARDENS

2612 Lane Park Road, Birmingham, 205-414-3900; www.bbgardens.org

Much more than just flowers, the botanical gardens offers tours, a garden maintained by the green thumbs at Southern Living magazine and a full calendar of events and classes. Don't miss the Japanese Garden, offering a bonsai collection and an authentic Japanese teahouse. And if you get hungry, there's a restaurant on the grounds.

Daily sunrise-sunset.

BIRMINGHAM CIVIL RIGHTS INSTITUTE

520 16th St. N., Birmingham, 205-328-9696, 866-328-9696; www.bcri.org

Exhibits and multimedia presentations portray the struggle for Civil Rights in Birmingham and across the nation from the 1920s to the present. "The March" exhibit in the Movement Gallery is particularly poignant as it uses audio and video to examine the March on Washington.

Admission: adults $11, seniors and students $5, children 4-12 $3, Tuesday-Saturday 10 a.m.-5 p.m., Sunday 1-5 p.m.

BIRMINGHAM-JEFFERSON CONVENTION COMPLEX

2100 Richard Arrington Jr. Blvd., Birmingham, 205-458-8400; www.bjcc.org

This complex covers seven square blocks and hosts events such as hunting expos, classic theatrical performances and sports tournaments. The center contains 220,000 square feet of exhibition space, a 3,000-seat concert hall, a 1,000-seat theater and an 18,000-seat coliseum.

BIRMINGHAM MUSEUM OF ART

2000 Rev Abraham Woods Jr. Blvd.., Birmingham, 205-254-2565; www.artsbma.org

Celebrated for its diverse collections, the museum is home to some 24,000 objects from almost every era of artistic production across the globe. Don't miss its collection of Asian art, including a 15th-century temple mural from China; its decorative arts, including the largest collection of Wedgwood outside of England; and the historical and contemporary work from Native American artists.

Tuesday-Saturday 10 a.m.-5 p.m., Sunday noon-5 p.m.

BIRMINGHAM-SOUTHERN COLLEGE

900 Arkadelphia Road, Birmingham, 205-226-4600; www.bsc.edu

A favorite of college guides, BSC boasts a pristine 192-acre campus on wooded rolling hills. Stop to see the Robert R. Meyer Planetarium, Alabama's first. Daily.

BIRMINGHAM ZOO

2630 Cahaba Road, Birmingham, 205-879-0409; www.birminghamzoo.com

Where else in Alabama can you see an Indochinese tiger, a red panda and a host of sea lions within a few acres of one another? Nurture your wild side by checking out the nearly 800 animals that reside here.

Admission: adults $12, seniors and children 2-12 $7, children under 2 free. Daily 9 a.m.-5 p.m.

MCWANE SCIENCE CENTER

200 19th St. N., Birmingham, 205-714-8300; www.mcwane.org

A natural history museum on the slopes of Red Mountain, the McWane Science Center offers plenty of adventure: explore the universe at the Challenger Learning Center, catch a flick on the five-story IMAX screen or visit with sea creatures at the center's World of Water Aquarium. Don't miss the walkway carved into the face of the mountain above the expressway, where you'll see more than 150 million years of geologic history. You also can do some picnicking there.

Admission: adults $11, seniors and children 2-12 $8, children under 2 free. September-May, Monday-Friday 9 a.m.-5 p.m., Saturday 10 a.m.-6 p.m., Sunday noon-6 p.m.; June-August, Monday-Saturday 10 a.m.-6 p.m., Sunday noon-6 p.m.

MILES COLLEGE

5500 Myron Massey Blvd., Fairfield, 205-929-1000; www.miles.edu

Miles College boasts an extensive collection of African-American literature, exhibits of African art forms and two historic landmark buildings. Daily.

OAK MOUNTAIN STATE PARK

200 Terrace Drive, Pelham, 205-620-2520; www.alapark.com

Peavine Falls and Gorge and two lakes sit amid 9,940 acres of the state's most rugged mountains. Enthusiasts cite Oak Mountain as one of the state's best places to mountain bike. Other activities include fishing, boating, hiking, backpacking, bridle trails, golf, tennis, picnicking, concessions, camping,

cabins and a demonstration farm.
Admission: adults $2, seniors and children $1. Daily.

RICKWOOD CAVERNS STATE PARK
370 Rickwood Park Road, Warrior, 205-647-9692; www.dcnr.state.al.us
Tour the "miracle mile," a stretch of colorful underground caverns that reveals 260-year-old limestone foundations. The 380-acre park also boasts an Olympic-sized swimming pool, hiking trails, a miniature train ride, carpet golf, a gift shop, concessions, picnic areas and camp sites.
Admission: $1, children under 6 free. Daily.

RUFFNER MOUNTAIN NATURE CENTER
1214-81st St. S., Birmingham, 205-833-8264; www.ruffnermountain.org
A 1,011-acre natural retreat from the bustle of Birmingham, the mountain offers 11 miles of hiking trails. Learn about the mountain's biology, geology and history at the center and then venture out to see Alabama wildlife.
Tuesday-Saturday 9 a.m.-5 p.m., Sunday 1-5 p.m.

SAMFORD UNIVERSITY
800 Lakeshore Drive, Birmingham, 205-726-2011; www.samford.edu
Stroll across Samford's 172-acre campus to see brick Georgian Colonial buildings, and then duck into the Rotunda to see the Samford Murals. Don't miss the Beeson Divinity Hall Chapel's copper-clad dome with a detailed ceiling mural on the interior. Daily.

SLOSS FURNACES NATIONAL HISTORIC LANDMARK
20 32nd St. N., Birmingham, 205-324-1911; www.slossfurnaces.com
Don't let the name fool you: this industrial museum offers more than a glimpse at old furnaces. Here you'll find captivating stories about the economic and social growth of the South. But beware: paranormal investigators have suggested that it is one of nation's most haunted places, so watch out for the ghosts of old workers.
Tuesday-Friday 10 a.m.-4 p.m, Sunday noon-4 p.m.

SOUTHERN MUSEUM OF FLIGHT/ALABAMA AVIATION HALL OF FAME
4343 73rd St. N., Birmingham, 205-833-8226; www.southernmuseumofflight.org
View a full-size Wright Flyer replica, try your hand at flying in two U.S. Air Force fighter jet cockpit simulators and wander through flight-related memorabilia.
Admission: adults $5, seniors and students $4, military and children under 4 free. Tuesday-Saturday 9:30 a.m.-4:30 p.m.

UNIVERSITY OF ALABAMA AT BIRMINGHAM
1400 University Blvd., Birmingham, 205-934-4011; www.uab.edu
Known for its excellent medical and technological programs, the UAB is home to more than 18,000 students. Reynolds Historical Library in the Lister Hill Library of the Health Sciences has collections of ivory anatomical mannequins, original manuscripts, and more than 13,000 rare medical and

scientific books; Alabama Museum of Health Sciences has memorabilia of Alabama doctors, surgeons and other medical practitioners as well as reproductions of turn-of-the-century doctors' and dentists' offices. Daily.

VULCAN
1701 Valley View Drive, Birmingham, 205-933-1409; www.visitvulcan.com
Vulcan, Roman god of fire and forge, legendary inventor of smithing and metalworking, stands as a monument to the city's iron industry atop Red Mountain. Since 1939, he has held a lighted torch aloft over the city from his perch on a 124-foot pedestal making him the largest cast iron statue in the world. A glass-enclosed elevator takes passengers to an observation deck. Vulcan's torch shines bright red for 24 hours after a traffic fatality in the city.
Admission: adults $6, seniors $5, children 5-12 $4, children under 5 free. Park: Daily 7 a.m.-10 p.m. Museum: Monday-Saturday 10 a.m.-6 p.m., Sunday 1-6 p.m.

SPECIAL EVENTS
CITY STAGES
1929 Third Ave. N., Birmingham, 205-251-1272; www.citystages.org
Billed as "Birmingham's World-Class Music Festival," City Stages features approximately 160 musical performances on 11 stages. Artists include both local and nationally known musicians, such as George Clinton, Al Green and Kid Rock.
Third weekend in June.

INTERNATIONAL FESTIVAL
205 20th St. N., Birmingham, 205-252-7652; www.bic-al.org
Each year, the Birmingham International Festival highlights the culture of a different country to promote education as well as business and trade relationships between Alabama and the selected country. A party early in the year kicks off a series of events to take place in the months to follow, which includes a trade expo, conferences, art exhibits, lectures and a black-tie dinner. The free educational programs bring musicians, performers and storytellers to Alabama schools.
February-May.

WHERE TO STAY
★★CLARION HOTEL
5216 Messer Airport Highway, Birmingham, 205-591-7900; www.clarionhotel.com
196 rooms. Restaurant, bar. Complimentary breakfast. Fitness center. Pool. $61-150

★★COURTYARD BIRMINGHAM HOMEWOOD
500 Shades Creek Parkway, Homewood, 205-879-0400, 800-321-2211; www.courtyard.com
140 rooms. Restaurant, bar. Fitness center. Pool. $61-150

★★EMBASSY SUITES

2300 Woodcrest Place, Birmingham, 205-879-7400, 800-362-2779;
www.embassy-suites.com

243 suites. Restaurant, bar. Complimentary breakfast. Business center. Fitness center. Pool. $61-150

★★★HAMPTON INN & SUITES BIRMINGHAM-DOWNTOWN-TUTWILER

2021 Park Place N., Birmingham, 205-322-2100, 877-999-3223; hamptoninn.hilton.com
The rooms in this comfortable hotel are big (choose between rooms with one king-sized bed or two queens), and amenities include 32-inch TVs, DVD players and plush duvets. You're also near golfing and local attractions such as the Civil Rights Institute.

149 rooms. Restaurant, bar. Complimentary breakfast. Business center. Fitness center. $251-350

★HAMPTON INN BIRMINGHAM-COLONNADE

3400 Colonnade Parkway, Birmingham, 205-967-0002, 800-861-7168;
www.hamptoninn.com

133 rooms. Complimentary breakfast. Business center. Fitness center. Pool. $61-150

★★★HILTON BIRMINGHAM PERIMETER PARK

8 Perimeter Park S., Birmingham, 205-967-2700, 800-774-1500; www.hilton.com
Located in an up-and-coming business and entertainment area, this large hotel is near Birmingham's downtown cultural and corporate destinations, making it an idea property for business travelers. Among the amenities in the attractive rooms are work desks, dual phone lines and wireless Internet access.

205 rooms. Restaurant, bar. Business center. Fitness center. $61-150

★LA QUINTA INN BIRMINGHAM

513 Cahaba Park Circle, Birmingham, 205-995-9990, 877-229-6668; www.lq.com
99 rooms. Complimentary breakfast. $61-151

★★★MARRIOTT BIRMINGHAM

3590 Grandview Parkway, Birmingham, 205-968-3775, 800-228-9290;
www.marriott.com

A mix of cozy and contemporary furnishings gives this hotel, just off Highway 280, an inviting and comfortable feel. Friendly staff, a huge array of amenities and a location close to many business headquarters and entertainment options make the Marriott a prime choice.

295 rooms. Restaurant, bar. Business center. $151-250

★★QUALITY INN BIRMINGHAM

1485 Montgomery Highway, Birmingham, 205-823-4300, 800-228-5151;
www.qualityinn.com

166 rooms. Restaurant, bar. Complimentary breakfast. Pool. $61-150

★★THE REDMONT HOTEL & RESIDENCES

2101 Fifth Ave., Birmingham, 205-324-2101, 800-536-2083; www.theredmont.com

114 rooms. Restaurant, bar. Business center. Fitness center. $61-150

★★RIME GARDEN INN & SUITES

5320 Beacon Drive, Birmingham, 205-951-1200, 888-828-1768; www.rimehotel.com

290 rooms. Restaurant, bar. Complimentary breakfast. Business center. Fitness center. Pool. $61-150

★★★SHERATON BIRMINGHAM HOTEL

2101 Richard Arrington Jr. Blvd. N., Birmingham, 205-324-5000, 800-325-3535;
www.sheraton.com

Located in downtown Birmingham, this hotel is a short stroll on the skywalk to the convention center. Explore the zoo, the art museum and Five Points South historical district nearby.

770 rooms. Restaurant, bar. Business center. Fitness center. Pool. $151-250

★★★THE WYNFREY HOTEL

1000 Riverchase Galleria, Birmingham, 205-987-1600, 800-996-3739;
www.wynfrey.com

The Wynfrey Hotel is one of Birmingham's best lodging options. Located on the edge of the city, this gracious hotel combines Southern hospitality with European panache. The rooms and suites offer comfort, style and plenty of amenities. The hotel is a favorite destination of shoppers, with special access to the city's renowned Riverchase Galleria. After a day of bargain hunting, guests retire to the Spa Japonika to recharge and relax, or enjoy a meal at one of the hotel's three restaurants.

329 rooms. Restaurant, bar. Business center. Fitness center. Pool. Spa. $151-250

WHERE TO EAT

★GOLDEN CITY CHINESE RESTAURANT

4647 Highway 280, Birmingham, 205-991-3197

Chinese. Lunch, dinner. $16-35

★★★HIGHLANDS

2011 11th Ave. S., Birmingham, 205-939-1400; www.highlandsbarandgrill.com

This French bistro has been one of Birmingham's premiere restaurants for many years. The food has a southern emphasis, which has become the chef's signature style. The duck two ways is particularly tasty, served with pearl onions, local turnips and sweet peas in a warm sherry sauce.

French. Dinner. Closed Sunday-Monday. $36-85

★★NIKI'S WEST

233 Finley Ave. W., Birmingham, 205-252-5751; www.nikiswest.com

American. Lunch, dinner. Closed Sunday. $16-35

CULLMAN
See also Birmingham, Decatur

Col. John G. Cullmann, a German immigrant whose dream was to build a self-sustaining colony of other German refugees and immigrants, founded Cullman in the early 1870s. In 1873, five German families settled on the 5,400 square miles of land he had purchased from the Louisville & Nashville Railroad. Notice the town's 100-foot-wide streets, a gift from Cullmann when he laid out the town. Today, Cullman is part of metropolitan Birmingham.

WHAT TO SEE
AVE MARIA GROTTO
1600 St. Bernard Drive S.E., Cullman, 256-734-4110; www.avemariagrotto.com

Brother Joseph Zoettl, a Benedictine monk, spent nearly 50 years building some 150 miniature replicas of famous churches, buildings and shrines, including the Basilica of St. Peter's, the California missions and famous buildings from Jerusalem and the Holy Land, using such materials as cement, stone, bits of jewelry and marble. The miniatures cover 4 acres of a terraced, landscaped garden.

Admission: adults $7, seniors $5, children 6-12 $4.50, children under 6 free. April-September, daily 8 a.m.-6 p.m.; October-March, daily 8 a.m.-5 p.m.

CLARKSON COVERED BRIDGE
Highway 278 W., Cullman, 256-734-3369; www.cullmancountyparks.com

One of the largest covered bridges in Alabama, the truss-styled Clarkson is 270 feet long and 50 feet high. The site of the Civil War Battle of Hog Mountain, the bridge is now on the National Register of Historic Places. It also offers a dogtrot cabin and gristmill, a nature trail and picnic facilities. Daily.

HURRICANE CREEK PARK
22600 U.S. Highway 31, Vinemont, 256-734-2125;
www.hurricanecreek.homestead.com

Come see the park's 500-foot-deep gorge with an observation platform, trail over the swinging bridge, unusual rock formations, earthquake fault and waterfalls. Picnic tables are available if you want to make a day of it.

Admission: adults $3, children $2.50. Wednesday-Friday, noon-5 p.m., Saturday-Sunday 9 a.m.-5 p.m.

SPORTSMAN LAKE PARK
1536 Sportsman Lake Road N.W., Cullman, 256-734-3052;
www.cullmancountyparks.com

Stocked with bream, bass, catfish and other fish, this appropriately-named lake also offers land-based activities such as miniature golf, kiddie rides, picnicking and camping. Daily.

WILLIAM B. BANKHEAD NATIONAL FOREST
Highway 278, Double Springs, 205-489-5111; www.fs.fed.us/r8/alabama

A place primed for adventure, the 180,000 acres contain bubbling streams, diverse wildlife and plenty of space to wander. The forest's crown jewel is Sipsey Wilderness, often called the "Land of a Thousand Waterfalls." Trek through the Sipsey to find the state's last remaining stand of old-growth hard-wood. There is also swimming, fishing, boating, hiking and horseback riding available. Daily.

WHERE TO EAT
★★ALL STEAK
314 Second Ave. Southwest, Cullman, 256-734-4322; www.theallsteak.com
Seafood, steak. Breakfast, lunch, dinner. Children's menu. $16-35

DAUPHIN ISLAND
See also Mobile
A barrier island with white sandy beaches and about 1,200 residents, Dauphin Island is rich in history. Native Americans first inhabited the island and built shell middens from discarded oyster shells and other waste from the sea. The Shell Mound still stands as a testament to Native American presence on the island. Later, Spaniards visited and mapped the area in the 16th century. French explorer Pierre le Moyne, Sieur d'Iberville, used the island as his base for a short time in 1699 as he scouted out French Louisiana. Today, the island is part of Mobile County and a playground for its citizens. It is also a haven for birds; a 60-acre sanctuary is home to many local and migratory species.

Reach Dauphin Island from the north on Highway 193, via a four-mile-long, high-rise bridge and causeway that crosses Grants Pass. The island also has a 3,000-foot paved airstrip. A ferry service to Fort Morgan operates year-round.

WHAT TO SEE
FORT GAINES
109 Bienville Blvd., Dauphin Island, 251-861-3607; www.dauphinisland.org
This five-sided fort was begun in 1821 and completed in the 1850s. Union forces captured the fort from the Confederates on August 23, 1864. Check out the museum on the premises. Daily.

DAUPHIN ISLAND CAMPGROUND
Dauphin Island, 251-861-2742; www.dauphinisland.org
A private path leads to secluded Gulf beaches, fishing piers and boat launches; a hiking trail brings you to the Audubon Bird Sanctuary. The campground also has recreation areas and tent and trailer sites. Daily.

DECATUR
See also Athens, Cullman, Huntsville
Decatur, center of northern Alabama's mountain lakes recreation area, is a thriving manufacturing and market city with historic districts and sprawling public parks.

President Monroe selected the town site in 1820, and Decatur, named for U.S. naval officer Commodore Stephen Decatur, was born. The Civil War was hard on the town, which found itself seesawing between invasion and resistance, frequently attacked and then abandoned. Only three buildings were left standing at war's end.

On the edge of the Tennessee River, Decatur today is a busy port and a bustling town where residents and visitors enjoy the area's many recreational activities.

WHAT TO SEE
MOORESVILLE
Six miles east on Highway 20, 413 N. Main St., Mooresville, 704-663-3800; www.mooresvillealabama.com/

History buffs must visit Mooresville for a glimpse of the South circa 1818. The state's oldest incorporated town, Mooresville is (not surprisingly) home to Alabama's oldest operational post office, which has original wooden call boxes and still hand-stamps the mail. Ghosts of presidents past linger here: President Andrew Johnson was a tailor's apprentice before his rise to the presidency, and President James Garfield preached here during the Civil War. Daily.

OLD DECATUR AND ALBANY HISTORIC DISTRICTS
719 Sixth Ave. S.E., Decatur, 256-350-2028; www.historicalbanyalabama.com

The walking tour of this Victorian neighborhood begins at the restored Old Bank on historic Bank Street and includes three antebellum and 194 Victorian structures. During the holiday season, there is a fantastic Christmas Tour of Homes through Albany and Old Decatur.

POINT MALLARD PARK
2901 Point Mallard Drive, Decatur, 256-341-4900, 800-350-3000; www.pointmallardpark.com

On the Tennessee River, this 500-acre park offers plenty of family fun. It includes a swimming pool, wave pool, water slide, beach, hiking and biking trails, an 18-hole golf course, tennis courts, an indoor ice rink, camping and a recreation center. Daily.

PRINCESS THEATRE
112 Second Ave. N.E., Decatur, 256-350-1745; www.princesstheatre.org

The renovated Art Deco-style theater features musical and dramatic performances and children's theater. The historic building also offers tours, which take you backstage and around the property. Daily.

WHEELER NATIONAL WILDLIFE REFUGE
2700 Refuge Headquarters Road, Decatur, 256-353-7243; wheeler.fws.gov

At 34,500 acres, this is Alabama's oldest and largest wildlife refuge. It's a wintering ground for waterfowl and home to numerous species of animal and plant life. Fishing, boating, picnicking, bird study and photography are available here. There's a visitor center and Waterfowl Observation Building as well.

March-September, Tuesday-Saturday 9 a.m.-4 p.m.; October-February, daily 9 a.m.-5 p.m.

SPECIAL EVENTS
ALABAMA JUBILEE HOT AIR BALLOON CLASSIC
Point Mallard Park, 1800 Point Mallard Drive S.E., Decatur, 800-232-5449, 256-350-2028; www.alabamajubilee.net
Since its beginnings in 1977, the Alabama Jubilee has become one of the most popular events in the state. Over the three-day Memorial Day weekend, more than 50,000 spectators gather to watch 60 pilots compete in five hot-air balloon races. The festival also offers a fireworks display, an antique tractor and classic car shows, entertainment and arts and crafts.
Memorial Day weekend.

CIVIL WAR REENACTMENT/SEPTEMBER SKIRMISH
Point Mallard Park, 1800 Point Mallard Drive S.E., Decatur, 800-524-6181; www.decaturcvb.org
This historical reenactment is held in honor of Confederate Generals "Fighting Joe" Wheeler and John Hunt. Events include craft fairs, displays of Civil War relics, a living history of daily camp life and battles between Confederate and Union "troops" dressed in authentic Civil War uniforms.
Labor Day weekend.

RACKING HORSE WORLD CELEBRATION
Celebration Arena, 67 Horse Center Road, Decatur, 256-353-7225; www.rackinghorse.com
Horses show off their high-stepping four-beat gait at this annual competition.
Last full week in September.

SOUTHERN WILDLIFE FESTIVAL
6250 Highway 31, Decatur, 800-524-6181; www.decaturcvb.org
The fest holds competitions and exhibits of wildlife carvings, artwork, photography and duck calling.
Third weekend in October.

SPIRIT OF AMERICA FESTIVAL
Point Mallard Park, 1800 Point Mallard Drive S.E., Decatur, 800-232-5449, 256-350-2028; www.spiritofamericafestival.com
One of the South's largest free Fourth of July celebrations, the Spirit of America Festival offers games, contests, a beauty pageant, concerts, exhibits and fireworks.
Early July.

WHERE TO STAY
★★COUNTRY INN & SUITES BY CARLSON DECATUR
807 Bank St. N.E., Decatur, 256-355-6800, 800-456-4000, 888-201-1746; www.countryinns.com
110 rooms. Restaurant, bar. Complimentary breakfast. Fitness center. Pool.
$61-150

WHERE TO EAT
★★SIMP MCGHEE'S
725 Bank St., Decatur, 256-353-6284; www.simpmcghees.com
Cajun/Creole, seafood. Dinner. Closed Sunday. $16-35

DOTHAN
See also Ozark

The self-proclaimed "Peanut Capital of the World," Dothan has more going for it than just nuts. It's enjoying an economic boom, thanks to growth in retail shops and restaurants. And its prime locale—almost equidistant from Atlanta, Birmingham, Jacksonville and Mobile—makes it a popular stop for visitors, so local businesses cater to out-of-towners.

WHAT TO SEE
ADVENTURELAND THEME PARK
3738 W. Main St., Dothan, 334-793-9100; www.adventurelandthemepark.com
A kid's dream, this park offers two 18-hole miniature golf courses, a go-cart track, bumper boats, batting cages, a snack bar and a game room. November-March, Monday-Friday noon-10 p.m., Saturday 10 a.m.-midnight, -Sunday noon-10 p.m.; April-October, Monday-Saturday 10 a.m.-midnight, Sunday noon-midnight.

LANDMARK PARK
430 Landmark Drive, Dothan, 334-794-3452; www.landmarkpark.com
This 100-acre park features a living-history farm from the 1890s, a natural science and history center, turn-of-the-century buildings (including a drug store with an old-fashioned soda fountain). Star gaze in the planetarium or meander along the nature trails and elevated boardwalk.
Admission: adults $6, children 4-15 $3, children under 4 free. Monday-Saturday 9 a.m.-5 p.m., Sunday noon-6 p.m.

OPERA HOUSE
115 N. St. Andrews St., Dothan, 334-615-4376
Built in 1915 and recently refurbished, this 590-seat theater hosts concerts, dance recitals and choral performances. Daily.

WESTGATE PARK
501 Recreation Road, Dothan, 334-615-3760
This recreation complex has a little something for everyone. Water World water park offers a children's pool, triple-flume slide and wave pool. The recreation center has an indoor pool and ball fields, and tennis, racquetball and basketball courts.
May-August, daily.

SPECIAL EVENTS
AZALEA DOGWOOD FESTIVAL
Dothan Garden District, Dothan, 334-794-6622; www.dothanalcvb.com
Stroll through residential areas in early spring when the flowers reach peak bloom. Late March.

NATIONAL PEANUT FESTIVAL

National Peanut Festival Fairgrounds, 5622 Highway 231 S., Dothan, 334-793-4323;
www.nationalpeanutfestival.com
Celebrate America's peanuts, half of which are grown within 100 miles of
Dothan. The festival includes entertainment, sports events, arts and crafts,
livestock exhibits and a parade.
Late October-early November.

WHERE TO STAY
★★LA QUINTA INN & SUITES DOTHAN

3593 Ross Clark Circle N.W., Dothan, 334-793-9090, 800-474-7298; www.lq.com
122 rooms. Restaurant. Complimentary breakfast. Pool. $61-150

★★HOLIDAY INN DOTHAN-SOUTH

2195 Ross Clark Circle S.E., Dothan, 334-794-8711, 800-777-6611;
www.holiday-inn.com
144 rooms. Restaurant, bar. Complimentary breakfast. Pool. $61-150

EUFAULA
This city stands on a bluff rising 200 feet above Lake Eufaula, a 45,000-acre
lake known throughout the area for its excellent bass fishing.

WHAT TO SEE
EUFAULA NATIONAL WILDLIFE REFUGE

509 Old Highway 165, Eufaula, 334-687-4065; www.eufaula.fws.gov
Stretching from Alabama to Georgia, the refuge offers a feeding and resting area for waterfowl migrating between the Tennessee Valley and the Gulf
Coast. See ducks, geese, egrets and herons—along with more than 275 other
species of birds. The grounds also boast an observation tower, a nature trail,
hunting, and great photo opps. Daily.

LAKEPOINT RESORT STATE PARK

104 Lakepoint Drive, Eufaula, 334-687-8011; www.dcnr.state.al.us
This 1,220-acre picturesque park rests on the shores of Lake Eufaula. Swimming, fishing, boating, hiking, 18-hole golf, tennis, picnicking, concessions,
a restaurant, a resort inn, camping and cottages are among the park's offerings. Daily.

SETH LORE AND IRWINTON HISTORIC DISTRICT

211 N. Eufaula Ave., Eufaula, 334-687-5283
Architecture buffs should walk through the district for a look at Greek Revival, Italianate and Victorian homes, churches and commercial structures
built between 1834 and 1911. Daily.

SHORTER MANSION

340 N. Eufaula Ave., Eufaula, 334-687-3793; www.eufaulapilgrimage.com
Built in 1906, this neoclassical mansion houses antique furnishings, Con-
federate relics and memorabilia of six state governors from Barbour County.
Daily.

SPECIAL EVENT
EUFAULA PILGRIMAGE
917 W. Barbour St., Eufaula, 334-687-3793; www.eufaulapilgrimage.com
This event features daytime and candlelight tours of antebellum houses and churches, an antiques show and sales, historic reenactments and Civil War displays.
First weekend in April.

FLORENCE
See also Sheffield
A small town with a rich cultural life, Florence lays claim to some of Alabama's most famous residents: W.C. Handy, "Father of the Blues," was born here, and Helen Keller grew up nearby. The town is also the site of Alabama's only structure designed by Frank Lloyd Wright: the Rosenbaum House.

WHAT TO SEE
ELK RIVER
Florence
The river provides a prime spot for fishing, boating, picnicking, a playground and a group lodge. Daily.

INDIAN MOUND AND MUSEUM
1028 S. Court St., Florence, 256-760-6427; www.florenceal.org
Archeologists believe the mound—the largest in the Tennessee Valley—was the site of ceremonies and other tribal exercises. Visit the museum to see artifacts thought to be thousands of years old.
Admission: adults $2, students $.50. Tuesday-Saturday 10 a.m.-4 p.m.

NATCHEZ TRACE PARKWAY
This 444-mile parkway traces an ancient trail used by Natchez, Choctaw and Chickasaw Indians. The trail connected southern portions of the Mississippi River to central Tennessee through Alabama. Visitors can hike, bike, drive, ride horseback and camp along the trail. Stop by historic sites such as Colbert Ferry Park. Legend says George Colbert, a leading Chickasaw of the area, charged Andrew Jackson $75,000 to ferry Jackson's army across the river. Daily.

POPE'S TAVERN
203 Hermitage Drive, Florence, 256-760-6439; www.florenceal.org
General Andrew Jackson stayed in this stage stop, which served as a hospital for both Union and Confederate soldiers during the Civil War.
Admission: adults $2, students $.50. Tuesday-Saturday 10 a.m.-4 p.m.

W. C. HANDY HOME, MUSEUM AND LIBRARY
620 W. College St., Florence, 256-760-6434; www.florenceal.org
Blues lovers take note: the restored birthplace of the famous composer and the "Father of the Blues" houses handwritten sheet music, Handy's famous trumpet and the piano on which he composed "St. Louis Blues."
Admission: adults $2, students $.50. Tuesday-Saturday 10 a.m.-4 p.m.

WHEELER DAM
Highway 101, Elgin, 256-685-3306; www.alapark.com/JoeWheeler
Part of the Muscle Shoals complex, the dam is 72 feet high and stretches 6,342 feet across the Tennessee River. It's a good backdrop for swimming, fishing, boat liveries, tennis, picnic facilities and cabins. Daily.

WILSON DAM
704 S. Wilson Dam Road, Florence
Completed in 1924 and named after President Woodrow Wilson, the dam is owned and operated by the Tennessee Valley Authority. It is the TVA's only neo-classical dam; it combines hints of Greek and Roman architecture into one modern structure. Stretching 4,541 feet across the Tennessee River, the dam prevents floods, provides 650 miles of navigable channel and produces electricity for the area's residents, farms and industry. Daily.

WILSON LAKE
719 Highway 72 W., Tuscumbia, 256-383-0783; www.colbertcountytourism.org
The lake extends more than 15 miles upstream to Wheeler Dam. Go there for swimming, fishing or boating.
Monday-Friday 8:30 a.m.-5 p.m., Saturdays 9 a.m.-4 p.m.

SPECIAL EVENTS
ALABAMA RENAISSANCE FAIRE
Wilson Park, 541 Riverview Drive, Florence, 256-740-4141; www.visitflorenceal.com
Renaissance-era arts and crafts, music, food, entertainment bring you back to the old days. Fair workers in period costumes also set the mood. October.

HELEN KELLER FESTIVAL
Spring Park, 719 Highway 72 W., Florence, 256-383-0783; www.colbertcounty.org
Celebrate Keller's legacy of courage during this three-day celebration. Music, crafts and a parade are among the festivities.
Last weekend in June.

W. C. HANDY MUSIC FESTIVAL
115 1/2 E. Mobile, Florence, 256-766-7642; www.wchandyfest.com
This weeklong festival celebrates the musical heritage of northwest Alabama, particularly Handy's legacy. The offerings are impressive: see musical performances from jazz, blues and gospel groups.
First week in August.

FORT PAYNE
See also Gadsden
Fort Payne is in an area celebrated for natural wonders and Native American history. Sequoyah, who invented the Cherokee alphabet, lived in Will's Town, a Cherokee settlement near Fort Payne.

WHAT TO SEE
CLOUDMONT SKI AND GOLF RESORT
721 County Road 614, Mentone, 256-634-4344; www.cloudmont.com
Skiing in the South? You bet. Cloudmont doesn't let a little thing like the

weather stand in the way of a great run. It manufactures its own snow for about three months a year (mid-December to early March). The longest run is 1,000 feet, and the vertical drop is 150 feet. The resort offers a ski school, rentals, concessions, a snack bar and snow patrol. In the summer, visit Cloudmont for swimming, horseback riding, fishing, hiking and golf.
Monday-Friday 10 a.m.-4 p.m., 6-10 p.m.

DESOTO STATE PARK
13883 County Road 89, Fort Payne, 256-845-5380; www.desotostatepark.com
This 3,502-acre park includes Lookout Mountain, Little River Canyon and DeSoto Falls and Lake. Twenty miles of hiking trails cross the mountaintop and a scenic drive skirts the canyon. Enjoy the wildflowers and waterfalls, both in abundance. The park also offers a swimming pool, a bathhouse, fishing, a hiking trail, tennis, a playground, picnicking, a restaurant, a country store, a resort inn, a nature center, camping and cabins. Daily.

FORT PAYNE OPERA HOUSE
510 Gault Ave. N., Fort Payne, 256-845-2741; www.fortpaynechamber.com
Alabama's oldest opera house still in use, the building was restored and reopened in 1970 as a cultural arts center. Tours of the theater include historic murals.
By appointment.

LANDMARKS OF DEKALB MUSEUM
105 Fifth St. N.E., Fort Payne, 256-845-5714; www.fortpaynedepotmuseum.org
The museum features Native American artifacts from several different tribes, a turn-of-the-century house and farm items, railroad memorabilia and photographs and artwork of local historical significance.
Monday, Wednesday, Friday 10 a.m.-4 p.m., Sunday 2-4 p.m.

SEQUOYAH CAVERNS
1438 County Road 731, Fort Payne, 256-635-0024; www.sequoyahcaverns.com
Tour the caverns—once occupied by local Native Americans seeking shelter—and gaze into the Looking Glass Lakes. The caverns hold thousands of rock formations, and the homestead around the caverns is home to deer, buffalo and rainbow trout pools. The caverns also have a swimming pool, a picnic area and camping.
Admission: adults $12.95, children 4-12 $6.95, children under 4 free.
Monday-Saturday 8:30 a.m.-5 p.m., Sunday 1-5 p.m.

SPECIAL EVENT
DEKALB COUNTY VFW AGRICULTURAL FAIR
VFW Fairgrounds, 600 Golf Ave., Fort Payne, 256-845-4752; www.fortpayne.com
The fair attracts nearly 45,000 visitors annually and features live music, a beauty pageant for ladies 65 years and older and special events for kids.
Late September-early October.

GADSDEN

See also Anniston, Guntersville

Named for James Gadsden, who negotiated the purchase of Arizona and New Mexico in 1853, Gadsden has a charming downtown district, and plenty of natural beauty and a few fascinating historic tales.

WHAT TO SEE
CENTER FOR CULTURAL ARTS

501 Broad St., Gadsden, 256-543-2787; www.culturalarts.com

The center offers visual art exhibits from the U.S. and Europe, concerts and theatrical performances and the renowned Etowah Youth Orchestras. Imagination Place, the children's museum, keeps kids entertained with hands-on exhibits such as a tree house and miniature "walk-through" city.

Admission: adults $5, children $4. Monday-Friday 9 a.m.-6 p.m., Saturday 10 a.m.-6 p.m., Sunday 1-5 p.m.

GADSDEN MUSEUM OF ART

515 Broad St., Gadsden, 256-546-7365; www.gadsdenmuseum.com

Dedicated to celebrating Southern artists and preserving the region's history, the museum is home to numerous paintings, sculptures and prints.

Monday-Saturday, 10 a.m.-4 p.m.

HORTON MILL COVERED BRIDGE

Highway 75, Hendrix

This 22-foot-long structure is the highest covered bridge built over water in the U.S., in this case over the Black Warrior River. Daily.

NOCCALULA FALLS PARK

1500 Noccalula Road, Gadsden, 256-549-4663; www.gadsden-etowahtourismboard. com

This 100-foot waterfall comes with a tale of star-crossed love: according to local legend, an Indian chief's daughter, named Noccalula, leaped to her death instead of betraying her true love and marrying a man of her father's choosing. Lookout Mountain Parkway, a scenic drive that stretches all the way to Chattanooga, originates here. A swimming pool, a bathhouse, nature and hiking trails, miniature golf, a picnic area, a playground, camping, a petting zoo and an animal habitat house are all on offer. There's also a pioneer homestead and museum and botanical gardens. Daily.

WEISS DAM AND LAKE

590 E. Main St., Centre, 256-526-8467

Swim or fish on this 30,200-acre lake. When you tire of the sun and water, you can tour the nearby power plant, which harnesses the energy produced by the dam. Daily.

GULF SHORES

See also Mobile

Postcard-perfect beaches are the main attraction in Gulf Shores, located on the aptly named Pleasure Island. Swimming and fishing in the Gulf are excellent, and golfers will find plenty of nearby courses to keep them busy. Nature lovers will enjoy bike paths, hiking trails and even a few prime spots for canoeing.

WHAT TO SEE
ALABAMA GULF COAST ZOO
1204 Gulf Shores Parkway, Gulf Shores, 251-968-5732; www.alabamagulfcoastzoo.com
Located a few miles from the beach, this zoo has endured violent visits from hurricanes Ivan, Dennis and Katrina in recent years, but its comeback landed it a television series called The Little Zoo That Could on Animal Planet. Admission: adults $10, seniors $8, children 3-12 $7, children under 3 free. Daily 9 a.m.-4 p.m.

BON SECOUR NATIONAL WILDLIFE REFUGE
12295 State Highway 180, Gulf Shores, 251-540-7720; www.fws.gov/bonsecour
One of Alabama's 10 natural wonders, Bon Secour's 7,000 acres are home to endangered and threatened animals such as the nesting sea turtles and the Alabama beach mouse. You can commune with nature by swimming, hiking and even fishing here.
Schedule varies.

FORT MORGAN
Gulf Shores, 251-540-7125
Fort Morgan's most famous moment came during the Civil War's Battle of Mobile Bay, when Union Admiral Farragut commanded his troops: "Damn the torpedoes, full speed ahead!" (Farragut was referring to the Confederates' use of mines, known then as torpedoes.) Following the battle, the fort withstood a two-week siege before surrendering to Union forces. The fort was in active use during the Spanish-American War, World War I and World War II. Daily.

FORT MORGAN MUSEUM
Gulf Shores, 251-540-7127
Just can't get enough military history? The museum, built in 1967 and designed after the 10-sided citadel damaged in 1864, displays military artifacts from the War of 1812 through World War II. Daily.

FORT MORGAN PARK
51 Highway 180, Gulf Shores
Explored by the Spanish in 1519, this area on the western tip of Mobile Point is a history buff's dream. Between 1519 and 1813, Spain, France, England and finally the U.S. held this strategic point. The park also has a fishing pier, picnicking and concessions. Daily.

GULF STATE PARK
20115 State Highway 135, Gulf Shores, 251-948-7275; www.dcnr.state.al.us
The 6,000-acre park boasts more than two miles of white-sand beaches on the Gulf and freshwater lakes. There's swimming, a bathhouse, waterskiing, surfing, fishing, a marina and boathouse, hiking, bicycling, tennis, 18-hole

golf, a picnic area, a pavilion, grills, a restaurant, a resort inn, cabins and camping.
Daily.

SPECIAL EVENTS
MARDI GRAS CELEBRATION
3150 Gulf Shores Parkway, Gulf Shores, 251-968-6904; www.gulfshores.com
Don't let New Orleans fool you: Alabama was actually the site of the first Mardi Gras celebration in this neck of the woods. In Gulf Shores, catch a parade of boats on the water and rock bands on flatbed trailers on the roads.
Late February.

NATIONAL SHRIMP FESTIVAL
Highways 59 and 182, Gulf Shores, 251-968-6904; www.gulfshores.com
Although fabulous seafood is the main draw at this annual festival, visitors will also enjoy live music, a kids' art show and a sandcastle contest.
Second weekend of October.

WHERE TO STAY
★AMERICA'S BEST INN & SUITES
1517 S. McKenzie St., Foley, 251-943-3297, 888-800-8000; www.foleyabis.com
86 rooms. Complimentary breakfast. Fitness center. Pool. $61-150

★★BEST WESTERN ON THE BEACH
337 E. Beach Blvd., Gulf Shores, 251-948-2711, 800-788-4557; www.bestwestern.com
111 rooms. Restaurant. Pool. Beach. $61-150

WHERE TO EAT
★ORIGINAL OYSTER HOUSE
701 Gulf Shores Parkway, Gulf Shores, 251-948-2445; www.theoysterhouse.com
Seafood. Lunch, dinner. Outdoor seating. $16-35

★SEA-N-SUDS
405 E. Beach Blvd., Gulf Shores, 251-948-7894; www.sea-n-suds.com
Seafood. Lunch, dinner. Closed Sunday (off-season). Outdoor seating. $16-35

GUNTERSVILLE
See also Gadsden, Huntsville
On a peninsula surrounded by water, Guntersville is a beautiful backdrop for plenty of recreational activities. Landlubbers will enjoy hiking or mountain biking in the Appalachian foothills. Visitors who prefer to play in the water will be thrilled by the sparking waters of Lake Guntersville.

The town has a unique history: Cherokee Indians and European settlers lived together peacefully here for many decades. The Cumberland River Trail, the route Andrew Jackson took on his way to the Creek War in 1813, passed through Guntersville, and Cherokees from this area joined and fought bravely with Jackson's troops against the Creeks. But in 1837, General Winfield Scott—under the direction of Andrew Jackson—rounded up the area's Cherokees and moved them westward.

WHAT TO SEE
BUCK'S POCKET STATE PARK
393 County Road 174, Guntersville, 256-659-2000; www.dcnr.state.al.us
A secluded natural pocket of the Appalachian mountain chain, this park offers breathtaking vistas. Fishing, a boat launch, hiking trails, picnic facilities, a playground, a concession, camping and a visitor center are all available at the park. Daily.

GUNTERSVILLE DAM AND LAKE
1155 Lodge Drive, Guntersville, 256-582-3263; www.tva.gov/sites/guntersville.htm
A playground for fishermen, swimmers and boaters, Guntersville Lake is Alabama's largest lake. The lake holds largemouth bass, bream, crappie and catfish, among other species of fish. Daily.

LAKE GUNTERSVILLE STATE PARK
Highway 227, Guntersville, 256-571-5455, 800-548-4553; www.dcnr.state.al.us
Overlooking the Guntersville Reservoir, the 6,000-acre park is a nature lover's dream. A beach, waterskiing, a fishing center, boating, hiking, bicycling, golf, tennis, nature programs, picnicking, camping, a playground, a restaurant, chalets, lakeside cottages and a resort inn on Taylor Mountain keep the park busy. Daily.

WHERE TO STAY
★COVENANT COVE RESORT AND MARINA
7001 Val Monte Drive, Guntersville, 256-582-1000; www.covenantcove.com
53 rooms. Bar. Complimentary breakfast. Pool. $61-150

★★HOLIDAY INN
2140 Gunter Ave., Guntersville, 256-582-2220, 888-882-1160; www.holiday-inn.com
100 rooms. Restaurant, bar. Pool. $61-150

HAMILTON
See also Montgomery
Settled in the 1880s, Hamilton spans "Military Road," a passage carved out of the wilderness by volunteer soldiers from Tennessee returning to their homes after fighting the British in New Orleans in 1815. General Andrew Jackson ordered the road created as a shortcut between New Orleans and Nashville and today a bike and hiking path is under way to commemorate this historic path.

WHAT TO SEE
HORSESHOE BEND NATIONAL MILITARY PARK
11288 Horseshoe Bend Road, Daviston, 256-234-7111; www.nps.gov/hobe
The park is the site of an 1814 clash between General Andrew Jackson's army and Upper Creek Indian warriors—the bloodiest battle of the Creek War. Jackson's army of 3,300 men attacked about 1,000 Upper Creek warriors, who had vowed to defend their land and their customs from the growing number of white settlers. More than 800 Upper Creeks died, making this the deadliest single battle for Native Americans in U.S. history. The peace

treaty that followed cost the Creeks more than 20 million acres of land, opening a vast and rich domain to settlement—a move that eventually led to Alabama's statehood in 1819. For Jackson, Horseshoe Bend was the beginning; for the Creek Nation, it was the beginning of the end. Thanks in part to his military fame, Jackson was elected president of the United States in 1829. A year later, he signed the Indian Removal Bill, which forced all Native American tribes living east of the Mississippi River to move to Oklahoma. The Cherokees named this trek the "Trail of Tears." Located on the banks of the Tallapoosa River, the park contains 2,040 acres of forested hills. A museum at the visitor center depicts the battle with a slide presentation and an electric map exhibit. A three-mile loop road tour with seven interpretive markers crosses the battle area. Nature trails, picnic areas and a boat ramp are all available.
Daily 8 a.m.-5 p.m.

NATURAL BRIDGE OF ALABAMA
Highway 278 W. Natural Bridge, 205-486-5330
Two spans of sandstone, the longest at 148 feet, were created by natural erosion of a tributary stream more than 200 million years ago. Scenic picnic spots are plentiful. Daily.

WHERE TO STAY
★★ECONO LODGE INN & SUITES
2031 Military St. S., Hamilton, 205-921-7831, 800-553-2666; www.econolodge.com
80 rooms. Restaurant. $61-150

HUNTSVILLE
See also Athens, Decatur, Guntersville
Huntsville might deceive you. This little city at the foot of a mountain in northern Alabama is intimately involved in space exploration, thanks to NASA's Space and Rocket Center, which is headquartered here. Aspiring astronauts (or just curious earth-bound folks) head to Huntsville for Space Camp, where kids and families learn what it takes to cruise the universe. But rockets aren't the only attraction. Huntsville is rich in Civil War history, natural beauty, golf courses and good ol' Southern cooking. Don't miss the hush puppies, fried catfish and pecan pie.

WHAT TO SEE
ALABAMA CONSTITUTION VILLAGE
109 Gates Ave., Huntsville, 256-564-8100; www.earlyworks.com
This re-created complex of buildings commemorates Alabama's entry into the Union at the 1819 Constitutional Convention. The village offers period craft demonstrations and activities, and guides in period dress.
Admission: adults $10, seniors $8, youth $8, toddlers $4. March-October, Tuesday-Saturday 10 a.m.-4 p.m.

BURRITT MUSEUM & PARK
3101 Burritt Drive, Huntsville, 256-536-2882; www.burrittonthemountain.com
The 167-acre park atop Round Top Mountain offers a little something for

everyone. The former home of eccentric Dr. William Henry Burritt, the mansion houses rotating exhibits, most of which have regional or local themes. The historic park has restored 19th-century buildings—including a blacksmith shop and a smokehouse—and volunteers in period dress. You'll also find nature trails, gardens and a panoramic view of the city.

Admission: adults $7, seniors and military $6, children 13-17 $5, children 3-12 $4, children under 2 free. April-October, Tuesday-Saturday 9 a.m.-5 p.m., Sunday 9 a.m.-noon; November-March, Tuesday-Saturday 10 a.m.-4 p.m., Sunday 9 a.m.-noon.

HUNTSVILLE DEPOT

320 Church St., Huntsville, 256-564-8100, 800-678-1819; www.earlyworks.com

Opened in 1860 as a "passenger house" and eastern division headquarters for the Memphis & Charleston Railroad Company, the Huntsville Depot was captured by Union troops and used as a prison; Civil War graffiti is still there. Kids can climb aboard real trains and Huntsville's first ladder truck.

Admission: adults $10, seniors $8, youth $8, toddlers $4. March-December, Tuesday-Saturday 10 a.m.-4 p.m.

HUNTSVILLE MUSEUM OF ART

300 Church St., Huntsville, 256-535-4350; www.hsvmuseum.org

Named one of the state's top 10 destinations by the Alabama Bureau of Tourism and Travel, the museum has seven galleries, which host traveling exhibits and display work from the museum's own collection. Tours, lectures, concerts and films round out the offerings.

Admission: adults $7, seniors, military and students $6, children 6-11 $3, children under 6 free. Tuesday-Wednesday, Thursday 10 a.m.-8 p.m., Friday-Saturday 10 a.m.-5 p.m., Sunday 1-5 p.m.

MONTE SANO STATE PARK

5105 Nolan Ave., Huntsville, 256-534-3757; www.dcnr.state.al.us

Spanish for "mountain of health," Monte Sano reaches 1,600 feet above sea level. Hiking trails, picnicking, a playground, concessions, camping, cabins and an amphitheater keep the park humming. Daily.

TWICKENHAM HISTORIC DISTRICT

500 Church St., Huntsville, 256-551-2230; www.huntsville.org

A living museum of antebellum architecture, the district contains Alabama's largest concentration of antebellum houses. Several of the houses are occupied by descendants of original builders or owners. Daily.

U.S. SPACE AND ROCKET CENTER

1 Tranquility Base, Huntsville, 256-837-3400, 800-637-7223; www.spacecamp.com

If you've ever dreamed of climbing aboard a rocket and blasting off, this is the place for you. Experience a rocket launch in Space Spot, a simulated ride that shoots riders 140 feet in the air in 2.5 seconds. Visit the Mars exhibit, where you can climb Olympus Mons, the tallest volcano in the solar system. In the museum, check out the Apollo capsule and space shuttle objects returned from orbit. The Omnimax Theater, with a tilted dome screen, seats

280 and shows 45-minute space shuttle and science films photographed by astronauts. NASA bus tours take visitors through Marshall Space Flight Center, featuring mission control, space station construction and the tank where astronauts simulate weightlessness. The U.S. Space Camp offers programs for children fourth grade and up, families and even corporate executives. Daily 9 a.m.-5 p.m.

VON BRAUN CENTER
700 Monroe St., Huntsville, 256-533-1953; www.vonbrauncenter.com
This is the largest multipurpose complex in northern Alabama, named for noted space pioneer Dr. Wernher von Braun. The center hosts concerts, touring Broadway performances, ballets and other shows.

SPECIAL EVENTS
BIG SPRING JAM
Big Spring International Park, 700 Monroe St., Huntsville, 256-533-1953;
www.bigspringjam.org
Three days, five stages, more than 80 musical acts—what else do you want? Wynonna Judd, Lynyrd Skynyrd and Jewel have performed in recent years. Late September.

PANOPLY ARTS FESTIVAL
Big Spring International Park, 700 Monroe St., Huntsville, 256-519-2787;
www.panoply.org
A haven for art lovers of all kinds, the festival showcases work by visual artists, dancers, musicians and actors. Enjoy dance performances at the choreography competition and interactive art activities at Artrageous. Don't miss the final round of excitement at Panoply Idol.
Last weekend of April.

WHERE TO STAY
★★COURTYARD HUNTSVILLE
4804 University Drive, Huntsville, 256-837-1400, 800-321-2211; www.marriott.com
149 rooms. Restaurant, bar. Fitness center. Pool. $61-150

★★FOUR POINTS BY SHERATON HUNTSVILLE AIRPORT
1000 Glenn Hearn Blvd., Huntsville, 256-772-9661, 888-625-5144; www.fourpoints.com
146 rooms. Restaurant, bar. Business center. Fitness center. $61-150

★GUESTHOUSE SUITES PLUS HUNTSVILLE
4020 Independence Drive N.W., Huntsville, 256-837-8907, 800-331-3131; www.guest-houseintl.com
112 rooms. Complimentary breakfast. $61-150

★★HOLIDAY INN EXPRESS
3808 University Drive, Huntsville, 256-721-1000, 800-345-7720; www.hiexpress.com
112 rooms. Restaurant, bar. Pool. $61-150

★★HOLIDAY INN HUNTSVILLE DOWNTOWN
401 Williams Ave., Huntsville, 256-533-1400; www.holidayinn.com
279 rooms. Restaurant, bar. Business center. Fitness center. Pool. $61-150

★LA QUINTA INN HUNTSVILLE SPACE CENTER
3141 University Drive N.W., Huntsville, 256-533-0756, 800-687-6667;
www.laquinta.com
130 rooms. Complimentary breakfast. Pool. $61-150

★★★HUNTSVILLE MARRIOTT
5 Tranquility Base, Huntsville, 256-830-2222; www.marriott.com
Enjoy the comfort of this fine hotel, with rooms specifically designed for the business traveler. The Space and Rocket Museum is next door and hiking and biking trails abound nearby. Tech-savvy travelers will enjoy the new high-speed Internet and satellite flat-screen TVs in each room.
290 rooms. Restaurant, bar. Business center. $61-150

★QUALITY INN UNIVERSITY
3788 University Drive, Huntsville, 256-533-3291, 800-228-5150; www.qualityinn.com
67 rooms. Complimentary breakfast. Pool. $61-150

★★RADISSON SUITE HOTEL HUNTSVILLE
6000 Memorial Parkway S., Huntsville, 256-882-9400, 800-333-3333;
www.radisson.com
153 suites. Restaurant, bar. Fitness center. Pool. $61-150

WHERE TO EAT
★★OL' HEIDELBERG
6125 University Drive N.W., Huntsville, 256-922-0556
American, German. Lunch, dinner. $16-35

MOBILE
See also Dauphin Island, Gulf Shores; Pascagoula, MS
Mobile, Alabama's largest port city, blends old Southern grace with new Southern enterprise. The city began in 1702 as the first capital of French Louisiana. Thanks to its prime location on the water and easy access to the Gulf of Mexico, it flourished. After the Civil War, Mobile grew into a ship-building port, and increased military production buoyed the town's economy during World War II. In fact, one of the nation's first submarines was built in Mobile. Today, the city is a vibrant industrial seaport that has preserved its air of antebellum graciousness. Its historic charm is on display in the Church Street, DeTonti Square, Oakleigh Garden and Old Dauphinway historical districts. So indulge in fresh Gulf seafood, enjoy the city's diverse architectural styles and breathe in the salty air of Alabama's "Port City."

WHAT TO SEE
BATTLESHIP MEMORIAL PARK, USS ALABAMA
2703 Battleship Parkway, Mobile bay, 251-433-2703; www.ussalabama.com
Visitors may tour the 35,000-ton *USS Alabama*, which serves as a memo-

rial to the state's men and women who served in World War II, the Korean conflict, Vietnam and Desert Storm. Don't miss the submarine *USS Drum*, World War II aircraft, a B-52 bomber and an A-12 Blackbird spy plane. Admission: adults $12, children 6-11 $6, children under 6 free. October-March, daily 8 a.m.-4 p.m.; April-September, daily 8 a.m.-6 p.m.

BELLINGRATH GARDENS AND HOME
12401 Bellingrath Gardens Road, Mobile, 251-973-2217, 800-247-8420;
www.bellingrath.org
Travels to world-famous gardens abroad inspired the Bellingraths to create these majestic gardens in the 1920s. Approximately 250,000 azalea plants of 200 varieties bloom on the estate alongside camellias, roses and water lilies. In the center of the gardens, you'll find the Bellingrath house, furnished with antiques, fine china and rare porcelain. The riverboat Southern Belle provides 45-minute cruises along the nearby Fowl River.
Daily 8 a.m.-5 p.m.

BRAGG-MITCHELL MANSION
1906 Springhill Ave., Mobile, 251-471-6364; www.braggmitchellmansion.com
This Greek Revival 20-room mansion sits amid 12 acres of landscaped grounds. The restored interior includes extensive faux-grained woodwork and stenciled moldings as well as period furnishings. The circular staircase is not to be missed.
Admission: adults $5, children 6-18 $3, children under 6 free. Tuesday-Friday 10 a.m.-4 p.m.

CATHEDRAL OF THE IMMACULATE CONCEPTION
2 S. Claiborne, Mobile, 251-434-1565; www.mobilecathedral.org
Begun in 1835 and consecrated in 1850, the cathedral has German art-glass windows, a bronze canopy over the altar and hand-carved stations of the cross. Daily.

CONDE-CHARLOTTE MUSEUM HOUSE
104 Theatre St., Mobile, 251-432-4722; www.condecharlottemuseum.com
Mobile's first jail, the museum house now gives you a quick look at Mobile through its history, period kitchen and walled Spanish garden.
Admission: adults $5, children 6-18 $2, children under 6 free. Tuesday-Saturday 10 a.m.-4 p.m.

MALBIS GREEK ORTHODOX CHURCH
10145 Highway 90, Daphne, 251-626-3050
Inspired by a similar church in Athens, Greece, this Byzantine church is a Greek wonder. Pentelic marble is from the same quarries that supplied the Parthenon. Skilled artists from Greece created the authentic paintings; hand-carved figures and ornaments were brought from Greece. Visitors enjoy the stained-glass windows, dome with murals and many works of art depicting the life of Christ. Guided tours are by appointment. Daily.

MOBILE MEDICAL MUSEUM

1664 Springhill Ave., Mobile, 251-415-1109; www.mobilemedicalmuseum.com

Prepare to be fascinated—and a little grossed out. The museum houses rare medical artifacts, tools and photographs. Imagine life as a Civil War solider when you see the tools a Civil War surgeon used, including bullet extractors and amputation saws.

Monday-Friday 10 a.m.-4 p.m.

MOBILE MUSEUM OF ART

4850 Museum Drive, Mobile, 251-208-5200; www.mobilemuseumofart.com

The permanent collection includes African and Asian art, contemporary glass as well as American and European 19th-century paintings and prints. It also houses traveling exhibits.

Admission: adults $10, children $6. Monday-Saturday 10 a.m.-5 p.m., Sunday 1-5 p.m.

MUSEUM OF MOBILE

111 S. Royal St., Mobile, 251-208-7569; www.museumofmobile.com

See 300 years of history in one place. You'll find artifacts from Mobile's French, British, Spanish and Confederate periods, costumes from Mardi Gras celebrations, ship models and arms collection. It is all housed in the Bernstein-Bush House, an Italianate town house dating back to 1872.

Admission: adults $5, seniors $4, children 6-18 $3, children under 6 free. Monday-Saturday 9 a.m.-5 p.m., Sunday 1-5 p.m.

PHOENIX FIRE MUSEUM

111 S. Royal St., Mobile, 251-208-7569; www.museumofmobile.com

This museum, within a restored fire station from the 1800s, showcases fire-fighting equipment, memorabilia dating from Mobile's first volunteer company, steam fire engines and a collection of silver trumpets and helmets.

Tuesday-Saturday 9 a.m.-5 p.m., Sunday 1-5 p.m.

RICHARDS-DAR HOUSE

256 N. Joachim St., Mobile, 251-208-7320; www.richardsdarhouse.com

This restored Italianate town house features elaborate ironwork, a curved suspended staircase and period furniture. The elaborate white cast-iron façade depicts the four seasons and is stunning.

Admission: adults $5, children $2. Monday-Friday 11 a.m.-3:30 p.m., Saturday 10 a.m.-4 p.m., Sunday 1-4 p.m.

UNIVERSITY OF SOUTH ALABAMA

307 University Blvd., Mobile, 251-460-6101; www.southalabama.edu

Theater productions are presented during the school year at Laidlaw Performing Arts Center and at Saenger Theatre. Of architectural interest on campus are Seaman's Bethel Theater from 1860; the Plantation Creole House 1828), a reconstructed Creole cottage dating back to 1828; and Mobile town house, a 1870 federal-style building showing Italianate and Greek Revival influences that also houses the USA campus art gallery. Daily.

SPECIAL EVENTS
AZALEA TRAIL RUN FESTIVAL AND FESTIVAL OF FLOWERS1 S.

Water St., Mobile, 800-566-2453; www.mobilebay.org

Strap on your running shoes and enjoy the Azalea Trail 10 K Run, one of the nation's premier road races. Not much of an athlete? You can still enjoy this fragrant event. A 35-mile-long driving tour winds through the floral streets in and around Mobile. The Convention & Visitors Corporation has further details and maps for self-guided tours of the Azalea Trail and local historic sites.

Late March.

BAY FEST

2900 Dauphin St., Mobile, 251-470-7730; www.bayfest.com

Musicians occupy nine stages for three days every fall for this energetic festival. Past performers include B.B. King, 3 Doors Down and Keith Urban.

First weekend in October.

BLESSING OF THE FLEET

13790 S. Wintzell, Bayou La Batre, 251-824-2415; www.fleetblessing.org

A special Mass, a live crab race and a parade are just some of the activities at this annual church festival.

Early May.

GREATER GULF STATE FAIR

1035 Cody Road, Mobile, 251-344-4573; www.mobilefair.com

The state fair has all the makings of a great time: carnival rides, a rodeo, livestock shows, food and entertainment.

Late October.

SENIOR BOWL FOOTBALL GAME

Ladd-Peebles Stadium, 1621 Virginia St., Mobile, 251-438-2276, 888-736-2695; www. seniorbowl.com

This unique annual football game stars all of the nation's leading NFL draft prospects on teams coached by NFL coaches.

Late January.

WHERE TO STAY
★★ASHBURY HOTELS AND SUITES

600 W I-65 Service Road S., Mobile, 251-344-8030; www.ashburyhotel.com

236 rooms. Restaurant, bar. Complimentary breakfast. Business center. Pool. $61-150

★DAYS INN AND SUITES MOBILE

5472-A Inn Road, Mobile, 251-660-1520; www.daysinn.com

118 rooms. Complimentary breakfast. Fitness center. Pool. $61-150

★★HOLIDAY INN

5465 Highway 90 W., Mobile, 251-666-5600, 800-465-4329; www.holiday-inn.com

160 rooms. Restaurant, bar. Business center. Fitness center. Pool. $61-150

★LA QUINTA INN
816 W. I-65 Service Road South, Mobile, 251-343-4051, 800-531-5900;
www.laquinta.com
122 rooms. Complimentary breakfast. Outdoor pool. $61-150

★★★MARRIOTT GRAND HOTEL
1 Grand Blvd., Point Clear, 251-928-9201, 800-544-9933; www.marriott.com
Guests can indulge in fun and relaxation at this full-service beach resort on 550 landscaped acres on Mobile Bay. A historic Civil War cemetery is onsite. Be sure to set aside enough time to visit the 20,000-square-foot spa. Guest rooms are newly renovated with views of either the bay or the pool and verdant gardens.
371 rooms. Restaurant, bar. Business center. Fitness center. Pool. Spa. Beach. Golf. Tennis. $151-250

★★RADISSON ADMIRAL SEMMES HOTEL
251 Government St., Mobile, 251-432-8000, 800-333-3333; www.radisson.com
170 rooms. Restaurant, bar. Business center. Pool. $61-150

★★RIVERVIEW PLAZA
64 S. Water St., Mobile, 251-438-4000, 800-922-3298; www.marriott.com
374 rooms. Restaurant, bar. $151-250

WHERE TO EAT
★★★THE GRAND DINING ROOM
1 Grand Blvd., Point Clear, 251-928-9201; www.marriott.com
Part of the Marriott's Grand Hotel Resort & Golf Club, this signature restaurant with a picture-perfect view offers generous buffet dining during breakfast and lunch and romantic, festive dinners.
American. Breakfast, lunch, dinner. Closed Sunday-Monday. $16-35

★★★THE PILLARS
1757 Government St., Mobile, 251-471-3411; www.thepillarsmobile.com
Treat yourself to a delicious meal in a beautiful historic house. The menu reads like a surf-and-turf lover's dream: Gulf crab, shrimp, plenty of fresh fish and any cut of steak you could want. Owner Filippo Milone is the perfect host, warmly greeting guests and watching over his attentive staff.
American. Dinner. Closed Sunday. $16-35

★★★RUTH'S CHRIS STEAK HOUSE
2058 Airport Blvd.., Mobile, 251-476-0516; www.ruthschris.com
Now an international presence, this restaurant group started in New Orleans, so portions are generous and the menu is dotted with food inspired by the founder's hometown. The custom-aged Midwestern beef is never frozen and cooked in a 1,800-degree broiler to customers' tastes.
Steak. Dinner. $36-85

MONTGOMERY

See also Hamilton, Selma, Troy, Tuskegee

Known as the birthplace of the Civil War and civil rights, Montgomery is not just Alabama's state capital; it is a city that holds history important to the entire nation. It served as the Confederacy's first capital, from which Confederate leaders sent the "Fire on Fort Sumter" telegram that began the Civil War. About 100 years later, when black seamstress Rosa Parks refused to give up her bus seat to a white man, Montgomery again found itself embroiled in battle, this time for civil rights.

Montgomery has turned that turbulent history into rich cultural offerings. Here you'll find the nation's first Civil Rights Memorial, the famed Alabama Shakespeare Festival, fine art museums and historic buildings.

WHAT TO SEE
ALABAMA DEPARTMENT OF ARCHIVES AND HISTORY
624 Washington Ave., Montgomery, 334-242-4435; www.archives.state.al.us
This place houses a historical museum and genealogical research facilities. Artifact collections include exhibits on the 19th century, the military and early Native American. It also has an interactive children's gallery. Monday-Friday 8:30 a.m.-4:30 p.m.

ALABAMA SHAKESPEARE FESTIVAL
1 Festival Drive, Montgomery, 334-271-5353, 800-841-4273; www.asf.net
What started as a six-week summer festival held in a stuffy high school auditorium has become one the nation's finest year round theaters. Each year, ASF actors perform three Shakespearean plays in addition to other classics by playwrights such as Tennessee Williams, George Bernard Shaw and Thornton Wilder. The company also produces musicals and commissions new works. Schedules and prices vary.

CIVIL RIGHTS MEMORIAL
400 Washington Ave., Montgomery; www.tolerance.org/memorial
Designed by Vietnam Veterans Memorial artist Maya Lin, the memorial is inscribed with the names of people who lost their lives in the fight for civil rights. Daily.

DEXTER AVENUE KING MEMORIAL BAPTIST CHURCH
454 Dexter Ave., Montgomery, 334-263-3970; www.dexterkingmemorial.org
See the pulpit from which Dr. Martin Luther King, Jr. first preached his message of non-violent activism. King directed the Montgomery bus boycott from this church, where he served as pastor from 1954 to 1960. The church is now home to the mural and original painting "The Beginning of a Dream." To see the church, go on a guided tour (Monday-Thursday 10 a.m., 2 p.m.), walk through (Friday 10 a.m.) or make an appointment (Saturday 10:30 a.m.-1:30 p.m.). Sunday worship is at 10:30 a.m. Tuesday-Friday 10 a.m.-4 p.m., Saturday 10 a.m.-2 p.m.

F. SCOTT AND ZELDA FITZGERALD MUSEUM
919 Felder Ave., Montgomery, 334-264-4222
The famous author and his wife lived in this house from 1931 to 1932. The museum contains personal artifacts detailing the couple's public and private lives. It includes paintings by Zelda, letters and photographs, plus a 25-minute video presentation.
Admission: adults $5, seniors $2, children $2. Wednesday-Friday 10 a.m.-2 p.m., Saturday-Sunday 1-5 p.m.

FIRST WHITE HOUSE OF THE CONFEDERACY
644 Washington Ave., Montgomery, 334-242-1861
Confederacy President Jefferson Davis and his family lived here while Montgomery was the Confederate capital. Moved from its original location at Bibb and Lee streets in 1920, it is now a Confederate museum containing period furnishings, Confederate mementos, personal belongings and paintings of the Davis family.
Monday-Friday 8 a.m.-4:30 p.m.

FORT TOULOUSE/JACKSON PARK NATIONAL HISTORIC LANDMARK
2521 W. Fort Toulouse Road, Montgomery, 334-567-3002; www.fttoulousejackson.org
At the confluence of the Coosa and Tallapoosa rivers, Fort Toulouse was originally a French fort, built in 1717 to keep those pesky Brits at bay. The French abandoned it in 1763, and more than 50 years later, Andrew Jackson built a fort on the same site. Today, you can see a reconstructed Fort Toulouse and a partially reconstructed Fort Jackson. Don't miss the mounds, nearly 1,000 years old. The park features a boat ramp, nature walks, picnicking, improved camping and a museum. A living history program can be seen the third weekend of each month.
Admission: adults $1, seniors and children $.50. Daily.

MAXWELL AIR FORCE BASE
55 S. LeMay Plaza, Montgomery, 334-953-1110; www.au.af.mil
Wilbur Wright began the world's first flying school on this site in 1910. His brother Orville made his first flight in Montgomery on March 26, 1910. Named in 1922 for Lieutenant William C. Maxwell of Alabama, who was killed while serving in the Third Aero Squadron in the Philippines, it is now the site of Air University. Daily.

MONTGOMERY MUSEUM OF FINE ARTS
1 Museum Drive, Montgomery, 334-244-5700; www.mmfa.org
The museums holds collections of 19th- and 20th-century American art, European works on paper, regional and decorative arts. It also offers hands-on children's exhibits, lectures and concerts.
Tuesday-Saturday 10 a.m.-5 p.m., Sunday noon-5 p.m.

MONTGOMERY ZOO
2301 Coliseum Parkway, Montgomery, 334-240-4900; www.montgomeryal.gov
More than 500 animals from five continents reside here in natural, barrier-

free habitats. The zoo's Overlook Café gives visitors a unique peek at the zoo, and a train ride helps them get a lay of the land.
Admission: adults $8, seniors and children 3-12 $5, children under 3 free. Daily 9 a.m.-5 p.m.

OLD ALABAMA TOWN

301 Columbus St., Montgomery, 334-240-4500, 888-240-1850; www.oldalabamatown. com
In the heart of historic Montgomery, this six-block stretch of restored 19th- and 20th-century buildings includes an 1820s log cabin, an urban church circa 1890, a country doctor's office and a corner grocer, among many others. Hosts in period dress give you an inside look into Alabama's history.
Admission: adults $8, children 6-18 $4, children under 6 free. Monday-Saturday 9 a.m.-3 p.m.

ST. JOHN'S EPISCOPAL CHURCH

113 Madison Ave., Montgomery, 334-262-1937; www.stjohnsmontgomery.org
Built in 1855, this church has seen much of Alabama's history up close. Confederacy President Jefferson Davis worshipped here with his family. Today, visitors come to see the church's stained-glass windows, Gothic pipe organ and Jefferson's pew. Daily.

SPECIAL EVENTS
ALABAMA NATIONAL FAIR

Garrett Coliseum, 1555 Federal Drive, Montgomery, 334-272-6831;
www.alnationalfair.org
Don't miss the festivities, which include concerts, a circus, children's rides and the famed pig races. October.

SOUTHEASTERN LIVESTOCK EXPOSITION AND RODEO

Garrett Coliseum, 1555 Federal Drive, Montgomery, 334-265-1867; www.bamabeef.org
Some of the nation's best cowboys and cowgirls compete in this PRCA event, the largest rodeo east of the South.
Mid-March.

WHERE TO STAY
★ECONO LODGE & SUITES

5924 Monticello Drive, Montgomery, 334-272-1013; www.choicehotels.com
46 rooms. Complimentary breakfast. Business center. Fitness center. Pool. $61-150

★RED ROOF INN MONTGOMERY

5601 Carmichael Road, Montgomery, 205-270-0007, 800-228-2800; www.fairfieldinn.com
133 rooms. Complimentary breakfast. Pool. $61-150

★★HOLIDAY INN

1185 Eastern Bypass, Montgomery, 334-272-0370, 800-465-4329;
www.himontgomery.com
211 rooms. Restaurant, bar. Business center. Fitness center. Pool. $61-150

★KINGS INN

1355 East Blvd., Montgomery, 334-277-2200, 800-240-2200; www.ramada.com
152 rooms. Restaurant, bar. Complimentary breakfast. Pool. $61-150

★LA QUINTA INN

1280 Eastern Blvd., Montgomery, 334-271-1620, 800-531-5980; www.laquinta.com
130 rooms. Complimentary breakfast. Pool. $61-150

WHERE TO EAT
★MARTHA'S PLACE

458 Sayre St., Montgomery, 334-263-9135
American. Breakfast, lunch. Reservations recommended. $15 and under.

★★★VINTAGE YEAR

405 Cloverdale Road, Montgomery, 334-264-8463
Located in Montgomery's historic Cloverdale District, this restaurant serves unique appetizers and desserts. The modern décor with intimate lighting makes it a great spot for a romantic dinner. You can't go wrong with either the seafood or a steak.
Seafood. Dinner. Closed Sunday-Monday. $16-35

ORANGE BEACH

See also Gulf Shores
This town on the Gulf Coast offers plenty of white sand and warm breezes. Orange Beach and its neighbor town, Gulf Shores, make up one of Alabama's best playgrounds. Golf, hike, swim, fish—or just lounge on the beach.

WHERE TO STAY
★★HILTON GARDEN INN ORANGE BEACH BEACHFRONT

23092 Perdido Beach Blvd., Orange Beach, 251-974-1600; www.hiltongardeninn.com
137 rooms. Business center. Fitness center. Pool. Beach. $61-150

★★★PERDIDO BEACH RESORT

27200 Perdido Beach Blvd., Orange Beach, 251-981-9811, 800-634-8001;
www.perdidobeachresort.com
Directly on the Gulf of Mexico, this wonderful Mediterranean-style resort offers everything you need for a relaxing beachside vacation. Enjoy the white sand beaches, boating, deep-sea fishing, parasailing and scuba diving. Guest rooms are spacious and include balconies overlooking either the pool or the Gulf.
346 rooms. Restaurant, bar. Fitness center. Pool. Beach. Tennis. $151-250

WHERE TO EAT
★HAZEL'S FAMILY RESTAURANT

25311 Perdido Beach Blvd., Orange Beach, 251-981-4628;
www.hazelsseafoodrestaurant.com
American. Breakfast, lunch, dinner. $16-35

SELMA

See also Montgomery

High on a bluff above the Alabama River, Selma has had a front-row seat to some of American history's most tumultuous battles. During the Civil War, Selma was one of the Confederacy's prime military manufacturing centers, which made it a target for Union armies. The city fell on April 2, 1865, during a bloody siege by Union forces, which destroyed Selma's arsenal and factories, along with much of the city. With defeat came an end to the era of wealthy plantation owners and leisurely living. One hundred years after Selma fell to Union forces, it was entangled in another battle. On March 7, 1965, nearly 600 African-American residents of Selma marched east toward Montgomery. In the weeks before the march, discrimination and intimidation had prevented much of Selma's black population from registering to vote, and the marchers hoped Governor George Wallace would take notice of their plight when they arrived in the state's capital. Instead, Wallace declared the march a threat to public safety, and the marchers only made it as far as Selma's Edmund Pettus Bridge before they were driven back into town by police officers with clubs, whips and tear gas. This violence gave the day its name: "Bloody Sunday." Marchers, led by Dr. Martin Luther King Jr. tried again unsuccessfully two days later. They finally made it to Montgomery on their third attempt.

WHAT TO SEE
BLACK HERITAGE TOUR
Chamber of Commerce, 513 Lauderdale St., Selma, 334-875-7241;
www.selmaalabama.com
Learn about Selma's role in the fight for civil rights. Visit Brown Chapel A.M.E. Church (also a part of the Martin Luther King Jr. self-guided street walking tour), the Edmund Pettus Bridge, the National Voting Rights Museum, Selma University, the Dallas County Courthouse and the Wilson Building. Daily.

CAHAWBA
9518 Cahaba Road, Selma, 334-872-8058; www.selmaalabama.com
This ghost town has a fascinating history. From 1820 to 1826, Cahawba served as Alabama's first permanent capital. Its low elevation made it vulnerable to frequent flooding, and the capital was moved to Tuscaloosa in 1826. The town survived until the Civil War, when the Confederate government tore up the railroad to extend a railroad nearby and established a lice-infested prison for captured Union troops. After the war, freemen used the courthouse as a meeting place to discuss how to gain political power, and former slave families created a new rural community. By 1900, the town was again abandoned and most of the buildings had collapsed or been burned. Today, visitors can stroll the deserted streets, chat with archeologists onsite and view the town's ruins. Daily

NATIONAL VOTING RIGHTS MUSEUM AND INSTITUTE
1012 Water Ave., Selma, 334-418-0800; www.nvrm.org
Located near the foot of Edmund Pettus Bridge, this museum offers a pictorial history of the voting rights struggle. It displays an exceptional record of

events and participants, including Viola Liuzzo, who was killed by Ku Klux Klan members after the voting-rights march, and Marie Foster, who made voting rights history.
Admission: adults $6, seniors and students $4. Monday-Friday 9 a.m.-5 p.m., Saturday 10 a.m.-3 p.m.

OLD DEPOT MUSEUM

4 Martin Luther King Jr. St., Selma, 334-874-2197; www.selmaalabama.com
Visit this interpretive history museum to see artifacts from Selma and Alabama's "black belt" region. Admission: adult $4, seniors $3, students $2, children under 5 free.
Monday-Saturday 10 a.m.-4 p.m.

OLD TOWN HISTORIC DISTRICT

Chamber of Commerce, 513 Lauderdale St., Selma, 334-875-7241; www.selmaalabama.com
Alabama's largest historic district, Old Town comprises more than 1,200 structures, including museums, specialty shops and restaurants. Daily.

STURDIVANT HALL

713 Mabry St., Selma, 334-872-5626; www.sturdivanthall.com
This beautiful home is an excellent example of Greek Revival architecture. Designed by Thomas Helm Lee, cousin of Robert E. Lee, it features massive Corinthian columns, original wrought iron on the balconies and belvedere on the roof. It's fully restored with period furnishings; the kitchen has slave quarters above; plus there's a smokehouse, wine cellar, carriage house and garden. One-hour guided tours are available.
Admission: adults $5, children $2. Tuesday-Saturday 10 a.m.-4 p.m.

SPECIAL EVENTS
HISTORIC SELMA PILGRIMAGE

109 Union St., Selma, 800-457-3562; www.pilgrimage.selmaalabama.com
If you want to wander through Selma's beautiful historic homes, this is your chance. Each year, guides take curious onlookers through privately owned historic homes. At twilight, take the living history tour at Old Live Oak cemetery. The annual event also includes an antiques show.
Mid-March.

REENACTMENT OF THE BATTLE OF SELMA

Battlefield Park, 205-755-1990; www.battleofselma.com
The Yankees are coming! One weekend each year, residents of Selma relive the battle between Union troops and the Confederacy. The battles take place on Saturday and Sunday, and other activities include a ladies' home tour and the Grand Military Ball.
Late April.

SHEFFIELD

See also Huntsville

Sheffield sits on the edge of the Tennessee River, a perfect spot for swimmers, fishermen and boaters. Locals are particularly proud of the area's musical heritage. Legends such as the Rolling Stones, Cher and Lynyrd Skynyrd recorded their music at Muscle Shoals Sound Studio, and musicians still trek to this northwest corner of Alabama to record their work.

WHAT TO SEE
ALABAMA MUSIC HALL OF FAME

617 Highway 72 W., Tuscumbia, 256-381-4417, 800-239-2643; www.alamhof.org

Rock on, Alabama: The Hall of Fame honors the contributions Alabamians have made to music of all genres—rock, rhythm and blues, gospel, contemporary and country music. Exhibits celebrate the accomplishments of performers such Hank Williams, also Nat King Cole and Lionel Richie. A recording studio is available to record personal cassettes or videos. Admission: adults $8, seniors and students $7, children 6-12 $5, children under 5 free. Monday-Saturday 9 a.m.-5 p.m., Sunday 1-5 p.m.

IVY GREEN

300 W. North Commons, Tuscumbia, 256-383-4066; www.helenkellerbirthplace.org

Helen Keller was born here in 1880. Deaf and blind from the age of 19 months, she learned to sign her first words at the water pump out back from her teacher Annie Sullivan. The play The Miracle Worker captures the turbulent and eventually triumphant relationship between Sullivan and Keller. Admission: adults $6, seniors $5, children 5-18 $2, children under 5 free. Monday-Saturday 8:30 a.m.-4 p.m.

SPECIAL EVENTS
HELEN KELLER FESTIVAL

Ivy Green, 300 N. Commons St. W., Tuscumbia, 256-383-4066; www.helenkellerfestival.com

First held in 1979, this festival includes Braille and sign language lessons as well as performances of The Miracle Worker.
Late June.

THE MIRACLE WORKER

300 N. Commons St. W., Tuscumbia, Ivy Green, 256-383-4066; www.helenkellerbirthplace.org

This is an outdoor performance of William Gibson's prize-winning play based on Helen Keller's life. A limited number of tickets are available at the gate; advance purchase is recommended. The price includes a tour of Ivy Green preceding the play.
Admission: $8. Mid-June-mid-July, Friday-Saturday 8 p.m.

WHERE TO STAY
★★HOLIDAY INN

4900 Hatch Blvd., Sheffield, 256-381-4710, 800-465-4329, 800-111-000; www.holiday-inn.com

204 rooms. Restaurant, bar. Fitness center. Pool. $61-150

WHERE TO EAT
★★GEORGE'S STEAK PIT
1206 Jackson Highway, Sheffield, 256-381-1531; www.georgessteakpit.com
American. Dinner. Closed Sunday-Monday. $36-85

★SOUTHLAND
1309 Jackson Highway, Sheffield, 256-383-8236; www.thesouthlandrestaurant.com
Southern. Lunch, dinner. Closed Monday. $16-35

TALLADEGA
See also Anniston, Birmingham, Sylacauga
Famous for its Talladega Speedway, this town is also home to Talladega College, founded by two former slaves. Love the great outdoors? Check out Logan Martin Lake to the northwest of Talladega and Talladega National Forest to the east.

WHAT TO SEE
CHEAHA STATE PARK
19644 Highway 281, Delta, 256-488-5111; www.dcnr.state.al.us
Visit the observation tower at the top of Mount Cheaha, the state's highest point at 2,407 feet. Nearly 2,800 acres of rugged forest country surround the mountain. But you may want to stick to the swimming in Lake Cheaha. Daily.

INTERNATIONAL MOTORSPORTS HALL OF FAME
3198 Speedway Blvd., Talladega, 256-362-5002; www.motorsportshalloffame.com
This is the official hall of fame of motor sports, with memorabilia and displays of more than 100 vehicles. Try the racecar simulator or pick up a nice souvenir at the gift shop. The annual hall of fame induction ceremony takes place in late April.
Admission: adults $10, children 7-17 $5, children under 7 free. Daily 9 a.m.-5 p.m.

SILK STOCKING DISTRICT
25 W. 11th St., Talladega, 256-761-2108
Stroll by antebellum and turn-of-the-century houses along tree-lined streets. Talladega Square, in the heart of town, dates to 1834 and includes the renovated Talladega County Courthouse, the oldest courthouse in continuous use in Alabama.

TALLADEGA NATIONAL FOREST
Forest Supervisor, 2946 Chestnut St., Montgomery, 256-362-2909; www.fs.fed.us
On the Southern edge of the Appalachian Mountains, this forest comprises more than 360,000 acres of beauty. The forest has high ridges with spectacular views of wooded valleys, waterfalls and streams. There's lake swimming, fishing and hiking trails, including the 100-mile Pinhoti National Recreation Trail, a national byway extending from Highway 78 to Cheaha State Park. Daily.

TALLADEGA SUPERSPEEDWAY

5200 Speedway Blvd., Eastaboga, 256-362-5002, 877-462-3342;
www.talladegasuperspeedway.com

Race mavericks say this is one of the world's fastest speedways, with 33-degree banks in the turns. Stock-car races include the EA Sports 500, Aaron's 499, and Aaron's 312. Ticket prices vary.
Daily 8 a.m.-4 p.m.

TUSCALOOSA

See also Bessemer

The Crimson Tide—otherwise known as the University of Alabama—calls Tuscaloosa home, and college football rules supreme here. But the city, located on the Black Warrior River, has a strong sense of history beyond its football traditions. Tuscaloosa was the capital of Alabama from 1826 to 1846, when profits from cotton padded farmers' pockets funded extravagant parties. When cotton prices fell, the capital moved to Montgomery and the Civil War ravaged Tuscaloosa (Choctaw for "black warrior"). Thanks to the expansion of the university and growing industry, today the city is a vibrant community, especially when the Tide is rollin'.

WHAT TO SEE

BATTLE-FRIEDMAN HOUSE

1010 Greensboro Ave., Tuscaloosa, 205-758-6138; www.historictuscaloosa.org

Local plantation owner Alfred Battle built this magnificent house when Tuscaloosa was the capital of Alabama. Financially ravaged by Confederate investments, Battle was forced to sell the house to Hungarian immigrant Bernard Friedman. Preserved and restored, today it contains fine antiques and its period gardens occupy a half block.
Admission: adults $5, children under 12 free. Tuesday-Saturday 10 a.m.-noon, 1-4 p.m.

CHILDREN'S HANDS-ON MUSEUM

2213 University Blvd., Tuscaloosa, 205-349-4235; www.chomonline.org

The exhibit highlights at this kiddie museum include a Choctaw Indian Village, an art studio, a planetarium, a beaver's den and a TV studio. There's also a computer and science lab resource center for enterprising little minds.
Admission: adults $7, seniors $6, children 1-3 $4, children under 1 free.
Monday-Friday 9 a.m.-5 p.m., Saturday 10 a.m.-4 p.m.

GORGAS HOUSE

Ninth Avenue and Capstone Drive, Tuscaloosa, 205-348-5906; gorgashouse.ua.edu

The three-story brick structure was named for General Josiah Gorgas, a former university president. One of the school's original structures, Gorgas now houses a museum with historical exhibits. Get a look at the Spanish Colonial silver display.
Admission: adults $2. Tuesday-Saturday 10 a.m.-4 p.m.

MOUNDVILLE ARCHAEOLOGICAL PARK

100 Mound Parkway, Moundville, 205-371-2234; www.moundville.ua.edu

The park maintains a group of more than 20 Native American ceremonial mounds dating back to A.D. 1000-1450. The Jones Archaeological Museum traces the prehistory of southeastern Native Americans and exhibits products of this aboriginal culture. There are also nature trails along the river, picnic facilities and tent and trailer sites.

Admission: adults $5, seniors $4, students and children 5-18 $3, children under 5 free. Daily 8 a.m.-8 p.m.

OLD TAVERN

500 28th Ave., Tuscaloosa, 205-758-2238; www.historictuscaloosa.org

Governor Gayle and members of the Alabama legislature frequented this former inn and stagecoach stop when Tuscaloosa was the state's capital. Tuesday-Friday 10 a.m.-noon, 1-4 p.m.

UNIVERSITY OF ALABAMA

801 University Blvd. E., Tuscaloosa, 205-348-6010; www.ua.edu

Roll Tide! Alabama's first public university, Bama has 21,000 students. On the campus is an art gallery in Garland Hall with changing exhibits, a museum of natural history, a 60-acre arboretum and the Paul W. Bryant Museum. The Frank Moody Music Building holds concerts and is the home of the largest pipe organ in the Southeast. Daily.

SPECIAL EVENT
MOUNDVILLE NATIVE AMERICAN FESTIVAL

Moundville Archaeological Park, 100 Mound Parkway, Tuscaloosa, 205-371-2572; www.moundville.ua.edu/festival.html

Celebrate the culture of the southeastern Native Americans with craft demonstrations, songs, dances and folktales. The final day is Indian Market Day, when artisans exhibit their wares.

Early October.

WHERE TO STAY
★BEST WESTERN PARK PLAZA MOTOR INN

3801 McFarland Blvd., Tuscaloosa, 205-556-9690, 800-235-7282; www.bestwestern.com

118 rooms. Complimentary breakfast. Fitness center. Pool. $61-150

★★HOTEL CAPSTONE

320 Paul Bryant Drive, Tuscaloosa, 205-752-3200, 888-625-5144; www.fourpoints.com

152 rooms. Restaurant, bar. Business center. Fitness center. Pool. $61-150

★HAMPTON INN TUSCALOOSA-UNIVERSITY

600 Harper Lee Drive, Tuscaloosa, 205-553-9800, 800-426-7866; www.hamptoninn.com

102 rooms. Complimentary breakfast. Business center. Fitness center. Pool. $61-150

WHERE TO EAT
★★HENSON'S CYPRESS INN
501 Rice Mine Road N., Tuscaloosa, 205-345-6963; www.cypressinnrestaurant.com
American. Lunch, dinner. $16-35

TUSKEGEE
See also Auburn, Montgomery
For more than 100 years, Tuskegee has witnessed great accomplishments by African-Americans. In 1881, Booker T. Washington founded the Tuskegee Normal School for Colored Teachers, which eventually became the Tuskegee Institute and then Tuskegee University. One of the institute's most famous instructors, George Washington Carver taught former slaves how to farm and be self-sufficient. In the early 1940s, the town's famous Tuskegee Airmen became America's first black military airmen.

WHAT TO SEE
BOOKER T. WASHINGTON MONUMENT
Tuskegee, 540-721-2094; www.nps.gov/bowa
The larger-than-life bronze figure honors the institute's first principal, who advocated "lifting the veil of ignorance" from the heads of freed slaves. Daily 9 a.m.-5 p.m.

CHAPEL, TUSKEGEE UNIVERSITY
Tuskegee University campus, Tuskegee, 334-727-8322; www.tuskegee.edu
Paul Rudolph designed this unusual structure with saw-toothed ceilings and deep beams. Adjacent are the graves of George Washington Carver and Booker T. Washington. Daily.

GEORGE WASHINGTON CARVER MUSEUM
Tuskegee, 334-727-3200; www.nps.gov

Born a slave, George Washington Carver eventually earned an advanced degree in agriculture from Iowa Agricultural College. He accepted a position at Tuskegee Institute in 1896, where he taught and researched for 47 years. The museum includes Carver's original laboratory, the array of products he developed, and his extensive collection of native plants, minerals, needlework, paintings, drawings and personal belongings.
Daily 9 a.m.-5 p.m.

TUSKEGEE INSTITUTE NATIONAL HISTORIC SITE
1212 W. Montgomery Road, Tuskegee, 334-727-6390; www.nps.gov/tuin
The Tuskegee Institute opened on July 4, 1881—a date that celebrated freedom for all citizens, including the black students who enrolled. The institute focused on giving students the skills they would need to find work and on building its students' moral character. Many of these students went on to become educators who took their knowledge and skills to rural areas, where they taught people how to implement these ideas. The school's reputation as a progressive institution grew, and in 1974, Congress established Tuskegee Institute National Historic Site to include "The Oaks," home of Booker T. Washington; the George Washington Carver Museum; and the Historic Cam-

pus District. The 5,000-acre campus comprises more than 160 buildings. Daily 9 a.m.-4:30 p.m.

TUSKEGEE NATIONAL FOREST
125 National Forest Road 949, Tuskegee, 334-727-2652; www.stateparks.com
This beautiful slice of southeastern country offers plenty of outdoor fun. There's fishing, hunting and hiking on Bartram National Recreation Trail; Atasi and Taska picnic sites; and camping. See the area's native animals at the Tsinia Wildlife Viewing Area. Daily.

WHERE TO STAY
★★KELLOGG CONFERENCE CENTER
Tuskegee University, Tuskegee Institute, 334-727-3000, 800-949-6161; www.tuskegeekelloggcenter.com
110 rooms. Restaurant, bar. Business center. Fitness center. Pool. $61-150

ARKANSAS

OUTDOOR ENTHUSIASTS OF EVERY STRIPE THINK ARKANSAS IS HEAVEN ON EARTH—AND they just might be right. The Natural State has been well endowed by Mother Nature, and its beautiful terrain inspires people to trade in laptops and cell phones for mountain bikes and spelunking lanterns. The Ozark and Ouachita mountain ranges, separated by the Arkansas River, offer splendid forests. Pine and hardwood trees shade streams filled with enough black bass, bream and trout to restore any angler's faith. There are deer, geese, ducks and quail to hunt and feast on in season, and if you just want to see wildlife, the White River National Wildlife Refuge is a haven for a diverse population of animals and plants. Caves, springs, meadows, valleys, bayous, rice and cotton fields and magnificent lakes and rivers dot the state. For an enjoyable backwoods vacation, a visitor can't go wrong bunking in a quiet rustic resort or indulging in cosmopolitan Hot Springs National Park—the renowned spa dedicated to sophisticated pleasures and therapeutic treatment.

For much of its early American history, Arkansas was rugged land on the western frontier, and a spirit of adventure still lives here, as does an appreciation for the cultural offerings that make Arkansas unique. Bluegrass music rules, and it's almost as necessary as good food at many of the town's annual festivals.

Arkansas also has several great cities. Hot Springs, in the midst of wooded hills and valleys, has been a vacation hot spot—literally—since the 19th century. The town offers a mixture of spa-inspired luxury and hearty outdoor fun. Little Rock, the state's capital, enjoyed its time in the nation's spotlight when the 42nd president of the United States, Bill Clinton, once the governor, moved into the White House. Today, Little Rock—so named for its place on the Arkansas River—has a revived downtown scene that attracts fun-seekers looking for live entertainment, eclectic dining and a healthy dose of retail therapy. For a totally different scene, check out Eureka Springs, a tourist destination admired for its European flavor, Victorian homes and steep, winding streets.

People who have already discovered Arkansas' rich offerings don't want the secret to get out, but there's plenty of room in Arkansas' wide-open spaces for a few more guests. So regardless of whether you come to party at Little Rock's riverfront, indulge in a hot-spring-fed spa or wander along quiet mountain trails, you'll find a surprising slice of paradise in Arkansas.

ALTUS
See also Clarksville
This itty-bitty town (population about 800) packs a serious punch for lovers of wine and Paris Hilton. The first season of The Simple Life, starring Hilton and Nicole Richie, was filmed here.

WHAT TO SEE
WIEDERKEHR WINE CELLARS
3324 Swiss Family Drive, Altus, 479-468-9463, 800-622-9463;www.wiederkehrwines.com
Take a guided wine-tasting tour (there's a gourmet and nonalcoholic bever-

age tasting for visitors under 21) or a self-guided tour of the vineyards. Stop by the observation tower, restaurant and gift shop along the way.
Daily 9 a.m.-4:30 p.m.

WHERE TO EAT
★★★WEINKELLER RESTAURANT
3324 Swiss Family Drive, Altus, 479-468-3551; www.wiederkehrwines.com
Listed on the National Register of Historic Places, this restaurant sits on the site of the first Wiederkehr wine cellar, dug in 1880. The menu offers Old World cuisine with classic European favorites.
Swiss, European. Lunch, dinner. $16-35

ARKADELPHIA
See also Hot Springs, Malvern
On a bluff overlooking the Ouachita River, Arkadelphia is an outdoor lover's dream: Hikers trek along Ouachita National Forest, the South's oldest national forest, while others take to the woods with a mountain bike or via horseback. Arkadelphia will also delight fishermen, boaters and swimmers, thanks to DeGray Lake and Ouachita River.

WHAT TO SEE
ARKANSAS POST MUSEUM
5530 Highway 165 S., Gillett, 870-548-2634; www.arkansas.com
The museum and five buildings house artifacts of early settlers on the grand prairie of Arkansas. Highlights include a colonial kitchen, an 1877 log house with period furnishings, Civil War memorabilia and a child's three-room finished playhouse.
Admission: adults $3, children 6-12 $2, children under 6 free. Tuesday-Saturday 8 a.m.-5 p.m., Sunday 1-5 p.m.

ARKANSAS POST NATIONAL MEMORIAL
1741 Old Post Road, Gillett, 501-548-2207; www.nps.gov/arpo
The Arkansas Post began as a trading post, established by French lieutenant Henri De Tonti in 1686. The French's first semi-permanent settlement in the lower Mississippi River Valley, the Post grew to an impressive garrison of 40 men by 1759. As European forces fought for control over the expanding American territory, Spain, England and France controlled this land at different points in American history until the U.S. bought it as part of the Louisiana Purchase in 1803. It became the capital of the new Arkansas Territory and home of Arkansas' first newspaper, The Arkansas Gazette. Both moved to Little Rock in 1821, and eventually, the Civil War and numerous floods finally destroyed the little town. Today, you can enjoy fishing, hiking and picnicking on the 389 acres of this wildlife sanctuary.
Daily 8 a.m.-5 p.m.

DEGRAY LAKE RESORT STATE PARK
Highway 7, Arkadelphia, 870-865-2801, 501-865-2801; www.degray.com
A great spot for family fun, this resort park offers something for everyone. More than 200 miles of shoreline make the 13,000-acre lake a perfect place

to waterski, fish or swim, or simply lounge on the shoreline. DeGray is one of Arkansas' "diamond lakes," renowned for its clear water. Other park activities include hiking, 18-hole golf, tennis, picnicking and playing on the playground. If you are in the mood to camp, a general store, laundry facility, restaurant and lodge may come in handy. Daily.

OUACHITA BAPTIST UNIVERSITY
410 Ouachita St., Arkadelphia, 870-245-5000; www.obu.edu
Located on the banks of the Ouachita River, and surrounded by the foothills of the Ouachita Mountains, McClellan Hall contains the official papers and memorabilia of U.S. Senator John L. McClellan. Daily.

WHERE TO STAY
★★BEST WESTERN CONTINENTAL INN
136 Valley St., Arkadelphia, 870-246-5592, 800-780-7234; www.bestwestern.com
59 rooms. Restaurant. Complimentary breakfast. Pool. $61-150

BENTONVILLE
See also Fayetteville, Rogers, Springdale
Bentonville is the headquarters for Wal-Mart. But that's not the only thing it has going. Cultural events, nearby state parks and a historic town square give visitors plenty to do.

WHAT TO SEE
PEEL MANSION & HISTORIC GARDENS
400 S. Walton Blvd., Bentonville, 479-273-9664; www.peelmansion.org
This villa tower Italianate mansion—built by Colonel Samuel West Peel, the first native-born Arkansan to serve in the U.S. Congress—has been restored and refurnished in the Victorian style. The 180-acre property also has an outdoor museum of historic roses, perennials and native plants. The pre-Civil War Andy Lynch log cabin serves as the gatehouse and is worth checking out.
Admission: adults $3, children $1. Tuesday-Saturday 10 a.m.-4 p.m.

WHERE TO STAY
★TRAVELODGE BENTONVILLE
2307 S.E. Walton Blvd., Bentonville, 479-273-9727, 800-780-7234; travelodge.com
54 rooms. Complimentary breakfast. Business center. Pool. $61-150

★HOLIDAY INN EXPRESS HOTEL & SUITES
2205 S.E. Walton Blvd., Bentonville, 479-271-2222; www.holiday-inn.com
84 rooms. Complimentary breakfast. $61-150

WHERE TO EAT
★★FRED'S HICKORY INN
1502 N. Walton Blvd., Bentonville, 479-273-3303; www.fredshickoryinn.net
Steak. Lunch, dinner. $16-35

BERRYVILLE

See also Eureka Springs, Harrison

Book worms, rejoice! Berryhill is a great place to find rare or unusual books, thanks to many antique shops and flea markets that specialize in collectible or used tomes. Some of Arkansas' beloved writers spend time here, too.

WHAT TO SEE
CARROLL COUNTY HERITAGE CENTER MUSEUM

403 Public Square, Berryville, 870-423-6312; www.rootsweb.com
Local historical exhibits and genealogical material are housed in this old courthouse, which dates back to 1880.
Admission: adults $2, children $1. Monday-Friday 9 a.m.-4 p.m.

COSMIC CAVERN

6386 Highway 21, Berryville, 870-749-2298; www.cosmiccavern.com
This limestone cave in the Ozarks has two "bottomless" lakes—cave divers have never found the bottom. One section of the cave, discovered in 1993, has one of the longest soda-straw formations—beautiful and fragile mineral tubes. A visitor center and picnic area are also on the premises.
Admission: adults $14, children 5-12 $7.50, children under 5 free. September-May, daily 9 a.m.-5 p.m.; June-August, daily 9 a.m.-6 p.m.

SAUNDERS MEMORIAL MUSEUM

115 E. Madison, Berryville, 870-423-2563; www.arkansas.com
Here you'll find an eclectic collection of loot amassed by C. Burton Saunders during a lifetime of adventure. See guns once used by Jesse James, Billy the Kid and Buffalo Bill Cody. You'll also find items as diverse as Sitting Bull's war bonnet and an Arab sheik's tent.
Admission: adults $3, children 6-12 $1.50, children under 6 free. Mid-April-November, Monday-Saturday 10:30 a.m.-5 p.m.

CAMDEN

See also El Dorado, Magnolia

This little town on the Ouachita River has seen its fair share of historical events—including the Civil War Battle of Poison Springs in 1864, three performances by Elvis Presley in 1955 and a parade of politicians stumping for different causes over the last 200 years.

WHAT TO SEE
MCCOLLUM-CHIDESTER HOUSE

926 Washington St. N.W., Camden
Once a stage coach headquarters, this historic house was used as a base at various times by Confederate General Sterling Price and Union General Frederick Steele. It contains original furnishings and mementos of the Civil War period. It was the setting for segments of the TV miniseries North and South.
Admission: adults $5, children $2. Wednesday-Saturday 9 a.m.-4 p.m.

POISON SPRING BATTLEGROUND HISTORICAL MONUMENT
Highway 76, Bluff City, 870-836-6426, 501-682-1191
This was the site of Union defeat during Union General Frederick Steele's "Red River Campaign" into southwest Arkansas. Exhibits and dioramas trace troop movement. There's also a trail to a small spring and a picnic area. Daily.

WHITE OAK LAKE STATE PARK
986 Highway 387, Bluff City, 870-685-2748; www.arkansasstateparks.com/whiteoaklake
Go swimming; fishing for bass, crappie and bream; or boating on this 2,765-acre lake. Land-based fun abounds with hiking trails, picnicking and camping. Daily.

CONWAY
See also Little Rock
"The City of Colleges," Conway is home to the University of Central Arkansas, Central Baptist College and Hendrix College. Like many towns in Arkansas, Conway offers residents and visitors opportunities to enjoy the outdoors, and the colleges and community groups provide cultural activities, such as theatrical performances and concerts.

WHAT TO SEE
CADRON SETTLEMENT PARK
6298 Highway 60 W. Conway, 501-329-2986; www.swl.usace.army.mil
Part of the Cherokee Trail of Tears runs through the park. You'll also find a replica of a blockhouse built by early settlers in the 1770s. Daily.

HENDRIX COLLEGE
1600 Washington Ave., Conway, 501-450-1462; www.hendrix.edu
This private liberal arts college has long been a favorite of college guides. Stroll the campus and see why. The Mills Center houses congressional office contents and some personal papers of former Congressman Wilbur D. Mills, chairman of the House Ways and Means Committee and graduate of Hendrix College. Daily.

WOOLLY HOLLOW STATE PARK
82 Woolly Hollow Road, Greenbrier, 501-679-2098; www.arkansasstateparks.com/woollyhollow
A peaceful getaway in the Ozark foothills, the park surrounds Lake Bennett, where visitors can fish and swim. Woolly Cabin, a restored one-room log structure built in 1882, gives you a glimpse of early settlers' lives. A swimming beach, fishing, boating, hiking trails, picnicking, a playground, camping, and a snack bar are all nearby. Daily.

SPECIAL EVENT
TOAD SUCK DAZE
1234 Main St., Conway, 501-327-7788; www.toadsuck.org
According to local lore, the name "Toad Suck" comes from a description locals used to describe steamboat captains and crews who traveled down the

Arkansas River and stopped to imbibe at the local tavern. Wary locals said the visitors sucked on liquor bottles "until they swelled up like toads." The festival features carnival rides; arts and crafts; bluegrass, country and gospel music; and of course, toad races.

First weekend of May.

WHERE TO STAY
★★BEST WESTERN CONWAY
816 E. Oak St., Conway, 501-329-9855, 800-780-7234; www.bestwestern.com
70 rooms. Restaurant. Complimentary breakfast. Pool. $61-150

★QUALITY INN
150 Highway 65 N., Conway, 501-329-0300; www.qualityinn.com
60 rooms. Complimentary breakfast. Pool. $61-150

WHERE TO EAT
★FU LIN
195 Farris Road, Conway, 501-329-1415
Chinese. Lunch, dinner. $16-35

DUMAS
See also Little Rock

Dumas, Ark., and Dumas, Texas, have been in a bit of a scuffle over a song written in the 1930s. Both towns lay claim to the song "I'm a Ding Dong Daddy From Dumas," a knee-slapping song written by Phil Baxter and Carl Moore. The tune, which was a big hit, prompted the town to erect big signs on the highway entrances to Dumas, proclaiming "Welcome to Dumas, home of the Ding Dong Daddies."

WHAT TO SEE
LAKE CHICOT STATE PARK
2542 Highway 257, Lake Village, 870-265-5480; www.arkansas.com
The park surrounds Arkansas' largest natural lake (formed centuries ago when the Mississippi changed its course), which is famous for its bream, crappie, catfish and bass fishing. But you also have your choice of swimming in a pool, boating, picnicking, frolicking on the playground, camping or staying in cabins. Sporty types can take archery lessons in the summer. Daily.

EL DORADO
See also Camden, Magnolia

Legend tells us that one day around 1830, pioneer Matthew F. Rainey's wagon broke down in a forest of hardwood and pine. Discouraged and tired, he offered his goods for sale. The farmers in the area were such eager customers that Rainey decided to open a store on the spot and call the place El Dorado. The town led a quiet existence until oil was discovered in 1921. Soon it was inundated with drillers, speculators, engineers and merchants. The vivacity of the '20s continues today in El Dorado, especially in its lively and beautiful downtown district.

WHAT TO SEE
ARKANSAS MUSEUM OF NATURAL RESOURCES
3853 Smackover Highway, Smackover, 870-725-2877; www.amnr.org
The 10-acre outdoor exhibit depicts working examples of oil production from the 1920s to the present. Aside from the museum exhibits, there's a research center, gift shop and picnic area.
Monday-Saturday 8 a.m.-5 p.m., Sunday 1-5 p.m.

SOUTH ARKANSAS ARBORETUM
501 Timberlane, El Dorado, 870-862-8131; www.goeldorado.com
The 13-acre arboretum features indigenous trees and plants, including exotic species of azaleas and camellias. The grounds also have nature trails and wooden bridges.
Daily 8 a.m.-4 p.m.

WHERE TO STAY
★★ECONO LODGE CONFERENCE CENTER
1920 Junction City Road, El Dorado, 870-862-5191; www.econolodge.com
131 rooms. Restaurant. Business Center. Pool. $61-150

EUREKA SPRINGS
See also Berryville, Harrison, Rogers
Eureka Springs is one of Arkansas' most popular tourist destinations. Visitors are drawn to its European flavor, Victorian buildings and steep, winding streets. In the 19th century, Eureka Springs was a well-known health spa. Thousands of people flocked to the city because its springs, which gushed from limestone crevices, had a reputation for healing a wide variety of illnesses. Today, the town attracts tourists who simply want to enjoy the town's many art galleries, boutiques, restaurants and charm.

WHAT TO SEE

EUREKA SPRINGS & NORTH ARKANSAS RAILWAY
299 N. Main St. (Highway 23), Eureka Springs, 479-253-9623; www.esnarailway.com
Travel through the hills of the Ozarks and imagine life in the 19th century, when the first settlers rode into Eureka Springs. Dining cars are available on certain trips.
Admission: adults $12, children 4-10 $6, children under 4 free. April-October, Tuesday-Saturday 10:30 a.m., noon, 2 p.m., 4 p.m.

EUREKA SPRINGS HISTORICAL MUSEUM
95 S. Main St., Eureka Springs, 479-253-9417; www.eshm.org
Eureka Springs has a history worth investigating, and the museum is a good spot to begin your exploration. Artifacts from the 19th century, including photographs and furniture, are on display in this beautiful house.
Admission: adults $5, students $2.50, children under 10 free. Monday-Saturday 9:30 a.m.-4 p.m., Sunday 11 a.m.-4 p.m.

FROG FANTASIES MUSEUM

151 Spring St., Eureka Springs, 479-253-7227; www.arkansas.com

This museum displays more than 7,000 man-made frog trinkets, from Christmas ornaments and plush toys to a diamond-encrusted pin. There's also a gift shop so you can pick up your own froggie souvenirs. Daily.

HAMMOND MUSEUM OF BELLS

2 Pine St., Eureka Springs,

More than 30 lighted exhibits trace the history and structure of bells from 800 B.C. to the present. The collection of bells on display is impressive, from primitive antiques to examples of musical fine art. There's a narrated audio tour.

Admission: adults $3, children free. Monday-Friday 9:30 a.m.-5 p.m., Sunday 11:30 a.m.-4 p.m.

PIVOT ROCK AND NATURAL BRIDGE

1708 Pivot Rock Road, Eureka Springs, 479-253-8860; www.arkansas.com

Hidden in a forest, these unusual rock formations will surprise you. The top of Pivot Rock is 15 times as wide as the bottom yet it is perfectly balanced. Nearby are a natural bridge and caves, where locals believe Jesse James once hid.

April-mid-November, daily.

ROSALIE HOUSE

282 Spring St., Eureka Springs, 479-253-7377; www.therosalie.com

The house was built of handmade brick with gingerbread trim. It has its original interior, with gold leaf molding, ceiling frescoes, handmade woodwork and period furnishings. It is a popular destination for weddings and special events.

Thursday-Monday 11 a.m.-5 p.m.

BIBLE MUSEUM

935 Passion Play Road, Eureka Springs, 866-566-3565 www.greatpassionplay.com

This museum carries rare Bibles, artifacts and more than 6,000 volumes in 625 languages, including works on papyrus, parchment and clay cylinders and cones dating from 2000 B.C.

Admission: adults $15, children 6-15 $10, children under 6 free. Daily noon-5 p.m.

CHRIST OF THE OZARKS

935 Passion Play Road, Eureka Springs, 866-566-3565; www.greatpassionplay.com

Erected in 1966, this seven-story-tall statue of Jesus weighs more than 1 million pounds and has an arm span of 65 feet.

Daily.

NEW HOLY LAND

935 Passion Play Road, Eureka Springs, 866-566-3565; www.greatpassionplay.com

This facility contains Old and New Testament exhibits with costumed guides, including full-size replica of Moses' tabernacle and Last Supper re-creation.

Admission: adults $15, children 6-15 $10, children under 6 free. Monday-Saturday.

THORNCROWN CHAPEL
12968 Highway 62 W., Eureka Springs, 479-253-7401; www.thorncrown.com
This sensational glass chapel structure is tucked in the woods in the Ozarks. It was designed by noted Arkansas architect E. Fay Jones.
April-November, daily 9 a.m.-5 p.m.; December, March, daily 11 a.m.-4 p.m. Closed January-February.

WITHROW SPRINGS STATE PARK
Highway 23 N., Huntsville, 479-559-2593; www.arkansasstateparks.com
This 700-acre recreation area stretches across mountains and valleys along the bluffs of War Eagle River. The waters of a large spring gush from a shallow cave at the foot of a towering bluff. Get active canoeing, hiking, playing tennis, picnicking or camping. Daily.

SPECIAL EVENTS
THE GREAT PASSION PLAY
Mount Oberammergau, Passion Play Road, Eureka Springs, 479-253-9200, 866-566-3565; www.greatpassionplay.com
Performed five nights a week from late April to late October, the play portrays the life of Jesus from Palm Sunday through the Ascension in an outdoor amphitheater.
Monday-Tuesday, Thursday-Saturday.

OZARK FOLK FESTIVAL
36 S. Main St., Eureka Springs, 888-855-7823; www.ozarkfolkfestival.com
The festival attracts national headliners and other musical acts, and also offers a beauty pageant, Gay '90s costume parade and other events.
Early October.

WHERE TO STAY
★★★1886 CRESCENT HOTEL & SPA
75 Prospect Ave., Eureka Springs, 877-342-9766, 800-342-9766;
www.crescent-hotel.com
Built atop Eureka Springs' highest point, this grand hotel offers gorgeous views of the valley. Guests will feel as if they have traveled back in time when they pass through the front door into the opulent lobby. Guest rooms are decorated in Victorian style with wallpaper and period furnishings. Stake out a spot by the pool or indulge in a spa treatment at the property's New Moon Spa and Salon. Adventure seekers will find plenty of activities in the area such as ghost tours, fishing, hiking, kayaking, canoeing, and car and motorcycle tours. After a busy day, The Crystal Dining Room is the perfect spot for an elegant meal, followed by drinks at Dr. Baker's Lounge, where guests can enjoy panoramic views of the Ozarks and live entertainment on the weekends.
72 rooms. Restaurant, bar. Pool. Spa. $61-150

★★BEST WESTERN INN OF THE OZARKS

207 W. Van Buren, Eureka Springs, 479-253-9768, 800-780-7234;
www.innoftheozarks.com
122 rooms. Restaurant. Business center. Pool. Tennis. $61-150

★★NEW ORLEANS HOTEL & SPA

63 Spring St., Eureka Springs, 479-253-8630, 800-243-8630; www.neworleanshote-
landspa.com
21 rooms. Restaurant, bar. Spa. $61-150

WHERE TO EAT
★BUBBA'S BARBECUE

166 W. Van Buren, Eureka Springs, 479-253-7706
Barbecue. Lunch, dinner. Closed Sunday. $16-35

★★★THE CRYSTAL DINING ROOM

75 Prospect Ave., Eureka Springs, 479-253-9766, 800-342-9766;
www.crescent-hotel.com/dining
Located off the lobby of the historic 1886 Crescent Hotel & Spa, The Crystal Dining Room offers beautiful Victorian-style surroundings with hardwood floors, high ceilings and sparkling chandeliers, formal but friendly service and a stellar menu of inventive American cuisine. Dinner options may include espresso-glazed filet of sirloin or mesquite-seared salmon. Breakfast, lunch and a Sunday champagne brunch are also served; dishes like three-layer pancakes with wild berry compote and a classic Reuben on marble rye satisfy every palate.
American. Breakfast, lunch, dinner, Sunday brunch. Reservations recommended. Children's menu. $36-85

FAYETTEVILLE

See also Bentonville, Rogers, Springdale
Home of the University of Arkansas Razorbacks, Fayetteville is often ranked among the nation's best places to live, thanks to its reputation for affordable living, natural beauty, temperate climate and easy access to outdoor activities.

WHAT TO SEE
ARKANSAS AIR MUSEUM

4290 S. School St., Fayetteville, 479-521-4947; www.arkairmuseum.org
Aspiring pilots and curious air travelers will enjoy the exhibits here, which span the history of manned flight. Don't miss the racing planes from the 1920s and '30s, the Lear Jet 23 and the Cobra Helicopter, one of the first modern combat helicopters.
Admission: adults $8, children 6-12 $4, children under 6 free. Sunday-Friday 11 a.m.-4:30 p.m., Saturday 10 a.m.-4:30 p.m.

DEVIL'S DEN STATE PARK

11333 Highway 74 W., West Fork, 479-761-3325; www.arkansasstateparks.com
In a scenic valley in the Boston Mountains, this 2,000-acre park in the heart

of rugged Ozark terrain includes unusual sandstone formations and the Devil's Icebox, where the temperature never goes above 60 F. If you want to get moving, go swimming in the pool, fishing, canoeing, hiking or mountain biking on the trails. There's also a horse camp and a visitor center with exhibits, camping and backpack equipment rentals. Daily.

PRAIRIE GROVE BATTLEFIELD STATE PARK
14262 Highway 62, Prairie Grove, 479-846-2990; www.arkansasstateparks.com
Here you'll find the site where more than 22,000 Union and Confederate forces fought on December 7, 1862. The armies suffered a combined loss of 2,700 dead, wounded or missing. The Hindman Hall Museum houses a visitor center with exhibits, a battle diorama, artifacts and an audiovisual presentation. The park is also home to historic structures.
Admission: adults $3, children 6-12 $2, children under 6 free. Daily 8 a.m.-5 p.m.

WHERE TO STAY
★BEST WESTERN WINDSOR SUITES
1122 S. Futrall, Fayetteville, 479-587-1400, 800-780-7234; www.bestwestern.com
68 rooms. Complimentary breakfast. Business center. Pool. $61-150

★★CLARION CARRIAGE HOUSE INN AT THE MILL
3906 Great House Springs Road, Johnson, 479-443-1800; www.innatthemill.com
48 rooms. Restaurant. Complimentary breakfast. $151-250

★DAYS INN
2402 N. College Ave., Fayetteville, 479-443-4323, 800-329-7466; www.daysinn.com
149 rooms. Complimentary breakfast. Pool. $61-150

★★COSMOPOLITAN HOTEL FAYETTEVILLE
70 N. East Ave., Fayetteville, 479-442-5555, 800-333-3333; www.radisson.com/fayettevillear
235 rooms. Restaurant, bar. Fitness center. Pool. $61-150

FORT SMITH
See also Van Buren
It's hard to imagine today, but Fort Smith was once the edge of the Wild West. The original fort was built on the Arkansas River in 1817 to promote peace between the warring Osages and the Cherokees. It also gave protection to traders, trappers and explorers.

In 1848, when gold was discovered in California, Fort Smith immediately became a thriving supply center and starting point for gold rush wagons heading south across the plains. Bandits, robbers and gamblers moved in. Without peace officers, the territory was wild and tough until 1875, when Judge Isaac C. Parker—known later as "The Hanging Judge"—arrived to clean it up. Parker was judge of the Federal District Court at Fort Smith for 21 years; during his first 14 years, there were no appeals of his decisions. Under Parker's rule, 151 men were sentenced to die and about 80 hanged, sometimes as many as six at a time. The town has preserved much of its history, which makes it a great stop for travelers who want to see the place where the Old West meets the Old South.

WHAT TO SEE
FORT SMITH ART CENTER
423 N. Sixth St., Fort Smith, 479-784-2787; www.ftsartcenter.com
Originally built in 1879 as a residence, the art center now offers changing monthly exhibits and art classes.
Tuesday-Saturday 9:30 a.m.-4:30 p.m.

FORT SMITH MUSEUM OF HISTORY
320 Rogers Ave., Fort Smith, 479-783-7841; www.fortsmithmuseum.com
The museum gives a glimpse into regional history with a period pharmacy with a working soda fountain and a transportation exhibit with an 1899 steam fire pumper.
Admission: adults $5, children 6-15 $2, children under 6 free. June-August, Tuesday-Saturday 10 a.m.-5 p.m., Sunday 1-5 p.m.; September-May, Tuesday-Saturday 10 a.m.-5 p.m.

FORT SMITH NATIONAL HISTORIC SITE
301 Parker Ave., Fort Smith, 479-783-3961; www.nps.gov/fosm
The park includes foundations of the first Fort Smith, the famous Judge Parker's courtroom, jail (known during Judge Parker's reign as "Hell on the Border") and reconstructed gallows.
Admission: adults $4. Daily 9 a.m.-5 p.m.

WHITE ROCK MOUNTAIN RECREATION AREA
Highway 215, in the Boston Mountain range of the Ozark National Forest, Alma, 501-369-4128; www.whiterockmountain.com
At the summit of 2,287-foot White Rock peak, this primitive area has beautiful panoramic views. It's a great spot for picnicking and camping. Daily.

SPECIAL EVENTS
ARKANSAS-OKLAHOMA STATE FAIR
Kay Rodgers Park, 4400 Midland Blvd., Fort Smith, 479-783-6176, 800-364-1080; www.kayrodgerspark.com
Kay Rodgers Park is home to a number of events throughout the year, including the Arkansas-Oklahoma State Fair, held nine days in September and October. The fair features live musical entertainment, a youth talent contest, a circus, a demolition derby, monster-truck racing, a carnival, and livestock, poultry and horticulture exhibits.
Late September-early October.

OLD FORT DAYS RODEO
Kay Rodgers Park, 4400 Midland Blvd., Fort Smith, 479-783-6176, 800-364-1080
This fast-paced rodeo has it all: calf roping, wild-horse racing, steer wrestling and rodeo clown bullfighting.
Late May-early June.

WHERE TO STAY
★ASPEN HOTEL & SUITES
2900 S. 68th, Fort Smith, 501-452-9000, 800-627-9417; www.aspenhotelandsuites.com
49 rooms. Complimentary breakfast. Business center. Pool. $61-150

★★HOLIDAY INN FORT SMITH CITY CENTER
700 Rogers Ave., Fort Smith, 479-783-1000, 800-465-4329; www.holiday-inn.com
255 rooms. Restaurant, bar. Business center. Fitness center. Pool. $61-150

WHERE TO EAT
★CALICO COUNTY
2401 S. 56th St., Fort Smith, 479-452-3299; www.calicocounty.net
American. Breakfast, lunch, dinner. $16-35

HARRISON
See also Berryville, Eureka Springs
Scenic Harrison, headquarters for a rustic resort area in the wild and beautiful Ozarks, is an excellent vacation spot. Don't miss the gorgeous drive along Highway 7.

WHAT TO SEE
BOONE COUNTY HERITAGE MUSEUM
110 S. Cherry, Harrison, 870-741-3312; www.bchrs.org
The museum preserves history and antiques from the Civil War and the Missouri and North Arkansas Railroad Co., Native American artifacts, old clocks, and medical and domestic tools from the 1800s.
Admission: adults $2, children under 12 free. March-November, Monday-Friday 10 a.m.-4 p.m.; December-February, Thursday 10 a.m.-4 p.m.

MYSTIC CAVERNS

Highway 7 S., Dogpatch, 870-743-1739; www.mysticcaverns.com
Mystic has two caves with large formations, a 35-foot "pipe organ" formation and an eight-story crystal dome. The one-hour walking tour can be strenuous so come prepared.
Admission: adults $14.99, Children 4-12 $6.99, children under 4 free. March-December, Monday-Saturday 9 a.m.-5 p.m.

SPECIAL EVENTS
HARVEST HOMECOMING
Harrison, 870-741-4889; www.arkansas.com
During the first weekend in October, the people of Harrison flock to the downtown area to take part in the city's largest festival. The Harvest Homecoming celebrates Harrison's history with activities the whole family can enjoy. In addition to autumn food and live entertainment, the festival features a farmers' market, working craftsmen, children's activities, a car show, tractor races and a scarecrow-decorating contest. October.

NORTHWEST ARKANSAS BLUEGRASS MUSIC FESTIVAL

Northwest Arkansas Fairgrounds, 1400 Fairgrounds Road, Harrison, 870-427-3342; www.southshore.com

Festival-goers camp out and enjoy impromptu jam sessions when they're not busy catching the scheduled stage acts.

August.

WHERE TO STAY

★COMFORT INN

1210 Highway 62-65 N., Harrison, 870-741-7676, 800-228-5150; www.choicehotels.com

93 rooms. Complimentary breakfast. Pool. $61-150

★DAYS INN

1425 Highway 62/65 N., Harrison, 870-391-3297, 800-329-7466; www.daysinn.com

82 rooms. Restaurant, bar. Complimentary breakfast. Business center. Pool. $61-150

★★RED APPLE INN RESORT

1000 Country Club, Heber Springs, 501-362-3111, 800-733-2775; www.redappleinn.com

57 rooms. Restaurant, bar. Restaurant, bar. Fitness center. Pool. Golf. Tennis. $61-150

WHERE TO EAT

★★CAFE KLASER

600 W. Main St., Heber Springs, 501-206-0688; www.cafeklaser.com

Steak. Lunch, dinner. Closed Sunday-Monday. $16-35

★★OL' ROCKHOUSE

416 S. Pine St., Harrison, 870-741-8047

American. Lunch, dinner. $16-35

★★RED APPLE DINING ROOM

1000 Club Road, Heber Springs, 501-362-3111; www.redappleinn.com

American. Breakfast, lunch, dinner, Sunday brunch. $16-35

HELENA

See also Clarksdale

Mark Twain once described Helena as occupying "one of the prettiest situations on the Mississippi." This spot has more than good looks. Some of the nation's best blues musicians cut their teeth here. Sunnyland Slim, Memphis Slim and Roosevelt Sykes all played here in the 1940s and '50s.

WHAT TO SEE

OZARK NATIONAL FOREST

Highway 44, Helena, 479-964-7200, 870-295-5278; www.fs.fed.us/oonf/ozark

In beautiful Ozark National Forest, you'll find the Boston Mountains, the state's tallest mountain, Mount Magazine, and an amazing underground cave, Blanchard Springs Caverns. Trek the 165-mile Ozark Highlands Trail, paddle Richland Creek and check out the waterfalls and camp along Shores Lake (especially in April, when dogwoods are in bloom). Daily.

PHILLIPS COUNTY MUSEUM
623 Pecan St., Helena, 870-338-7790
At this museum, you'll find Native American artifacts, Civil War relics, a local history collection, glass, china, paintings and costumes.
Tuesday-Saturday 10 a.m.-4 p.m.

SPECIAL EVENT
ARKANSAS BLUES HERITAGE FESTIVAL
Cherry St., Helena, 870-338-8798; www.bluesandheritage.org
Formerly the King Biscuit Blues Festival, this celebration of blues is one of the South's best. For three full days, nearly 100,000 people enjoy blues music and culture.
October.

HOPE
See also Texarkana
Before he was the 42nd president of the United States, William Jefferson Clinton was a little kid in Hope, Ark. Today, the town celebrates its native son who told delegates at the 1992 Democratic National Convention: "I still believe in a place called Hope." Hope's second claim to fame is its Watermelon Festival, where farmers compete to win awards for the largest melon.

WHAT TO SEE
CLINTON BIRTHPLACE HOME
117 S. Hervey, Hope, 870-777-4455; www.clintonbirthplace.org/hometour.htm
This was the first home of President Bill Clinton; he lived here from the time of his birth in 1946 until his mother married Roger Clinton in 1950. It's a National Register Historic Site. There's also a visitor center and gift shop.
Admission: adults $5, seniors $4, children 7-18 $3, children under 7 free.
Monday-Saturday 10 a.m.-5 p.m.

HOPE WATERMELON FESTIVAL
108 W. Third St., Hope, 870-777-3640; www.hopemelonfest.com
Celebrate the great melon for four days. The festival tradition began in the 1920s, when trains cut through this small town and local watermelon growers would sell their fruit to parched travelers. These days, people flock to the four-day festival to enjoy good food, buy arts and crafts, attend the antique car show and compete in the Watermelon Olympics, which includes a seed-spitting contest and a melon toss. The big event, though, is the competition to see the biggest watermelon. Most years, the winner weighs between 150 and 200 pounds.
Early August.

WHERE TO STAY
★BEST WESTERN OF HOPE
1800 Holiday Drive, Hope, 870-777-9222, 800-429-4494; www.bestwestern.com
75 rooms. Complimentary breakfast. Pool. $61-150

HOT SPRINGS AND HOT SPRINGS NATIONAL PARK
See also Arkadelphia, Benton, Malvern
One of the most popular destinations in the United States, the colorful city of Hot Springs surrounds portions of Hot Springs National Park. Known as "America's spa," Hot Springs has long attracted vacationers in search of healing or relaxation.

Nearly 1 million gallons of thermal water flow daily from the 47 springs within the park. At an average temperature of 147 F, the water flows to a reservoir under the city's headquarters building; here it is distributed to bathhouses and spas through insulated pipes. Bathhouses mix cooled and hot thermal water to regulate bath temperatures.

Hot Springs, however, is more than a spa. It is a cosmopolitan city in the midst of beautiful wooded hills, valleys and lakes of the Ouachita region. The town's art scene is one of the best in the South, and its downtown area offers delicious restaurants and charming shops. Swimming, boating and water sports are available at nearby Catherine, Hamilton and Ouachita lakes. All three offer good year-round fishing for bream, crappie, bass and rainbow trout.

WHAT TO SEE
ARKANSAS ALLIGATOR FARM & PETTING ZOO
847 Whittington Ave., Hot Springs, 501-623-6172; www.arkansasalligatorfarm.com
We're not sure you'll actually want to pet the alligators, but this stop has plenty for you to see. It's also home to rhesus monkeys, mountain lions, llamas, pygmy goats, ducks and other animals.
Admission: adults $6.50, children 3-12 $5.50, children 2 free. Daily 9:30 a.m.-5 p.m.

AUTO TOURS
Fountain Street and Hot Springs Mountain Drive, Hot Springs, 501-321-2277; www. hotsprings.org
Just north of Bathhouse Row, drive from the end of Fountain Street up Hot Springs Mountain Drive to scenic overlooks at Hot Springs Mountain Tower and a picnic area on the mountaintop. West Mountain Drive, starting from either Prospect Avenue (on the south) or from Whittington Avenue (on the north), also provides excellent vistas of the city and surrounding countryside. Daily.

COLEMAN'S CRYSTAL MINE
5387 N. Highway 7, Jesseville, 501-984-5328; www.jimcolemancrystals.com
Visitors may dig for quartz crystals or just take a spin through the massive collection of already-found gems.
Admission: adults $10, children under 10 free. Daily 8 a.m.-5 p.m.

FORDYCE BATHHOUSE MUSEUM & HOT SPRINGS NATIONAL PARK VISITOR CENTER

300 Central Ave., Hot Springs, 501-624-2308; www.hotsprings.org

Multiple exhibits on the history of the Hot Springs are on display in this renovated 1915 original bathhouse structure with stained glass ceilings, marble walls and carved statues.

Daily 9 a.m.-7 p.m.

HOT SPRINGS MOUNTAIN TOWER

401 Hot Springs Mountain Drive, Hot Springs, 501-623-6035

The tower rises 216 feet above Hot Springs National Park. Ride its glass-enclosed elevator up 1,256 feet above sea level for spectacular views of the Ouachita Mountains. Enjoy the fully enclosed viewing area and higher up, an open-air deck.

Admission: adults $7, seniors $6, children 5-11 $4, children under 5 free. Daily.

JOSEPHINE TUSSAUD WAX MUSEUM

250 Central Ave., Hot Springs, 501-623-5836; www.rideaduck.com

Set in the former Southern Club, which was the city's largest casino and supper club until the late 1960s, this museum displays more than 100 wax figures.

Admission: adults $9, children 3-12 $5.50, children under 3 free. May-September, Sunday-Thursday 9 a.m.-8 p.m., Friday-Saturday 9 a.m.-9 p.m.; October-April, Sunday-Thursday 9:30 a.m.-5 p.m., Friday-Saturday 9:30 a.m.-8 p.m.

MID-AMERICA SCIENCE MUSEUM

500 Mid-America Blvd., Hot Springs, 71913; 501-767-3461; www.midamericamuseum.org

Spend a day contemplating the wonders of the world—or at least, of Arkansas. Travel through "Underground Arkansas," an indoor cave with bridges, chambers, tunnels and slides. Catch the laser light show and trap your shadow—à la Peter Pan—in the Shadow Trapper. Before you leave, check out the 35,000-gallon freshwater aquarium. There's also a snack bar and a gift shop.

Admission: adults $8, seniors, military and children 2-12 $7, children under 2 free. June-August, daily 9:30 a.m.-6 p.m.; September-May, Tuesday-Sunday 10 a.m.-5 p.m.

NATIONAL PARK DUCK TOURS

418 Central Ave., Hot Springs, 501-321-2911, 800-682-7044; www.rideaduck.com

The "Amphibious Duck" travels on both land and water. Board in the heart of Hot Springs and proceed onto Lake Hamilton and around St. John's Island. Ticket prices vary.

March-October, daily; November-February, weather permitting.

OUACHITA NATIONAL FOREST

100 Reserve St., Hot Springs, 501-321-5202; www.hotspringsar.com

The Ouachita ("WASH-i-taw") is 1.8 million acres of natural beauty in west central Arkansas and southeast Oklahoma. Hike, mountain bike or ride horseback along the park's many trails. Fish, swim or boat in any one of eight lakes, or canoe down one of its nine navigable rivers. Daily.

PARK HEADQUARTERS AND VISITOR CENTER

101 Reserve St., Hot Springs, 501-624-3383; www.hot.springs.national-park.com
The center offers an exhibit on the workings and origin of the hot springs. A self-guided nature trail starts here and follows the Grand Promenade. The visitor center is in the Hill Wheatley Plaza at the park entrance. Daily.

WHERE TO STAY
★★★ARLINGTON RESORT HOTEL AND SPA

239 Central Ave., Hot Springs, 501-623-7771, 800-643-1502; www.arlingtonhotel.com
Guests will find total relaxation and enjoyment at this resort in the beautiful Ouachita Mountains of Hot Springs National Park. You can unwind in twin cascading pools or in the refreshing outdoor mountainside hot tub.
484 rooms. Restaurant, bar. Pool. Spa. $151-250

★★★THE AUSTIN HOTEL & CONVENTION CENTER

305 Malvern Ave., Hot Springs, 501-623-6600, 877-623-6697; www.theaustinhotel.com
This wonderful getaway is in Hot Springs Park with a spectacular view of the Ouachita Mountains. Guests can rejuvenate with a visit to the famous spa in the park or enjoy art galleries and music shows only a few miles away. Convenient for business travelers, the hotel is connected to the Hot Springs Convention Center via a covered walkway.
200 rooms. Restaurant, bar. Pool. Spa. $151-250

★DAYS INN

106 Lookout Point, Hot Springs, 501-525-5666, 800-995-9559; www.daysinn.com
58 rooms. Complimentary breakfast. Pool. $61-150

★HAMPTON INN
151 Temperance Hill Road, Hot Springs, 501-525-7000, 800-426-7866;
www.hamptoninn.com
82 rooms. Complimentary breakfast. Business center. Pool. $61-150

WHERE TO EAT
★CAJUN BOILERS
2806 Albert Pike Highway, Hot Springs, 501-767-5695
Cajun. Dinner. Closed Sunday-Monday. $16-35

★★COY'S STEAK HOUSE
300 Coy St., Hot Springs, 501-321-1414; www.coyssteakhouse.com
Seafood, steak. Dinner. $36-85

★★★HAMILTON HOUSE
132 Van Lyell Trail, Hot Springs, 501-520-4040; www.hamiltonhouseestate.com
The town's best fine dining experience, the restaurant occupies four stories of an old estate home. The house sits on a quiet peninsula on beautiful Lake

Hamilton and the cozy dining rooms will charm you.
American. Dinner. $36-85

★★HOT SPRINGS BRAU-HOUSE
801 Central Ave., Hot Springs, 501-624-7866
German. Dinner. Closed Monday. $15 and under

★MCCLARD'S BAR-B-Q
505 Albert Pike, Hot Springs, 501-623-9665; www.mcclards.com
Barbecue. Lunch, dinner. Closed Sunday-Monday. $15 and under

JONESBORO
See also Little Rock
The largest city in northeast Arkansas, Jonesboro is on Crowley's Ridge, an unusual geological formation that rises 250 to 500 feet above the Mississippi Delta; the ridge runs nearly 200 miles from Missouri to Helena, Ark., more or less parallel to the Mississippi. Jonesboro is home to Arkansas State University and to more than 75 churches, earning it the nickname "The City of Churches."

WHAT TO SEE
ARKANSAS STATE UNIVERSITY
106 N. Caraway, Jonesboro, 870-972-2100; www.astate.edu
Nine colleges and a graduate school are spread throughout the verdant 941-acre campus. Daily.

CROWLEY'S RIDGE STATE PARK
2092 Highway 168, Walcott, 870-573-6751; www.arkansasstateparks.com
Once a campground for the Quapaw, this park has two lakes and miles of wooded hills. The ridge is named for Benjamin Crowley, whose homestead and burial place are here. You also have your choice of swimming, fishing, boating, hiking and picnicking. Daily.

LAKE FRIERSON STATE PARK
7904 Highway 141, Jonesboro, 870-932-2615; www.arkansasstateparks.com
Famous for its brilliant array of dogwood blossoms in spring, this 135-acre park is on the eastern shore of Lake Frierson, which fronts the western edge of Crowley's Ridge. Daily.

WHERE TO STAY
★★HOLIDAY INN
3006 S. Caraway Road, Jonesboro, 870-935-2030; www.holiday-inn.com
179 rooms. Restaurant, bar. Business center. Fitness center. Pool. $61-150

★HOLIDAY INN EXPRESS
2407 Phillips Drive, Jonesboro, 870-932-5554, 800-465-4329; www.hiexpress.com
103 rooms. Complimentary breakfast. Business center. Pool. $61-150

WHERE TO EAT
★FRONT PAGE CAFE
2117 E. Parker, Jonesboro, 870-932-6343
American. Breakfast, lunch, dinner. $15 and under

LITTLE ROCK
See also Benton, Pine Bluff
Little Rock, the state capital, got its name from French explorers who dubbed this site on the Arkansas River "La Petite Roche" to distinguish it from larger rock outcroppings up the river. By 1831, the town was incorporated.

More than 175 years later, Little Rock is a historic city with the sophistication and spunk of a metropolitan mecca. Little Rockers—as the city's residents are called—enjoy beautiful river walks, chic restaurants, fine museums and plenty of recreational and cultural activities. One of the hottest spots in town is River Market in downtown Little Rock, home to a large indoor market where shoppers can buy everything from fresh vegetables to instruments. At night, River Market is the place to find live entertainment, often provided by the city's up-and-coming musicians.

Another lively neighborhood, the Heights on the north central side of town has a friendly vibe. Exclusive boutiques, antique shops, coffee houses and cafés—all frequented by the yuppies who live nearby—are worth a visit. The area gets its name from the bluffs on which many of the posh residential homes sit.

WHAT TO SEE
ARKANSAS ARTS CENTER
MacArthur Park, 501 E. Ninth St., Little Rock, 501-372-4000; www.arkarts.com
Exhibits at this arts center include paintings, drawings, prints, sculpture and ceramics. Public classes in visual and performing arts are available. Plus, the facility also features a library, restaurant and theater. You can catch a performance by the Arkansas Arts Center Children's Theater here.
Tuesday-Saturday 10 a.m.-5 p.m., -Sunday 11 a.m.-5 p.m.

BURNS PARK
1 Eldor Johnson Drive, North Little Rock, 501-791-8537; www.northlittlerock.ar.gov
One of the largest city-owned parks in the country, 1,500-acre Burns Park offers a little something for everyone. Fishing, boating, wildlife trails, 27-hole golf, miniature golf, tennis and even camping are available. The park's more unusual activities include amusement rides and nine-hole Frisbee golf. Daily.

CLINTON PRESIDENTIAL LIBRARY AND MUSEUM
1200 Clinton Ave., Little Rock, 501-374-4242
The library and museum archives contain over 76 million pages of documents, over a million photographs and 84,600 artifacts that preserve the written record of our presidents. The museum also offers educational programs, exhibits and special events and includes replicas of the Oval Office and Cabinet Room. President Reagan described the presidential libraries as "classrooms of democracy."

Admission: adults $7, seniors and students $5, children $3. Monday-Saturday 9 a.m.-5 p.m., Sunday 1-5 p.m.

DECORATIVE ARTS MUSEUM

501 E. Ninth St., Little Rock, 501-372-4000; www.arkarts.com

The restored 1839 Greek Revival mansion houses decorative art objects ranging from Greek and Roman period to contemporary American. You'll see ceramics, glass, textiles, crafts and Asian works of art.

Tuesday-Saturday 10 a.m.-5 p.m., -Sunday 11 a.m.-5 p.m.

HISTORIC ARKANSAS MUSEUM

200 E. Third St., Little Rock, 501-324-9351; www.arkansashistory.com

Built between the 1820s and 1850s, the restoration includes four houses, out-buildings and a log house arranged to give a realistic picture of pre-Civil War Arkansas. The museum houses Arkansas-made exhibits and a crafts shop. Admission: adults $2.50, seniors $1.50, children $1. Monday-Saturday 9 a.m.-5 p.m., Sunday 1-5 p.m.

LITTLE ROCK ZOO

1 Jonesboro Dr,, Little Rock, 501-666-2406; www.littlerockzoo.com

What began in 1926 with an abandoned timber wolf and a circus-trained brown bear has grown into one of Little Rock's best attractions. More than 700 animals live here, many of them on the endangered species list. Be sure to check out the antique Over-the-Jumps carousel that dates back to the 1880s.

Admission: adults $10, seniors and children 1-12 $8, children under 1 free. Daily 9 a.m.-5 p.m.

MUSEUM OF DISCOVERY

500 President Clinton Ave., Little Rock, 501-396-7050, 800-880-6475; www.amod.org

This hands-on museum houses exhibits that will fascinate you and your kids. Check out the eerily empty mummy's coffin; its owner hasn't been found. Or chill out with a tarantula, an alligator or even the famed blue-tongued skink. Other exhibits cover energy, technology, the human body, foreign nations and much more.

Admission: adults $8, seniors and children 1-12 $7, children under 1 free. Monday-Saturday 9 a.m.-5 p.m., Sunday 1-5 p.m.

OLD MILL

Lakeshore and Fairway avenues, North Little Rock, 501-791-8537; www.northlr.org

This scenic city park is famous for its cameo in the opening scene of *Gone with the Wind*. On the road to the mill are original milestones laid out by Confederate President Jefferson Davis. Daily.

THE OLD STATE HOUSE

300 W. Markham St., Little Rock, 501-324-9685; www.oldstatehouse.com

Originally designed by Kentucky architect Gideon Shryock, this beautiful Greek Revival building was the capitol from 1836 to 1911. It now houses a museum of Arkansas history. Features include the restored governor's of-

fice and legislative chambers; Granny's Attic, a hands-on exhibit; a President William J. Clinton exhibit; and an interpretive display of Arkansas' first ladies' gowns.
Monday-Saturday 9 a.m.-5 p.m., Sunday 1-5 p.m.

PINNACLE MOUNTAIN STATE PARK
9420 Highway 300, Roland, 501-868-5806; www.arkansasstateparks.com
A cone-shaped mountain juts 1,000 feet above this heavily forested, 1,800-acre park, bordered on the west by 9,000-acre Lake Maumelle. Fishing, boating, hiking, backpacking, picnicking and a playground provide lots to do. There's also a gift shop and visitor center with natural history exhibits. Daily.

QUAPAW QUARTER HISTORIC NEIGHBORHOODS
1315 Scott St., Little Rock and North Little Rock, 501-371-0075; www.quapaw.com
Named for Arkansas' native Quapaw Indians, this nine-square-mile area oozes charm and old-fashioned style. The neighborhoods contain sites and structures from the 1820s to the present. The original town of Little Rock grew up here, and you'll find more than 150 buildings listed on the National Register of Historic Places. A tour of historic houses in the area is held the first weekend of May. Daily.

STATE CAPITOL
1 State Capitol, Little Rock, 501-682-5080; www.sosweb.state.ar.us
This slightly smaller replica of the nation's capitol has stood in for its big brother in several films, including the 1986 TV movie *Under Siege*. You can explore some of the grounds on your own, but you might opt for the free, guided tour to get the scoop on the building's history and some of the state's liveliest politicians. When the legislature is in session—beginning the second Monday in January of odd-numbered years—take a seat in the House or Senate chamber and watch the politicos debate. If you get tired of the wrangling, escape to the south lawn's 1,600-bush rose garden.
Monday-Friday 9 a.m.-5 p.m.

TOLTEC MOUNDS ARCHEOLOGICAL STATE PARK
490 Toltec Mounds Road, Scott, 501-961-9442; www.arkansasstateparks.com
The park is one of the largest and most complex prehistoric Native American settlements in the Lower Mississippi Valley. Native Americans inhabited this site from A.D. 600 to 1050, and the park preserves several mounds and a remnant of an embankment. Tours depart from the visitor center, which has exhibits that explain the site's history. The center also offers audiovisual programs and an archaeological laboratory.
Admission: adults $3, children 6-12 $2. Monday-Saturday 8 a.m.-5 p.m., Sunday noon-5 p.m.

WILD RIVER COUNTRY
6820 Crystal Hill Road, North Little Rock, 501-753-8600; www.wildrivercountry.com
Cool off in Arkansas' largest water park and enjoy rides with names like Vertigo, Vortex and Cyclone.

A CLINTON DRIVING TOUR

Former President Bill Clinton may reside in New York now, but much of his history lives in Arkansas. Little Rock is the place to learn about Clinton's political career, but to explore his life before he stepped into the limelight, you'll need to visit Hope, Clinton's birthplace, and Hot Springs, where he spent much of his childhood.

From I-30 in Hope, follow signs to the visitor center at the train depot on Main and Division streets. (You might recognize the small depot with a large green "HOPE" sign from Clinton's presidential campaign videos.) Four blocks from the visitor center, Clinton's birthplace—a modest home on Hervey Street where he lived until he was eight years old—is now an historic site and museum.

Next, head east on I-30 toward Hot Springs; once in town, head north on Highway 278 toward downtown. Clinton went to grade school and high school here, and the town is full of sites where he studied, worked and played long before he moved into the White House. Off Highway 7, at the south end of Bathhouse Row, a city visitor center distributes a map of 16 Clinton-related sites, including his church, a local bowling alley and his favorite hamburger joint. Hot Springs High School, from which Clinton graduated in 1964, is now the William Jefferson Clinton Cultural Campus, a residential community art center that features a restored theater and presidential museum from Clinton's high school days. And if you still haven't gotten enough presidential history, take I-30 east to Little Rock, where Clinton made his political debut as attorney general of Arkansas in 1976.

Admission: adults $29.99, children 2-12 $19.99, seniors and children under 2 free. June-August, Monday-Saturday 10 a.m.-8 p.m., Sunday noon-8 p.m.

SPECIAL EVENTS
ARKANSAS STATE FAIR AND LIVESTOCK SHOW
2300 W. Roosevelt Road, Little Rock, 501-372-8341; www.arkansasstatefair.com
Enjoy some down-home fun at this popular fair, which attracts more than 400,000 people during its 10-day run. Live music, motor sports, rodeos and children's shows, as well as a 10-acre Midway with carnival rides, food and games will thrill every member of the family.
Mid-October.

RIVERFEST
Riverfront Park, Little Rock, 501-255-3378; www.riverfestarkansas.com
This arts and music festival brings some of the nation's best performers to Little Rock. There's something for art lovers of all kinds: ballet, symphony, opera, theater, jazz, bluegrass and rock groups. There's also a children's area, bike race and five-mile run.
Memorial Day weekend.

WHERE TO STAY
★BEST WESTERN GOVERNORS SUITES
1501 Merrill Drive, Little Rock, 501-224-8051, 800-422-8051; www.bestwestern.com
49 rooms. Complimentary breakfast. Business center. Pool. $61-150

★★★THE CAPITAL HOTEL
111 W. Markham St., Little Rock, 501-374-7474, 800-766-7666; www.capitalhotel.com
After nearly two years of renovations, this historic downtown hotel earns

high marks for its modern amenities, outstanding service and vintage southern charm. First opening its doors in 1872, the Capital Hotel is conveniently located across the street from the Statehouse and only a short stroll from the Clinton Library, the Arkansas Art Center, the Rivermarket and other Little Rock must-sees. Bright, airy guest rooms benefit from neutral hues, floor-to-ceiling windows, flat-screen TVs and Frette bath linens. No visit is complete without a meal at Ashley's restaurant where dishes such as rice grits with tasso and rock shrimp and chicken and parsnip bacon cornbread pudding remind you that there's more to Southern cooking than fried chicken.
125 rooms. Restaurant, bar. $151-250

★★COURTYARD BY MARRIOTT WEST
10900 Financial Centre Parkway, Little Rock, 501-227-6000, 800-321-2211; www.courtyard.com
149 rooms. Restaurant, bar. Fitness center. Pool. $61-150

★★★EMPRESS OF LITTLE ROCK
2120 S. Louisiana, Little Rock, 501-374-7966, 877-374-7966; www.theempress.com
Scarlett O'Hara would approve of this 1888 Queen Anne-style mansion, carefully restored in the 1990s. This Victorian masterpiece offers antique-filled suites and gourmet breakfasts. Ask the innkeeper about the house's fascinating history. All rooms are named after historic Arkansas figures.
8 rooms. Complimentary breakfast. $151-250

★HAMPTON INN LITTLE ROCK
6100 Mitchell Drive, Little Rock, 501-562-6667, 800-426-7866; www.hamptoninn.com
122 rooms. Complimentary breakfast. Business center. Fitness center. Pool. $61-150

★★LA QUINTA INN
11701 Interstate-30, Little Rock, 501-455-2300, 800-687-6667; www.laquinta.com
145 rooms. Restaurant, bar. Complimentary breakfast. Pool. $61-150

★★★★THE PEABODY LITTLE ROCK
Three Statehouse Plaza, Little Rock, 501-906-4000; www.peabodylittlerock.com
Travelers to historic Little Rock would be hard-pressed to find a place more luxurious than The Peabody, located on the banks of the Arkansas River. One of Little Rock's most unusual—and endearing—spectacles happens here: At 11 a.m. each day, the hotel's beloved ducks march on a red carpet from their duck palace in the lobby to the fountain, while John Philip Sousa's King Cotton March plays. At 5 p.m., they march back to their digs. If the ducks are treated this well, imagine how much pampering the hotel's human guests enjoy. Guest rooms are small and in need of a facelift, but the accommodating staff more than makes up for the tired décor. One treat not to be missed: gourmet dining at Capriccio, famous for steaks and Italian favorites.
417 rooms. Restaurant, bar. Business center. Fitness center. $151-250

WHERE TO EAT
★★1620
1620 Market St., Little Rock, 501-221-1620; www.1620restaurant.com
American. Dinner. $16-35

★BROWNING'S
5805 Kavanaugh Blvd., Little Rock, 501-663-9956; www.browningsmexican.com
Mexican, American. Breakfast, lunch, dinner. Closed Sunday. $16-35

★BRUNO'S LITTLE ITALY
315 N. Bowman Road, Little Rock, 501-224-4700; www.brunoslittleitaly.com
Italian. Dinner. Closed Sunday. $16-35

★BUFFALO GRILL
1611 Rebsamen Park Road, Little Rock, 501-663-2158
American. Lunch, dinner. Closed Sunday. $15 and under

★CHIP'S BARBECUE
9801 W. Markham St., Little Rock, 501-225-4346
Barbecue, Southern. Lunch, dinner. Closed Monday. $15 and under

★FADED ROSE
1619 Rebsamen Park Road, Little Rock, 501-663-9734; www.thefadedrose.com
American, Cajun. Lunch, dinner. $16-35

★★GRAFFITI'S
7811 Cantrell Road, Little Rock, 501-224-9079
Italian. Dinner. Closed Sunday. $16-35

★★SIR LOIN'S INN
801 W. 29th St., North Little Rock, 501-753-1361
Steak. Dinner. Closed Sunday. $36-85

MAGNOLIA
See also Camden, El Dorado
Named for the fragrant white blossoms that dot its landscape, Magnolia is home to Southern Arkansas University (the Muleriders). The small town's other big claim to fame is the World Championship Steak Cook-Off, held each May during the Magnolia Blossom Festival.

WHAT TO SEE
LOGOLY STATE PARK
31 Columbia 459, McNeil, 870-695-3561; www.arkansasstateparks.com/logoly
Logoly is the first state park in Arkansas dedicated to environmental education. The 368 acres of forested coastal plain offer a "living laboratory" for students and researchers. Enjoy well-marked hiking trails, observation sites and the park's 11 natural springs. Picnicking and camping are available. The visitor center displays flora, fauna and history of the area.
Daily 8 a.m.-5 p.m.

SOUTHERN ARKANSAS UNIVERSITY

100 E. University St., Magnolia, 870-235-4000; www.saumag.edu

On the north edge of Magnolia, the campus is home to a Greek theater and model farm. The Carl White Caddo Native American Collection is on permanent display in the Magale Library. Daily.

WHERE TO STAY
★★COACHMAN'S INN MAGNOLIA

420 E. Main St., Magnolia, 870-234-6122, 800-237-6122

80 rooms. Restaurant. Complimentary breakfast. $61-150

MENA

See also Arkadelphia

This pretty little town sits at the base of Rich Mountain in the Ouachita Mountains. Outdoor enthusiasts flock here for the bounty of recreational activities.

WHAT TO SEE
QUEEN WILHELMINA STATE PARK

3877 Highway 88 W., Mena, 479-394-2863, 800-264-2477; www.queenwilhelmina.com

With views fit for royalty, this park atop Rich Mountain is the perfect antidote to cabin fever or too much time in the office. The Kansas City Railroad Company built the original inn here in 1898 as a luxurious retreat; financed by Dutch investors, the inn was named for the reigning queen of the Netherlands, Queen Wilhelmina. The current building is a reconstruction of the original. The park also offers hiking trails, miniature golf, picnicking, a playground, a store, a restaurant, camping and shower facilities. Daily.

TALIMENA SCENIC DRIVE

524 Sherwood Ave., Mena, 501-394-2912; www.talimenascenicdrive.com

This 54-mile roller-coaster drive through the Ouachita National Forests to Talihina, Okla., passes through the park and other interesting and beautiful areas. In addition to campgrounds in the park, there are other camping locations along the drive. The trip may be difficult in the winter. Daily.

MORRILTON

See also Conway, Russellville

The common story on how Morrilton got its name is that two farmers donated some land to the railroad being built here in the late 1800s. Each farmer wanted the train stop to bear his name and the two flipped a coin. Mr. Morrill won (hence Morrilton), though if you swing through the downtown streets, you'll also see Mr. Moose's name.

WHAT TO SEE
MUSEUM OF AUTOMOBILES

8 Jones Lane, Morrilton, 501-727-5427; www.museumofautos.com

Founded by former Arkansas Governor Winthrop Rockefeller, the museum features impressive antique and classic cars. There are autos from Rockefeller's personal collection, as well as changing exhibits of privately owned cars.

Admission: adults $7, seniors $6.50, students $3.50, children under 6 free. Daily 10 a.m.-5 p.m.

PETIT JEAN STATE PARK
Highway 9, Morrilton, 501-727-5441, 800-264-2462; www.petitjeanstatepark.com
This rugged area is the oldest, and one of the most beautiful, of the Arkansas parks. The park and its forested Petit Jean Mountain are named for a French girl who disguised herself as a boy to accompany her sailor sweetheart to America. In the New World, she got sick and died, and legend tells us that friendly Native Americans buried her on the mountain. Among the park's most spectacular sights are Cedar Falls—a magnificent waterfall—and Cedar Creek Canyon. More than 20 miles of hiking trails will take you to these and other jewels of the park. Daily.

SPECIAL EVENT
GREAT ARKANSAS PIGOUT FESTIVAL
120 N. Division St., Morrilton, 501-354-5400
The name says it all. After you stuff yourself silly, enjoy softball, volleyball and three-on-three basketball tournaments. Don't miss the hog-calling competition and the famed pig chase. Local and nationally known entertainment also take the stage.
First weekend in August.

MOUNTAIN VIEW
See also Little Rock
This retreat will provide a unique soundtrack to your vacation: The folk music heritage that early settlers brought to these mountains is still an important part of the community. Almost every night of the summer, if the weather is nice, people gather in Courthouse Square with chairs and instruments to hear and play music.

WHAT TO SEE
BLANCHARD SPRINGS CAVERNS
Highway 14, Mountain View, 870-757-2211, 888-757-2246;
These spectacular living caverns feature crystalline formations, an underground river and huge chambers. Guided tours depart from the visitor information center, which has an exhibit hall and free movie. There's a one-hour tour of the half-mile Dripstone Trail (year-round) and a 1 3/4-hour tour of the more strenuous Discovery Trail (summer only).
Admission: adults $10, children 6-15 $5, children under 6 free. April-October, daily 9:30 a.m.-6 p.m.; November-March, Wednesday-Sunday 9:30 a.m.-6 p.m.

OZARK FOLK CENTER STATE PARK
Highway 382, Mountain View, 870-269-3851, 800-264-3655; www.ozarkfolkcenter.com
Established to preserve and share the crafts, music and heritage of the Ozark region, the park hosts fascinating events, such as a cowboy folk humor and storytelling weekend and crafts workshops. In the living museum, artisans demonstrate basketry, quilt-making and woodcarving. The park also includes

a lodge, restaurant, music auditorium and an outdoor stage with 300 covered seats. Special events are held all year. Daily.

SPECIAL EVENTS
ARKANSAS FOLK FESTIVAL
Mountain View, 870-269-8068; www.ozarkgetaways.com
Relax in the shade of blooming dogwood trees, browse the arts and crafts, and delight in local fare, all the while listening to acoustic folk music. Third weekend in April.

BEAN FEST AND GREAT ARKANSAS CHAMPIONSHIP OUTHOUSE RACE
Courthouse Square, Mountain View, 870-269-8068; www.ozarkgetaways.com
This three-day festival mixes traditional events—music, food and fun—with the unorthodox Parade of Outhouses and subsequent homemade outhouse races around Courthouse Square. Music, a bean cook-off and games add to the festivities.
Last Saturday in October.

HERB HARVEST FALL FESTIVAL
Ozark Folk Center, Highway 382, Mountain View, 870-269-3851;
www.ozarkfolkcenter.com
The fest ushers in the harvest with concerts, crafts demonstrations, races, a fiddlers' jamboree and contests.
Early October.

TRIBUTE TO MERLE TRAVIS: NATIONAL THUMBPICKING GUITAR CONTEST
Ozark Folk Center, Highway 382, Mountain View, 870-269-3851;
www.ozarkfolkcenter.com
This two-day event and contest honors Merle Travis, the guitarist, singer and composer who mastered the thumb and finger guitar technique.
Mid-May.

WHERE TO STAY
★BEST WESTERN FIDDLERS INN
601 Sylamore Ave., Mountain View, 870-269-2828, 800-780-7234;
www.bestwestern.com
48 rooms. Pool. $61-150

PINE BLUFF
See also Stuttgart
Any loyal citizen of Pine Bluff will tell you that the Civil War began right here. In April 1861, several days before the war's first official shots rang out at Fort Sumter, a musket shot was fired across the bow of a federal gunboat in the Arkansas River. The vessel and its supplies were confiscated. On October 25, 1863, Union troops took control of Pine Bluff and it remained in Union hands until the end of the Civil War.

Today Pine Bluff anchors the southeast corner of Arkansas. The "Bass

Capital of the World," this area hosts as many as 35 bass-fishing tournaments each year.

WHAT TO SEE
ARKANSAS ENTERTAINERS HALL OF FAME
1 Convention Center Plaza, Pine Bluff, 870-536-7600
Arkansas has given the world entertainment greats Johnny Cash, Glenn Campbell, Billy Bob Thornton and Al Green, among many others. Trace their careers and check out stars' personal memorabilia.
Monday-Friday 9 a.m.-5 p.m.

JEFFERSON COUNTY HISTORICAL MUSEUM
201 E. Fourth St., Pine Bluff, 870-541-5402
The museum features exhibits on the history of Pine Bluff and Jefferson County; development of area transportation, including river, roads and rail; displays of Victorian artifacts; and clothing used by early settlers.
Admission: adults $4, children 3-12 $1. Monday-Saturday 11 a.m.-4 p.m.

WHERE TO STAY
★★RAMADA
Two Convention Center Drive, Pine Bluff, 870-535-3111; www.ramada.com
84 rooms. Restaurant, bar. Complimentary breakfast. Business center. Fitness center. Pool. $61-150

ROGERS
See also Bentonville, Fayetteville
This pleasant town in the Ozark area is where Sam Walton built the first Wal-Mart. Its proximity to the mountains makes it a prime spot for outdoor sports year-round.

WHAT TO SEE

BEAVER LAKE
2260 N. Second St., Rogers, 479-636-1210
A huge reservoir with a 500-mile shoreline is a prime spot for swimming, waterskiing, fishing and boating. The lake also offers hunting, picnicking, a playground and camping. Daily.

DAISY INTERNATIONAL AIRGUN MUSEUM
202 W. Walnut, Rogers, 479-986-6873; www.daisymuseum.com
Daisy Outdoor Products, which manufactures the famed Red Ryder B-B Gun ("You'll shoot your eye out!"), established this museum, which has a large display of guns, some dating to the late 18th century.
Admission: adults $2, children under 16 free. Monday-Saturday 9 a.m.-5 p.m.

PEA RIDGE NATIONAL MILITARY PARK
15930 E. Highway 62, Garfield, 479-451-8122; www.nps.gov/peri
More than 26,000 troops clashed here on March 7-8, 1862, in a decisive Civil War battle that gave the Union control of Missouri. Three Confederate generals—McCulloch, McIntosh and Slack—died in the battle. The park

preserves the battles site and a 2 1/2-mile section of the Trail of Tears. Admission: $7. Daily 8 a.m.-5 p.m.

ROGERS HISTORICAL MUSEUM (HAWKINS HOUSE)
322 S. Second St., Rogers, 479-621-1154; www.rogersarkansas.com/museum
The museum shows exhibits on local history, re-created turn-of-the-century businesses and Victorian-era furnishings. There's also a hands-on children's discovery room.
Tuesday-Saturday 10 a.m.-4 p.m.

WAR EAGLE CAVERN
21494 Cavern Road, Rogers, 479-789-2909; www.wareaglecavern.com
The cavern's spectacular natural entrance leads to huge rooms full of interesting geologic formations. Learn about the cave's history and the bandits, warriors, squatters and draft dodgers who've holed up in the cavern over the years.
Admission: adults $11.50, children 4-12 $6.75, children under 4 free. Mid-March-November, daily 9:30 a.m.-5 p.m.

WHERE TO EAT
★★THE BEAN PALACE
11045 War Eagle Road, Rogers, 479-789-5343; www.wareaglemill.com
American. Breakfast, lunch. Closed January-February. $15 and under

RUSSELLVILLE
See also Rogers
Headquarters for the Ozark and St. Francis National Forests, Russellville is a haven for people who love the great outdoors. Nearby state parks, a wildlife refuge and the scenic Highway 7 make this town a popular destination for travelers.

WHAT TO SEE
HOLLA BEND NATIONAL WILDLIFE REFUGE
Highway 1, Dardanelle, 479-229-4300; www.fws.gov/HollaBend
This refuge provides a safe home for thousands of migratory birds that fly south each winter, so the best time to visit is between late November and February. Ducks, geese, golden and bald eagles, herons, egrets, sandpipers and scissor-tailed flycatchers call this spot home for at least part of the year. Daily.

MOUNT NEBO STATE PARK
1 State Park Drive, Dardanelle, 479-229-3655, 800-264-2458;
www.arkansasstateparks.com
Mount Nebo has gorgeous vistas, miles of hiking trails and several campsites. It is also one of two state parks that offer launch sites for hang gliders. Bench Trail, a 4 1/2-mile mountain bike path is perfect for novice bikers. The drive from the base to the summit winds up the eastern side of the mountain; the drive is not recommended for trailers over 15 feet, thanks to a few hairpin turns. There's also a swimming pool, fishing, biking and hiking trails, tennis,

picnicking, a playground, a store, camping and cabins. The visitor center provides exhibits and interpretive programs. Daily.

OZARK NATIONAL FOREST
605 W. Main St., Russellville, 479-968-2354
In beautiful Ozark National Forest, you'll find the Boston Mountains, the state's tallest mountain, Mount Magazine, and an amazing underground cave, Blanchard Springs Caverns. The park's 1.2-million acres are the perfect playground for outdoor enthusiasts. Daily.

WHERE TO STAY
★★HOLIDAY INN
2407 N. Arkansas, Russellville, 479-968-4300, 800-465-4329; www.holiday-inn.com
149 rooms. Restaurant. Complimentary breakfast. Pool. $61-150

SPRINGDALE
See also Bentonville, Fayetteville, Rogers
Springdale calls itself the heart of northwest Arkansas. It has much of Arkansas' natural beauty and—as a bonus—colorful vineyards nearby. The best are a few miles west on Highway 68 near Tontitown, a community settled by Italian immigrants in 1897.

WHAT TO SEE
ARTS CENTER OF THE OZARKS
214 S. Main, Springdale, 479-751-5441; www.artscenteroftheozarks.org
"Come play with us" is the center's motto—a tempting invitation for art lovers of any kind. Catch a show or concert in the theater, amble through the art gallery or take an art or a music class.
Prices vary. Monday-Saturday.

SHILOH MUSEUM OF OZARK HISTORY
118 W. Johnson Ave., Springdale, 479-750-8165
Long before Angelina Jolie and Brad Pitt named their baby Shiloh, the title belonged to a community that would become Springdale. The museum tells the history of the Ozarks through interactive exhibits, photographs, Native American artifacts and other historic items. Check out the 1855 log cabin, a post office/general store dating back to 1871 and country doctor's office.
Monday-Saturday 10 a.m.-5 p.m.

SPECIAL EVENT
RODEO OF THE OZARKS
Parsons Stadium, 1433 E. Emma Ave., Springdale, Old Missouri Road, 877-927-6336; www.rodeooftheozarks.org
Nothing says Independence Day quite like a rodeo, so the folks in Springdale celebrate each July with a professional one. Spectators watch seven professional events, including steer wrestling, bareback riding and the ever-popular bull riding. A parade, pageant, "denim & lace" dance and other activities round out the festivities.
Early July.

WHERE TO STAY
★HAMPTON INN
1700 S. 48th St., Springdale, 479-756-3500, 800-426-7866;
www.hamptoninnspringdale.com
102 rooms. Complimentary breakfast. Business center. Fitness center. Pool. $61-150

★★HOLIDAY INN
1500 S. 48th St., Springdale, 479-751-8300, 800-465-4329; www.holiday-inn.com
206 rooms. Restaurant, bar. Pool. $61-150

WHERE TO EAT
★A. Q. CHICKEN HOUSE
1207 N. Thompson, Springdale, 479-751-4633; www.aqchickenhouse.net
American, Southern. Lunch, dinner. $16-35

STUTTGART
See also Pine Bluff
If you show up in Stuttgart and everyone's wearing camouflage, don't panic. The small town is one of the nation's best areas for duck hunting, and from November through January, duck hunters from around the world descend on Stuttgart.

WHAT TO SEE
MUSEUM OF THE ARKANSAS GRAND PRAIRIE
921 E. Fourth St., Stuttgart, 870-673-7001; www.grandprairiemuseum.org
The museum tells the history of pioneer life and prairie farming with unique displays, including a replica prairie village, a model of an early newspaper office with a working printing press, a wildlife exhibit and a simulated duck hunt. Tuesday-Friday 8 a.m.-4 p.m., Saturday 10 a.m.-4 p.m.

WHITE RIVER NATIONAL WILDLIFE REFUGE
57 S. CC Camp Road, St. Charles, 870-282-8201
Migratory birds make their home here, which makes the refuge an excellent spot to bird-watch. Keep an eye out for the other animals that live here, including raccoons, alligators, deer and bears. Hunting is permitted for duck, deer, turkey, squirrel and raccoon. There's also fishing, boat access, picnicking and primitive camping.
March-October, daily.

SPECIAL EVENT
WINGS OVER THE PRAIRIE FESTIVAL
Downtown Stuttgart, 870-673-1602
The kick-off to duck-hunting season, the festival includes the famous World Championship Duck Calling Contest, which is featured in the bestselling book *1,000 Places to See Before You Die* by Patricia Schultz. Other highlights include a carnival, the 10-K Great Duck Race (for people, not birds) and the Duck Gumbo Cook-off.
Thanksgiving week.

WHERE TO STAY
★BEST WESTERN DUCK INN
704 W. Michigan St., Stuttgart, 870-673-2575; www.bestwestern.com
70 rooms. Complimentary breakfast. Pool. $61-150

TEXARKANA
See also Hope
Folks flock from surrounding states to Texarkana each year to attend the annual fair and rodeo. Cowboy hat not required.

SPECIAL EVENT
FOUR STATES FAIR & RODEO
Fairgrounds, Loop 245 and East 50th St., Texarkana, 870-773-2941, 800-776-1836; www.fourstatesfair.com
Dating back to 1945, the fair and rodeo features live entertainment, livestock exhibits and a Demolition Derby. There is even a Miss Four States Fair Rodeo beauty contest. September.

WHERE TO STAY
★★AMERICA'S BEST VALUE KINGS ROW INN & SUITES
4200 State Line Ave., Texarkana, 870-774-3851, 800-643-5464; www.kingsrowinn.com
116 rooms. Restaurant. Complimentary breakfast. Pool. $61-150

WASHINGTON
See also Hope
Soak up a bit of history by stepping foot in Washington, which became the Confederate capital for the state after Little Rock was captured in 1863.

WHAT TO SEE
OLD WASHINGTON HISTORIC STATE PARK
Highways 195 and 278, Washington, 870-983-2684; www.oldwashingtonstatepark.com
This historic village will transport you to the 19th century, when the town of Washington was a convenient stop on the Southwestern Trail. The park preserves and interprets the town's past from 1824 to 1875.
Daily 8 a.m.-5 p.m.

SPECIAL EVENTS
FRONTIER DAYS
Old Washington Historic State Park, Highways 195 and 278,Washington, 870-983-2684
Curious about what 19th-century pioneers did for fun? Visit this festival, where you'll see park staff create and throw knives, make lye soap, render lard and shoot turkeys.
Third weekend in October.

JONQUIL FESTIVAL
Old Washington Historic State Park, Highways 195 and 278,Washington, 870-983-2684
The fest coincides with the blooming of jonquils planted by early settlers. It also has craft demonstrations and bluegrass music.
Mid-March.

KENTUCKY

FAMOUS FOR HORSERACING, MINT JULEPS AND THE BLUEGRASS, KENTUCKY SPENDS A FEW minutes each May in the world's spotlight when all eyes turn to Louisville's Churchill Downs and the Derby. But the commonwealth offers much more than "the most exciting two minutes in sports." This is the place where President Abraham Lincoln was born, where explorer Daniel Boone carved out a path on young America's western edge for pioneers, and where Harriet Beecher Stowe witnessed the auctioning of slaves and found inspiration for Uncle Tom's Cabin. It's also home to flourishing art communities, hip urban neighborhoods and an eclectic music scene. And even though the Derby might be Kentucky's biggest party, the rest of the year, Kentuckians celebrate everything from bluegrass music and barbecue to beauty queens and Scottish traditions. The pioneer spirit meets Southern charm in this diverse state.

Kentucky stretches from Virginia to Missouri, a geographic and historic bridge in the westward flow of American settlement. The commonwealth can be divided into four sections: the Bluegrass, the south-central cave country, the eastern mountains and the western lakes. Each region will surprise visitors with its unique geography and culture. The Lexington plain, a circular area in the north-central part of Kentucky, is Bluegrass Country, home of fast horses and gentlemen farmers. South of this region is cave country, where you'll find Mammoth Cave National Park, the world's longest cave system. And outdoor enthusiasts will enjoy the Appalachian Mountains in the east, which provide a beautiful backdrop for outdoor activities, and the western lakes, an ideal place for boating, fishing and canoeing.

The Cumberland Gap, a natural passageway through the mountains that sealed the Kentucky wilderness off from Virginia, was the gateway of the pioneers. Dr. Thomas Walker, the first recorded explorer to make a thorough land expedition into the area, arrived in 1750. Daniel Boone and a company of axmen hacked the Wilderness Road through the Cumberland Gap and far into the wild. The first permanent settlement was at Harrodsburg in 1774, and less than 20 years later in 1792, Congress admitted Kentucky into the Union. During the Civil War, Kentucky supported the Union but opposed abolition, a position that highlights its place as a bridge between the Old South and the Yankee North. Ironically, President Abraham Lincoln and Confederate President Jefferson Davis were both born in Kentucky—less than one year and 100 miles apart. Countless museums, restored historical sites and festivals pay tribute to Honest Abe, the commonwealth's most famous native son.

Of course, Kentucky didn't just give the nation bourbon, horses and politicians. Heavyweight boxing champion Muhammad Ali, actor Johnny Depp, TV journalist Diane Sawyer and country music legend Loretta Lynn all hail from the Bluegrass State. As if that weren't enough, this is where Kentucky Fried Chicken got its start, where Louisville Slugger baseball bats were born and where all the Corvettes in the world are produced.

So if you miss the most exciting two minutes in sports each May, you'll still find plenty of ways to fill the time until the next Derby Day.

ASHLAND

See also Olive Hill

Set in the highlands of northeastern Kentucky, Ashland enjoys a prime spot on the Ohio River. The small town is the first unofficial stop on the Country Music Highway (Highway 23).

WHAT TO SEE
BENNETT'S MILL BRIDGE
Ashland, eight miles west on Highway 125 off Highway Seven

One of Kentucky's longest single-span covered bridges at 195 feet, Bennett's Mill Bridge was built in 1855 to serve mill customers. Its original footings and frame are intact, but it's closed to traffic. Daily.

GREENBO LAKE STATE RESORT PARK
Ashland, 18 miles west via Highway 23 to Highway 1, 606-473-7324; www.parks.ky.gov/findparks/resortparks/go

Get active at this state park with a swimming pool, fishing, boating, hiking, bicycle rentals and tennis. If you want to stay awhile, check out the lodge, tent and trailer sites. The new amphitheater offers concerts and shows and there's a recreation program for children. Daily.

HIGHLANDS MUSEUM & DISCOVERY CENTER
1620 Winchester Ave., Ashland, 606-329-8888; www.highlandsmuseum.com

Visit this interactive museum to learn about Kentucky's unique heritage. Exhibits include a tribute to country music's history in the state, a glimpse at life in the 19th century and a look at the Kentuckians who fought in the wars of the 20th century.

Admission: adults $5.50, seniors and children 2-18 $4.50, children under 2 free. Tuesday-Saturday 10 a.m.-5 p.m.

PARAMOUNT ARTS CENTER
1300 Winchester Ave., Ashland, 606-324-3175; www.paramountartscenter.com

This intimate theater hosts all kinds of performances, from country music concerts to touring Broadway shows. The center also prides itself on sharing the arts with the rest of the community, especially youths. The restored 1930s Art Deco theater was originally a movie theater. Daily.

SPECIAL EVENT
POAGE LANDING DAYS FESTIVAL
Central Park, Winchester Avenue, Ashland, 606-329-1007, 800-377-6249; www.poage-landingdays.com

This fiddle festival features national and local entertainers. Also on offer are arts and crafts and children's activities.

Third weekend in September.

WHERE TO STAY
★DAYS INN
12700 Highway 180, Ashland, 606-928-3600, 800-329-7466; www.daysinn.com

63 rooms. Complimentary breakfast. Fitness center. Pool. $61-150

★FAIRFIELD INN ASHLAND

10945 Highway 60, Ashland, 606-928-1222, 800-228-2800; www.fairfieldinn.com
63 rooms. Complimentary breakfast. $61-150

★★JESSE STUART LODGE AT GREENBO LAKE STATE RESORT

Ashland, 606-473-7324, 800-325-0083; www.parks.ky.gov/findparks/resortparks/go/
36 rooms. Restaurant. Pool. $61-150

THE COUNTRY MUSIC HIGHWAY

A stretch of Highway 23 that runs almost the entire length of Eastern Kentucky is the perfect introduction to the state's rich history and musical heritage. Dubbed the "Country Music Highway," the path will take you by towns where country music stars such as Loretta Lynn, Wynona and Naomi Judd, Dwight Yoakam and Patty Loveless once lived. You'll also learn about Kentucky's fascinating history, so find a little country music on the radio and explore, y'all.

Begin in Ashland at the Paramount Art Center (606-324-3175), where music legends including Kentucky natives Billy Ray Cyrus and Wynona and Naomi Judd have played. Originally a movie theater, this restored theater also hosts up-and-comers in its intimate space. Not far away, the Highlands Museum and Discovery Center (606-329-8888) celebrates Eastern Kentucky heritage. Kids will enjoy the Karaoke Korner, where they can make their own music.

Head south to Louisa and Kentucky Pavilion (606-638-9998), a shrine to country music. The five-story building houses country stars' costumes, signed guitars, photographs—even Elvis Presley's Exxon gas card.

Continue south to the remote mining town of Butcher Hollow, where Loretta Lynn was born. Visitors can stop by the cabin where Lynn grew up. (Her autobiographical song "Coal Miner's Daughter" is based on her life here.)

Your next stop is Prestonburg, about 15 miles from Butcher Hollow. Here you'll find the Kentucky Opry (888-459-8704) at the Mountain Arts Center. Catch a country, bluegrass or gospel show by local favorites or national headliners to round out your trip along one of America's most historic highways.

BARBOURVILLE

See also Corbin

There's something in the water in Barbourville: The city has produced two Kentucky governors, a lieutenant governor, three U.S. congressmen and a slew of politicians who serve outside of Kentucky. Thanks to its location in the valley of the scenic Cumberland River, this little town has opportunities for fishing, swimming and other outdoor activities.

WHAT TO SEE

DR. THOMAS WALKER STATE HISTORIC SITE

4929 Kentucky 459, Barbourville, 606-546-4400;
www.parks.ky.gov/findparks/histparks/tw

See a replica of the original log cabin built in 1750 by Dr. Thomas Walker surrounded by 12 acres of parkland. The site also includes a miniature golf course, picnic area and playground. Daily.

SPECIAL EVENT
DANIEL BOONE FESTIVAL
Knox and Daniel Boone Drive, Barbourville, 606-546-4300

Get a little pioneer spirit at this annual celebration of Boone's adventures in Kentucky. Activities include square dancing, musket shooting, a reenactment of Native American treaty signing, a horse show, a parade, old-time fiddling, antique displays, arts and crafts and entertainment. The Cherokee make an annual pilgrimage to the city.

Early October.

BARDSTOWN
See also Elizabethtown

Folks in Bardstown are proud of their town's Southern charm, their beautiful city—and their bourbon. In fact, Bardstown is the heart of the Kentucky Bourbon Trail, featured in Patricia Schultz's bestseller book *1,000 Places to See Before You Die*.

WHAT TO SEE
BARDSTOWN HISTORICAL MUSEUM
114 N. Fifth St., Bardstown, 502-348-2999; www.whiskeymuseum.com

The museum features items covering 200 years of local history. Exhibits include Native American artifacts, Lincoln documents, Stephen Foster memorabilia, Civil War artifacts, gifts from King Louis Philippe and King Charles X of France, pioneer items, period costumes from the late 1800s and a natural science display.

May-October, Monday-Friday 10 a.m.-5 p.m., Saturday 10 a.m.-4 p.m., Sunday noon-4 p.m.; November-April, Tuesday-Saturday 10 a.m.-4 p.m., Sunday noon-4 p.m.

BERNHEIM FOREST
State Highway 245,14 miles northwest on Highway 245, Shepherdsville, 502-955-8512; www.bernheim.org

This arboretum is an ideal spot to relax, take a walk and admire Kentucky's foliage. The Garden Pavilion is particularly magnificent during summer months when the water lilies are in full bloom.

Admission: Monday-Friday free, Saturday-Sunday $5 per car. Daily 9 a.m.-5 p.m.

JIM BEAM AMERICAN OUTPOST
149 Happy Hollow Road, Shepherdsville, 502-543-9877; www.jimbeam.com

Visitors can tour the historic Beam family home and stroll the grounds. Check out the craft shop before enjoying a free tasting.

Monday-Saturday 9 a.m.-4:30 p.m., Sunday 1-4 p.m.

LINCOLN HOMESTEAD STATE PARK
5079 Lincoln Park Road, Bardstown, 859-336-7461; www.parks.ky.gov/findparks/recparks/lh/

This park is full of Lincoln family history. See the Berry House, where Nancy Hanks, Abe's mother, lived while Thomas Lincoln was courting her. You'll also

find replicas of the cabin and blacksmith shop where Thomas Lincoln grew up and learned his trade. And if that's not enough, stop by the house where Lincoln's favorite uncle—Mordecai Lincoln—lived (on its original site).
Admission: adults $2, children $1.50. May-October, daily.

MY OLD KENTUCKY DINNER TRAIN
602 N. Third St., Bardstown, 502-348-7300; www.kydinnertrain.com
Go on a scenic dining excursion aboard elegant restored dining cars from the 1940s. A round-trip ride through the countryside includes a three-course lunch or four-course dinner.
February-December, Tuesday-Saturday.

MY OLD KENTUCKY HOME STATE PARK
501 E. Stephen Foster Ave., Bardstown, 502-348-3502; www.myoldkentuckyhome.com
Costumed guides lead you through this beautiful Georgian-style mansion and its gardens. The composer Stephen Foster occasionally visited his cousin, Judge John Rowan, at the stately 1795 house, Federal Hill. These visits may have inspired him in 1852 to write "My Old Kentucky Home," Kentucky's state song. The grounds include a golf course, picnic area, playground, tent and trailer sites, gardens and an amphitheater.
Admission: adults $5.50, seniors $5, children $3.50. Daily 9 a.m.-4:45 p.m.

OSCAR GETZ MUSEUM OF WHISKEY HISTORY
114 N. Fifth St., Bardstown, 502-348-2999; www.whiskeymuseum.com
Whiskey is a big deal in Kentucky, and this museum chronicles the history of the liquor from pre-colonial days to the Prohibition era. Check out copper stills, manuscripts, old advertising art, a moonshine still and even Abe Lincoln's liquor license.
May-October, Monday-Friday 10 a.m.-5 p.m., Saturday 10 a.m.-4 p.m., Sunday noon-4 p.m.; November-April, Tuesday-Saturday 10 a.m.-4 p.m., Sunday noon-4 p.m.

SPALDING HALL
114 N. Fifth St., Bardstown, 502-348-2999; www.whiskeymuseum.com
Once part of St. Joseph College, Spalding Hall was used as a hospital in the Civil War. The former dormitory now houses art.
May-October, Monday-Friday 10 a.m.-5 p.m., Saturday 10 a.m.-4 p.m., Sunday noon-4 p.m.; November-April, Tuesday-Saturday 10 a.m.-4 p.m., Sunday noon-4 p.m.

ST. JOSEPH PROTO-CATHEDRAL
310 W. Stephen Foster Ave., Bardstown, 502-348-3126; www.bardstown.com/~stjoe/
This is the first Catholic cathedral west of the Allegheny Mountains. Paintings were donated by Pope Leo XII.
Daily 9 a.m.-5 p.m.

SPECIAL EVENTS
KENTUCKY BOURBON FESTIVAL
1 Court Square, Bardstown, 800-638-4877; www.kybourbonfestival.com
Folks in Bardstown have been making bourbon since 1776, and at this annual festival, they celebrate their favorite spirit. Festivities include art exhibits, a black-tie gala and, of course, plenty of bourbon tasting.
Mid-September.

STEPHEN FOSTER, THE MUSICAL
J. Dan Talbott Amphitheater, My Old Kentucky Home State Park, Bardstown,
502-348-5971, 800-626-1563; www.stephenfoster.com
More than 50 songs in this musical tell the story of American composer Stephen Foster's triumphs and romance. The show is performed in an outdoor amphitheater.
Admission: adults $23, seniors $16, children ages 6-12 $10, children under 6 free. Early June-late August, Tuesday-Sunday 8:30 p.m.

WHERE TO STAY
★BEST WESTERN GENERAL NELSON
114 W. Stephen Foster Ave., Bardstown, 502-348-3977, 800-225-3977;
www.generalnelson.com
48 rooms. Complimentary breakfast. Pool. $61-150

★HAMPTON INN
985 Chambers Blvd., Bardstown, 502-349-0100; www.hamptoninn.com
106 rooms. Complimentary breakfast. Fitness center. Pool. $61-150

★★QUALITY INN
1875 New Haven Road, Bardstown, 502-348-9253, 866-348-6900; www.qualityinnof-bardstown.com
101 rooms. Restaurant, bar. Fitness center. Pool. $61-150

WHERE TO EAT
★★KURTZ
418 E. Stephen Foster Ave., Bardstown, 502-348-5983, 800-732-2384;
American. Lunch, dinner. $16-35

BEREA
See also Lexington
This community in the foothills of the Cumberland Mountains is known as the "Folk Arts and Crafts Capital of Kentucky." Antique shops, craft stores and working studios line the streets. If you're looking for a handmade souvenir from your trip through Kentucky, Berea is a good place to look.

WHAT TO SEE
BEREA COLLEGE
107 Jackson St., Berea, 859-985-3000, 800-326-5948; www.berea.edu
Berea College, the first coeducational, integrated college in the South, mirrors the town's unique approach to hard work and creativity. The college

charges no tuition; instead, students work in the college's Labor Program to cover the cost of their education. Daily.

STUDIO CRAFTSPEOPLE OF BEREA
Berea, 859-986-2540; www.berea.com
An organization of craftspeople working in various media invites visitors to their studios. You'll see everything from glass-blowing to woodworking to oil painting. And the best part? There's no pressure to buy. Daily.

SPECIAL EVENT
BEREA CRAFT FESTIVAL
Indian Fort Theater at Berea College, Berea, 859-986-2258, 800-598-5263;
www.bereacraftfestival.com
For more than 25 years, artisans from across the country have presented their work at this annual festival.
Three days in mid-July.

WHERE TO STAY
★★BOONE TAVERN HOTEL
100 Main St. North, Berea, 859-986-9358, 800-366-9358; www.boonetavernhotel.com.
58 rooms. Restaurant. $61-150

WHERE TO EAT
★DINNER BELL
Interstate-75 Plaza, Berea, 859-986-2777
American. Breakfast, lunch, dinner. $15 and under

★PAPALENO'S
108 Center St., Berea, 859-986-4497; www.papalenos.com
Italian. Lunch, dinner. $16-35

BOWLING GREEN
See also Elizabethtown
This city is where Corvettes are born: every Corvette made in the world today is produced in Bowling Green, so there are plenty of attractions for car lovers. But if motors and chrome aren't your thing, don't dismay. Bowling Green is also home to beautiful historic mansions, natural wonders (think underground boat tours) and even an amusement park.

WHAT TO SEE
CAPITOL ARTS CENTER
416 E. Main St., Bowling Green, 270-782-2787; www.capitolarts.com
This restored Art Deco building plays host to national and local live presentations and gallery exhibits throughout the year.

RIVERVIEW AT HOBSON GROVE
Hobson Grove Park, 1100 W. Main St., Bowling Green, 270-843-5565;
www.bgky.org/riverview
A stunning example of the Italianate style, this hilltop home is furnished with

a collection of Victorian furniture from 1860 to 1890. The house was used as an armory by the Confederates when they occupied Bowling Green during the winter of 1861.

Admission: adults $5, students $2.50, children under 6 free. February to mid-December, Tuesday-Saturday 10 a.m.-4 p.m., Sunday 1-4 p.m.

KENTUCKY LIBRARY AND MUSEUM
1 Big Red Way, Western Kentucky University, Bowling Green, 270-745-2592; www.wku. edu/Library/museum

The library contains 30,000 books, manuscripts, maps, broadsides, photographs, sheet music, scrapbooks and materials relating to Kentucky and genealogical research of Kentucky families. The museum also offers educational lectures and programs open to the public.

Admission: adults $5, seniors and children 6-16 $2.50, children under 6 free. Monday-Saturday 9 a.m.-4 p.m., Sunday 1-4 p.m.

NATIONAL CORVETTE MUSEUM
350 Corvette Drive, Bowling Green, 270-781-7973; www.corvettemuseum.com

Sports car aficionados drool over this place, which has hands-on educational exhibits and displays about the history of this classic American car. Open since 1953, the museum also has an impressive collection of full-scale dioramas, advertisements and videos. More than 50 vintage cars are available for viewing.

Admission: adults $8, children 6-16 $4.50, children under 6 free. Daily 8 a.m.-5 p.m.

WHERE TO STAY
★★BEST WESTERN MOTOR INN
166 Cumberland Trace Road, Bowling Green, 270-782-3800, 800-780-7234; www. bestwestern.com

177 rooms. Restaurant. Pool. $61-150

★FAIRFIELD INN
1940 Mel Browning St., Bowling Green, 270-782-6933, 800-228-2800; www.fairfieldinn.com

105 rooms. Complimentary breakfast. $61-150

★HAMPTON INN
233 Three Springs Road, Bowling Green, 270-842-4100, 800-426-7866; www.hamptoninn.com

131 rooms. Complimentary breakfast. Fitness center. Pool. $61-150

WHERE TO EAT
★★MARIAH'S
801 State St., Bowling Green, 270-842-6878; www.mariahs.com

American. Lunch, dinner. $16-35

BREAKS INTERSTATE PARK
See also Berea

This park's main attraction is the "Grand Canyon of the South," where the

Russell Fork of the Big Sandy River plunges through the mountains. The 1,600-foot-deep gorge stretches for five miles through this park on the Kentucky-Virginia border. From the park's entrance, a paved road winds through an evergreen forest and then skirts the canyon rim. Overlooks along the route provide spectacular views of the "Towers," a huge pyramid of rocks. You'll also find caves, springs and fields of rhododendron in this natural wonder.

The visitor center houses historical and natural exhibits. Laurel Lake is stocked with bass and bluegill. It also has a swimming pool, pedal boats, hiking, bridle and mountain bike trails, picnicking, playground and camping. In addition, a motor lodge and cottages are available.

WHERE TO STAY
★★BREAKS INTERSTATE
Highway 1, Breaks, 540-865-4414, 800-982-5122, 276-865-4413; www.breakspark.com
34 rooms. Restaurant. Pool. $61-150

CADIZ
See also Gilbertsville, Hopkinsville
Time has almost stopped in this small town. Many of Cadiz's original buildings are preserved, making it a great place to see architecture from the 19th century. Its location on a 170,000-acre wooded peninsula between Kentucky Lake and Lake Barkley gives this pretty town a gorgeous backdrop.

WHAT TO SEE
LAKE BARKLEY STATE RESORT PARK
3500 State Park Road, Cadiz, 270-924-1131, 800-325-1708; www.parks.ky.gov/find-parks/resortparks/lb/
This park on the shores of Lake Barkley provides almost every outdoor activity you can imagine: a swimming beach, pool, bathhouse, fishing, boating, canoeing, hiking, backpacking, horseback riding, 18-hole golf, tennis, trapshooting, shuffleboard, basketball, picnicking, and camping. Children's programs are offered as well. Daily.

ORIGINAL LOG CABIN
22 Main St., Cadiz, 270-522-3892; www.gocadiz.com
This four-room log cabin was occupied by a single family for more than a century. The building is furnished with 18th- and 19th-century artifacts including a Beckwith pump organ, Victorian settee and a 150-year-old cradle. Monday-Friday 9 a.m.-5 p.m.

WHERE TO STAY
★★LAKE BARKLEY STATE RESORT PARK
3500 State Park Road, Cadiz, 270-924-1131, 800-325-1708; www.parks.ky.gov
124 rooms. Restaurant. $61-150

CARROLLTON
See also Louisville
Where the Ohio and Kentucky rivers meet, Carrollton was named in honor of Charles Carroll, one of the signers of the Declaration of Independence.

Today, this place has small-town charm, a beautiful state park and several great antique shops.

WHAT TO SEE
EDGE OF SPEEDWAY CAMPGROUND
4125 Highway 1130, Sparta, 859-576-2161; www.edgeofspeedway.com
This well-manicured campground overlooks the Kentucky Speedway and has space for 200 campers. Gravel roads and large sites set it apart from other camping spots in the area. Daily.

GENERAL BUTLER STATE RESORT PARK
1608 Highway 227, Carrollton, 502-732-4384; www.parks.ky.gov/findparks/resortparks/gb/
The Ohio and Kentucky Rivers meet here, making the park a scenic site for outdoor activities of all kinds. Swim, fish and boat at the 30-acre lake; or play nine-hole golf or tennis. Picnic sites, a playground, cottages, a lodge and dining room, tent and trailer camping are also available. Daily.

SPECIAL EVENT
KENTUCKY SCOTTISH WEEKEND
Carrollton, 502-239-2665; www.kyscottishweekend.org
At this celebration of Scottish heritage, you'll find bands and bagpipers, the Scottish Athletic Competition (where athletes wear kilts), Celtic music, a Highland dance competition and a British auto show.
Second weekend in May.

WHERE TO STAY
★★GENERAL BUTLER LODGE AND COTTAGES
1608 Highway 227, Carrollton, 502-732-4384, 800-325-0078
77 rooms. Restaurant. $61-150

95

CAVE CITY
See also Bowling Green
True to its name, the city in the heart of Cave Country primarily serves tourists passing through the region en route to Mammoth Cave and other commercially operated caves nearby.

WHAT TO SEE
CRYSTAL ONYX CAVE
8709 Happy Valley Road, Cave City, 270-773-2359; www.cavecity.com/cavetours.htm
Geologic wonders of all kinds fill this cave. Helectites, stalagmites, stalactites, onyx columns and rare crystal onyx rim-stone formations will amaze you. So will the knowledge that Native Americans used the 54-degree cave as a burial site more than 2,700 years ago. Guided tours depart every 45 minutes.
Admission: adults $8.50, children $5.50. June-August, daily 9 a.m.-6 p.m.; September-May, daily 9 a.m.-5 p.m.

KENTUCKY ACTION PARK

3057 Mammoth Cave Road, Cave City, 270-773-2560, 800-798-0560;www.kentuckyactionpark.com

Ride to the top of the mountain on a chairlift and slide 1/4 mile down in an alpine sled. The action keeps going with go-karts, bumper boats and cars and horseback riding.

Admission: adults and children $5, children under 6 free.

WHERE TO STAY
★BEST WESTERN KENTUCKY INN

1009 Doyle Ave., Cave City, 270-773-3161, 800-780-7234; www.bestwestern.com

50 rooms. Complimentary breakfast. Pool. $61-150

WHERE TO EAT
★SAHARA STEAK HOUSE

413 E. Happy Valley St., Cave City, 270-773-3450

Steak. Lunch, dinner. $16-35

CORBIN

See also Berea

Feel like some finger-lickin' good chicken? There's plenty to eat in Corbin, home to the first Kentucky Fried Chicken restaurant. Just make sure to wait an hour before diving into the nearby 5,600-acre lake.

WHAT TO SEE
COLONEL HARLAND SANDERS' ORIGINAL RESTAURANT

Corbin, two miles north on Highway 25, 606-528-2163; www.chickenfestival.com

There really was a Colonel Sanders. See this authentic restoration of his first Kentucky Fried Chicken restaurant. Displays include an original kitchen, artifacts and the motel where Sanders worked as a chef. The original dining area is still in use.

Daily 10 a.m.-10 p.m.

LAUREL RIVER LAKE

1433 Laurel Lake Road, London, 606-864-6412

A 5,600-acre lake offers fishing and boating. If you're more of a landlubber, take a hike on one of the many nature trails. Daily.

SPECIAL EVENT
NIBROC FESTIVAL

101 N. Depot St., Corbin, 800-528-7123; www.corbinky.org

This fest highlights mountain arts and crafts. A parade, square dancing, a beauty pageant, a midway and entertainment round out the event.

Early August.

WHERE TO STAY
★BEST WESTERN CORBIN INN
2630 Cumberland Falls Highway, Corbin, 606-528-2100, 800-780-7234;
www.bestwestern.com
63 rooms. Complimentary breakfast. Pool. $61-150

★★CUMBERLAND FALLS STATE PARK LODGE AND COTTAGES
7351 Highway 90, Corbin, 606-528-4121, 800-325-0063; www.parks.ky.gov
78 rooms. Restaurant. $61-150

★HAMPTON INN
125 Adams Road, Corbin, 606-523-5696, 800-426-7866; www.hamptoninn.com
67 rooms. Complimentary breakfast. Business center. Fitness center. Pool.
$61-150

COVINGTON (CINCINNATI AIRPORT AREA)
See also Carrollton
Five broad bridges spanning the Ohio River link Covington to Cincinnati, but this city doesn't need help from Ohioans to have fun. Covington, named for a hero of the War of 1812, has had a renaissance in the last 20 years. Real estate developers and the city government invested in the city's riverfront and infrastructure, and eclectic restaurants and cool shops followed. To experience this revival, check out Covington Landing, a floating restaurant and entertainment complex.

WHAT TO SEE
CARROLL CHIMES BELL TOWER
Covington, west end of village
Completed in 1979, this 100-foot tower has a 43-bell carillon and mechanical figures that portray the legend of the Pied Piper of Hamelin. Daily.

CATHEDRAL BASILICA OF THE ASSUMPTION
1400 Madison Ave., Covington, 859-431-2060; www.covcathedral.com
Patterned after the Abbey of St. Denis and the Cathedral of Notre Dame in France, the basilica has massive doors, classic stained-glass windows (including one of the largest in the world), murals and mosaics by local and foreign artists.
Monday-Saturday 9:30 a.m.-4 p.m.

DEVOU PARK
Park Drive and Montague Road, Covington, 859-292-2151
This 550-acre park has a lake overlooking the Ohio River. Available activities include golf, tennis and picnicking. A number of outdoor concerts are held here as well during the summer months. Daily.

BEHRINGER-CRAWFORD MUSEUM
1600 Montague Road, Covington, 859-491-4003; www.bcmuseum.org
The museum keeps exhibits on local archaeology, paleontology, history, fine art and wildlife.

Admission: adults $7, seniors $6, children $4. Tuesday-Saturday 10 a.m.-5 p.m., Sunday 1-5 p.m.

MAINSTRASSE VILLAGE

406 W. Sixth St., Covington, 859-491-0458; www.mainstrasse.org

Approximately five square blocks in Covington's old German area make up this historic district of residences, shops and restaurants. It has more than 20 restored buildings dating back to the mid to late 1800s.

Monday-Saturday 11 a.m.-5 p.m., Sunday noon-5 p.m.

NEWPORT ON THE LEVEE

1 Levee Way, Newport, 859-750-4995; www.newportonthelevee.com

This 10-acre entertainment district on the river includes a trendy shopping center; 12 stylish restaurants; a state-of-the-art, 20-screen movie theater; and the acclaimed Newport Aquarium.

VENT HAVEN MUSEUM

33 W. Maple Ave., Fort Mitchell, 859-341-0461; www.venthavenmuseum.net

The only one of its kind in the world, this quirky museum houses more than 700 ventriloquist figures—"dummies"—who stare wide-eyed at visitors. The museum also contains pictures and collectibles.

Admission: $5. May-September, by appointment only.

WORLD OF SPORTS

7400 Woodspoint Drive, Florence, 859-371-8255; www.landrumgolf.com

Grab your clubs and check out this family entertainment complex, which has an 18-hole golf course, a 25-station lighted practice range, nine covered tees and a miniature golf course. When you tire of the woods and irons, you can play at the billiard hall, video arcade, five racquetball/volleyball courts and three slam-dunk basketball courts. A snack bar is available for refueling.

Sunday-Thursday 9 a.m.-11 p.m., Friday-Saturday 9 a.m.-1 p.m.

SPECIAL EVENTS

MAIFEST

MainStrasse Village, 605 Philadelphia St., Covington, 859-491-0458;
www.mainstrasse.org

Organizers say this traditional festival celebrates the spring's first wines, but you'll find plenty of that other German brew here, too. Maifest meshes traditional German fare—like polka bands and sauerkraut—with Kentucky treats, like Southern rock bands and artisans' crafts.

Third weekend in May.

OKTOBERFEST

MainStrasse Village, 605 Philadelphia St., Covington

Any self-respecting German historic neighborhood must celebrate Oktoberfest, and MainStrasse doesn't disappoint. Grab a beer and a brat and enjoy the full schedule of German music, ranging from rock 'n' roll to oompah music. Each day begins with the legendary Keg Tapping Ceremony.

Early September.

RIVERFEST

Covington, banks of Ohio River, 859-581-2260; www.nkycvb.com
One of the largest fireworks displays in the country, Riverfest shoots its pyrotechnics from barges moored on the river.
Labor Day weekend.

WHERE TO STAY
★★DRAWBRIDGE INN

2477 Royal Drive, Fort Mitchell, 859-341-2800, 800-354-9793; www.drawbridgeinn.com
488 rooms. Restaurant, bar. Fitness center. Pool. $61-150

★★EMBASSY SUITES

10 E. River Center Blvd., Covington, 859-261-8400, 800-362-2779; www.embassysuites1.hilton.com
226 suites. Restaurant, bar. Complimentary breakfast. Business center. Fitness center. Pool. $61-150

★HAMPTON INN

200 Crescent Ave., Covington, 859-581-7800; www.hamptoninn.com
151 rooms. Complimentary breakfast. Business center. Fitness center. Pool. $61-150

★★★MARRIOTT AT RIVERCENTER

10 W. River Center Blvd., Covington, 859-261-2900, 800-228-9290; www.marriott.com
Situated along the Ohio River, this soaring hotel offers close proximity to Cincinnati, as well as direct access to the Northern Kentucky Convention Center, a great perk for business travelers. The updated rooms are spacious and boast waterfront views and wireless Internet access.
321 rooms. Restaurant, bar. Business center. Fitness center. $61-150

★★★★★KENTUCKY

★★★RADISSON HOTEL CINCINNATI RIVERFRONT

668 W. Fifth St., Covington, 859-491-1200; www.radisson.com
The guest rooms supply views of the beautiful Ohio River, the lush wooded hills of northern Kentucky or scenic downtown Cincinnati. Nearby attractions include the Cincinnati Reds and Bengals and the Cincinnati Zoo.
220 rooms. Restaurant, bar. Fitness center. Pool. $61-150

★★RESIDENCE INN CINCINNATI AIRPORT

2811 Circleport Drive, Erlanger, 859-282-7400, 800-331-3131; www.residenceinn.com
150 rooms. Complimentary breakfast. Fitness center. Pool. $61-150

WHERE TO EAT
★★DEE FELICE CAFE

529 Main St., Covington, 859-261-2365; www.deefelice.com
Cajun, Creole. Dinner. $16-35

★★MIKE FINK

One Ben Bernstein Place, Covington, 859-261-4212; www.mikefink.com
Seafood. Lunch, dinner, Sunday brunch. $16-35

★★RIVERVIEW REVOLVING RESTAURANT
668 W. Fifth St., Covington, 859-491-5300
American. Breakfast, lunch, dinner. $16-35

★★★WATERFRONT
14 Pete Rose Pier, Covington, 859-581-1414; www.jeffruby.com
This bustling steak and lobster house has a stunning view of the Cincinnati skyline and a sit-down sushi bar.
Steak. Dinner. Closed Sunday. $16-35

CUMBERLAND FALLS STATE RESORT PARK
See also Corbin
The park's main attraction is a magnificent waterfall, 65 feet high and 125 feet wide. Surrounded by Daniel Boone National Forest, this awesome waterfall is the second largest east of the Rockies. By night, when the moon is full and the sky clear, a mysterious moonbow appears in the mist—a phenomenon you can't find anywhere else in the Western Hemisphere. The park also offers a swimming pool, fishing, nature trails, a nature center, riding, tennis, picnicking, a playground, a lodge, cottages, tent and trailer campsites.

WHAT TO SEE
BLUE HERON MINING COMMUNITY
Cumberland, in Big South Fork National River/Recreation Area (KY side), south via Highways 27 and 92 to Stearns, then nine miles west on Highway 742 (Mine 18 Road), 606-376-3787; www.nps.gov/biso/bheron.htm
Once a thriving mining community, Blue Heron was abandoned when the mine was closed in 1962. Today, the re-created town comprises metal-frame "ghost structures" that tell the stories of life here in the mid-20th century. Begin your tour at the depot, which has exhibits on the town's history. A scenic railway line connects Blue Heron with the town of Stearns. Daily.

SHELTOWEE TRACE OUTFITTERS
117 Hawkins Ave., Somerset, 606-376-5567, 800-541-7238; www.ky-rafting.com
Go on river rafting, canoeing and "funyak" trips in the scenic Cumberland River below the falls. Appointments are required for the five- to seven-hour trips. Prices vary.
June-September, daily; March-May and October, Saturday-Sunday.

CUMBERLAND GAP NATIONAL HISTORICAL PARK
See also Lexington
The famous Cumberland Gap served as the early pioneers' primary route through the central Appalachian Mountains. Long before settlers used the passage, Native Americans followed migratory animals along the gap, which was prime hunting territory. Then in 1775, Daniel Boone and 30 axmen cut a 208-mile swath through the forests from Kingsport, Tenn. to the Kentucky River, passing through the Cumberland Gap. Settlers poured through the pass and along Boone's "Wilderness Road," and in 1777, Kentucky became Virginia's westernmost county. After the Revolution, the mainstream of west-

ern settlement went through Cumberland Gap and slowed only when more direct northerly routes opened.

The park captures the gap's history with several historic buildings and structures preserved on 22,000 acres. Visitors will be amazed by the park's dramatically beautiful countryside, ready to be explored on more than 70 miles of hiking trails.

WHAT TO SEE
HENSLEY SETTLEMENT
Cumberland Gap, National Historical Park, Highway 25E, Corbin, 606-248-2817; www. nps.gov/cuga
An isolated mountain community until 1951, Hensley is now a restored historic site. To get here, hike 3 1/2 miles up the Chadwell Gap trail or take the shuttle from the visitor center.
Daily 8 a.m.-5 p.m.

DANIEL BOONE NATIONAL FOREST

These 707,000 acres contain some of Kentucky's most spectacular scenery. Among the park's famous attractions is Red River Gorge Geological Area, known for its natural arches and colorful rock formations as tall as 300 feet. A scenic loop drive of the gorge begins north of Natural Bridge State Resort Park on Highway 77. The nearest camping facilities are at Koomer Ridge, on Highway 15 between the Slade and Beattyville exits of Mount Parkway.

Another must-see is the forest's section of Sheltowee Trace National Recreation Trail, which runs the length of the national forest (and stretches more than 260 miles from Morehead, Kentucky, to Pickett State Rustic Park in Tennessee). If you're looking for a spectacular drive, take Forest Development Road 918—the main road to Zilpo Recreation Area on Cave Run Lake. The 11.2-mile road winds through hardwood forests and offers great views of Cave Run Lake.

After glimpses of it from afar, don't miss Cave Run Lake. It has swimming beaches, boat ramps and camping at Twin Knobs and Zilpo recreation areas. Laurel River Lake has boat ramps and camping areas at Holly Bay and Grove. Clay Lick (Cave Run Lake), Grove and White Oak (Laurel River Lake) have boat-in camping as well. Hunting and fishing are permitted in most parts of the forest under Kentucky regulations; backpacking is permitted on forest trails.

PINNACLE OVERLOOK
Cumberland Gap, National Historical Park, Highway 25E, Corbin, 606-248-2817; www. nps.gov/cuga
The overlook (at 2,440 feet) offers spectacular views into Kentucky, Virginia and Tennessee. To get there, take the Skyline Road up the mountain. Vehicles more than 20 feet in length and all trailers are prohibited. Daily.

DANVILLE
See also Harrodsburg
The birthplace of Kentucky government, Danville has had a front-row seat for much of the state's history. Ten years after the city was founded, it became the first capital of the Kentucky district of Virginia. The state constitution was signed here in 1792, and in the years leading up to statehood, Danville was one of the largest settlements on the Wilderness Road. Danville is the site of

the state's first college, first log courthouse, first post office, first school for the deaf and first law school.

WHAT TO SEE
CONSTITUTION SQUARE STATE SHRINE
134 S. Second St., Danville, 859-239-7089; www.parks.ky.gov/findparks/histparks/cs/
An authentic reproduction of Kentucky's first courthouse square stands at the exact site where the first state constitution was framed and adopted in 1792. The original post office is here as well as replicas of the jail, courthouse and meetinghouse. Governor's Circle has a bronze plaque of each Kentucky governor. A museum store and art gallery are also on the grounds. Daily.

HERRINGTON LAKE
1200 Gwinn Island Road, Danville, 859-236-4286; gwinnmarina.com
Formed by Dix Dam, one of the world's largest rock-filled dams, Herrington has 333 miles of shoreline. A balanced fish population is maintained through a conservation program. Fishing, a boat launch, camping hookups and cabins are all available. Daily.

MCDOWELL HOUSE AND APOTHECARY SHOP
125 S. Second St., Danville, 859-236-2804; www.mcdowellhouse.com
On Christmas Day 1809, Dr. Ephraim McDowell removed a 22.5-pound ovarian tumor from a woman without the benefit of anesthesia or antisepsis, neither of which had been invented yet. Amazingly, the surgery was a success. McDowell's residence and shop are restored and refurbished with period pieces. You'll see a large apothecary-ware collection. The surrounding gardens include trees, wildflowers and herbs of the period.
Admission: adults $7, seniors $5, students $3, children 5-12 $2, children under 5 free. Monday-Saturday 10 a.m.-noon, 1-4 p.m., Sunday 2-4 p.m.

PERRYVILLE BATTLEFIELD STATE HISTORIC SITE
1825 Battlefield Road, Perryville, 859-332-8631; www.parks.ky.gov/findparks/histparks/pb/
A 300-acre park, once a field, appears much as it did on October 8, 1862, when Confederate forces and Union troops clashed. A total of 4,241 Union soldiers and 1,822 Confederate troops were killed, wounded or missing. Still standing are the Crawford House, used by Confederate General Bragg as headquarters, and Bottom House, the site of some of the heaviest fighting. A mock battle is staged each year (weekend nearest October 8). At the north end of the battle line is a 1902 memorial to remember the Confederate dead and one built in 1931 to honor the Union dead. A museum houses artifacts from the battle. Take a gander at a 9-by-9-foot detailed battle map and battle dioramas.
April-October, daily; November-March, by appointment.

PIONEER PLAYHOUSE VILLAGE-OF-THE-ARTS
840 Stanford Road, Danville, 859-236-2747; www.pioneerplayhouse.com
This reproduction of an 18th-century Kentucky village features a drama school and museum on its on a 200-acre site.
May-October, daily.

SPECIAL EVENT
PIONEER PLAYHOUSE
Pioneer Playhouse Village-of-the-Arts, 840 Stanford Road, Danville, 859-236-2747;
www.pioneerplayhouse.com
Kentucky's oldest outdoor theater, this summer stock theater puts on five
shows each summer.
June-August, Tuesday-Saturday.

WHERE TO STAY
★★COUNTRY HEARTH INN-DANVILLE
Highway 127, Danville, 859-236-8601; www.countryhearth.com
81 rooms. Restaurant. Fitness center. Pool. $61-150

★HOLIDAY INN EXPRESS
96 Daniel Drive, Danville, 859-236-8600; www.hiexpress.com
63 rooms. Complimentary breakfast. Pool. $61-150

ELIZABETHTOWN
See also Bardstown, Fort Knox, Shepherdsville
With a starring role in Cameron Crowe's 2005 movie, Elizabethtown could
have gotten a Hollywood-sized ego. Instead, this little town is as laid-back
and charming as it ever was. The town plays a big role in President Abraham
Lincoln's family story: Thomas Lincoln, the president's father, owned property and worked here, and he brought his bride Nancy Hanks to the area after
their wedding. Honest Abe's older sister Sarah was born here, and after his
first wife's death, Thomas returned here to marry Sarah Bush Johnston.

WHAT TO SEE
BROWN-PUSEY COMMUNITY HOUSE
128 N. Main St., Elizabethtown, 270-765-2515; www.touretown.com
This former stagecoach inn is an excellent example of Georgian Colonial architecture; General George Custer lived here from 1871 to 1873. It's restored
as a historical genealogy library and community house.
Tuesday-Saturday 10 a.m.-4 p.m.

LINCOLN HERITAGE HOUSE
Elizabethtown, one mile north on Highway 31 W., in Freeman Lake Park, 270-765-2175,
800-437-0092; www.touretown.com
Pioneer Hardin Thomas lived in this double log cabin, and Thomas Lincoln,
father of President Abraham Lincoln, created the unusual trim work. It show-
cases pioneer implements, early surveying equipment and period furniture.
Park facilities include pavilions, paddle and row boats and canoes.
June-September, Tuesday-Sunday 10 a.m.-5 p.m.

SCHMIDT MUSEUM OF COCA-COLA MEMORABILIA
109 Buffalo Creek Drive, Elizabethtown, 270-234-1100; www.schmidtmuseum.com
Have a Coke and a smile at this museum, the world's largest private collection of Coca-Cola memorabilia with more than 80,000 items, some dating
back to 1886. More than 1,100 pieces are on display in the museum at any

given time. Expect to see artifacts like old Coca-Cola toys, bottles, Santas, trays and vending machines.

Admission: adults $5, seniors $4, students $2, children under 5 free.

Monday-Saturday 10 a.m.-6 p.m., Sunday 1-5 p.m.

SPECIAL EVENT
KENTUCKY HEARTLAND FESTIVAL
Freeman Lake Park, 111 W. Dixie Ave., Elizabethtown, 270-765-4334;
www.touretown.com

The festival offers an antique auto show, arts and crafts, a canoe race, a running event, a hot-air balloon, bluegrass music, games and lots of food.

Last weekend in August.

WHERE TO STAY
★BEST WESTERN ATRIUM GARDENS
1043 Executive Drive, Elizabethtown, 270-769-3030; www.bestwestern.com

133 rooms. Complimentary breakfast. Fitness center. $61-150

★KENTUCKY CARDINAL INN
642 E. Dixie Ave., Elizabethtown, 270-765-6139, 800-528-1234

54 rooms. Restaurant. Fitness center. Pool. $61-150

WHERE TO EAT
★JERRY'S
654 E Dixie Ave., Elizabethtown, 270-769-2336

American. Breakfast, lunch, dinner. $16-35

★★STONE HEARTH
1001 N. Mulberry St., Elizabethtown, 270-765-4898; www.stonehearthetown.com

American. Lunch, dinner. $16-35

FORT KNOX
See also Elizabethtown, Louisville

This military post established in 1918 is home to the U.S. Army Armor Center and School and the Army's home of Mounted Warfare. Named for Major General Henry Knox, the first secretary of war, the post has been a major installation since 1932.

WHAT TO SEE
PATTON MUSEUM OF CAVALRY AND ARMOR
4554 Fayette Ave., Fort Knox, 502-624-3812; www.generalpatton.org

The Armor Branch Museum was named in honor of General George S. Patton Jr. The collection includes U.S. and foreign armored equipment, weapons, art and uniforms as well as mementos of General Patton's military career, including the sedan in which he was riding when he was fatally injured in 1945. Also on display are a 10-by-12-foot section of the Berlin Wall and foreign armored equipment from Operation Desert Storm.

Monday-Friday 9 a.m.-4:30 p.m., Saturday-Sunday 10 a.m.-4:30 p.m.

UNITED STATES BULLION DEPOSITORY

Fort Knox, Gold Vault Road, www.usmint.gov

It turns out that the old song about "all the gold in Fort Knox" refers to real gold. Opened in 1937, this two-story granite, steel and concrete building houses part of the nation's gold reserves. The depository and the surrounding grounds are not open to the public. Daily.

WHERE TO STAY
★RADCLIFF INN

438 S. Dixie Blvd., Radcliff, 270-351-8211, 800-421-2030; www.radcliffinn.com

83 rooms. Complimentary breakfast. Fitness center. Pool. $61-150

FRANKFORT

See also Lexington

The Kentucky River runs through the heart of Frankfort, and wooded hills rise up around it, making the city one of the most picturesque state capitals in the country. But don't let the scenery fool you: Against this serene backdrop, politics rule when the legislature is in session. Catch the politicos at play and tour the city's historic sites. This place has real charm, good stories and plenty for visitors to do.

WHAT TO SEE
DANIEL BOONE'S GRAVE

215 E. Main St., in Frankfort Cemetery, Frankfort, 502-227-2403

This monument is for Boone and his wife. Boone died in Missouri but his remains were brought here in 1845. Daily.

FLORAL CLOCK

300 Capitol Ave., Frankfort, 502-564-3449

This functioning outdoor timepiece is adorned with thousands of plants and elevated above a reflecting pool. The mechanism moves a 530-pound minute hand and a 420-pound hour hand. Visitors toss thousands of dollars in coins into the pool, all of which are donated to state child-care agencies. Daily.

KENTUCKY HISTORICAL SOCIETY

100 W. Broadway St., Frankfort, 502-564-1792; www.history.ky.gov

The center features exhibits pertaining to the history and development of the state and the culture of its people. The Historical Society's campus also includes the Old State Capitol, a library with an impressive genealogical archive and the Kentucky Military History Museum.
Admission: adults $4, children 6-18 $2, children under 6 free. Tuesday-Saturday 10 a.m.-5 p.m.

KENTUCKY STATE UNIVERSITY

400 E. Main St., Frankfort, 502-597-6000; www.kysu.edu

Historically, KSU was a black liberal studies institution. Campus highlights include Jackson Hall, which has art and photo gallery exhibits, and Carver Hall, featuring the King Farouk butterfly collection. Daily.

KENTUCKY VIETNAM VETERANS MEMORIAL

300 Coffee Tree Road, Frankfort; www.kyvietnammemorial.net

This unique memorial is a 14-foot sundial that casts a shadow across veterans' names on the anniversaries of their deaths. The memorial contains more than 1,000 names.

Daily.

LIBERTY HALL

218 Wilkinson St., Frankfort, 502-227-2560; www.libertyhall.org

The first U.S. senator from Kentucky, John Brown, built this home near the end of the 18th century. It has been restored to its original state and furnished with family heirlooms. Take a stroll through the surrounding period gardens.

Admission: adults $4, seniors $3, children 4-18 $1, children under 4 free. Tuesday-Saturday, sunrise-sunset.

OLD GOVERNOR'S MANSION

420 High St., Frankfort, 502-564-3449; www.kentucky.gov

The official residence of the governor is styled after the Petit Trianon, Marie Antoinette's villa at Versailles. The outfitted parlor and dining room have hosted such heavyweights as Theodore Roosevelt, Henry Clay and the Marquis de Lafayette.

Guided tours are given Monday, Tuesday and Thursday from 1:30 to 3:30 p.m.

OLD STATE CAPITOL BUILDING

Broadway and Lewis streets, Frankfort; 502-564-1792; www.history.ky.gov

Kentucky's third capitol building was used as the capitol from 1830 to 1909 and was the first Greek Revival statehouse west of the Alleghenies. Completely restored and furnished in period style, the building features an unusual self-balanced double stairway.

Admission: adults $4, children 6-18 $2, children under 6 free. Tuesday-Saturday 10 a.m.-4 p.m.

ORLANDO BROWN HOUSE

202 Wilkinson St., Frankfort, 502-227-2560; www.libertyhall.org

This early Greek Revival house was built for Orlando Brown, son of Senator John Brown. The home has its original furnishings and artifacts.

Admission: adults $4, seniors $3, children 4-18 $1, children under 4 free. Tuesday-Saturday 10 a.m.-5 p.m.

STATE CAPITOL

700 Capitol Ave., Frankfort, 502-564-3449; www.finance.ky.gov/properties/capitol.htm

The stately Beaux-Arts building has French influences. The dome over the rotunda was designed to look like the one over Napoleon's tomb in Paris, and the Paris Grand Opera House inspired the massive marble stairways to the second floor. You can watch the politicians do their thing when the legislature is in session. Admire great men of history when you walk by the rotunda's statues of Abraham Lincoln, Jefferson Davis, Henry Clay, Dr. Ephraim Mc-

Dowell and Alben Barkley, vice president under Harry S. Truman. Guided tours are available.
Monday-Friday 8:30 a.m.-3:30 p.m.

SPECIAL EVENTS
CAPITAL EXPO FESTIVAL
405 Mero St., Capital Plaza Complex, Frankfort, 502-695-7452; www.capitalexpofestival.com
Traditional music, country music and fiddling fill the air at this fest. Workshops, demonstrations, arts and crafts, balloon races, dancing, games, contests, puppets, museum exhibitions, ethnic and regional foods all add to the fun.
First weekend in June.

GOVERNOR'S DERBY BREAKFAST
700 Capitol Ave., Frankfort, 502-564-2611
Kentuckians, nearly 13,000 of them, start Derby Day right with a hearty breakfast served on the Capitol grounds. The staff here serves 2,080 pounds of country ham, 20,000 eggs and 15,000 cups of coffee. Music and crafts round out the festivities.
First Saturday in May.

WHERE TO STAY
★BEST WESTERN PARKSIDE INN
80 Chenault Road, Frankfort, 502-695-6111, 800-938-8376; www.bestwestern.com
99 rooms. Complimentary breakfast. Fitness center. Pool. $61-150

★★CAPITAL PLAZA HOTEL
405 Wilkinson Blvd., Frankfort, 502-227-5100; www.holiday-inn.com
189 rooms. Restaurant, bar. $61-150

WHERE TO EAT
★JIM'S SEAFOOD
950 Wilkinson Blvd., Frankfort, 502-223-7448
Seafood. Lunch, dinner. Closed Sunday. $16-35

GEORGETOWN
See also Frankfort, Lexington, Paris
Georgetown may be small, but it has one big claim to fame: this is the place where Kentucky bourbon whiskey was first produced. Baptist minister the Reverend Elijah Craig invented the spirit in 1789 using water from Royal Spring, which still flows in the center of the city.

WHAT TO SEE
CARDOME CENTRE
800 Cincinnati Pike, Georgetown, 502-863-1575; www.cardomecenter.com
This place was the former house of Civil War Governor J. F. Robinson and later the home of the Academy of the Sisters of the Visitation. Now it houses Georgetown and Scott County Museum and serves as a community center.
Monday-Friday, also by appointment.

ROYAL SPRING PARK

West Main and South Water streets, Georgetown, 502-863-2547;
www.georgetownky.com

Kentucky's largest spring and the city's water source since 1775, Royal Spring is the site of the first bourbon distillation, which dates back to 1789. It's also the former site of McClelland's Fort 1776, the first paper mill in the West, a pioneer classical music school and state's first ropewalk. A cabin of a former slave was relocated and restored here for use as an information center.
Mid-May-mid-October, Tuesday-Sunday.

TOYOTA MOTOR MANUFACTURING, KENTUCKY, INC

1001 Cherry Blossom Way, Georgetown, 502-868-3027, 800-866-4485;
www.toyotageorgetown.com

About 400,000 cars and 350,000 engines are made here annually. The visitor center has interactive exhibits. One-hour tours of the plant (for those ages 6 and up) include a video presentation and tram ride through different levels of production.
Monday-Friday 9 a.m.-4 p.m.

GILBERTSVILLE

See also Madisonville

Fishing parties heading for Kentucky Lake stop in tiny Gilbertsville for last-minute provisions. The area also caters to tourists bound for the resorts and state parks.

WHAT TO SEE
BARKLEY LOCK AND DAM

Highways 62 and 641, Gilbertsville, 270-362-4236

Play on more than 1,000 miles of shoreline. A navigation lock, canal, hydro-electric generating plant and recreation areas are all onsite. Daily.

KENTUCKY DAM VILLAGE STATE RESORT PARK

Gilbertsville, 113 Administration Drive, 270-362-4271, 800-325-0146;
www.parks.ky.gov.com

The park, on Kentucky Lake, provides many ways to play: a swimming beach, pool, bathhouse, waterskiing, boating, hiking, 18-hole and miniature golf, tennis, picnicking, playground, shops, camping, lodge and cottages. Daily.

WHERE TO STAY
★★KENTUCKY DAM STATE RESORT PARK LODGE AND COTTAGES

Gilbertsville, 270-362-4271, 800-325-0146; www.parks.ky.gov
156 rooms. Restaurant. $61-150

WHERE TO EAT
★PATTI'S

1759 J. H. O'Bryan Ave., Grand River, 270-362-8844, 888-736-2515;
www.pattis-settlement.com
American. Lunch, dinner. $16-35

GLASGOW

See also Bowling Green

Not surprisingly, Glasgow has a bit o' Scottish flavor. It's famous for its Highland Games, which celebrate Celtic heritage and culture.

WHAT TO SEE
BARREN RIVER LAKE STATE RESORT PARK

1149 State Park Road, Lucas, 270-646-2151, 800-325-0057; www.parks.ky.gov

Near Mammoth Cave National Park, this resort park is near the 10,000-acre Barren River Lake. You'll have your choice of activities: swimming at the beach or pool, fishing, boating, hiking, horseback riding, bicycle trails, playing on the 18-hole golf course, tennis, picnicking and hanging around the playground. If you want to stay the night, tent and trailer sites, cottages and a lodge are available. Daily.

SPECIAL EVENT
HIGHLAND GAMES AND GATHERING OF SCOTTISH CLANS

1149 State Park Road, Lucas, 270-651-3161

There's something captivating about watching grown men in plaid kilts compete in the historic Highland Games. Athletic events include the stone toss, hammer throw and the caber throw, in which contestants toss a 19-foot, 120-pound pole end-over-end. The four-day festival also hosts live entertainment, food vendors and a banquet.

Weekend following Memorial Day.

WHERE TO STAY
★★BARREN RIVER LAKE STATE RESORT PARK LODGE AND COTTAGES

1149 State Park Road, Lucas, 270-646-2151, 800-325-0057; www.parks.ky.gov

51 rooms. Restaurant. $61-150

★DAYS INN

105 Days Inn Blvd., Glasgow, 270-651-1757; www.daysinn.com

59 rooms. Complimentary breakfast. Business center. Pool. $61-150

GREENVILLE

See also Bowling Green

Located in the heart of the western Kentucky coal, oil and natural gas fields, Greenville is also close to areas popular with hunters and fishermen.

WHAT TO SEE
LAKE MALONE STATE PARK

331 Highway 8001, Dunmore, 270-657-2111; www.parks.ky.gov

Steep sandstone bluffs and a wooded shoreline surround Lake Malone, making it a beautiful place to relax. If you get the urge to hike, take the easy 1 1/2-mile trek on Laurel Trail. Anglers will enjoy fishing for bass, bluegill and crappie. Daily.

HARRODSBURG

See also Danville

Settled in 1774, Harrodsburg (named for pioneer James Harrod) is Kentucky's oldest town. Its sulfur springs and historical sites make it a busy tourist center.

WHAT TO SEE
MORGAN ROW

220-222 S. Chiles St., Harrodsburg, 859-734-5985

One of the oldest standing row houses west of the Alleghenies, Morgan Row once was a stagecoach stop and tavern. Now it houses the Harrodsburg Historical Society Museum.

Tuesday 10 a.m.-4 p.m., Wednesday-Saturday 1-4 p.m.

OLD FORT HARROD STATE PARK

100 S. College, Harrodsburg, 859-734-3314; www.parks.ky.gov

This 28-acre park includes a reproduction of Old Fort Harrod, near where the original fort was built in 1774. Other structures on the site include pioneers' homes, which hold authentic cooking utensils, tools and furniture. The Mansion Museum includes the Lincoln Room, the Confederate Room, a gun collection and Native American artifacts. Lincoln Marriage Temple shelters the log cabin in which Abraham Lincoln's parents were married on June 12, 1806 (moved from its original site in Beech Fork). Picnic facilities, a playground and gift shop are there as well. Living history crafts programs are held in the fort.

OLD MUD MEETING HOUSE

Harrodsburg, four miles south off Highway 68, 859-734-5985

This is the first Dutch Reformed Church west of the Alleghenies. The original mud-thatch walls have been restored.

By appointment only.

SHAKER VILLAGE OF PLEASANT HILL

3501 Lexington Road, Harrodsburg, 859-734-5411; www.shakervillageky.org

What was once a flourishing society is now the nation's largest restored Shaker community. In the heart of horse country, this village has 34 buildings and 3,000 acres of farmland, much of which visitors can explore on foot, bike or horseback. Costumed interpreters in the village tell the stories of Shaker life. Craft shops offer reproductions of Shaker furniture and Kentucky craft items. A year-round calendar of special events includes music, dance and workshops. Daily.

April-October, daily 10 a.m.-5 p.m.

SPECIAL EVENT
THE LEGEND OF DANIEL BOONE

Harrodsburg

This outdoor drama tells the story of Boone, one of America's great explorers, in the James Harrod Amphitheater in Old Fort Harrod State Park.

Mid-June-August, Tuesday-Sunday.

WHERE TO STAY
★★★BEAUMONT INN
638 Beaumont Inn Dr., Harrodsburg, 859-734-3381, 800-352-3992; www.beaumontinn. com

Maintaining the style and tradition of the past, this property offers unique accommodations that reflect the area's rich heritage. Guests experience the meaning of "Southern decadence" when they treat themselves to dinner here.

31 rooms. Restaurant. $61-150

★DAYS INN HARRODSBURG
1680 Danville Road, Harrodsburg, 859-734-9431; www.daysinn.com

69 rooms. Complimentary breakfast. Pool. $61-150

WHERE TO EAT
★★TRUSTEES' HOUSE AT PLEASANT HILL
3501 Lexington Road, Harrodsburg, 859-734-5411; www.shakervillageky.org
American. Lunch, dinner. $16-35

HAZARD
See also London

In rugged mountain country, Hazard is a coal-mining town that earned a little name recognition from the 1980s TV hit *Dukes of Hazzard*, although the fictional Hazzard County was set in Georgia.

WHAT TO SEE
BOBBY DAVIS MEMORIAL PARK
Walnut Street, Hazard

Head to the park for its picnic area, reflecting pool, World War II Memorial and 400 varieties of shrubs and plants. Don't miss the Bobby Davis Park Museum, which houses local historical artifacts and photographs about life on Kentucky River waterways.

Monday-Friday 8 a.m.-4 p.m.

CARR FORK LAKE
843 Sassafras Creek Road, Sassafras, 606-642-3308; www.lrl.usace.army.mil/cfl/

The 710-acre lake makes for good fishing, boating and camping. Check out the observation points along the way. Daily.

SPECIAL EVENT
BLACK GOLD FESTIVAL
Main Street, Hazard, 606-436-0161; www.blackgoldfestival.com

The festival celebrates local coal resources with food and craft booths, games, an ugliest lamp contest, entertainment, a carnival and parade.

Third weekend in September.

WHERE TO STAY
★★BUCKHORN LAKE STATE RESORT PARK
4441 Highway 1833, Buckhorn, 606-398-7510, 800-325-0058; www.parks.ky.gov
36 rooms. Restaurant. $61-150

★SUPER 8
125 Village Lane, Hazard, 606-436-8888, 800-800-8000; www.super8.com
86 rooms. Complimentary breakfast. $61-150

HENDERSON
See also Owensboro
On a bluff overlooking the Ohio River, Henderson is a town of great natural beauty. It was once home to artist and naturalist John James Audubon, who lived here for nine years and painted life-size pictures of the wildlife nearby.

WHAT TO SEE
JOHN JAMES AUDUBON STATE PARK
3100 I-41 North, Henderson, 270-826-2247; www.parks.ky.gov
See the massive hardwood forests, woodland plants and two lakes that inspired Audubon's writings. The museum here holds the celebrated naturalist's art and personal memorabilia. The park also has a bathhouse, fishing, paddleboat rentals, nine-hole golf, picnicking, a playground, tent and trailer camping and cottages. Daily.

SPECIAL EVENTS
BLUEGRASS IN THE PARK
Henderson, 270-826-3128; www.bluegrassintheparkfestival.com
On the banks of the Ohio River, in Audubon Mill Park, this free festival hosts bluegrass acts from across the country. The festival includes a Folklife Festival, where locals celebrate folk music, crafts, cooking and storytelling. Early August.

W. C. HANDY BLUES & BARBECUE FESTIVAL
Atkinson Park, Elm St., Henderson, 800-648-3128, 270-826-3128; www.handyblues.org
Local legends says that W.C. Handy, the "father of the blues," was traveling back from the Chicago World's Fair in 1893 when he ran out of money in St. Louis and joined a band that played in the region. At a gig in Henderson, Handy met Elizabeth Price, the woman who would become his wife. W.C. Handy lived in Henderson for 10 years, and this festival celebrates the musical genre he helped create. Mid-June.

WHERE TO STAY
★COMFORT INN
2820 Highway 41 N., Henderson, 270-827-8191, 877-417-3251; www.comfortinn.com
55 rooms. Complimentary breakfast. Fitness center. Pool. $61-150

HODGENVILLE

See also Elizabethtown

Admirers of Abraham Lincoln will appreciate Hodgenville, where the 16th president of the United States was born in 1809. Almost all of the tourist attractions here relate to the city's most famous native son.

WHAT TO SEE
LINCOLN MUSEUM

66 Lincoln Square, Hodgenville, 270-358-3163; www.lincolnmuseum-ky.org
Dioramas at the museum tell the story of Lincoln's life, from his early childhood in Kentucky to his assassination at Ford's Theatre. The second floor holds rare newspaper clippings, memorabilia, campaign posters and an art gallery.
Monday-Saturday 8:30 a.m.-4:30 p.m., Sunday 12:30-4:30 p.m.

SPECIAL EVENTS
LINCOLN DAYS CELEBRATION

Lincoln Square, Hodgenville, 270-358-3411; www.laruecounty.org/civicclubs.shtml
Lincoln Days has a rail-splitting competition, pioneer games, a classic car show, arts and crafts exhibits and a parade.
Second weekend in October.

LINCOLN'S BIRTHDAY

2995 Lincoln Farm Road, Hodgenville, 270-358-3137; www.nps.gov/abli
A wreath-laying ceremony marks Abraham Lincoln's birthday.
February 12.

HOPKINSVILLE

See also Cadiz

The tobacco auctioneers' chant has long been the theme song of Hopkinsville. The town was the infamous site of the Night Rider War, brought on by farmers' discontent at the low prices they received for their dark tobacco. They raided the town in December 1907, burning several warehouses. In 1911, the culprits were tried and their group disbanded.
Hopkinsville was also a stop on the "Trail of Tears." The site of the Cherokee encampment is now a park with a museum and memorial dedicated to those who lost their lives.

WHAT TO SEE
FORT CAMPBELL

2334 19th St., Hopkinsville, 270-798-2151; www.campbell.army.mil/campbell.htm
The fort is one of the nation's largest military installations at 105,000 acres, and home of the 101st Airborne Division. Wickham Hall houses the Don F. Pratt Museum, which displays historic military items. Daily.

PENNYRILE FOREST STATE RESORT PARK

20781 Pennyrile Lodge Road, Dawson Springs, 270-797-3421; www.parks.ky.gov
You'll stay busy at the park with swimming at the beach and pool, a bathhouse, fishing, boating, hiking, riding, nine-hole and miniature golf, tennis,

picnicking and a playground. The grounds also have a grocery, cottages, a lodge, and tent and trailer sites. Daily.

PENNYROYAL AREA MUSEUM
217 E. Ninth St., Hopkinsville, 270-887-4270; www.hoptown.org
Exhibits feature the area's agriculture and industries, a miniature circus and old railroad items. The museum also highlights Civil War items, 1898 law office furniture and an Edgar Cayce exhibit.
Admission: $5. Monday-Friday 8:30 a.m.-4:30 p.m., Saturday 10 a.m.-3 p.m.

JEFFERSON DAVIS MONUMENT STATE SHRINE
In 1808, Jefferson Davis, the only president of the Confederate States of America, was born in Fairview, Ky. (Ironically, less than a year later, President Abraham Lincoln was born about 100 miles away.) This monument to Davis, a cast-concrete obelisk more than 350 feet tall, overlooks a 19-acre park. Visitors may take an elevator to the observation area at the top for a smal fee.

The son of a Revolutionary War officer, Davis graduated from West Point, became a successful cotton planter in Mississippi, was elected to the U.S. Senate, and served as secretary of war in President Franklin Pierce's cabinet. He had returned to the Senate when Mississippi seceded from the Union in 1860, a move that prompted Davis to resign his seat. Elected president of the Confederacy, he served for the duration of the war — about four years. Union troops captured him in Georgia, and Davis lost his citizenship and served two years in prison. May-October, daily.

SPECIAL EVENTS
LITTLE RIVER DAYS
1209 S. Virginia St., Hopkinsville, 270-885-9096
The festival consists of road races, canoe races, arts and crafts, entertainment and children's events.
Early May.

WESTERN KENTUCKY STATE FAIR
Hopkinsville, 270-885-9096; www.hopkinsvillechamber.com
The state fair keeps it festive with a midway, rides, concerts, local exhibits and events.
First week in August.

WHERE TO STAY
★BEST WESTERN HOPKINSVILLE
4101 Fort Campbell Blvd., Hopkinsville, 270-886-9000; www.bestwestern.com
107 rooms. Bar. Complimentary breakfast. Business center. Pool. $61-150

★★HOLIDAY INN
2910 Fort Campbell Blvd., Hopkinsville, 270-886-4413; www.holiday-inn.com
101 rooms. Restaurant, bar. Pool. $61-150

HORSE CAVE

See also Cave City, Glasgow

On the south side of Main Street, you'll find the reason for this city's unusual name: a large natural cave opening. Legend suggests that in the 19th century, horse was a synonym for large, hence the cave's—and the city's—unusual name.

WHAT TO SEE
KENTUCKY DOWN UNDER/KENTUCKY CAVERNS

3700 Land Turnpike Road N., Horse Cave, 270-786-2634, 800-762-2869; www.kdu.com

This Australian-themed animal park features free-roaming kangaroos, wallabies, emus and other animals native to Down Under. Walk into the exotic bird garden and feed colorful lorikeets while they sit on your head and shoulders. Learn about sheep herding in the sheep station area, or find out about Australia's aborigines and their way of life at Camp Corroboree. View bison from the Overlook Deck and then try not to feel guilty as you munch on a bison burger at the Outback Cafe. Admission to Kentucky Caverns (formerly Mammoth Onyx Cave) is included and lets visitors get up close and personal with the beautiful onyx formations found underground here in Kentucky's "Cave Country." The 45-minute guided cave tour reveals colorful stalactites and stalagmites, flowstone and hanging bridges and is leisurely enough to accommodate most people (though not those in wheelchairs). Best of all, the cave keeps to a comfortable 60 degrees year-round, so it stays open through the winter. Admission: adults $22, seniors $19.30, children 5-14 $13, children under 5 free. November-March, daily 9 a.m.-4 p.m.; April-May, daily 8 a.m.-5 p.m.; June-August, daily 8 a.m.-6 p.m.; September-November, daily 8 a.m.-5 p.m.

KENTUCKY REPERTORY THEATRE AT HORSE CAVE

107 E. Main St., Horse Cave, 800-342-2177; www.kentuckyrep.org

This is Southern Kentucky's resident professional festival theater. Six of the season's plays run in rotating repertory during the summer. An art gallery is also on the premises.

JAMESTOWN

See also Glasgow

It was here that Lake Cumberland was created, with the help of a 101-mile-long dam. Look for plenty of water sports, and more than a few activities—from golf to shuffleboard—for the landlubbers among us.

WHAT TO SEE
LAKE CUMBERLAND STATE RESORT PARK

5465 State Park Road, Jamestown, 270-343-3111, 800-325-1709; www.parks.ky.gov

This lake resort is a water sportsman's dream. It has a reputation as one of the best fishing spots in the eastern United States. The park also has swimming pools, boating, hiking, riding, nine-hole par-3 and miniature golf, tennis, shuffleboard, bicycling, picnicking, a playground, a lodge, rental houseboats, cottages and tent and trailer camping. Check out the nature center if there is time.

Daily.

WHERE TO STAY
★★LAKE CUMBERLAND STATE RESORT PARK LODGE
*5465 State Park Road, Jamestown, 270-343-3111, 800-325-1709; www.parks.ky.gov/
findparks/resortparks/lc*
106 rooms. Restaurant. $61-150

KENLAKE STATE RESORT PARK
See also Bowling Green
This park on Kentucky Lake has it all: beautiful scenery, four miles of shore-line and so many amenities you won't know where to begin your vacation. A pool, a bathhouse, waterskiing, fishing, boating, hiking, nine-hole golf, shuffleboard, tennis, picnicking, playgrounds, cottages, a dining room, a lodge and tent and trailer sites are all available here. Daily.

WHERE TO STAY
★★KENLAKE STATE RESORT PARK LODGE
542 Kenlake Road, Hardin, 270-474-2211, 800-425-0143; www.parks.ky.gov
82 rooms. Restaurant. $61-150

LAND BETWEEN THE LAKES
See also Hopkinsville
Welcome to one of the nation's biggest outdoor recreation areas. More than 170,000 acres make up this wooded peninsula that runs 40 miles from north to south between Kentucky Lake and Lake Barkley.
There are four major family campgrounds: Hillman Ferry, Piney, Energy Lake and Wranglers Campground, which is equipped for horseback riders. Eleven other lake-access areas offer more primitive camping. All areas of-fer swimming, fishing, boating, ramps and picnic facilities. Family camp-grounds have planned recreation programs.
There is a 5,000-acre wooded Environmental Education Area that includes the Nature Station, which presents interpretive displays of native plant and animal life. Within this area are several nature trails. Elk and Bison Prairie is a drive-through viewing area where you'll see plants and wildlife in their native habitat.

WHAT TO SEE
GOLDEN POND VISITOR CENTER
*Land Between the Lakes, 100 Van Morgan Drive, Golden Pond, 270-924-2000;
www.lbl.org*
This is the main orientation center for Land Between the Lakes visitors. Planetarium presentations take place here. Daily.

THE HOMEPLACE
*Land Between the Lakes, 100 Van Morgan Drive, Golden Pond, 270-924-2020;
www.lbl.org*
This working history farm provides an authentic look at farm life in the 19th century. Corn and tobacco are grown and harvested using tools and techniques of the era. The livestock and farm animals are "minor breeds"— historic breeds of domestic animals that are endangered species.

Admission: adults $4, children 5-12 $2, children under 5 free. April-October, Monday-Saturday 9 a.m.-5 p.m., Sunday 10 a.m.-5 p.m.; November, Wednesday-Saturday 9 a.m.-5 p.m., Sunday 10 a.m.-5 p.m.

WOODLANDS NATURE STATION
Land Between the Lakes, 100 Van Morgan Drive, Golden Pond, 270-924-2000; www. lbl.org

Inside you'll find the station's discovery center, and outside in "the Backyard," you'll see plants and animals from this corner of the world. Catch sight of a bobcat, red wolf and maybe even a bald eagle.

Admission: adults $4, children 5-12 $2, children under 5 free. April-October, Monday-Saturday 9 a.m.-5 p.m., Sunday 10 a.m.-5 p.m.; November, Wednesday-Saturday 9 a.m.-5 p.m., Sunday 10 a.m.-5 p.m.

LEXINGTON
See also Frankfort, Winchester

Lexington might be the "Horse Capital of the World," but don't mistake this city for a simple horse town. In the heart of Kentucky's Bluegrass region, Lexington benefits from smart urban planning, Southern sophistication and the allure of bourbon and horse racing. (Don't be fooled by the region's name: the legendary steel-blue tint of the bluegrass is visible only in May's early morning sunshine.) In 1775, an exploring party was camping here when members got news of the colonists' triumph at the Battle of Lexington in Massachusetts and decided to name their campsite in honor of the victory. Four years later, the city was established, and it quickly gained prominence in the expanding western territory. Pioneers who settled here brought their best horses from Maryland and Virginia, and as the citizens' wealth grew, they imported horses from abroad to improve the breed. The first races were held in Lexington in 1780, and the first jockey club was organized in 1797.

In the early 19th century, Lexington earned the nickname "Athens of the West," thanks to its vibrant cultural life—a spirit that continues today. The city's offerings include two ballet companies, a professional theater group and an outstanding opera program at the University of Kentucky.

WHAT TO SEE
AMERICAN SADDLEBRED MUSEUM
4093 Iron Works Parkway, Lexington, 859-259-2746;
www.americansaddlebredmuseum.org

The museum is dedicated to the American saddlebred horse, Kentucky's only native breed. Contemporary exhibits look at the development and uses of the American saddlebred. There's also a gift shop.

Admission: adults $15, seniors $14, children 7-12 $8, children under 7 free. June-August 9 a.m.-6 p.m.; September-May 9 a.m.-5 p.m.

ASHLAND
Richmond and Sycamore Roads, Lexington, 859-266-8581; www.henryclay.org

This estate on 20 acres of woodland was the home of Henry Clay, statesman, orator, senator and would-be president. Occupied by the Clay clan for five generations, Ashland is furnished with family possessions. The estate was named for the ash trees that surround it. A number of outbuildings still stand. Admission: adults $7, children 6-18 $4, children under 6 free. Tuesday-Saturday 10 a.m.-4 p.m., Sunday 1-4 p.m.

HEADLEY-WHITNEY MUSEUM
4435 Old Frankfort Pike, Lexington, 859-255-6653; www.headley-whitney.org
This museum exhibits decorative arts—furniture, metalwork, textiles and ceramics. Unusual buildings house displays of bibelots (small decorative objects) created with precious metals and jewels, Oriental porcelains, paintings, decorative arts, shell grotto and special exhibits.
Admission: adults $10, seniors and students $7, children under 5 free. Tuesday-Friday 10 a.m.-5 p.m., Saturday-Sunday noon-5 p.m.

HORSE FARMS
Lexington
More than 400 horse farms are in the area, most of them concentrated in Lexington-Fayette County. Although the majority are thoroughbred farms, some farms breed other varieties such as standardbreds, American saddle horses, Arabians, Morgans and quarter horses. You can see the farms by taking one of many tours offered by tour companies in Lexington.

HUNT-MORGAN HOUSE
201 N. Mill St., Lexington, 859-253-0362; www.bluegrasstrust.org
This mansion has been home to several of Kentucky's famous native sons. Built for John Wesley Hunt, Kentucky's first millionaire, it was later occupied by his grandson, General John Hunt Morgan, known as the "Thunderbolt of the Confederacy" for his guerilla tactics behind enemy lines. In 1866, Nobel Prize-winning geneticist Thomas Hunt Morgan was born in this house. Inside it, you'll see family furniture, portraits and porcelain. There's also a walled courtyard garden and gift shop.
Admission: adults $7, seniors $6, children $4. Wednesday-Friday 1-4 p.m., Saturday 10 a.m.-3 p.m., Sunday 1-4 p.m.

KENTUCKY HORSE PARK
4089 Iron Works Parkway, Lexington, 859-233-4303, 800-568-8813; www.imh.org
Dedicated to "man's relationship with the horse," this park has more than 1,000 acres of beautiful bluegrass. Its diverse offerings include the Man O' War grave and memorial, in honor of one of the world's greatest thoroughbred horses of all time. The visitor information center shows a widescreen film presentation, *Thou Shalt Fly Without Wings*. Also located within the park are the International Museum of the Horse, Parade of Breeds, Calumet Trophy Collection, Sears Collection of hand-carved miniatures, Hall of Champions stable that houses famous thoroughbreds and standardbreds, walking farm tour and antique carriage display. In addition, the park offers swimming, tennis, ball courts, picnic areas, playgrounds and a campground.
Admission: adults $15, children 7-12 $8, children under 7 free. Mid-March-October, daily 9 a.m.-5 p.m.; November-mid-March, Wednesday-Sunday 9 a.m.-5 p.m.

LEXINGTON CEMETERY

833 W. Main St., Lexington, 859-255-5522; www.lexcem.org

Buried on these 170 acres are Henry Clay, John C. Breckinridge, General John Hunt Morgan, the Todds (Mrs. Abraham Lincoln's family), coach Adolph Rupp (one of college basketball's most successful coaches) and many other notable persons, including 500 Confederate and 1,110 Union veterans. The grounds have sunken gardens, lily pools, a four-acre flower garden, extensive plantings of spring-flowering trees and shrubs. Daily.

MARY TODD LINCOLN HOUSE

578 W. Main St., Lexington, 859-233-9999; www.mtlhouse.org

The childhood residence of Mary Todd Lincoln is authentically restored and has period furnishings and personal items. The brick Georgian-style house was initially built as an inn in 1803.

Admission: adults $7, children 6-12 $4, children under 6 free. Mid-February-November, Monday-Saturday 10 a.m.-4 p.m.

TRANSYLVANIA UNIVERSITY

300 N. Broadway, Lexington, 859-233-8300; www.transy.edu

The oldest institution of higher learning west of the Allegheny Mountains, Transylvania has a list of distinguished alumni: two U.S. vice presidents, 36 state and territorial governors, 34 ambassadors, 50 senators, 112 members of the U.S. House of Representatives and Confederate President Jefferson Davis. Thomas Jefferson was one of Transylvania's early supporters. Henry Clay taught law courses and was a member of the university's governing board. The administration building, "Old Morrison," was used as a hospital during the Civil War. Tours of campus are available by appointment.

VICTORIAN SQUARE

401 W. Main St., Lexington, 859-252-7575; www.victoriansquareshoppes.com

This shopping area is in the downtown restoration project. Head there for specialty stores, restaurants and a children's museum. Daily.

WAVELAND STATE HISTORIC SITE

225 Waveland Museum Lane, Lexington, 859-272-3611; www.parks.ky.gov

For a glimpse into plantation life in the 19th century, visit this Greek Revival mansion. Slave quarters, outbuildings, an icehouse and a smokehouse still stand. There's also a playground. Daily.

WILLIAM S. WEBB MUSEUM OF ANTHROPOLOGY

S. Limestone Street and Euclid Avenue, Lexington, 859-257-8208; www.uky.edu

Exhibits include the cultural history of Kentucky and the evolution of man. Monday-Friday 8 a.m.-4:30 p.m.

SPECIAL EVENTS
BLUE GRASS STAKES

Keeneland Race Course, 4201 Versailles Road, Lexington, 859-254-3412;www.keeneland.com

The top contenders for the Derby face off in one of the last major prep races before Derby Day. Mid-April.

EGYPTIAN EVENT

Kentucky Horse Park, 4089 Iron Works Parkway, Lexington, 859-231-0771;
www.pyramidsociety.org

The event celebrates rare Egyptian Arabian horses, whose lineage can be traced back at least 3,500 years. There are show classes, a walk of stallions, a breeder's sale, native costumes, seminars, an art auction and an Egyptian bazaar.

Early June.

FESTIVAL OF THE BLUEGRASS

Kentucky Horse Park, 4089 Iron Works Parkway, Lexington, 859-846-4995;
www.festivalofthebluegrass.com

The festival attracts top names in bluegrass music with more than 20 bands appearing. It includes special shows for children and workshops with the musicians.

Second weekend in June.

GRAND CIRCUIT MEET

The Red Mile Track, 1200 Red Mile Road, Lexington, 859-255-0752;
www.theredmile.com

The Red Mile has been hosting harness racing since 1875, which makes it Lexington's oldest track. The Grand Circuit Meet features the Kentucky Futurity race, the final leg of harness racing's Triple Crown.

Late September-early October.

ROLEX KENTUCKY THREE-DAY EVENT

Kentucky Horse Park, 4080 Iron Works Parkway, Lexington, 859-233-2362; www.rk3de.org

This is a three-day endurance test for horses and riders in dressage, cross-country and stadium jumping. The fair also features boutiques.

Late April.

WHERE TO STAY

★★BEST WESTERN LEXINGTON CONFERENCE CENTER HOTEL

5532 Athens Boonesboro Road, Lexington, 859-263-5241, 800-780-7234; www.
bestwestern.com

150 rooms. Restaurant, bar. Complimentary breakfast. Fitness center. Pool. $61-150

★BEST WESTERN REGENCY/LEXINGTON

2241 Elkhorn Road, Lexington, 859-293-2202; www.bestwestern.com

112 rooms. Complimentary breakfast. Pool. $61-150

★COMFORT INN

2381 Buena Vista Drive, Lexington, 859-299-0302; www.choicehotels.com

122 rooms. Complimentary breakfast. Pool. $61-150

★★CROWNE PLAZA HOTEL LEXINGTON-THE CAMPBELL HOUSE

1375 S. Broadway, Lexington, 859-255-4281; www.crowneplaza.com

370 rooms. Restaurant, bar. Business center. Fitness center. $61-150

★★★DOUBLETREE GUEST SUITES LEXINGTON

2601 Richmond Road, Lexington, 859-268-0060, 800-262-3774; www.doubletree.com

This French-Quarter styled property blends southern hospitality with modern conveniences including ample in-room workspaces, a business center, luxury Sweet Dreams beds and Wolfgang Puck coffee makers in each room. The outdoor pool is very refreshing in summer.

155 suites. Restaurant, bar. Business center. Fitness center. Pool. $61-150

★★★GRATZ PARK INN

120 W. Second St., Lexington,859-231-1777, 800-752-4166 ,; www.gratzparkinn.com

Just steps from many of Lexington's attractions, this boutique inn pampers guests with distinctive charm. Each room is decorated differently with 19th-century antique reproductions, stately mahogany furniture and regional artwork. Guests can relax in the lobby, retreat to the library or enjoy a mouth-watering meal at chef Lundy's acclaimed restaurant, Jonathan at Gratz Park Inn.

41 rooms. Restaurant. $151-250

★HAMPTON INN

2251 Elkhorn Road, Lexington, 859-299-2613, 800-426-7866; www.hamptoninn.com

125 rooms. Complimentary breakfast. Business center. Fitness center. Pool. $61-150

★★★HILTON SUITES

245 Lexington Green Circle, Lexington, 859-271-4000, 800-774-1500; www.hilton.com

This hotel features deluxe two-room suites. It's near restaurants and a shopping mall and it is also less than seven miles from Bluegrass Airport, which makes it a convenient choice for business travelers.

174 suites. Restaurant, bar. Business center. Fitness center. Pool. $61-150

★★★HYATT REGENCY LEXINGTON

401 W. High St., Lexington, 859-253-1234; www.hyatt.com

This hotel is perfectly situated in the downtown business district at Triangle Park and Lexington Center, near shopping, restaurants, a convention center, sports and entertainment. Guest rooms offer views of historic Triangle Park and the city skyline, as well as iPod docks and flat-screen TVs.

365 rooms. Restaurant, bar. Business center. Fitness center. Pool. $151-250

★★LEXINGTON DOWNTOWN HOTEL & CONFERENCE CENTER

369 W. Vine St., Lexington, 859-231-9000; www.lexingtondowntownhotel.com

367 rooms. Restaurant, bar. Complimentary breakfast. Business center. Fitness center. Pool. $151-250

★★★MARRIOTT'S GRIFFIN GATE RESORT

1800 Newtown Pike, Lexington, 859-231-5100, 888-236-2427; www.marriott.com

This resort sits in the heart of Kentucky Bluegrass Country. Leisure guests will enjoy recreational facilities such as a championship golf course, tennis courts and an indoor and outdoor pool. Business travelers will appreciate the dataport-equipped phones, voicemail services, business center and corpo-

rate-team-challenge programs.
409 rooms. Restaurant, bar. Business center. pool. Tennis. $61-150

WHERE TO EAT
★★A-LA LUCIE
159 N. Limestone St., Lexington, 859-252-5277; www.alalucie.com
American. Lunch, dinner. Closed Sunday. $16-35

★★DESHA'S LEXINGTON
101 N. Broadway, Lexington, 859-259-3771; www.deshas.com
American. Lunch, dinner. $16-35

★★DUDLEY'S
380 S. Mill St., Lexington, 859-252-1010; www.dudleysrestaurant.com
Mediterranean. Lunch, dinner. $16-35

★★MALONE'S
3347 Tates Creek Road, Lexington, 859-335-6500; www.malonesrestaurant.com
Steak, American. Lunch, dinner. $36-85

★★★THE MANSION AT GRIFFIN GATE
1800 Newtown Pike, Lexington, 859-288-6142; www.mansionrestaurant.com
In this antebellum mansion, executive chef Brian Hove serves elegant entrées such as Kurobuta pork chops (served with baked grits and apricot bourbon glaze) and sesame-crusted ahi with coconut risotto, pineapple salsa and a sesame-soy sauce. The wine list is extensive, and the service professional.
American. Dinner. $36-85

★★MERRICK INN
1074 Merrick Drive, Lexington, 859-269-5417; www.murrays-merrick.com
American. Lunch, dinner. Closed Sunday. $16-35

★★MURRAY'S
3955 Harrodsburg Road, Lexington, 859-219-9922; www.murrays-merrick.com
American. Dinner. Closed Sunday. $36-85

★★REGATTA SEAFOOD GRILLE
161 Lexington Green Circle, Lexington, 859-273-7875; www.regattaseafood.com
Seafood. Lunch, dinner. $16-35

LONDON
See also Corbin
In the foothills of the Appalachian Mountains, London is close to the beautiful Daniel Boone National Forest, a prime spot for outdoor recreation.

WHAT TO SEE
LEVI JACKSON WILDERNESS ROAD STATE PARK
998 Levi Jackson Mill Road, London, 606-330-2130; www.parks.ky.gov
Descendants of pioneer farmer Levi Jackson deeded some of this land to the

state as a historical shrine to those who carved homes out of the wilderness. Boone's Trace and Wilderness Road pioneer trails converge in the park. Recreational facilities include a swimming pool, a bathhouse, hiking, an archery range, miniature golf, picnicking, playgrounds and camping. Daily.

MCHARGUE'S MILL

998 Levi Jackson Mill Road, London, 606-330-2130; www.parks.ky.gov
This is one of the largest collections of millstones in the world. The mill was built in 1812 and reconstructed on the present site in 1939. Tours and demonstrations are also available.
June-August, daily.

MOUNTAIN LIFE MUSEUM

998 Levi Jackson Mill Road, London, 606-330-2130; www.parks.ky.gov/findparks/rec-parks/lj
Split-rail fences enclose rustic cabins with household furnishings, pioneer relics, farm tools and Native American artifacts. There's also a smokehouse, blacksmith shop and barn with prairie schooner.
Admission: adults $3.50, children 3-12 $2.25, children under 3 free.
Monday-Thursday 9 a.m.-4 p.m., Friday-Saturday 9 a.m.-7 p.m., Sunday 9 a.m.-5 p.m.

WHERE TO STAY
★COMFORT INN

1918 W. Highway 192, London, 606-877-7848; www.choicehotels.com
62 rooms. Complimentary breakfast. Pool. $61-150

LOUISVILLE

See also Fort Knox, Shepherdsville
On the banks of the Ohio River, Louisville is sometimes called "the biggest small town in America." Its unique blend of Southern charm and urban sophistication is on display every year when the world watches the renowned Kentucky Derby, Louisville's biggest claim to fame. First run on May 17, 1875, and modeled after England's Epsom Derby, the Derby is the nation's oldest continually held race. The first Saturday in May each year, Churchill Downs hosts "the best two minutes in sports," played out against its backdrop of Edwardian towers and antique grandstands.

Louisville knows how to have a good time, and Derby festivities are the ultimate Southern party: they are a glamorous mélange of carnival, fashion show, spectacle and celebration of the horse. But if you can't make it to Louisville during these first days of May, you'll still find plenty to keep you entertained. Home to a growing art community and a hot underground music scene, the city takes its cultural life seriously. The public subscription Fund for the Arts subsidizes the Tony Award-winning Actors Theater, and the city boasts the Kentucky Center for the Arts, home of ballet, opera and music performances. For those interested in less formal entertainment, Louisville's Highlands neighborhood is a good bet. The funky district, which stretches along Bardstown Road, has nightclubs, upscale dining, art galleries and one-of-a-kind shops. Part of Louisville's charm comes from its ability to mesh its urban style with its colorful history. Founded in 1778 and named for French King Louis XVI for his help during the American Revolution, the city soon became a leader in the new nation's economic growth, thanks in part to its prime spot on the Ohio River. The city has been home to several giants of American history, too: President Zachary Taylor grew up nearby, and two Supreme Court justices—including Louis Brandeis—are from the city. F. Scott Fitzgerald was stationed at Camp Zachary Taylor during World War I and frequented the bar at the Seelbach Hotel, which was celebrated in *The Great Gatsby.*

WHAT TO SEE
AMERICAN PRINTING HOUSE FOR THE BLIND
1839 Frankfort Ave., Louisville, 502-895-2405; www.aph.org
Dating back to 1858, this is the largest and oldest publishing house for the blind in the nation. In addition to books and music in Braille, it issues talking books, magazines, large-type textbooks and educational aids. Tours are run from Monday to Thursday at 10 a.m. and 2 p.m.

CAVE HILL CEMETERY
701 Baxter Ave., Louisville, 502-451-5630; www.cavehillcemetery.com
This is the burial ground of George Rogers Clark, hero of the American Revolution and founder of the settlement that became Louisville. Colonel Harland Sanders, of fried chicken fame, is also buried here. The grounds have rare trees, shrubs and plants, as well as swans, geese and ducks. Daily.

CHURCHILL DOWNS
700 Central Ave., Louisville, 502-636-4400; www.churchilldowns.com
Founded in 1875, this historic and world-famous thoroughbred racetrack is the home of the Kentucky Derby, "the most exciting two minutes in sports." The Kentucky Derby is always held the first Saturday in May. Other races commence throughout the spring and fall.

E. P. "TOM" SAWYER STATE PARK
3000 Freys Hill Road, Louisville, 502-429-7270, www.parks.ky.gov
Named for Erbon Powers "Tom" Sawyer (father of television journalist Diane Sawyer), the park has 550 acres that make up one of Louisville's best playgrounds for outdoor enthusiasts. People come for the swimming, tennis, archery range, BMX track, ball fields, gymnasium and picnicking areas. Daily.

FARMINGTON HISTORIC HOME
3033 Bardstown Road N., Louisville, 502-452-9920; www.historicfarmington.org
This federal-style house was built from plans drawn by Thomas Jefferson. Abraham Lincoln visited here in 1841. It's furnished with pre-1820 antiques, plus it has a hidden stairway, octagonal rooms, a museum room, a blacksmith shop, a stone barn and a 19th-century garden.
Admission: adults $9, seniors $8, children 6-14 $4, children under 6 free. Tuesday-Saturday 10 a.m.-4:30 p.m.

FILSON HISTORICAL SOCIETY

1310 S. Third St., Louisville, 502-635-5083; www.filsonhistorical.org

The historical society houses a well-stocked library, a manuscript collection, photographs and a prints collection.

Monday-Friday 9 a.m.-5 p.m.

HISTORIC DISTRICTS

Old Louisville, between Breckinridge and Ninth streets, near Central Park

Old Louisville teems with historical districts. The West Main Street Historic District is a concentration of cast-iron buildings, many recently renovated, on Main Street between First and Eighth streets. Butchertown is a renovated 19th-century German community between Market Street and Story Avenue. Cherokee Triangle is a well-preserved Victorian neighborhood with diverse architectural details. And Portland is an early settlement and commercial port with Irish and French heritage.

JEFFERSON COUNTY COURTHOUSE

527 W. Jefferson St., Louisville

This Greek Revival-style courthouse was designed by Gideon Shryock. A cast-iron floor in the rotunda supports a statue of Henry Clay. The 68-foot rotunda also boasts a magnificent cast-iron monumental stair and balustrade. Statues of Thomas Jefferson and Louis XVI call the courthouse home, and there's a war memorial on the grounds. Guided tours are available by appointment.

Monday-Friday 9 a.m.-5 p.m.

KENTUCKY CENTER FOR THE ARTS

501 W. Main St., Louisville, 502-584-7777, 800-775-7777; www.kca.org

Three stages present national and international performers showcasing a wide range of music, dance and drama. A distinctive glass-arched lobby features a collection of 20th-century sculpture and provides a panoramic view of Ohio River and Falls Fountain. There is also a restaurant and gift shop.

KENTUCKY DERBY MUSEUM

704 Central Ave., Louisville, 502-637-1111; www.derbymuseum.org

A tribute to the classic "run for the roses," the museum features exhibits on thoroughbred racing and the Kentucky Derby. Experience the excitement of Derby Day when you watch The Greatest Day, featured in high definition on a 360-degree screen. Check out hands-on exhibits, artifacts, educational programs, a tour and special events. There's also an outdoor paddock area with thoroughbreds. In addition, there's a shop and a café serving lunch. Tours of Churchill Downs are available, weather permitting.

Monday-Saturday 8 a.m.-5 p.m., Sunday 8 a.m.-noon.

KENTUCKY FAIR AND EXPOSITION CENTER

937 Phillips Lane, Louisville, 502-367-5000; www.kyfairexpo.org

This gigantic complex includes a coliseum, exposition halls, a stadium and an amusement park. More than 1,500 events take place throughout the year, including basketball and the Milwaukee Brewers minor league affiliate team's home games.

LOCUST GROVE

561 Blankenbaker Lane, Louisville, 502-897-9845; www.locustgrove.org

This was the home of General George Rogers Clark from 1809 to 1818. The handsome Georgian mansion sits on 55 acres. It retains its original paneling, authentic furnishings and a lovely garden. There are eight restored outbuildings. The visitor center offers an audiovisual program.

Monday-Saturday 10 a.m.-4:30 p.m., Sunday 1:30-4:30 p.m.

LOUISVILLE SCIENCE CENTER & IMAX THEATRE

727 W. Main St., Louisville, 502-561-6100; www.louisvillescience.org

You don't have to keep your hands to yourself in this museum. Designed to encourage exploration, the museum has exhibits that test visitors' creative-thinking skills, teach them about space travel and introduce them to natural wonders, such as a mummy, polar bears and a Gemini trainer. There's also a theater with a four-story IMAX screen.

Monday-Thursday 9:30 a.m.-5 p.m., Friday-Saturday 9:30 a.m.-9 p.m., Sunday noon-6 p.m.

LOUISVILLE SLUGGER MUSEUM & BAT FACTORY

800 W. Main St., Louisville, 610-524-0822; www.sluggermuseum.org

Buy me some peanuts and Cracker Jacks...or just take me to this museum, a haven for baseball fans. See memorabilia and tour the factory, where Louisville Slugger baseball bats and PowerBilt golf clubs are made. No cameras are allowed. Children over 8 years only; they must be accompanied by adult. Tours are available.

Admission: adults $10, children $5, children under 6 free. Monday-Saturday 9 a.m.-5 p.m., also April-November, Sunday noon-5 p.m.

LOUISVILLE ZOO

1100 Trevilian Way, Louisville, 502-459-2181; www.louisvillezoo.org

More than 1,600 animals live in naturalistic settings here. Exhibits include Gorilla Forest, a four-acre display that gives visitors a look into the world of the gorillas; Herp Aquarium, the home of King Louie, a rare white alligator; and Islands, which highlights endangered species and habitats. Camel and elephant rides are available.

Admission: adults $11.95, children $8.50, children under 3 free. September-March, daily 10 a.m.-4 p.m.; April-August, daily 10 a.m.-5 p.m.

RAUCH MEMORIAL PLANETARIUM

First and Brandeis streets, Louisville, 502-852-6664; www.louisville.edu/planetarium/

Planetarium shows take place on Friday and Saturday afternoons.

RIVERBOAT EXCURSION

Riverfront Plaza, Fourth Street and River Road, Louisville, 502-574-2355;
www.belleoflouisville.org

Cruise the river during a two-hour afternoon trip on sternwheeler *Belle of Louisville* or the *Spirit of Jefferson*.

Memorial Day-Labor Day: Tuesday-Sunday.

SIX FLAGS KENTUCKY KINGDOM

937 Phillips Lane, Louisville, 502-366-2231; www.sixflags.com
This amusement and water park is filled with more than 110 rides and attractions, including five roller coasters.

SPEED ART MUSEUM

2035 S. Third St., Louisville, 502-634-2700; www.speedmuseum.org
Kentucky's oldest and largest art museum, Speed has a collection that spans more than 6,000 years of human history. It provides traditional and modern art, an English Renaissance Room and a sculpture collection. The museum also highlights local Kentucky artists. A café, shop and bookstore are on the premises; tours are available on request.
Tuesday-Wednesday, Friday 10:30 a.m.-4 p.m.; Thursday 10:30 a.m.-8 p.m.; Sunday noon-5 p.m.

THOMAS EDISON HOUSE

729-731 E. Washington St., Louisville, 502-585-5247; www.edisonhouse.org
This is the restored 1850 cottage where Edison lived while working for Western Union after the Civil War. The bedroom is decorated with period furnishings. Four display rooms have Edison memorabilia and inventions, including phonographs, records and cylinders and an early light bulb collection.
Tuesday-Saturday 10 a.m.-2 p.m., also by appointment.

UNIVERSITY OF LOUISVILLE

2301 S. Third St., Louisville, 502-852-5555, 800-334-8635; www.louisville.edu
This public university, home of the Cardinals, is known for its outstanding medical facilities, killer athletic programs and a recent boost in its endowment. If you tour the campus, don't miss the Ekstrom Library and the John Patterson rare book collection; the original town charter signed by Thomas Jefferson; and the Photo Archives, one of the largest photograph collections in the country. Also here is an enlarged cast of Rodin's sculpture The Thinker; a Foucault pendulum more than 73 feet high, which demonstrates the Earth's rotation; and one of the largest concert organs in the region. Two art galleries feature works by students and locals as well as national and international artists. The grave of Supreme Court Justice Louis D. Brandeis is under the School of Law portico.

WATER TOWER

Zorn Avenue and River Road, Louisville, 502-896-2146; www.cem.va.gov
A restored tower and pumping station was built in the classic style in 1860. The tower houses the Louisville Visual Art Association and the Center for Contemporary Art.Daily.

ZACHARY TAYLOR NATIONAL CEMETERY

4701 Brownboro Road, Louisville, 502-893-3852
The 12th president of the United States is buried here, near the site where he lived from infancy to adulthood. Established in 1928, this national cemetery surrounds the Taylor family plot. Daily.

SPECIAL EVENTS
CORN ISLAND STORYTELLING FESTIVAL
12019 Donohue Ave., Louisville, 502-245-0643; www.cornislandstorytellingfestival.org
The festival celebrates traditions of storytelling. Events are held at various sites in the city. Programs include ghost stories at night in E.P. "Tom" Sawyer State Park and storytelling cruises.
Third weekend in September.

KENTUCKY DERBY
Churchill Downs, 700 Central Ave., Louisville, 502-636-4400; www.kentuckyderby.com
This is the first jewel in the Triple Crown.
First Saturday in May.

KENTUCKY DERBY FESTIVAL
1001 S. Third St., Louisville, 502-584-6383, 800-928-3378; www.kdf.org
The two-week celebration kicks off with the Pegasus Parade, the Great Steamboat Race (between *Belle of Louisville* and *Delta Queen*), the Great Balloon Race, a mini-marathon, concerts and sports tournaments.
Two weeks prior to Kentucky Derby.

KENTUCKY STATE FAIR
Kentucky Fair and Exposition Center, 937 Phillips Lane, Louisville, 502-367-5002; www.kystatefair.org
America's largest air-conditioned fair, this event fills 1 million square feet of the Kentucky Exposition Center. The fair spills out into nearby fields, where fairgoers enjoy outdoor entertainment and exhibits. Livestock shows, a championship horse show, home and fine arts exhibits and a midway round out the entertainment.
August.

WHERE TO STAY
★★★21C MUSEUM HOTEL
700 W. Main St., Louisville, 502-217-6300, 877-217-6400; www.21cmuseumhotel.com
This museum and hotel hybrid (with a focus on contemporary art) puts a premium on good design. Sprinkled throughout the hotel are photographs, paintings and sculptures from some of the world's top contemporary artists (one guest room even boasts a Chuck Close portrait). Rooms are appropriately loaded with 21st-century amenities, including oversized plasma TVs and iPods (customized pre-arrival with your favorite music) as well as docking stations. The hotel includes an onsite spa and fitness center , and the acclaimed restaurant Proof on Main.
90 rooms. Restaurant, bar. Fitness center. Spa. $151-250

★BAYMONT INN AND SUITES LOUISVILLE
9400 Blairwood Road, Louisville, 502-339-1900; www.baymontinns.com
100 rooms. Complimentary breakfast. Business center. Fitness center. Pool. $61-150

★★★THE BROWN HOTEL
335 W. Broadway, Louisville, 502-583-1234, 888-888-5252; www.brownhotel.com
The beautifully restored lobby of this hotel exudes Southern elegance, with intricate plaster moldings, polished woodwork, stained glass and crystal chandeliers. Built by philanthropist J. Graham Brown in 1923, the property's Georgian Revival-style building hosts many of Louisville's swankiest parties.
293 rooms. Restaurant, bar. $151-250

★THE CHARIOT HOTEL
1902 Embassy Square Blvd., Louisville, 502-491-2577; www.thechariothotel.com
116 rooms. Complimentary breakfast. Business center. $61-150

★★★EXECUTIVE INN
978 Phillips Lane, Louisville, 502-367-6161, 800-626-2706
This property has an interesting Tudor-style design with all the charm and warmth of a European hotel. It has richly crafted woodwork and spacious, comfortable rooms overlooking a beautiful courtyard and heated pool. It's surrounded with magnolia trees and water wheels.
472 rooms. Restaurant, bar. Fitness center. Pool. $61-150

★★EXECUTIVE WEST HOTEL
830 Phillips Lane, Louisville, 502-367-2251, 800-626-2708; www.executivewest.com
611 rooms. Restaurant, bar. Pool. $61-150

★★THE GALT HOUSE HOTEL
140 N. Fourth Ave., Louisville, 502-589-5200, 800-626-1814; www.galthouse.com
1,296 rooms. Restaurant, bar. Business center. Fitness center. Pool. $151-250

★HAMPTON INN
800 Phillips Lane, Louisville, 502-366-8100; www.hamptoninn.com
130 rooms. Complimentary breakfast. Business center. Fitness center. $61-150

★★HOLIDAY INN
1325 S. Hurstbourne Parkway, Louisville, 502-426-2600, 800-465-4329; www.hihurstbourne.com
267 rooms. Restaurant, bar. $61-150

★★★HYATT REGENCY LOUISVILLE
320 W. Jefferson St., Louisville, 502-581-1234; www.hyatt.com
The hotel offers views of the Ohio River and the downtown area. it is connected to both the Commonwealth Convention Center and the Louisville Galleria shopping mall.
393 rooms. Restaurant, bar. $61-150

★★★THE SEELBACH HILTON LOUISVILLE

500 Fourth Ave., Louisville, 502-585-3200, 800-333-3399; www.seelbachhilton.com

Elegant and historic, the Seelbach Hotel provides a luxurious home away from home. Built in 1905 by brothers Otto and Louis Seelbach, this landmark in the heart of downtown Louisville is immortalized in F. Scott Fitzgerald's *The Great Gatsby* as the site of Tom and Daisy Buchanan's wedding. Magnificent belle époque architecture and glittering interiors reflect an era long past, but the Seelbach offers all the amenities a contemporary traveler could want. The rooms and suites are charming with period reproductions and rich fabrics. Don't miss the sensational Oakroom restaurant, a favorite of critics and sweetheart of "best of" lists.

321 rooms. Complimentary breakfast. Restaurant, bar. $151-250

★SIGNATURE INN LOUISVILLE SOUTH

6515 Signature Drive, Louisville, 502-968-4100, 800-822-5252; www.signatureinn.com

119 rooms. Complimentary breakfast. Fitness center. Pool. $61-150

WHERE TO EAT

★★CAFE METRO

1700 Bardstown Road, Louisville, 502-458-4830; www.cafemetrolouisville.com

American. Dinner. Closed Sunday. $16-35

★CAFE MIMOSA

1216 Bardstown Road, Louisville, 502-458-2233; www.cafemimosatogo.com

Chinese, Vietnamese. Lunch, dinner, Sunday brunch. $16-35

★★★THE ENGLISH GRILL

335 W. Broadway, Louisville, 502-583-1234; www.brownhotel.com

This ornate dining room in the Brown Hotel has a decidedly refined English feel and a menu by chef Joe Castro to match. The sophisticated service and a wine list heavy on Bordeaux complete the experience, considered by many to be the best in town.

American. Dinner. Closed Sunday. $36-85

★★EQUUS

122 Sears Ave., Louisville, 502-897-9721; www.equusrestaurant.com

American. Dinner. Closed Sunday. $36-85

★★FIFTH QUARTER STEAKHOUSE

1241 Durrett Lane, Louisville, 502-361-2363

American. Lunch, dinner. $16-35

★★JACK FRY'S

1007 Bardstown Road, Louisville, 502-452-9244; www.jackfrys.com

American. Lunch, dinner. $36-85

★JESSIE'S FAMILY RESTAURANT

9609 Dixie Highway, Louisville, 502-937-6332

American. Breakfast, lunch, dinner. $16-35

★★★LE RELAIS
2817 Taylorsville Road, Louisville, 502-451-9020; www.lerelaisrestaurant.com
This romantic French bistro is tucked away in the historic administration building in Bowman Field. The comfortable and elegant Art Deco dining room, wonderful service and creative French menu have made Le Relais one of the most beloved restaurants in Louisville. Fresh, seasonal ingredients fill the menu in dishes like herb-encrusted venison rack with braised cabbage, carrots and potatoes; certified Angus beef filet with roasted potato and root vegetables; and duck confit with sage polenta cake, flageolet beans and baby Brussels sprouts. A well-crafted wine list, which has been honored by Wine Spectator, beautifully complements every dish.
French. Dinner. Closed Monday. $36-85

★★★LILLY'S
1147 Bardstown Road, Louisville, 502-451-0447; www.lillyslapeche.com
A brightly colored neon sign marks the window of chef Kathy Cary's innovative dining room—a hint to the Art Deco interior that lies beyond the red-brick entrance. Her menu changes seasonally and has an eclectic, urban edge with dishes such as seared scallops in beurre blanc served with basil couscous.
International. Lunch, dinner. Closed Sunday-Monday. $36-85

★★LIMESTONE
10001 Forest Green Blvd., Louisville, 502-426-7477; www.limestonerestaurant.com
American. Dinner. Closed Sunday. $16-35

★★★PROOF ON MAIN
702 W. Main St., Louisville, 502-217-6360; www.proofonmain.com
Art collectors and Kentucky philanthropists Steve Wilson and Laura Lee Brown (heir to a liquor fortune built by brands such as Jack Daniel's) launched this cutting-edge restaurant in 2006. Along with the adjacent 21c Museum Hotel, Proof on Main (the name is a nod to their bourbon past) is a prime spot for showcasing top-notch contemporary art and food. Executive chef Michael Paley sources local ingredients and puts them to good use in dishes such as Kentucky bison tenderloin with buttered leeks and fingerling potatoes, or smoked chicken with grain mustard and roasted string beans. Desserts include twists on Southern classics such as chocolate bread pudding with sea salt caramel gelato.
American. Breakfast, lunch, dinner. $36-85

★★UPTOWN CAFE
1624 Bardstown Road, Louisville, 502-458-4212; www.uptownlouisville.com
American. Lunch, dinner. Closed Sunday. $16-35

★★★VINCENZO'S
150 S. Fifth St., Louisville, 502-580-1350; www.vincenzositalianrestaurant.com
Italian. Lunch, dinner. Closed Sunday. $36-85

★★WINSTON'S
3101 Bardstown Road, Louisville, 502-456-6505; www.sullivan.edu/winstons/index.asp
American. Lunch, dinner, Sunday brunch. Closed Monday-Thursday. $36-85

MADISONVILLE
See also Hopkinsville
Named for President James Madison, the town is in a region of hills, rivers and creek bottoms. Recent revitalization efforts have created a charming downtown district.

WHAT TO SEE
PENNYRILE FOREST STATE RESORT PARK
20781 Pennyrile Lodge Road, Madisonville, 270-797-3421, 800-325-1711; www.parks.ky.gov
Head here for a slew of activities: swimming in the beach or pool, a bathhouse, fishing, boating, hiking, riding, nine-hole and miniature golf, tennis, picnicking and playgrounds. There's also a grocery, cottages, a lodge and tent and trailer sites. Daily.

SPECIAL EVENT
HOPKINS COUNTY FAIR
Hopkins County Fairgrounds, Arch St., Madisonville, 270-821-0950
The county fair breaks out a carnival, horse shows, agricultural exhibits, pageants and a Demolition Derby.
Late July-early August.

WHERE TO STAY
★★BEST WESTERN PENNYRILE INN
Mortons Gap, Madisonville, 270-258-5201; www.bestwestern.com
59 rooms. Restaurant. Complimentary breakfast. Pool. $61-150

★★PENNYRILE FOREST STATE RESORT PARK
20781 Pennyrile Lodge Road, Madisonville, 270-797-3421, 800-325-1711; www.parks.ky.gov
24 rooms. Restaurant. $61-150

WHERE TO EAT
★★BARTHOLOMEW'S FINE FOODS
51 S. Main St., Madisonville, 270-821-1061; www.madisonvillebedandbreakfast.com
American. Lunch, dinner. Closed Sunday. $16-35

MAYSVILLE
See also Lexington
This Ohio River town, first known as Limestone, was established by the Virginia Legislature. By 1792, it had become a leading port of entry for Kentucky settlers. Daniel Boone and his wife maintained a tavern in the town for several years. Many buildings and sites in the eight-block historic district are included on the National Register of Historic places.

WHAT TO SEE
BLUE LICKS BATTLEFIELD STATE RESORT PARK
Highway 68 Maysville Road, Mount Olivet, 26 miles Southwest on Highway 68,
859-289-5507; www.parks.ky.gov

The park preserves about 150 acres on the site of one of the Revolutionary War's bloodiest battles (August 19, 1782, a year after Cornwallis surrendered). In this final battle in Kentucky, 60 Americans died, including Daniel Boone's son, Israel. A monument in the park honors pioneers killed in an ambush. Also here is a museum with exhibits and displays depicting the history of the area from the Ice Age through the Revolution. Recreational facilities include a swimming pool, fishing, miniature golf, picnic shelters, a playground and camping.

April-October, daily.

HISTORIC WASHINGTON
2215 Old Main St., Washington, 606-759-7411; www.washingtonky.com

The original seat of Mason County, Washington was founded in 1786 and soon was the second-largest town in Kentucky, with 119 cabins. Restored buildings include the Paxton Inn, Albert Sidney Johnston House, Old Church Museum and Cane Brake, thought to be one of the original cabins of 1790. Guided tours are available.

Mid-March-December, daily.

THE PIEDMONT ART GALLERY
115 W. Riverside Drive, Augusta, 606-756-2216

Located in one of the oldest settlements on the Ohio River, the gallery houses contemporary works by national and regional artists and craftspeople. It also spotlights antiques, paintings, sculpture, ceramics and American folk art.

Thursday-Sunday.

SPECIAL EVENTS
SIMON KENTON FESTIVAL
Old Main Street Historic District, Maysville, 606-564-9411; www.cityofmaysville.com

Kin of pioneer Simon Kenton (who explored Kentucky between 1785 and 1800) congregate in Old Washington during this festival to exchange genealogy. "Living historians" reenact scenes from 18th-century life, demonstrating skills and games of early pioneers such as knife- and tomahawk-throwing contests, blacksmithing and candle making.

Third weekend in September.

MOREHEAD
See also Lexington

In the foothills of the Appalachian Mountains, Morehead has much of the beautiful scenery that makes this part of Kentucky so appealing to travelers who seek outdoor recreation.

WHAT TO SEE
CAVE RUN LAKE

2375 Highway 801 S., Morehead, 606-784-5624; www.caverun.org

Take advantage of the beach, the bathhouse and seasonal interpretive programs at Twin Knobs and Zilpo campgrounds. Or go fishing for bass and muskie, use the 12 boat ramps, visit the two marinas with boat rentals, go hiking or camp at Twin Knobs and Zilpo campgrounds.

Mid-April-October, daily.

MINOR CLARK STATE FISH HATCHERY

120 Fish Hatchery Road, Morehead, 606-784-6872

Largemouth bass, smallmouth bass, walleye, muskellunge and rockfish are reared here. They are on display in an exhibition pool.

May-September, Monday-Friday.

MOREHEAD STATE UNIVERSITY

150 University Blvd., Morehead, 606-783-2221; www.moreheadstate.edu

On campus, see the historic one-room schoolhouse by appointment. The Folk Art Museum, on the first floor of Claypool-Young Art Building, is open Monday to Friday. Don't miss the MSU Appalachian Collection, which includes books, periodicals, genealogical materials and government documents. Special holdings are devoted to authors James Still and Jesse Stuart and there are displays of regional art. Daily.

SPECIAL EVENT
BLUEGRASS 'N MORE

150 University Blvd., Morehead, 606-784-6221; www.moreheadstate.edu

This week is devoted to the history and heritage of Appalachia in Kentucky. Partake in dances, concerts, arts and crafts and exhibitions. Late June.

MOUNT VERNON

See also Berea

Take a step back in time when you cross the threshold of the first brick house west of the Alleghenies.

WHAT TO SEE
WILLIAM WHITLEY HOUSE HISTORIC SITE

625 William Whitley Road, Mount Vernon, 606-355-2881; www.parks.ky.gov

The first brick house west of the Alleghenies, this building was used as a protective fort from Native Americans and as a haven for travelers on the Wilderness Road. This site is also home to the first circular racetrack built in the U.S., which earned the house the nickname "Sportsman's Hill." Unlike the tracks in England, this one ran counter-clockwise. The restored home is furnished with period pieces. Panels symbolizing each of the 13 original states are over the mantel in the parlor.

June-August, daily; September-May, Tuesday-Sunday

NATURAL BRIDGE STATE RESORT PARK

See also Winchester

The sandstone arch for which this park is named is 78 feet long and 65 feet high. Visitors can hike to the natural bridge or take the Skylift, which drops riders off a mere 600 feet from the bridge. The park offers plenty of opportunities for outdoor recreation, including an open-air patio at Hoedown Island, so named for its weekly square dances. A swimming pool, fishing, boating, nature trails and center, picnicking, a playground, a dining room, cottages, a lodge and tent and trailer sites will keep you busy. Daily.

WHERE TO STAY
★★NATURAL BRIDGE STATE PARK
2135 Natural Bridge Road, Slade, 606-663-2214, 800-325-1710; www.parks.ky.gov
35 rooms. Restaurant. $61-150

OLIVE HILL

See also Ashland, Morehead

If you can't find something to do in the thousands of acres of raw outdoors just waiting to be explored here, you're just not trying.

WHAT TO SEE
CARTER CAVES STATE RESORT PARK
344 Caveland Drive, Olive Hill, 606-286-4411; www.parks.ky.gov
This 1,350-acre park lies in a region of cliffs, streams and many caves, where you'll find a 30-foot underground waterfall, among other surprises. Activities abound: there's a swimming pool, boating, fishing, canoe trips, nine-hole and miniature golf, tennis, shuffleboard, picnicking, a playground, cottages, a lodge and tent and trailer sites. The park also hosts films, dances and festivals. Several guided cave tours are available. Daily.

GRAYSON LAKE STATE PARK
314 Grayson Lake Park Road, Olive Hill, 606-474-9727; www.parks.ky.gov
Nearly 75 miles of shoreline change from gentle slopes to canyons and offer a beautiful backdrop to a day on Grayson Lake. Fishing, boating, hiking, picnicking and camping all keep park visitors entertained. Daily.

WHERE TO STAY
★★CARTER CAVES STATE RESORT PARK
Olive Hill, 606-286-4411, 800-325-0059; www.parks.ky.gov
43 rooms. $61-150

OWENSBORO

See also Henderson

Owensboro knows how to party: the city has crowned itself "Festival City," a nod to its many citywide celebrations. The festivals begin in February and last until mid-December, but if you arrive during an off week, the city's regular offerings promise plenty of entertainment. A progressive arts program has provided Owensboro with a symphony orchestra, fine art museum, dance theater, science museum and theater workshop. And if you're just up for a stroll, amble along tree-lined Griffith Avenue to see historic homes, a walk that's sweetened in spring by dogwood and azalea blossoms.

WHAT TO SEE
BEN HAWES STATE PARK
400 Boothfield Road, Owensboro, 270-687-7134; www.parks.ky.gov
The park is spread across about 300 acres with hiking, nine-hole and 18-hole golf, picnicking and a playground. Daily.

OWENSBORO AREA MUSEUM OF SCIENCE & HISTORY
122 E. second St., Owensboro, 270-687-2732; www.owensboromuseum.com
The museum has crawly live insects and reptiles; archaeological, geological and ornithological displays; and historic items. Stop by the gift shop if there is time.
Monday 10 a.m.-8 p.m., Tuesday-Saturday 10 a.m.-5 p.m., Sunday 1-5 p.m.

OWENSBORO MUSEUM OF FINE ART
901 Frederica St., Owensboro, 270-685-3181; www.omfa.us
The permanent collection includes 16th- to 20th-century American, French and English paintings, drawings, sculpture, graphic and decorative arts. There's also a special collection of 19th- and 20th-century regional art and one of Appalachian folk art.
Tuesday-Sunday.

WINDY HOLLOW RECREATION AREA
10874 Highway 81, Owensboro, 270-785-4150; www.windyhollowcampground.com
Head to these 214 acres for swimming, a 240-foot water slide, fishing, miniature golf. The property includes a grocery and tent and trailer camping.
April-October, daily.

SPECIAL EVENTS
INTERNATIONAL BAR-B-Q FESTIVAL
Second St., Owensboro, 270-926-6938; www.bbqfest.com
About 80,000 people show up to inhale the smell of hickory-smoke fires and taste the glories of down-home barbecue. Cooks come with their best recipes for mutton, chicken and burgoo and battle to see who will be crowned King or Queen of the Grill. Folks who want to compete but can't cook might take part in the tobacco-spitting, pie-eating or fiddling contests. Arts and crafts, music and dancing also liven up the event.
Early May.

WHERE TO EAT
★★COLBY'S
202 W. Third St., Owensboro, 270-685-4239
American. Lunch, dinner. $16-35

PADUCAH

See also Gilbertsville

This art-friendly city has a growing underground music scene and a thriving arts community, thanks to its Artist Relocation Program. In the historic Lowertown Arts District, artists from across the country come to live and work together, and there are gourmet restaurants and funky coffee shops.

The city doesn't play favorites: Paducah has recently begun reviving its Middletown district to serve as a haven for musicians. One major part of the renaissance is the renovation of Maggie Steed's Metropolitan Hotel, the site where musicians such as Louis Armstrong, B.B. King and Tina Turner played in the early to mid-20th century.

WHAT TO SEE
MARKET HOUSE

121 S. Second St., Paducah, 270-443-7759

This cultural center now houses the Market House Museum. It features early Americana, including the complete interior of a drugstore that's more than 100 years old. Other offerings include river lore, Alben Barkley and Irvin S. Cobb memorabilia, Native American artifacts and Civil War exhibits.
March-December, Monday-Saturday.

MUSEUM OF THE AMERICAN QUILTER'S SOCIETY

215 Jefferson St., Paducah, 270-442-8856; www.quiltmuseum.org

More than 200 quilts are exhibited here, with special displays scheduled regularly. If you can't bear leaving without a quilt, stop at the gift shop before you go.
April-October, Monday-Saturday 10 a.m.-5 p.m., Sunday 1-5 p.m.

WHITEHAVEN

1845 Lone Oak Road, Paducah, 270-554-2077

This antebellum mansion was remodeled in Classical Revival style in 1903; it has elaborate plasterwork, stained glass and 1860s furnishings. The state uses a portion of the house as a tourist welcome center and rest area. Daily.

YEISER ARTS CENTER

200 Broadway, Paducah, 270-442-2453; www.theyeiser.org

The arts center has monthly changing exhibits, and its collection ranges from European masters to regional artists.
Tuesday-Sunday 10 a.m.-4 p.m.

SPECIAL EVENTS
KIWANIS WEST KENTUCKY-MCCRACKEN COUNTY FAIR

301 Joe Clifton Drive, Carson Park, Paducah,

The county fair offers Society and Western horse shows, harness racing, motorcycle racing and gospel singing.
Last full week in June.

SUMMER FESTIVAL

Riverfront, foot of Broadway, Paducah, 270-443-8783, 800-789-8224;
www.paducahsummerfestival.com

The fest ushers in summer with hot-air balloons, a symphony, fireworks and free entertainment nightly. Events are held along the riverfront and throughout the city.

Last week in July.

WHERE TO STAY
★★COURTYARD PADUCAH WEST

3835 Technology Drive, Paducah, 270-442-3600; www.marriott.com

100 rooms. $61-150

★DRURY INN

3975 Hinkleville Road, Paducah, 270-443-3313; www.druryinn.com

118 rooms. Complimentary breakfast. Pool. $61-150

★HOLIDAY INN EXPRESS

3994 Hinkleville Road, Paducah, 270-442-8874; www.hiexpress.com

76 rooms. Complimentary breakfast. $61-150

WHERE TO EAT
★C. C. COHEN

103 Market House Square, Paducah, 270-442-6391; www.cccohen.com

American. Lunch, dinner. Closed Sunday. $16-35

★JEREMIAH'S

225 Broadway, Paducah, 270-443-3991

American. Dinner. Closed Sunday. $16-35

★★WHALER'S CATCH

123 N. Second St., Paducah, 270-444-7701; www.whalerscatch.net

Southern-style seafood. Lunch, dinner. Closed Sunday. $36-85

PARIS

See also Lexington

Both Paris and Bourbon County were named in appreciation of France's aid to the colonies during the Revolution. While the French dynasty is long gone, the whiskey made in this county is a lasting tribute to the royal name.

WHAT TO SEE
DUNCAN TAVERN HISTORIC CENTER

323 High St., Paris, 859-987-1788

Daniel Boone joined fellow pioneers for entertainment in Duncan Tavern, constructed in 1788. Next door is the Anne Duncan House, built right next door by the innkeeper's widow, who ran the tavern for many years after his death. Both the tavern, which is made of local limestone, and the old clapboard house of log construction have been restored and furnished with period pieces.

Tuesday-Saturday.

OLD CANE RIDGE MEETING HOUSE

1655 Cane Ridge Road, Paris, 859-987-5350; www.caneridge.org

This is the birthplace of the Christian Church. The original log meetinghouse has been restored within an outer building of stone. In the early 1800s, revival meetings outside Old Cane Ridge attracted 20,000 to 30,000 people at a time.

Tours are available by appointment.

WHERE TO STAY
★BEST WESTERN PARIS INN

2011 Alverson Drive, Paris, 859-987-0779, 800-528-1234; www.bestwestern.com

49 rooms. Complimentary breakfast. Pool. $61-150

PINEVILLE

See also Barbourville

Picnics and playgrounds are just the tip of the iceberg in this outdoor-sport-saturated area.

WHAT TO SEE
PINE MOUNTAIN STATE RESORT PARK

1050 State Park Road, Pineville, 606-337-3066, 800-325-1712; www.parks.ky.gov

This 1,500-acre park, surrounded by 12,000-acre Kentucky Ridge State Forest, has a nature center, supervised recreation and Laurel Cove Amphitheater. It also has a swimming pool, 18-hole and miniature golf, shuffleboard, picnicking, playgrounds, cottages, a lodge and camping.

SPECIAL EVENT
MOUNTAIN LAUREL FESTIVAL

Pine Mountain State Resort Park, 1050 State Park Road, Pineville, 606-337-3066; www. parks.ky.gov

At this unique pageant, college women from across Kentucky compete for the Festival Queen title. The weekend includes picnics, a parade, sporting events, concerts, a grand ball and the coronation at Pine Mountain State Resort Amphitheater.

Memorial Day weekend.

WHERE TO STAY
★★PINE MOUNTAIN STATE RESORT PARK

1050 State Park Road, Pineville, 606-337-3066, 800-325-1712; www.kystateparks.com

50 rooms. Restaurant. $61-150

PRESTONSBURG

See also Pikeville

The Country Music Highway, known less glamorously as U.S. Route 23, runs through Prestonsburg. The highway celebrates country music history and the legends, which came from this neck of the woods, including Loretta Lynn, Patty Loveless and the Judds.

WHAT TO SEE
JENNY WILEY STATE RESORT PARK
75 Theatre Court, Prestonsburg, 606-886-1790, 800-325-0142; www.parks.ky.gov
This park has everything a guest could want: hiking trails through the mountainous terrain, water sports on 1,150-acre Dewey Lake, a disc golf course and even an outdoor amphitheater where guests can catch musical theater hits. There's also a swimming pool, fishing, boating, nine-hole golf, shuffleboard, picnicking, a playground, cottages, a lodge and tent and trailer sites.

MOUNTAIN ARTS CENTER
1 Hal Rogers Drive, Prestonsburg, 606-886-2623; www.macarts.com
This performance theater seats 1,054. It's the home of the Kentucky Opry. A variety of entertainment is scheduled year-round.

SPECIAL EVENT
KENTUCKY APPLE FESTIVAL
Paintsville, 11 miles North via Highway 23/460, 606-789-8710; www.kyapplefest.org
The festival features a parade, amusement rides, an antique car show, arts and crafts, a flea market, a 5K run, square dancing, music and entertainment. First Saturday in October.

WHERE TO STAY
★★HOLIDAY INN
1887 Highway 23 North, Prestonsburg, 606-886-0001; www.holiday-inn.com
117 rooms. Restaurant, bar. $61-150

★★JENNY WILEY STATE RESORT PARK
75 Theater Court, Prestonsburg, 606-886-1790
49 rooms. Restaurant. $61-150

RICHMOND
See also Berea, Lexington, Winchester
The scene of a major Civil War battle—the first Confederate victory in Kentucky—Richmond has one of Kentucky's finest restored 19th-century downtown districts, perfect for an afternoon stroll.

WHAT TO SEE
COURTHOUSE
Courthouse square, N. First and Main streets, Richmond
This Greek Revival courthouse in the downtown historic district was used as a hospital by Union and Confederate forces during the Civil War.

HUMMEL PLANETARIUM AND SPACE THEATER
521 Lancaster Ave., Richmond, on Eastern Kentucky University campus, 859-622-1547; www.planetarium.eku.edu
One of the largest and most sophisticated planetariums in the U.S., this place has state-of-the-art projection and audio systems and a large-format film system.

WHITE HALL STATE HISTORIC HOUSE

500 White Hall Shrine Road, Richmond, 859-623-9178; www.parks.ky.gov

This is the restored 44-room house of Cassius M. Clay, emancipationist, diplomat and publisher of The True American, an antislavery newspaper. The 1799 Georgian home has an Italianate addition from the 1860s. Period furnishings, some original, and personal mementos fill the space.
April-August, daily; September-October, Wednesday-Sunday.

WHERE TO STAY
★DAYS INN

2109 Belmont Drive, Richmond, 859-624-5769, 800-329-7466; www.daysinn.com

70 rooms. Complimentary breakfast. Pool. $61-150

★LA QUINTA INN

1751 Lexington Road, Richmond, 859-623-9121, 800-575-5339; www.laquinta.com

95 rooms. Complimentary breakfast. Pool. $61-150

SHEPHERDSVILLE

See also Elizabethtown, Fort Knox, Louisville

Shepherdsville offers the granddaddy of all arboretums, clocking in at 2,000 acres.

WHAT TO SEE
BERNHEIM ARBORETUM AND RESEARCH FOREST

Shepherdsville, six miles south on I-65, exit 112, then one mile east on Highway 245, 502-543-2451, 502-955-8512; www.bernheim.org

This 2,000-acre arboretum offers a nature center with trails, a nature museum, waterfowl lakes and a 12,000-acre research forest. The landscape arboretum features 1,800 species of plants.
Daily 7 a.m.-6 p.m.

WHERE TO STAY
★★BEST WESTERN SOUTH

211 S. Lakeview Drive, Shepherdsville, 502-543-7097, 877-543-5080; www.bestwestern.com

85 rooms. Restaurant, bar. $61-150

SOMERSET

See also Jamestown, London

Centrally located, Somerset is only four miles from Lake Cumberland. Many of the state's most popular attractions are within an hour's drive.

WHAT TO SEE
BEAVER CREEK WILDERNESS

Somerset, 15 miles south on Highway 27, 606-679-2010; www.fs.fed.us

Towering sandstone cliffs surround this hardwood forest, where a variety of wildlife lives. Hike through the wilderness to see streams, waterfalls, flowering trees and creatures such as foxes, white-tailed deer and wild turkeys. Trails, compass hiking, backpacking and scenic overlooks will lure outdoor types. Daily.

GENERAL BURNSIDE STATE PARK

Burnside, 10 miles south on Highway 27, 606-561-4104; www.parks.ky.gov

On General Burnside Island in Lake Cumberland, the park offers a swimming pool, fishing, boating, 18-hole golf, picnicking, a playground and tent and trailer sites. Daily.

LAKE CUMBERLAND

Highway 27, Somerset, 606-679-6337, 606-679-6394;
www.lakecumberlandtourism.com

This man-made lake with 1,255 miles of shoreline has five recreation areas with campsites. Swimming, fishing, commercial docks, houseboats and other boats for rent are available.

SOUTH UNION

See also Bowling Green

The Shakers, officially the United Society of Believers in Christ's Second Appearing, settled this town as a religious community in the 19th century. Crafters and farmers of great skill and ingenuity, the Shakers were widely known both for the quality of their products and for their religious observances. When "moved by the spirit," they performed a dance that earned them the name "Shakers." By 1922, the community had dwindled to only nine members. The property was sold at an auction, and the remaining members dispersed.

WHAT TO SEE
SHAKER MUSEUM

850 Shaker Museum Road, South Union, 270-542-4167; www.shakermuseum.com

Located in the original 1824 building, the museum houses Shaker crafts, furniture, textiles and tools.

Admission: adults $8, children $4, children under 6 free. March-mid-December, daily.

SPECIAL EVENTS
SHAKER FESTIVAL

Shaker Town Village, South Union, 800-811-8379

The fest offers a tour of historic buildings, Shaker foods, music and craft demonstrations.

June.

TOBACCO FESTIVAL

116 S. Main St., Russellville, 270-726-2206; www.loganleads.com/Chamber/tobacco_heritage/

The festival celebrates tobacco heritage with a parade, a reenactment of the Jesse James bank robbery, house tours in the historic district, tobacco displays, antiques, bicycle rides, a five-mile run and a 5k walk, along with entertainment.

One week in early October.

WINCHESTER

See also Lexington, Richmond

Located in Kentucky's horse country, Winchester has many of the attractions that draw visitors to the commonwealth: historical sites, natural beauty and Southern charm. This is the place where orator Henry Clay made his first and last Kentucky speeches, where the Kentucky soft drink Ale-8-One has been bottled since 1926 and where people celebrate the bluegrass culture and heritage.

WHAT TO SEE
FORT BOONESBOROUGH STATE PARK

4375 Boonsboro Road, Winchester, 859-527-3131; www.parks.ky.gov

This is the site of the settlement where Daniel Boone defended his fort against Native American sieges. The fort houses craft shops, where costumed "pioneers" produce wares; a museum with Boone memorabilia and other historical items; and an audiovisual program. Exhibits in cabins and block-houses re-create life at the fort. A sand beach, a swimming pool, a bathhouse, fishing, boating, miniature golf, picnicking, a playground, a snack bar, tent and trailer sites offer lots to do.

HISTORIC MAIN STREET

Main Street, Winchester

This historic block has a number of restored buildings, most from the Victorian era, and unique shops. A walking tour is available. Daily.

SPECIAL EVENT
DANIEL BOONE PIONEER FESTIVAL

34 S. Main St., College and Lynkins Parks, Winchester, 859-744-0556;
www.kyfestivals.com

This fest honoring Daniel Boone offers juried arts and crafts, antiques, street dance, a 5K run, a two-mile walk, concerts, music, food and fireworks. Labor Day weekend.

WHERE TO STAY
★★DAYS INN

1100 Interstate Drive, Winchester, 859-744-9111; www.daysinn.com

64 rooms. Restaurant. Complimentary breakfast. Pool. $61-150

★HAMPTON INN

1025 Early Drive, Winchester, 859-745-2000; www.hamptoninn.com

60 rooms. Complimentary breakfast. Pool. $61-150

WHERE TO EAT
★HALL'S ON THE RIVER

1225 Athens-Boonesborough Road, Winchester, 859-527-6620;
www.hallsontheriver.com

American. Lunch, dinner. $16-35

LOUISIANA

BORN OUT OF SWAMPS AND BAYOUS, CRAFTED FROM THE WORK AND TRADITION OF DOZENS of cultures and celebrated as the home of renowned music, food and legend, Louisiana is as colorful and varied as the characters on the streets of New Orleans during Mardi Gras.

Named by the French (for Louis XIV), Louisiana was settled by both the French and the Spanish. To prevent Louisiana from falling into the hands of the English, Louis XV of France gave it to his cousin, Charles III of Spain. In 1801, Napoleon regained it for France, though no one in Louisiana knew of this until 1803, only 20 days before the Louisiana Purchase made it U.S. territory. From its earliest days, the state was home to settlers of English, Irish and German origin.

The settlers were drawn to Louisiana for any number of reasons. For some, the unique landscape is a major selling point: Louisiana is semitropical, and beautifully unusual—a land of bayous with cypress and live oak overhung with Spanish moss. Today, some Louisianans live in isolation on the bayous and riverbanks, where they still fish, trap and do a little farming.

The northern and southern parts of the state are quite different topographically. In the southern area are fine old mansions and sugarcane plantation estates, many of which are open to the public. The north is more rural, with beautiful rivers, hills, forests and cotton plantation mansions. This is the area from which the colorful politician Huey Long came; he was born in Winnfield.

Petroleum and natural gas taken from far underground, shipped abroad or processed in large plants contribute to Louisiana's thriving industrial and manufacturing economy. As these businesses expand, the service sector continually grows to meet demands.

Hurricane Katrina hit Louisiana hard in 2005, but the affected cities and towns continue the hard work of rebuilding. The storm's floodwaters washed away homes, businesses and some of the state's most beloved landmarks but failed to touch Louisiana's charm. It remains the old Deep South at its best: gracious, cultured and hospitable.

ABITA SPRINGS

See also Covington

Since the late 19th century Abita Springs has been a popular resort getaway for New Orleans residents. Today it is best known for the Abita Brewing Company, which brews beer with water from the city's artesian wells.

WHAT TO SEE
ABITA MYSTERY HOUSE/UCM MUSEUM

22275 Highway 36, Abita Springs, 985-892-2624; www.ucmmuseum.com

Looking for something off the beaten path? Check out the comb collection, popsicle-stick marble machine or "Aliens vs. Airstream Trailer" exhibits in this museum, which bills itself as Louisiana's "most eccentric."

Daily 10 a.m.-5 p.m.

CAJUN COUNTRY

Among the bayous and swamps west of New Orleans lies Cajun Country, a 22-parish region with a noticeably French accent. The area's vibrant history stretches back to the 18th century, when French refugees forced out of Nova Scotia by the British sought refuge in the French colony of New Orleans.

Although Lafayette, "the Capital of French Louisiana," can be reached in two hours from New Orleans by interstate, Highway 90 offers a leisurely introduction to Cajun Country that could take a half-day or more. You can catch Highway 90 just west of the French Quarter, but you're better off bypassing suburban congestion by taking I-10 west to the I-310 spur south. Here the interstate bridge crosses a fierce bend of the Mississippi River barely contained by a high levee. West of the river, I-310 deposits you in the subtropical Cajun wetlands region onto Highway 90; follow this route west toward Gibson.

In New Iberia, a detour south on Highway 329 leads to Avery Island, home of the world-famous McIlhenny Tabasco Sauce, where you can visit the factory for free. After your detour, cross 90 and follow Bayou Teche ("Tesh") toward downtown New Iberia, settled by the Spanish in 1779. Here Shadows-on-the-Teche, built in 1834, opens a stately plantation house museum with an extensive garden of magnolias, oaks and Spanish moss on Highway 182 at 317 E. Main St.

Ten miles north of New Iberia on Highway 31, St. Martinville is famous for the live oak memorialized in Longfellow's epic poem Evangeline. The 1847 poem tells the story of Acadian lovers reunited under the venerable oak. Today, the Romero Brothers, a pair of local troubadours, croon Cajun standards beside the oak to re-create the romance. A statue of Evangeline stands outside the St. Martin de Tours Church in the small downtown square nearby. At the Longfellow Evangeline Commemorative Area a mile north of town, guides offer tours of the 19th-century sugar plantation house.

Farther up Bayou Teche via Highway 31, Breaux Bridge proclaims itself "Crawfish Capital of the World." The town's annual Crawfish Festival on the first full weekend in May features crawfish races, a crawfish-eating contest, the crowning of the Crawfish King and Queen and continuous Cajun and zydeco music. But at any time, you can find people dancing away at Mulate's ("MOO-lots"), 1/4 mile west of Highway 31, practically spitting distance south of I-10. Follow the signs.

In downtown Breaux Bridge, near the drawbridge over Bayou Teche, Cafe des Amis operates out of an old general store built in 1925, retaining the stamped tin ceiling, ceiling fans and brick walls. Stay overnight at the adjacent Maison des Amis.

To reach Lafayette, take State Road 94 south and west. Founded as Vermilionville alongside the Bayou Vermilion in 1821, Lafayette was later renamed in honor of the Marquis de Lafayette. Today the historic attraction of Vermilionville re-creates a 19th century village, with guides in period costume, craft demonstrations and Cajun music in the barn house. It's open daily at 1600 Surrey St. Across the bayou at Jean Lafitte National Historic Park (501 Fisher Road, 337-232-0789), a 30-minute film dramatizes the story of the British removal of the Acadians from Nova Scotia in 1755.

Two of the region's most famous restaurants are north of Lafayette off I-49. Find crawfish and blackened Cajun specialties at Prejean's or farther north in Carenco at Enola Prudhomme's Cajun Cafe, named for the sister of internationally famous chef Paul. After a visit to Cajun Country, you can easily loop back to New Orleans along I-10 East. It's approximately 350 miles.

WHERE TO EAT
★ABITA BREW PUB
72011 Holly St., Abita Springs, 985-892-5837; www.abiteabrewpub.com
Since 1986, the Abita Brewery has been gaining a following across the state with its five flagship brews and seasonal favorites. Today, the company brews more than 62,000 barrels of beer each year, including some sold in the brewery's pub. American. Lunch, dinner. $16-35

ALEXANDRIA
Alexandria may be two hours from most of Louisiana's large cities and three hours from New Orleans, but locals and visitors don't need to travel far for big-city events and culture. With art museums, a zoological center and year-round live theater, the Central Louisiana city on the banks of the Red River has plenty to offer.

WHAT TO SEE
ALEXANDRIA MUSEUM OF ART
933 Main St., Alexandria, 318-443-3458; www.themuseum.org
This art museum, housed in an historic bank building dating back to 1898 and listed on the National Histoic Register, has national and regional exhibits. Admission: adults $4, students $2. Tuesday-Saturday.

BRINGHURST PARK
3016 Masonic Drive, Alexandria, 318-473-1385
The park offers tennis, nine-hole golf, picnicking and a playground. Daily.

KENT HOUSE
3601 Bayou Rapides Road, Alexandria, 318-487-5998; www.kenthouse.org
Built in 1796, this restored French colonial plantation house is one of Louisiana's oldest standing structures. Tour the house and outbuildings, including a millhouse, a barn, cabins, a detached kitchen, a carriage house, a sugar mill and a spinning and weaving cottage. Walk through the herb and formal gardens and check out the open-hearth cooking demonstration. Admission: adults $6, seniors $5. Daily.

KISATCHIE NATIONAL FOREST
2500 Shreveport Hwy, Pineville, 318-473-7160; www.southernregion.fs.fed.us/kisatchie
Louisiana's only national forest covers 600,000 acres. Dogwood and wild azalea bloom in the shadows of longleaf, loblolly and slash pine. Wild Azalea National Recreation Trail, the state's longest hiking trail, is in the Evangeline District. Swimming, waterskiing, fishing, hunting, off-road vehicles, picnicking, camping are also popular draws. Daily.

WHERE TO STAY
★BEST WESTERN OF ALEXANDRIA INN & SUITES & CONFERENCE CENTER
2720 N. Macarthur Drive, Alexandria, 318-445-5530; www.bestwestern.com
190 rooms. Bar. Complimentary breakfast. Fitness center. Pool. Pets accepted. $61-150

WHERE TO EAT
★★★BISTRO ON THE BAYOU
1321 Chappie James Ave., Alexandria, 318-445-7574; www.bistroonthebayou.com

The dining room at Bistro on the Bayou, along with the adjoining lounge, occupies an expansive space in the Parc England. Low lighting and a gurgling fountain create a serene and intimate atmosphere. A dramatic focal point is the glassed-in courtyard, filled with lush foliage and lit with fairy lights. Live jazz is offered Friday and Saturday nights. Just minutes from the airport, it is in a suburban setting on the grounds of the former England Air Force Base in Alexandria, which is now the England Air Park.

American. Lunch, dinner. Closed Sunday. $36-85

★★★RESTAURANT EVE
110 S. Pitt St., Alexandria, 703-706-0450; www.restauranteve.com

Chef Cathal Armstrong has earned well-deserved praise for his creative, seasonal cooking. A native of Dublin, Ireland, he cooked personal meals for Senators Kennedy and Clinton as well as President Bush who, once served, asked when he was going to open his own restaurant. The result: a place that features both a 34-seat Tasting Room and a more informal 66-seat bistro. The warm and inviting Tasting Room offers a five- or nine-course prix fixe meal and a seasonal menu featuring Creation (appetizers), Ocean (seafood), Earth and Sky (meats and game), Age (cheese) and Eden (desserts). The inviting, less-formal bistro offers favorites such as the confit of house-cured pork belly and Hawaiian king prawns with risotto.

American. Lunch, dinner. Closed Sunday. $36-85

BASTROP
See also Monroe

From woodlands and bayous to 150 years of Morehouse Parish history, there's plenty to keep you busy in Bastrop.

WHAT TO SEE
BUSSEY BRAKE RESERVOIR
5373 Boat Dock Road, Bastrop, 318-281-4507

Go fishing, boating or camping on these 2,200 acres.

CHEMIN-A-HAUT STATE PARK
14656 State Park Road, Bastrop, 318-283-0812, 888-677-2436; www.crt.state.la.us/ parks

More than 500 wooded acres are found at the intersection of bayous Chemin-a-Haut and Bartholomew. A portion of the "high road to the South" was originally a Native American trail. Visitors can swim, fish, rent a boat, hike or spend the night at one of many tent and trailer sites. Daily.

SNYDER MEMORIAL MUSEUM
1620 E. Madison Ave., Bastrop, 318-281-8760; www.museumsusa.org/museums

The museum covers 150 years of Morehouse Parish history. See antique furniture, kitchen utensils, farm equipment, clothing and Native American artifacts. The gallery features changing art and photographic exhibits. Daily.

BATON ROUGE

See also Hammond, Jackson, New Orleans

Named by its French founders for a red post that marked the boundary between the lands of two Native American tribes, Baton Rouge, the busy capital of Louisiana, is also a major Mississippi River port. Clinging to its gracious past, the area has restored antebellum mansions, gardens, tree-shaded university campuses, splendid Cajun and Creole cuisine, and historic attractions that reflect the culture and struggle of living under ten flags over a period of three centuries.

When Hurricane Katrina hit the Gulf Coast in August 2005, Baton Rouge endured some minor damage, but the most pronounced effect from the storm was the influx of residents from New Orleans and other cities on the Gulf, causing a boost in population that remains today.

Baton Rouge is divided into distinct neighborhoods, each with its own flavor. One of the most popular is Spanish Town, near downtown, which attracts an eclectic crowd because of its restored historic buildings, big Mardi Gras parade and inclusive attitude. The Garden District is a good place for a casual stroll and a peek at some of the city's most beautiful historic homes, and Beauregard Town, in downtown Baton Rouge, is worth a visit; it one of the city's oldest neighborhoods.

WHAT TO SEE
BREC'S BATON ROUGE ZOO
3601 Thomas Road, Baton Rouge, 225-775-3877; www.brzoo.org

Walkways overlook 140 acres of enclosed habitats for more than 1,800 animals and birds. Take in views of some of the fish, reptiles and amphibians of Louisiana at L'aquarium de Louisiane or take the kids to the Safari Playground or a live elephant show. Daily.

BREC'S MAGNOLIA MOUND PLANTATION
2161 Nicholson Drive, Baton Rouge, 225-343-4955; www.magnoliamound.org

An early 19th-century Creole-style building was restored to emphasize the lifestyle of colonial Louisiana. See more of that lifestyle with weekly demonstrations of open-hearth Creole cooking and costumed docents. Then meander over to the visitor center and gift shop.
Tuesday-Sunday.

COTTAGE PLANTATION
10528 Cottage Lane, St. Francisville, 225-635-3674; www.cottageplantation.com

The oldest part of the main house was built during Spanish control of the area. Outbuildings include a smokehouse, a school, kitchens and slave cabins. Accommodations and breakfast are available. Daily.

GOVERNOR'S MANSION
1001 Capitol Access Road, Baton Rouge, 225-342-5855;
www.lamansionfoundation.org

On a Greek Revival/Louisiana-style plantation, the mansion was built in 1963 to replace an earlier official residence.
Tours are available Monday through Friday.

HERITAGE MUSEUM AND VILLAGE

1606 Main St., Baker, 225-774-1776

The turn-of-the-century Victorian house showcases period rooms and exhibits. Also check out the rural village with a church, a school, a store and town hall replica buildings.
Monday-Saturday.

HOUMAS HOUSE

40136 Highway 92, Burnside, 225-473-9380, 888-323-8314; www.houmashouse.com

This large restored sugar plantation features a Greek Revival mansion with early Louisiana-crafted furnishings, a spiral staircase, a belvedere and hexagonal garconnieres in gardens. The house and grounds have been used as a set for 11 films and TV shows.
Monday-Tuesday 9 a.m.-5 p.m., Wednesday-Sunday 9 a.m.-7 p.m.

LAURENS HENRY COHN, SR., MEMORIAL PLANT ARBORETUM

12056 Foster Road, Baton Rouge, 225-775-1006

This unusual 16-acre tract of rolling terrain contains more than 120 species of native and adaptable trees and shrubs; several major plant collections; an herb/fragrance garden; and a tropical collection in a greenhouse. Daily.

LOUISIANA ART & SCIENCE MUSEUM

100 S. River Road, Baton Rouge, 225-344-5272; www.lasm.org

Originally a railroad depot, this building houses fine art, sculpture, cultural and historical exhibits, an Egyptian exhibition, Discovery Depot (for children ages 6 months to 9 years), hands-on galleries and science exhibits for kids. The Irene W. Pennington Planetarium features large-format films and laser shows. Outside, visitors can explore a sculpture garden and a restored five-car train. Additional fees are charged for Space Theater shows.
Tuesday-Saturday 10 a.m.-4 p.m., Sunday 1-4 p.m.; planetarium also open Friday-Saturday 7-10 p.m.

LOUISIANA STATE LIBRARY

701 N. Fourth St., Baton Rouge, 225-342-4913; www.state.lib.la.us

The library houses some 350,000 books, including an extensive section of Louisiana historical tomes, maps and photographs.
Monday-Friday 8 a.m.-4:30 p.m.

INDIAN MOUNDS

Field House and Dalrymple Drives, Baton Rouge

These mounds are believed to have served socio-religious purposes and date from 3300 to 2500 B.C.

LSU TIGERS

Nicholson and North Stadium drives, Baton Rouge, 800-960-8587; www.lsusports.net

Louisiana State University fields 20 athletic teams and draws some of the largest crowds in college athletics. The LSU mascots are Mike the Tiger, Mike VI (a live Bengal tiger that hosts daily feedings at the Tiger Cage) and Ellis Hugh (an inflatable acrobatic tiger). LSU adopted its Fighting Tigers nickname in 1896 from a Civil War volunteer company from New Orleans called the Tiger Rifles.

MEMORIAL TOWER

Highland Road and Dalrymple Drive, Baton Rouge, 225-388-4003; www.lsu.edu/campus/locations/MEMT.html

Built in 1923 as a monument to Louisianans who died in World War I, the tower houses the LSU Museum of Art and features original 17th- through mid-19th-century rooms from England and America.

MUSEUM OF NATURAL SCIENCE

119 Foster Hall, Baton Rouge, 225-578-2855; appl003.lsu.edu/natsci/lmnh.nsf/index

The museum features an extensive collection of birds from around the world; wildlife scenes include Louisiana marshlands and swamps, the Arizona desert, alpine regions and Honduran jungles.

Monday-Saturday.

THE MYRTLES PLANTATION

7747 Highway 61, St. Francisville, 225-635-6277; www.myrtlesplantation.com

Known as one of America's most haunted mansions, this carefully restored house of French influence boasts outstanding examples of wrought iron, ornamental plasterwork and period furniture. Visitors looking for signs of haunting can take a mystery tour on Friday and Saturday evenings.

Daily.

NOTTOWAY PLANTATION

30970 Highway 405, White Castle, 225-545-2730, 866-527-6884; www.nottoway.com

One of the South's most imposing houses, the 50,000-square-foot Nottoway has 64 rooms, 200 windows and 165 doors. In a near-perfect state of "originality," the house is famous for its all-white ballroom. Also on the premises are a restaurant and overnight accommodations. Daily.

OAKLEY HOUSE

Audubon State Historic Site, Highway 965, St. Francisville, 225-635-3739, 888-677-2838; www.nps.gov/history/nr/travel/louisiana/okl.htm

While living at Oakley and working as a tutor, John James Audubon painted 32 of his Birds of America. Spanish colonial Oakley is part of the Audubon State Historic Site, a 100-acre tract set aside as a wildlife sanctuary. Daily.

OLD ARSENAL MUSEUM

State Capitol grounds, 900 Capital Lake Drive, 225-342-0401; www.sos.louisiana.gov

This one-time military garrison dates back to 1838. On the south side are formal gardens that focus on a sunken garden with a monumental statue erected over the grave of Huey P. Long, who was buried here in 1935 after being assassinated in the Capitol.

OLD GOVERNOR'S MANSION

502 North Blvd., Baton Rouge, 225-387-2464; www.oldgovernorsmansion.org

The mansion is restored to the period of the 1930s, when it was built for Gov.

Huey P. Long. It includes original furnishings and memorabilia of former governors.
Tuesday-Friday 10 a.m.-4 p.m.

OLD STATE CAPITOL

100 North Blvd., Baton Rouge, 225-342-0500; www.nps.gov/history/NR/travel/louisiana/ocap.htm
Completed in 1849, Louisiana's old state capitol may be the country's most extravagant example of the Gothic Revival style popularized by the British Houses of Parliament. The richly ornamented building was enlarged in 1881 and abandoned as the capitol in 1932.
Tuesday-Sunday.

PARLANGE PLANTATION

8211 False River Road, Baton Rouge, 225-638-8410; www.nps.gov/history/nr/travel/louisiana/par.htm
Owned by relatives of the builder, this working plantation is a National Historic Landmark. It includes a French colonial home with a rare example of bousillage construction. Doorways and ceiling moldings are of hand-carved cypress; two octagonal brick dovecotes flank the driveway. Daily.

PENTAGON BARRACKS MUSEUM

959 Third St., Baton Rouge, 225-342-1866;www.nps.gov/history/nr/travel/louisiana/pen.htm
Built in 1822 as part of a U.S. military post, the columned, galleried buildings later became the first permanent home of Louisiana State University.

BUTLER GREENWOOD PLANTATION

6838 Highland Road, St. Francisville, 225-655-4475; www.butlergreenwood.com
The same family has owned and lived on this plantation since it was first settled in the 1790s. Today, Greenwood is still a working plantation producing cattle, hay and pecans. Tour the house and if you like it, spend the night—it's also a bed and breakfast.
Daily 9 a.m.-5 p.m.

PLAQUEMINE LOCK STATE HISTORIC SITE

57730 Main St., Plaquemine, 225-687-7158, 877-987-7158; www.crt.state.la.us/crt/parks/plaquemine lock/plaqlock.htm
Built between 1895 and 1909 to control the water level between the Bayou Plaquemine and the Mississippi, the locks were eventually closed in 1961 following the construction of larger locks at Port Allen. Designed by George Goethals, who later designed the Panama Canal, the Plaquemine Locks once had the highest freshwater lift in the world, at 51 feet. The area features the original lockhouse and locks. There's also an interpretive center with displays. Daily.

PORT HUDSON STATE HISTORIC SITE

236 Highway 61, Jackson, 225-654-3775, 888-677-3400;
www.crt.state.la.us/crt/parks/porthud/pthudson.htm

This 650-acre area encompasses part of a Civil War battlefield, site of the longest siege in American military history. The site features a 40-foot viewing towers, Civil War guns and trenches and hiking trails. Interpretive programs tell the 1863 story of how 6,800 Confederates held off a Union force of 30,000 to 40,000 men. Daily.

ROSEDOWN PLANTATION AND GARDENS

12501 Highway 10, St. Francisville, 225-635-3332, 888-376-1867;
www.crt.state.la.us/parks

This magnificently restored 1835 antebellum mansion has many original furnishings. The 28 acres of formal gardens include century-old camellias and azaleas, fountains, gazebos and an allée of moss-draped live oaks. Daily.

RURAL LIFE MUSEUM

4600 Essen Lane, Baton Rouge, 225-765-2437; www.rurallife.lsu.edu

The three-acre museum complex of 25 buildings is divided into plantation, folk architecture and exhibits. The plantation includes a blacksmith shop, an open-kettle sugar mill, a commissary and a church.
Admission: adults $7, children $5, children under 5 free. Daily.

STATE CAPITOL

N. Third Street and State Capitol Drive, Baton Rouge, 225-342-7317,
800-527-6843;www.nps.gov/history/NR/travel/louisiana/cap.htm

Built during Huey P. Long's administration, the 34-story, 450-foot moderne skyscraper capitol is decorated with 26 different varieties of marble. The Memorial Hall floor is laid with polished lava from Mount Vesuvius; the ceiling is leafed in gold. An observation tower offers views of the city. Lorado Taft sculpture groups on either side of the entrance symbolize the pioneer and patriotic spirit. Daily.

USS KIDD

305 S. River Road, Baton Rouge, 225-342-1942; www.usskidd.com

Visitors may roam the decks of the World War II Fletcher-class destroyer and explore its interior compartments. A unique dock allows the ship to be exhibited completely out of water when the Mississippi River is in its low stages. The adjacent museum houses a ship model collection, maritime artifacts and a restored P-40 Flying Tiger plane. There's a visitor center and an observation tower that overlooks the river. The Memorial Wall is dedicated to service personnel.

WEST BATON ROUGE MUSEUM

845 N. Jefferson Ave., Port Allen, 225-336-2422; www.westbatonrougemuseum.com

Exhibits include a large-scale 1904 model sugar mill, a bedroom featuring American Empire furniture and a sugar plantation slave cabin and French Creole house.
Tuesday-Saturday 10 a.m.- 4:30 p.m., Sunday 2-5 p.m.

SPECIAL EVENT
BLUES WEEK
730 North Blvd., Baton Rouge, 225-383-0968; www.louisianasmusic.com
The weeklong event features blues, jazz, Cajun, zydeco and gospel music.
Traditional Louisiana cuisine is served.
Late April-early May.

WHERE TO STAY
★BEST WESTERN RICHMOND SUITES HOTEL
5668 Hilton Ave., Baton Rouge, 225-924-6500, 800-332-2582; www.bestwestern.com
141 rooms. Complimentary breakfast. Fitness center. Pool. Pets accepted.
$61-150

★★EMBASSY SUITES
4914 Constitution Ave., Baton Rouge, 225-924-6566, 800-433-4600;
www.embassybatonrouge.com
223 suites. Restaurant, bar. Complimentary breakfast. Business center. Fitness center. Pool. $151-250

★★HOLIDAY INN
9940 Airline Highway, Baton Rouge, 225-924-7021, 888-814-9602;
www.holiday-inn.com
334 rooms. Restaurant, bar. $61-150

★★★MARRIOTT BATON ROUGE
5500 Hilton Ave., Baton Rouge, 225-924-5000; www.marriott.com
299 rooms. Restaurant, bar. Business center. $61-150

★★★NOTTOWAY PLANTATION RESTAURANT & INN
31025 Louisiana Highway 1, White Castle, 225-545-2730, 866-527-6884;
www.nottoway.com
This Victorian-style inn was built in 1859. Today, the home retains its original
hand-painted Dresden doorknobs, elaborate plaster frieze work and marble
fireplaces. A lovely plantation-style restaurant serves Cajun and Southern
cuisine.
15 rooms. Restaurant. Complimentary breakfast. $61-150

★QUALITY INN
9138 Bluebonnet Centre Blvd., Baton Rouge, 225-293-1199, 800-228-5151;
www.qualityinn.com
120 rooms. Restaurant, bar. Complimentary breakfast. $61-150

★★★SHERATON BATON ROUGE CONVENTION CENTER HOTEL
102 France St., Baton Rouge, 225-242-2600; www.sheraton.com
300 rooms. Restaurant, bar. Business center. Fitness center. Pool. $151-250

WHERE TO EAT
★CABIN
Highways 22 and 44, Burnside, 225-473-3007; www.thecabinrestaurant.com
Cajun. Lunch, dinner. $16-35

★★DON'S SEAFOOD & STEAK HOUSE
6823 Airline Highway, Baton Rouge, 225-357-0601
Seafood, steak. Lunch, dinner. $16-35

★★★JUBAN'S
3739 Perkins Road, Baton Rouge, 225-346-8422; www.jubans.com
Diners will find fine Southern Louisiana cuisine with a Creole-American influence. For a sure thing, order the veal T-bone with shitake mushroom hash and a port wine demi-glace or the hallelujah crab topped with Creolaise sauce.
Creole. Lunch, dinner. Closed Sunday. $36-85

★★MIKE ANDERSON'S
1031 W. Lee Drive, Baton Rouge, 225-766-7823; www.mikeandersonsbr.com
Seafood. Lunch, dinner. $16-35

★★PARRAIN'S SEAFOOD RESTAURANT
3225 Perkins Road, Baton Rouge, 225-381-9922
Seafood. Lunch, dinner. $16-35

★★★RUTH'S CHRIS STEAK HOUSE
4836 Constitution Ave., Baton Rouge, 225-925-0163; www.ruthschris.com
The excellent service and atmosphere are on par with the steaks at this upscale national chain.
Steak. Lunch, dinner. Closed Sunday. $36-85

BOSSIER CITY
See also Shreveport
Located on the east bank of the Red River, Bossier City is a gambler's paradise: The city of a little more than 56,000 people has three major casinos and a thoroughbred racetrack in and around the city limits.

WHAT TO SEE
EIGHTH AIR FORCE MUSEUM
Barksdale Air Force Base, 841 Fairchild Ave., Bossier City, 318-456-
3067;www.8afmuseum.net
Aircraft on display include a B-52D Stratofortress, a P-51 Mustang and an F-84F Thunderstreak. Desert Storm memorabilia is available and there's a gift shop.
Daily 9:30 a.m.-4 p.m.

WHERE TO STAY
★★HOLIDAY INN

2015 Old Minden Road, Bossier City, 318-742-9700, 800-465-4329;www.holiday-inn.com
212 rooms. Restaurant, bar. Business center. Fitness center. $61-150

★LA QUINTA INN

309 Preston Blvd., Bossier City, 318-747-4400, 800-687-6667; www.laquinta.com
130 rooms. Complimentary breakfast. Pool. Pets accepted. $61-150

★ISLE OF CAPRI INN

711 Isle of Capri Blvd., Bossier City, 318-678-7777, 800-843-4753; www.isleofcaprica-sino.com
245 rooms. Bar. Complimentary breakfast. $61-150

WHERE TO EAT
★★RALPH & KACOO'S

1700 Old Minden Road, Bossier City, 318-747-6660; www.ralphandkacoos.com
Cajun. Lunch, dinner, Sunday brunch. $16-35

COVINGTON

See also New Orleans
Covington is in a wooded area north of Lake Pontchartrain, which is crossed via the 24-mile Lake Pontchartrain Causeway from New Orleans. With mild winters and semitropical summers, Covington is a town of vacation houses, recreational opportunities and pecan, pine and oak woods. A number of thoroughbred horse farms are also in the area.

WHAT TO SEE
FONTAINEBLEAU STATE PARK

67825 Highway 190, Mandeville, 985-624-4443, 888-677-3668; www.lastateparks.com/fontaine/fontaine.htm
A live oak allée forms the entrance to this 2,700-acre park on the north shore of Lake Pontchartrain; on the grounds are the ruins of a plantation brickyard and sugar mill. Swimming, fishing, boating and picnicking are available. Daily.

PONTCHARTRAIN VINEYARDS & WINERY

81250 Highway 1082 (Old Military Road), Bush, 985-892-9742;www.pontchartrainvine-yards.com
About an hour from New Orleans, the Pontchartrain Vineyards & Winery produces wines to complement the unique cuisine of Southern Louisiana. To sample the wines, you can drive out to the winery for a tasting, buy a case at a local spirits shop or order a bottle with your meal in any number of fine New Orleans restaurants.
Wednesday-Sunday noon-4p.m.

TAMMANY TRACE

Covington, Highway 59, 800-438-7223,985-867-9490; www.tammanytrace.org
This follows the old Illinois Central Railroad corridor for 31 miles, ending

in Slidell. There's a paved hiking/biking trail and an unpaved equestrian trail. Daily.

WHERE TO STAY
★★HOLIDAY INN
501 N. Highway 190, Covington, 985-893-3580, 888-465-4329; www.holiday-inn.com
156 rooms. Restaurant, bar. Business center. Fitness center. Pool. $61-150

FRANKLIN
See also Morgan City, New Iberia
Reportedly named by founder Guinea Lewis for Benjamin Franklin, this town on the Bayou Teche is in the center of the Cajun Coast. It has much of the beautiful scenery outsiders imagine when they think of Louisiana's coast. Boating, fishing and hunting are popular diversions at the nearby Atchafalaya Basin.

WHAT TO SEE
CHITIMACHA CULTURAL CENTER
490 Decater St., Charenton, 504-589-3882; www.nps.gov/Jela
Museum exhibits, crafts and a ten-minute video focus on the history and culture of the Chitimacha tribe of Louisiana. Walking tours are available. This center is a unit of Jean Lafitte National Historical Park. Daily.

CYPREMORT POINT STATE PARK
306 Beach Lane, Franklin, 337-867-4510;
www.lastateparks.com/cypremor/cyprempt.htm
This 185-acre site offers access to the Gulf of Mexico. The man-made beach in the heart of a natural marsh affords fresh and saltwater fishing and other seashore recreation opportunities. Daily.

GREVEMBERG HOUSE
St. Mary Parish Museum, 407 Sterling Road, Franklin, 337-828-2092;
www.grevemberghouse.com
The Greek Revival house maintains a fine collection of antique furnishings dating from the 1850s, children's toys, paintings and Civil War relics. Daily.

OAKLAWN MANOR PLANTATION
3296 E. Oaklawn Drive, Franklin, 337-828-0434; www.oaklawnmanor.com
Restored in 1927, this massive Greek Revival house has 20-inch-thick walls, is furnished with European antiques, and is surrounded by one of the largest groves of live oaks in the U.S. It's also the home of former Louisiana Gov. Mike Foster.
Admission: adults $10, students $6. Tuesday-Sunday 10 a.m.-4 p.m..

WHERE TO STAY
★★BEST WESTERN FOREST MOTOR INN
1909 Main St., Franklin, 337-828-1810, 800-828-1812; www.bestwestern.com
85 rooms. Restaurant. Complimentary breakfast. Business center. Pool. $61-150

HOUMA

See also Morgan City

Situated on Bayou Terrebonne and the Intracoastal Waterway, Houma is known as the "Venice of America," famous for its Cajun food and hospitality.

WHAT TO SEE
ANNIE MILLER'S SWAMP & MARSH TOURS

3718 Southdown Mandalay, Houma, 985-868-4758; www.annie-miller.com

Boat trips travel through winding waterways in swamps and wild marshlands. See birds, alligators, wild game, tropical plants and flowers. March-October, daily.

SOUTHDOWN PLANTATION HOUSE/TERREBONNE MUSEUM

1208 Museum Drive, Houma, 985-851-0154; www.southdownmuseum.org

The first floor, Greek Revival in style, was built in 1859; the second floor, late Victorian/Queen Anne in style, was added in 1893. The 21-room house includes stained glass, a Boehm and Doughty porcelain bird collection, a Terreboone Parish history room, a re-creation of Allen Ellender's Senate office, antique furniture and Mardi Gras costumes. Tuesday-Saturday 10 a.m.-4 p.m.

JACKSON

See also Baton Rouge

From Renaissance to Greek Revival, Jackson is a bastion of Southern architecture, with 20,000 acres of parklands to help you stretch your legs when you venture outside.

WHAT TO SEE
JACKSON HISTORIC DISTRICT

The district includes 123 structures covering approximately 65 percent of town. Architectural styles range from Renaissance and Greek Revival to Queen Anne and California stick-style bungalow. Daily.

MILBANK HISTORIC HOUSE

3045 Bank St., Jackson, 225-634-5901; www.milbankbandb.com/milbank.htm

The Revival town house, originally built as a banking house for the Clinton-Port Hudson Railroad, features first- and second-floor galleries supported by 12 30-foot columns. Daily.

JENNINGS

See also Lake Charles

A small town known for its Cajun food, music and museums—including one on the history of the telephone—Jennings is also notable for its outdoor recreational opportunities, including fishing, boating and hiking. The city hosts a main street farmers market every Saturday and live country music on the last Saturday of each month.

WHAT TO SEE
W. H. TUPPER GENERAL MERCHANDISE MUSEUM
311 N. Main St., Jennings, 337-821-5532, 800-264-5521; www.tuppermuseum.com
More than 10,000 items are on display re-creating the atmosphere of early 20th-century life in rural Louisiana. You'll see a toy collection, period clothing, drugs, toiletries and Native American basketry.
Admission: adults $3, students $1. Monday-Friday 9 a.m.-5 p.m.

ZIGLER MUSEUM
411 Clara St., Jennings, 337-824-0114
The museum contains galleries of wildlife and natural history, as well as European and American art.
Tuesday- Sunday.

WHERE TO STAY
★★ HOLIDAY INN
603 Holiday Drive, Jennings, 337-824-5280, 800-465-4329; www.holiday-inn.com
131 rooms Restaurant, bar. $61-150

KENNER
See also New Orleans
Slot machines, poker and blackjack all vie for attention at Kenner's many casinos.

WHAT TO SEE
TREASURE CHEST CASINO
5050 Williams Blvd., Kenner, 504-443-8000, 800-298-0711; www.treasurechest.com
This 25,767-square-foot riverboat docked in Lake Pontchartrain holds 1,000 slot machines and table games ranging from blackjack to Caribbean stud. Food choices are an all-you-can-eat buffet or the upscale Bobby G's restaurant, while the Caribbean Showroom offers live entertainment. Daily.

WHERE TO STAY
★★★HILTON NEW ORLEANS AIRPORT
901 Airline Drive, Kenner, 504-469-5000, 800-872-5914; www.hilton.com
This first-class hotel caters to business travelers, but with a 21-station fitness center, outdoor pool and whirlpool, tennis courts and putting green, it is great for leisure travelers as well.
317 rooms. Restaurant, bar. Business center. Fitness center. Pool. Tennis. Golf. $61-150

LACOMBE
See also Covington, New Orleans
Nestled near the Gulf of Mexico, Lacombe is a city of 7,000 residents and plenty of sizzling Southern dishes.

WHERE TO EAT
★★★LA PROVENCE
25020 Highway 190, E. Lacombe, 985-626-7662; www.laprovencerestaurant.com
For three decades, residents of New Orleans (and beyond) have been treated to the rustic, traditional cuisine of Southern France at La Provence, lovingly prepared by chef Randy Lewis. The restaurant was opened in 1972 by innovative chef Chris Kerageorgiou, and La Provence and has paid homage to Kerageorgiou's Mediterranean cooking ever since with steaming dishes brimming with garlic, tomatoes, olives and fresh herbs.
French. Lunch, dinner, brunch. Closed Monday-Tuesday. $16-35

LAFAYETTE
See also New Iberia
The heart of Cajun Country lies in Lafayette, a city with French, Spanish and Caribbean traditions still present in the speech patterns, cooking and daily life of its residents. Lafayette is home to top-notch Cajun and Creole restaurants, historic homes and a backyard of outdoor activities worth exploring.
In the late 18th century, Acadians from Nova Scotia came to the Lafayette area to escape persecution by the British who took control of French Canada. Many of today's descendents of the French Acadians maintain a strong feeling of kinship with Nova Scotia and France.
Despite its urban rhythm and growing population, Lafayette has retained its small-town charm. Live oaks and azaleas bloom all around town, as do clumps of native irises. These blooms offer color to an already vibrant place.

WHAT TO SEE
ACADIAN VILLAGE: A MUSEUM OF ACADIAN HERITAGE AND CULTURE
200 Greenleaf Drive, Lafayette, 337-981-2364, 800-962-9133; www.acadianvillage.org
This restored 19th-century Acadian village features fine examples of unique Acadian architecture with houses, a general store and a chapel. Crafts are on display and for sale. Daily.

CHRÉTIEN POINT PLANTATION
665 Chrétien Point Road, Lafayette, 337-662-7050; www.chretienpoint.com
This restored 1831 Greek Revival mansion was the site of a Civil War battle. Daily.

LAFAYETTE MUSEUM
1122 Lafayette St., Lafayette, 337-234-2208
Once the residence of Alexandre Mouton, the first Democratic governor of the state, the house is now a museum with antique furnishings, Civil War relics and carnival costumes.
Tuesday-Sunday.

LAFAYETTE NATURAL HISTORY MUSEUM AND PLANETARIUM
637 Girard Park Drive, Lafayette, 337-291-5544
The planetarium has various programs and changing exhibits. Daily

UNIVERSITY ART MUSEUM
East Lewis and Girard Park Drives, Lafayette, 337-482-5326; www.louisiana.edu/UAM
There are two locations: The permanent collection is at 101 Girard Park Drive (Monday-Friday); changing exhibits are staged at Fletcher Hall, East Lewis and Girard Park Circle (Monday-Friday, Sunday).
Tuesday-Saturday 10 a.m.-5 p.m.

UNIVERSITY OF LOUISIANA AT LAFAYETTE
200 E. University Ave., Lafayette, 337-482-1000; www.louisiana.edu
Founded in 1900, the university is now home to more than 16,000 students. The tree-shaded campus serves as an arboretum with many Southern plant species, while Cypress Lake, a miniature Louisiana cypress swamp, has fish, alligators and native irises. Daily.

SPECIAL EVENT
FESTIVAL INTERNATIONAL DE LOUISIANE
735 Jefferson St., Lafayette, 337-232-8086; www.festivalinternational.com
The festival offers international and local performances, visual arts and cuisine.
Last weekend in April.

WHERE TO STAY
★★BEST WESTERN HOTEL ACADIANA
1801 W. Pinhook Road, Lafayette, 337-233-8120, 800-826-8386;www.bestwestern.com
290 rooms. Restaurant, bar. $61-150

★★COMFORT INN
1421 S.E. Evangeline Thruway, Lafayette, 337-232-9000, 800-800-8752;
www.choicehotels.com
200 rooms. Restaurant, bar. Complimentary breakfast. Fitness center. Pool. $61-150

★★★HILTON LAFAYETTE AND TOWERS
800-1521 W. Pinhook Road, Lafayette, 337-235-6111; www.hilton.com
327 rooms. Restaurant, bar. Fitness center. Pool. Pets accepted. $151-250

WHERE TO EAT
★BLAIR HOUSE
1316 Surrey St., Lafayette, 337-234-0357
American, Cajun, French. Lunch, dinner. $16-35

★★BLUE DOG CAFE
1211 W. Pinhook Road, Lafayette, 337-237-0005; www.bluedogcafe.com
Cajun/Creole, seafood, steak. Lunch, dinner, brunch. $16-35

★★DON'S SEAFOOD & STEAK HOUSE
301 E. Vermilion St., Lafayette, 337-235-3551; www.donsdowntown.com
Cajun, seafood, steak. Lunch, dinner. $16-35

★★I MONELLI
4017 Johnston St., Lafayette, 337-989-9291
Italian. Lunch, dinner. Closed Sunday-Monday. $16-35

★★LA FONDA
3809 Johnston St., Lafayette, 337-984-5630
Mexican. Lunch, dinner. Closed Sunday-Monday. $16-35

★★POOR BOY'S RIVERSIDE INN
240 Tubing Road, Lafayette, 337-235-8559; www.poorboysriversideinn.com
Cajun, seafood. Lunch, dinner. Closed Sunday. $16-35

★PREJEAN'S RESTAURANT
3480 I-49N, Lafayette, 337-896-3247; www.prejeans.com
Cajun. Breakfast, lunch, dinner. $16-35

★RANDOL'S
2320 Kaliste Saloom Road, Lafayette, 337-981-7080, 800-962-2586; www.randols.com
Seafood. Dinner. Bar. $16-35

★★★RUTH'S CHRIS STEAK HOUSE
620 W. Pinhook Road, Lafayette, 337-237-6123; www.ruthschris.com
Prime steaks broiled in a custom-built oven and served sizzling in a pool of butter on a very hot plate characterize this upscale chain. À la carte vegetables include creamed spinach; asparagus with hollandaise sauce; and baked, mashed, lyonnaise, or au gratin potatoes.
Steak. Lunch, dinner. $36-85

LAKE CHARLES
See also Jennings
With more than 75 festivals each year, Lake Charles and the surrounding cities of Southwest Louisiana are proud to be known as the "Festival Capital" of the state. Visitors who want to bask in the tropical climate can fish or hike the Creole Nature Trail, while those looking for more temperate entertainment can take in one of the city's several museums.

WHAT TO SEE
BRIMSTONE HISTORICAL SOCIETY MUSEUM
800 Picard Road, Sulphur, 337-527-7142; www.brimstonemuseum.org/brimstone.asp
The museum commemorates the turn-of-the-century birth of the local sulfur industry with exhibits explaining the development of the Frasch mining process; other exhibits deal with southwest Louisiana.
Monday-Friday.

CREOLE NATURE TRAIL NATIONAL SCENIC BYWAY
1205 N. Lakeshore Drive, Sulphur, 800-456-7952; www.creolenaturetrail.org
The nature trail follows Highway 27 in a circular route ending back at Lake Charles. It's a unique composite of wildflowers, animals, shrimp, crab and many varieties of fish, plus one of the largest alligator populations in the world; a winter habitat of thousands of ducks and geese; views of several

bayous, Intracoastal Waterway, oil platforms, beaches, four wildlife refuges and a bird sanctuary. Take the automobile nature trail or the walking nature trail. Daily.

HISTORIC "CHARPENTIER"
Lake Charles
The district includes 20 square blocks of downtown area; architectural styles range from Queen Anne, Eastlake and Carpenter's Gothic (known locally as "Lake Charles style") to Western stick-style bungalows. Daily.

IMPERIAL CALCASIEU MUSEUM
204 W. Sallier St., Lake Charles, 337-439-3797; www.imperialcalcasieumuseum.org
Items of local historical interest, a toy collection and rare Audubon prints can be found at this museum. The Gibson-Barham Gallery houses art exhibits. On the premises is the 300-year-old Sallier oak tree.
Tuesday-Saturday.

SAM HOUSTON JONES STATE PARK
107 Sutherland Road, Lake Charles, 888-677-7264;
www.lastateparks.com/sanhoust/Shjones.htm
The approximately 1,000 acres includes lagoons in a densely wooded area at the confluence of the west fork of the Caslcasieu and Houston Rivers and the Indian Bayou. Fishing, boating, nature trails, hiking, picnicking, tent and trailer sites, cabins provide lots of recreation. Daily.

SPECIAL EVENT
CONTRABAND DAYS
Lake Charles Civic Center, 900 Lake Shore Drive, Lake Charles, 337-436-5508,
800-456-7952; www.contrabanddays.com
This event honors "gentleman pirate" Jean Lafitte. Boat races, midway, concerts and an arts and crafts display are some of the planned activities. Two weeks in early May.

WHERE TO STAY
★BEST WESTERN RICHMOND SUITES HOTEL
2600 Moeling St., Lake Charles, 337-433-5213, 800-643-2582; www.bestwestern.com
140 rooms. Complimentary breakfast. Fitness center. Pool. Spa. $61-150

WHERE TO EAT
★★PAT'S OF HENDERSON
1500 Siebarth Drive, Lake Charles, 337-439-6618; www.patsofhenderson.com
Cajun. Lunch, dinner. $16-35

★★PEKING GARDEN
2433 E. Broad St., Lake Charles, 337-436-3597
Chinese. Lunch, dinner. $16-35

★★PUJO STREET CAFE
901 Ryan St., Lake Charles, 337-439-2054; www.pujostreet.com
Creole. Lunch, dinner. Closed Sunday. $15 and under.

★STEAMBOAT BILL'S
732 Martin Luther King Highway, Lake Charles, 337-494-1700;www.steamboatbills.com
Creole. Lunch. $15 and under.

★TONY'S PIZZA
335 E. Prien Lake Road, Lake Charles, 337-477-1611; www.tonyspizzainc.com
Italian. Lunch, dinner. $15 and under.

MANDEVILLE
See also Lacombe
Located on the north shore of Lake Pontchartrain, across from New Orleans, Mandeville boasts a rich musical history of jazz and blues.

WHERE TO EAT
★★★TREY YUEN
600 N. Causeway, Mandeville, 985-626-4476;
www.treyyuen.com/treyyuenmandeville.htm
Fresh local seafood defines the restaurant's unorthodox Chinese menu, which includes alligator dishes, soft-shell crab items and crawfish creations. Koi ponds, footbridges and custom-built carvings outside give diners a hint of Asia.
Chinese. Lunch, dinner. $16-35

MANY
See also Alexandria
See 19th-century army living quarters or peer into blooming gardens in this small town in the heart of the state.

WHAT TO SEE
FORT JESUP STATE HISTORIC SITE
32 Geohagan Road, Many, 318-256-4117, 888-677-5378;
www.lastateparks.com/fortjes/ftjesup.htm
This fort on 21 acres, established in 1822 by Zachary Taylor (before he took his post at the White House), features a restored 1830s army kitchen, reconstructed officers' quarters and a museum. Daily.

HODGES GARDENS
110 Hodges Loop, Many, 318-586-3523; www.hodgesgardens.com
Wild and cultivated flowers and plants grow year-round on 4,700 acres of gardens and greenhouses. There's also a 225-acre lake. The Terrazzo map commemorates the Louisiana Purchase. Wildlife, fishing boat rentals and picnic facilities are available. Special events include Easter service, July Fourth festival and Christmas lights festival. Daily.

SPECIAL EVENTS
BATTLE OF PLEASANT HILL RE-ENACTMENT
18 miles north on Highway 175, north of Pleasant Hill, 318-872-1310; www.battleofpleasanthill.com
The three-day event includes a beauty pageant, Confederate ball, parade and battle reenactment.
Early April.

SABINE FREE STATE FESTIVAL
237 W. Port Arthur Ave., Florien, 318-586-7286
This festival offers a beauty pageant; syrup-making, basket-weaving and quilting demonstrations; arts and crafts exhibits; and a flea market.
First weekend in November.

METAIRIE
See also Kenner, New Orleans
This suburb of New Orleans lures locals and out-of-towners alike to see the Zephyrs baseball team.

WHAT TO SEE
NEW ORLEANS ZEPHYRS
6000 Airline Highway, Metairie, 504-734-5155; www.zephyrsbaseball.com
The Zephyrs first took the field in 1993 as the AAA farm team for the Houston Astros. They play ball at the 10,000-seat Zephyr Field, cheered on by team mascots Boudreaux D. Nutria and his wife, Clotile, as well as their numerous offspring. (Nutria is a species of water-dwelling rodent, which are beneficial in Louisiana and Texas but viewed as destructive in other areas.)
Early April-August.

WHERE TO STAY
★★DOUBLETREE HOTEL
3838 N. Causeway Blvd., Metairie, 504-836-5253, 800-222-8733; www.doubletreelakeside.com
210 rooms. Restaurant, bar. $151-250

★★FOUR POINTS BY SHERATON NEW ORLEANS AIRPORT
6401 Veterans Memorial Blvd., Metairie, 504-885-5700; www.starwoodhotels.com
181 rooms. Business center. Fitness center. Pool. $151-250

WHERE TO EAT
★★★ANDREA'S
3100 19th St., Metairie, 504-834-8583; www.andreasrestaurant.com
Italian. Lunch, dinner, Sunday brunch. $36-85

★★IMPASTATO'S
3400 16th St., Metairie, 504-455-1545; www.impastatos.com
Italian. Dinner. Closed Sunday-Monday. $36-85

★MORNING CALL

3325 Severn Ave., Metairie, 504-885-4068; www.morningcallcoffeestand.com
Deli. Breakfast, lunch, dinner, late-night. $15 and under.

★★MOSCA'S

4137 Highway 90 W., Avondale, 504-436-8950
Italian. Dinner. Closed Sunday-Monday; August. $36-85

MINDEN

See also Bossier City, Shreveport
Named after a town in Germany, Minden hosted the wedding of country
singer Hank Williams Sr. in 1952.

WHAT TO SEE
GERMANTOWN MUSEUM

120 Museum Road, Minden, 318-377-6061; www.mindenusa.com
The museum includes three buildings completed in 1835 by Germans seeking freedom from persecution; replicas of a communal smokehouse and a
blacksmith shop; as well as records and artifacts used by settlers.
Wednesday-Sunday.

LAKE BISTINEAU STATE PARK

*103 State Park Road, Minden, 318-745-3503, 888-677-2478;www.lastateparks.com/
lakebist/bistino.htm*
This 750-acre park in the heart of a pine forest includes a large lake. Swimming, waterskiing, fishing, boating, tent and trailer sites and cabins are
among the offerings. Daily.

MONROE AND WEST MONROE

See also Shreveport
Located on the Ouachita River across from West Monroe, its smaller twin
city, Monroe is home to more than 50,000 residents and a University of Louisiana campus with some 8,000 students. The city is proud of its business
history; Monroe was the first location west of the Mississippi to brew Coca-
Cola and the birthplace of Delta Airlines.

WHAT TO SEE
BRY HALL ART GALLERY

700 University Ave., Monroe, 318-342-1375
The gallery shows art exhibits, including photographs by American and for-
eign artists, students and faculty.
February-mid-December, Monday-Friday.

BIEDENHARN FAMILY HOUSE

2006 Riverside Drive, Monroe, 800-362-0983; www.bmuseum.org
This historic home is located at the Biedenharn Museum & Gardens. Built
by Joseph Biedenharn, first bottler of Coca-Cola in 1914, the home contains
antiques, fine furnishings, silver dating from the 18th century and Coca-Cola
memorabilia.

ELSONG GARDENS & CONSERVATORY

2006 Riverside Drive, Monroe, 800-362-0983; www.bmuseum.org

Located at the Biedenharn Museum & Gardens, these formal gardens enclosed within brick walls, were originally designed to accommodate musical events. Today, visitors trigger background music when they amble through separate gardens linked by winding paths. There are four fountains, including one from the garden of Russian Empress Catherine the Great.

LOUISIANA PURCHASE GARDENS AND ZOO

1405 Bernstien Park Drive, Monroe, 318-329-2400; www.monroezoo.org

Formal gardens, moss-laden live oaks, waterways and winding paths surround naturalistic habitats for more than 850 exotic animals in this 80-acre zoo. Boat and miniature train rides are also available, as are areas for picnics and concessions.

Admission: adults $4.50, children $3.00, children under 3 free. Daily 10 a.m.-5 p.m.

MUSEUM OF ZOOLOGY

700 University Ave., Monroe, 318-342-1799

The fish collection at this intimate museum is one of the largest and most complete in the nation.

February-mid-August, mid-September-December, Monday-Friday.

WHERE TO STAY

★★HOLIDAY INN

1051 Highway, 165 Bypass, Monroe, 318-387-5100, 800-465-4329;

www.holiday-inn.com

260 rooms. Restaurant, bar. Complimentary breakfast. Fitness center. Pool. Pets accepted. $61-150

★LA QUINTA INN

1035 Highway, 165 Bypass, Monroe, 318-322-3900, 800-531-5900; www.laquinta.com

130 rooms. Complimentary breakfast. Pets accepted. $61-150

WHERE TO EAT

★★CHATEAU

2007 Louisville Ave., Monroe, 318-325-0384

American, Italian. Lunch, dinner. Closed Sunday. $16-35

★★WAREHOUSE NO. 1

1 Olive St., Monroe, 318-322-1340; www.warehouseno1.com

Seafood. Dinner. Closed Sunday. $36-85

MORGAN CITY

See also Franklin, Thibodaux

Morgan City is an ideal jumping-off point for almost any destination in Louisiana, located 70 miles west of New Orleans, 60 miles east of Lafayette and 60 miles south of Baton Rouge. The city is home to Louisiana's oldest harvest festival—the Shrimp and Petroleum Festival held each year over Labor

Day weekend, complete with a horseshoe tournament, gospel concerts and the crowning of festival royalty.

WHAT TO SEE
BROWNELL MEMORIAL PARK & CARILLON TOWER
3359 Highway 70, Morgan City, 985-384-2283
The park preserves swamp in its natural state; on the property is a 106-foot carillon tower with 61 bronze bells. Daily.

CAJUN JACK'S
112 Main St., Morgan City, 985-395-7420; www.cajunjack.com
See how Cajun people lived more than 200 years ago. And explore the area where the first Tarzan movie was filmed.
Daily tours: 9 a.m., 2:30 p.m.

KEMPER WILLIAMS PARK
Patterson, eight miles west via Highway 90, Cotton Road exit in Patterson,985-395-2298; www.stmaryparishdevelopment.com
This 290-acre park offers nature and jogging trails, tennis courts, a golf driving range, baseball diamonds, picnicking and camping.
Daily. 9 a.m.-6 p.m.

SCULLY'S SWAMP TOURS & RESTAURANT
3141 Highway 70, Morgan City, 985-385-2388
See local wildlife while enjoying authentic Cajun seafood on two-hour tours through the swamp.
Tuesday-Saturday.

SWAMP GARDENS AND WILDLIFE ZOO
In Heritage Park, 725 Myrtle St., Morgan City, 985-384-3343
Outdoor exhibits depict both the history of the human settlement of the great Atchafalaya Basin and the natural flora and fauna of the swamp. Daily.

SPECIAL EVENT
LOUISIANA SHRIMP AND PETROLEUM FESTIVAL AND FAIR
715 second St., Morgan City, 985-385-0703; www.shrimp-petrofest.org
A great party with a strange name, the festival honors the men and women who work to keep the Cajun Coast afloat economically—in the fishing and petroleum industries.
Labor Day weekend.

WHERE TO STAY
★★HOLIDAY INN
520 Roderick St., Morgan City, 985-385-2200; www.holiday-inn.com
224 rooms. Restaurant, bar. Pool. Fitness center. Pets accepted. $61-150

NATCHITOCHES

See also Many

On and off the big screen (the city was the setting for the film *Steel Magnolias*), Natchitoches shines with its historic charms and outdoor attractions. Visitors can tour historic homes, working plantations or nature preserves. The city's 33-block Historic Landmark District, home to historic houses, churches and businesses, is worth a visit.

WHAT TO SEE
FORT ST. JEAN BAPTISTE STATE HISTORIC SITE
155 Rue Jefferson, Natchitoches, 318-357-3101; 888-677-7853;www.lastateparks.com/ fortstj/ftstjean.htm
On this 5-acre site is a replica of the fort as it was when first built to halt Spanish movement into Louisiana; the restoration includes barracks, a warehouse, a chapel and a mess hall.
Daily 9 a.m.-5 p.m.

MELROSE PLANTATION
3533 Highway 119, Natchitoches, 318-379-0055; www.nps.gov
The complex of eight plantation buildings includes Yucca House, the original cabin, the Big House and the African House. It originally was the residence of Marie Therese Coincoin, a former slave whose son developed the Spanish land grant into a thriving antebellum plantation. Melrose was restored at the turn of the 20th century by "Miss Cammie" Garrett Henry, who turned it into a repository of local arts and crafts.
Tuesday-Sunday noon-4 p.m.

NATIONAL FISH HATCHERY & AQUARIUM
615 Highway 1 S., Natchitoches, 318-352-5324; www.fws.gov
The aquarium has 16 tanks of indigenous fish, turtles and alligators. Daily.

NORTHWESTERN STATE UNIVERSITY
College Avenue St., Natchitoches, 318-357-6011; www.nsula.edu
The 916-acre campus is on Chaplin's Lake. On the 9,400-student campus are the Louisiana Sports Writers Hall of Fame in Prather Coliseum, the Archives Room of Watson Memorial Library, the Folklife Center, the Williamson Archaeological Museum in Kyser Hall and the Normal Hill Historic District.

SPECIAL EVENTS
CHRISTMAS FESTIVAL OF LIGHTS
781 Front St., Natchitoches, 318-352-8072, 800-259-1714; www.christmasfestival.com
More than 140,000 lights are turned on after a full day of celebration to welcome the Christmas season.
First Saturday in December.

MELROSE PLANTATION ARTS & CRAFTS FESTIVAL
3533 Highway 119, Natchitoches, 318-379-0055; www.nps.gov
The festival features juried works of more than 100 artists and craftspeople. Admission: adults $5, children $2. Second weekend in June, 9 a.m.-5 p.m.

NATCHITOCHES-NORTHWESTERN FOLK FESTIVAL

NSU Prather Coliseum, 938 S. Jefferson St., Natchitoches, 318-357-4332;
www.nsula.edu

The festival spotlights a different industry or occupation each year and works to preserve Louisiana folk art forms: music, dance, crafts, storytelling, and cuisine.

Third weekend in July.

NATCHITOCHES PILGRIMAGE

781 Front St., Natchitoches, 318-352-8072; www.natchitochesfalltour.com

Take city and Cane River tours of houses and plantations, or try the candle-light tour.

Second weekend in October.

WHERE TO STAY
★COMFORT INN

5362 Highway 6, Natchitoches, 318-352-7500, 800-228-5150;
59 rooms. Complimentary breakfast. Pool. $61-150

WHERE TO EAT
★★LANDING

530 Front St., Natchitoches, 318-352-1579; www.thelandingrestaurantandbar.com
Cajun. Lunch, dinner, Sunday brunch. Closed Monday. $16-35

★LASYONE MEAT PIE KITCHEN

622 Second St., Natchitoches, 318-352-3353; www.lasyones.com
American, Cajun. Breakfast, lunch, dinner. Closed Sunday. $16-35

★★MARINERS SEAFOOD & STEAK HOUSE

5948 Highway 1 Bypass, Natchitoches, 318-357-1220; www.marinersrestaurant.com
Seafood, steak. Dinner, Sunday brunch. $16-35

NEW IBERIA

See also Franklin, Lafayette

Located in the heart of Cajun country, New Iberia is home to a variety of attractions ranging from farmers markets to historic buildings (the city is home to the country's oldest rice mill) to the 200-acre Jungle Gardens. New Iberia is known for a few Louisiana classics: swamps, bayous and alligators. Visitors looking to add some spice to their trip can watch the bottling and packing operations at the McIlhenny Company Tabasco Factory and Company Store.

WHAT TO SEE
AVERY ISLAND

Seven miles southwest via Highway 14

Surrounded by a bayou, the island is a haven for colorful wildlife, including blue herons, white-tailed deer and small black bears. This unusual Eden is also where Tabasco sauce has been made for nearly 140 years.

BOULIGNY PLAZA

On Main Street in center of New Iberia

In the park are depictions of the history of the area as well as a gazebo, historic landmarks and a beautiful view along the bayou.

JUNGLE GARDENS

200 Center St., New Iberia Avery Island, 337-369-6243; www.junglegardens.org

Avery Island's most spectacular feature was developed by the late Edward Avery McIlhenny of Tabasco fame. Camellias, azaleas, irises and tropical plants, in season, form a beautiful display. Enormous flocks of egrets, cranes and herons, among other species, are protected here and may be seen in early spring and summer; ducks and other wild fowl can be spotted in winter. The Chinese Garden contains a fine Buddha dating from A.D. 1000.
Admission: adults $6.25, children $4.50. Daily.

KONRIKO RICE MILL AND COMPANY STORE

309 Ann St., New Iberia, 337-364-7242, 800-551-3245; www.conradricemill.com

Take a tour of the oldest rice mill in the U.S.; next door is a replica of the original company store, with antique fixtures and merchandise typical of Acadiana and Louisiana.
Monday-Saturday.

MCILHENNY COMPANY

Highway 329, Avery Island, 337-365-8173; www.tabasco.com

Spice up your day with a tour of the Tabasco factory and Country Store. The gift shop provides some good souvenir options. Monday-Saturday.

RIP VAN WINKLE GARDENS

5505 Rip Van Winkle Road, New Iberia, 337-359-8525; www.ripvanwinklegardens.com

Stroll through 20 acres of landscaped gardens and nature preserves. Also on the premises is the Victorian residence of 19th-century actor Joseph Jefferson. Stop in the restaurant and gift shop.
Admission: adults $10, children $8. Daily.

SHADOWS-ON-THE-TECHE

317 E. Main St., New Iberia, 337-369-6446; www.shadowsontheteche.org

The red brick and white-pillared Greek Revival house was built on the banks of the Bayou Teche in 1834 by sugar planter David Weeks. Home to four generations of his family, it served as the center of an antebellum plantation system. The house was restored and its celebrated gardens created in the 1920s by the builder's great-grandson, Weeks Hall, who used the estate to entertain such celebrities as D. W. Griffith, Anaïs Nin and Walt Disney. The house is surrounded by three acres of azaleas, camellias and massive oaks draped in Spanish moss. It's a National Trust for Historic Preservation property.
Daily 9 a.m.-4:30 p.m.

WHERE TO STAY
★★HOLIDAY INN

2915 Highway 14, New Iberia, 337-367-1201, 800-465-4329; www.holidayinn.com
177 rooms. Restaurant, bar. $61-150

WHERE TO EAT
★LITTLE RIVER INN

833 E. Main St., New Iberia, 337-367-7466; www.poorboysriversideinn.com
Cajun, seafood. Lunch, dinner. Closed Sunday. $16-35

NEW ORLEANS

See also Baton Rouge, Kenner, Slidell
New Orleans is a beguiling combination of old and new, and in the wake of Hurricane Katrina, it has become a symbol of both hardship and rebirth. Though many homes, businesses and historic landmarks were heavily damaged by the 2005 storm, Katrina failed to wash away the city's spirit, charm or storied past.

Named for the Duc d'Orleans, Regent of France, New Orleans was founded by the French, ruled by the Spanish, purchased by the United States and captured by Union forces—all in the span of about 100 years. Of course, this eclectic history has helped make New Orleans a must-see for travelers in search of great food (served with a side of music), gorgeous architecture and the colorful characters who call the "Big Easy" home.

New Orleans has a reputation for being seductive and decadent, magical and sensual. That reputation is still well deserved, even after Katrina—and subsequent broken levees—flooded the city and destroyed some of its most precious institutions. Parts of New Orleans are still recovering, but many of the city's historic districts did not flood—a hint of mercy in the midst of so much destruction. These areas, including the French Quarter and the Garden District, have been open for business for a while now, and visitors are rushing in to enjoy the famous cuisine and jazz and blues clubs that make New Orleans one of the country's most beloved destinations.

Food rules here. Locals believe they have the best cuisine in the nation, much of it influenced by Cajun and Creole cultures that flourish in Louisiana and featuring seafood from the Gulf of Mexico. Do not leave without eating a shrimp or hot sausage po' boy, gumbo, shrimp rémoulade, white-chocolate bread pudding and a few beignets.

Visitors also come for the amazing nightlife. Walking down Bourbon Street, you will hear music pouring from every doorway: Cajun, zydeco, jazz. The bottom line is that no one comes home from New Orleans disappointed.

WHAT TO SEE
AMPERSAND

1100 Tulane Ave., New Orleans, 504-587-3737; www.clubampersand.com
Sophisticatedly naughty, this converted bank building features two levels, two bars, a huge dance floor, an outdoor courtyard and several sitting rooms, one in the former bank vault. Appealing to serious clubbers of all stripes, Ampersand offers DJs from around the world spinning music of the techno and industrial persuasion.
Friday-Saturday at 11 p.m.

AUDUBON AQUARIUM OF THE AMERICAS

1 Canal St., Riverfront Area, New Orleans, 504-861-2537, 800-774-7394; www.auduboninstitute.org

True to its name, this aquarium houses more than 10,000 aquatic creatures from all areas of the Americas. For total immersion without getting wet, walk through the aquatic tunnel in the Caribbean Reef section or catch a glimpse of a rare white alligator through the River View window in the Mississippi section. Boasting the largest collection of jellyfish in the world, the aquarium also houses penguins, sea otters and sharks—brave visitors can touch one. Combination Aquarium/Zoo, Aquarium/IMAX and Aquarium/IMAX/Zoo tickets are available.

Sunday-Tuesday 10 a.m.-5 p.m., Friday-Saturday 10 a.m.-7 p.m.

AUDUBON NATURE INSTITUTE

6500 Magazine St., New Orleans, 504-861-2537; 800-774-7394;
www.auduboninstitute.org

This 400-acre park designed by the Olmsted brothers is nestled between St. Charles Avenue and the Mississippi River and is surrounded by century-old live oak trees. The park features a par-62 18-hole golf course, bicycle and jogging paths and tennis courts.

Daily.

AUDUBON ZOO

6500 Magazine St., New Orleans, 504-861-2537, 800-774-7394;
www.auduboninstitute.org/zoo

More than 1,800 animals from every continent call this top-ranked zoo, part of the Audubon Nature Institute, home. Check out kangaroos from Australia, llamas from South America, white tigers from Asia and zebras from Africa, all in naturalistic habitats. Indigenous furry, feathered and scaly creatures are featured at the Louisiana Swamp Exhibit. You can get up close during the sea lion show and in the Embraceable Zoo. Discovery walks, the EarthLab and other interactive programs make the zoo an educational experience. (Just don't tell the kids.) Combination Zoo/Aquarium and Zoo/Aquarium/IMAX tickets are available.

Daily 10 a.m-4 p.m.

BAYOU BARRIERE GOLF COURSE

7427 Highway 23, Belle Chasse, 504-394-9500; www.bayoubarriere.com

This course is fairly flat but strives to offer variety from hole to hole. The fairways differ in width and water comes into play, but at different points in each hole. The prices are reasonable, and the course is open year-round. With 27 holes onsite, the facility accommodates high levels of traffic well, and you can explore various combinations of holes to find your favorite 18. The most challenging nine is the third, as the tee boxes are mostly on the course's levee.

BEAUREGARD-KEYES HOUSE AND GARDEN

1113 Chartres St., New Orleans, 504-523-7257; www.neworleansmuseums.com

This Greek Revival, Louisiana-raised cottage was restored by its former owner, the novelist Frances Parkinson Keyes. Confederate Army General Pierre G. T. Beauregard lived here for more than a year following the Civil War. Exhibits include the main house and servant quarters, which together form a handsome shaded courtyard. (Keyes actually lived informally in the servant quarters, which are filled with her books, antiques and family heirlooms.) To the side of the main house is a formal garden (visible from both Chartres and Ursulines streets) that is part of the guided tour conducted by costumed docents.

Admission: adults $5, seniors $4, children $2. Monday-Saturday 10 a.m.-3 p.m.

BOURBON STREET

French Quarter, New Orleans, 504-525-5801; www.bourbonstreetexperience.com

No place in the world can match Bourbon Street for round-the-clock fun. With elegant hotels next door to garish strip clubs, Bourbon Street contains the ever-beating heart of the French Quarter. Visit its shops and restaurants in the daytime if you're not up for the always-rowdy nighttime crowds. But if you're visiting the Big Easy to let the good times roll, there's no better place to start a night of rambunctious partying.

THE CABILDO

701 Chartres St., New Orleans, 504-523-3939; www.friendsofthecabildo.org

Part of the Louisiana State Museum, the Cabildo offers exhibits on life in early New Orleans, including plantation and slave life. Construction was completed in 1799 and the building housed the city council and the Louisiana Supreme Court at various times. In 1803, the transfer of the Louisiana Purchase took place here. The museum covers diverse topics such as burial customs, women's roles in the South and immigrants' fate.

Admission: adults $12, seniors $10, children free. Tuesday-Sunday 10 a.m.-1.30 p.m.

CATHEDRAL GARDEN

615 Pere Antoine Alley, New Orleans, 504-525-9585; www.stlouiscathedral.org

The monument in the center of the garden was erected in honor of French marines who died while nursing New Orleans' citizens during a yellow fever outbreak. Picturesque, narrow Pirate's Alley, bordering the garden, is a favorite spot for painters. On the Alley is the house in which William Faulkner lived when he wrote his first novel. The garden is also called St. Anthony's Square in memory of a beloved priest known as Pere Antoine. Daily.

CEMETERY & VOODOO HISTORY TOUR

334-B Royal St., New Orleans, 504-947-2120; www.tourneworleans.com

The two-hour tour features St. Louis Cemetery No. 1, the oldest and most significant burial ground in New Orleans; visits to a practicing voodoo priestess at her temple; Congo Square, the site of early slave gatherings; and a stop at the home of legendary Voodoo Queen Marie Laveau.

Monday-Saturday 10 a.m., 1 p.m., Sunday 10 a.m.

CENTER OF BANKING

Royal Street, New Orleans

The old Louisiana State Bank was designed in 1821 by Benjamin Latrobe, one of the architects of the Capitol in Washington. The 343 Royal building was completed in the early 1800s for the old Bank of the United States. The old Bank of Louisiana, 334 Royal, was built in 1826; it is now the French Quarter Police Station.

CITY PARK

1 Palm Drive, New Orleans, 504-482-4888; www.neworleanscitypark.com

The 1,500 acres of City Park provide room for all sorts of family fun. Step into Storyland to glide down the dragon-flame slide, board Captain Hook's ship or engage with actors portraying storybook characters. Hop aboard one of two minitrains and mount a steed on one of the oldest wooden carousels in the U.S. Get some spray from Popp Fountain, get a license and catch some fish in one of the many lagoons, or bask in Marconi Meadow and catch some rays. Admire a range of architectural styles in various buildings and bridges. Appreciate the natural beauty in the Botanical Garden and see more mature oak trees than any other place in the world. Get active and rent a boat or play tennis, golf or softball in the park's facilities. The options are endless.

CONTEMPORARY ARTS CENTER

900 Camp St., New Orleans, 504-528-3805; www.cacno.org

Established in 1976, the Contemporary Arts Center (CAC) is housed in an award-winning building that was renovated in 1990. Each year, CAC hosts as many as two dozen exhibitions in its 10,000 square feet of gallery space. Taking a multidisciplinary approach, the center promotes art forms as traditional as painting, photography and sculpture, and as diverse as performance art, dance, music and video. Artists Studio Days offer children and their elders a glimpse into the creative process. The Dog & Pony Theater company-in-residence presents workshops, rehearsals and dance and theater productions. CAC also hosts the annual Black Theater Festival during the first two weekends in October.

Tuesday-Sunday 11 a.m.-5 p.m.

CRESCENT CITY FARMERS MARKET

700 Magazine St., New Orleans, 504-861-4488, 504-495-1459; www.crescentcityfarmersmarket.org

Choose the day and location to suit your needs. At this market, regional vendors offer fresh produce, seafood, baked goods and other edibles, as well as cut flowers and bedding plants. Each location offers frequent cooking demonstrations with area chefs and a variety of food-related events. Market founders promote sound ecological and economic development in the greater New Orleans area.

The Tuesday Market takes place between Levee and Broadway in the parking lot of Uptown Square, at 200 Broadway from 10 a.m. to 1 p.m. The Wednesday Market is between French Market Place and Governor Nicholls Street from 10 a.m. to 2 p.m. The Thursday Market sits on the renovated American Can Company residential development at 3700 Orleans Avenue from 3 to 7 p.m. The Saturday Market is in the downtown neighborhood

THE FRENCH QUARTER

New Orleans practically begs visitors to stroll her scenic streets, and the city's most prestigious addresses are all on Royal Street, which is lined with historic buildings, fine restaurants and some of the nation's most exclusive antique shops. The most refined street in the Quarter, Royal is only a block south and a world away from party-hearty Bourbon Street. Even if you cannot afford to buy the Louis XVI carved mahogany loveseat, this strip is a great place to wander and window-shop.

A good starting point for exploring this part of New Orleans is behind St. Louis Cathedral, a block up from Jackson Square, where a lush collection of tropical plants fills the compact St. Anthony's Garden. Follow the alleyway upriver to 324 Pirates Alley, where author William Faulkner lived in 1925. His fans still flock to that corner, now the home of a popular bookstore featuring the works of this bard of Southern letters. Continue down Pirates Alley and away from the river along St. Peter to return to Royal Street.

Near St. Peter and Royal streets, the brick LaBranche buildings, with their dramatic cast-iron galleries, were built starting in 1835. Proceed upriver along Royal Street. Beyond Toulouse Street, the 1798 Court of Two Lions at 541 Royal Street features marble lions atop the entry posts. The same architect built the neighboring house (527-533 Royal Street) in 1792. Now home to the Historic New Orleans Collection, the house museum displays exhibits on the city's history.

Between St. Louis and Conti streets, the huge State Supreme Court Building dominates the block; the baroque edifice is made of white Georgia marble. Further down, between Conti and Bienville streets, the block-long Monteleone Hotel is a posh, 600-room home-away-from-home.

Head north on Iberville to Bourbon Street, pass restaurants, nightclubs and saloons, and then drop down St. Ann Street back to Royal, where the Café des Exiles marks the historical gathering spot of French refugees from the Revolution. Further downriver, a detour down Dumaine lands you in front of Madame John's Legacy (632 Dumaine, 504-568-6968). This French cottage was one of the few structures to survive the fire that destroyed most of the city in 1794. Return to Royal and proceed downriver to the cornstalk fence at 915 Royal, a site that draws onlookers and carriage tours that stop to admire the intricate tasseled design of the ironwork.

The Gallier House at 1118-32 Royal Street was built in the 1860s by acclaimed local architect James Gallier Jr. Then head down Ursulines Avenue to the old Ursulines Convent at the corner of Chartres Street. The 1745 convent is among the oldest structures in the city. Continue down Ursulines toward the river to visit the French Market, or return upriver along Chartres Street to get back to Jackson Square.

known as the Warehouse District (originally known as the American Sector), at Magazine and Girod streets, at 700 Magazine Street from 8 a.m. to noon.

DESTREHAN PLANTATION
13034 River Road, Destrehan, 985-764-9315, 877-453-2095;
www.destrehanplantation.org
Built in 1787, this is the oldest plantation house left intact in the lower Mississippi Valley, with ancient live oaks adorning the grounds. Daily.

ENTERGY IMAX THEATRE
1 Canal St., New Orleans, 504-581-4327, 800-774-7394;
www.auduboninstitute.org/imax
Adjacent to the Audubon Aquarium of the Americas and part of the Audubon Nature Institute, this theater showcases several films at a time in larger-than-

life format and hosts a summer film festival. Combination IMAX/Aquarium and IMAX/Aquarium/Zoo tickets are available. Daily.

F & F BOTANICA

801 N. Broad St., New Orleans, 504-482-9142

The oldest and largest spiritual supply store in the French Quarter, F & F Botanica offers herbs, oils, potions, candles, incense—whatever you need to enhance your spiritual practice. The store offers free spiritual consultations to help you figure out how to find what your spirit seeks. At least one staffer is sure to speak Spanish to help customers who share owner Felix Figueroa's heritage.

Monday-Saturday 8 a.m.-6 p.m.

FAIR GROUNDS RACE COURSE

1751 Gentilly Blvd., New Orleans, 504-944-5515; www.fairgroundsracecourse.com

The horses have been darting out of the starting gates at this Mid-City race-track since 1852, making it the oldest track still operating in the United States. When you're not placing bets and watching the fast-paced action, wander through the Racing Hall of Fame, which honors 110 of the sport's most revered, such as legendary jockey Bill Shoemaker and Duncan Kenner, the founding father of racing in this country. The 145-acre facility also hosts the city's annual Jazz and Heritage Festival.

Mid-November-March.

FRENCH MARKET

800 Decatur St. New Orleans, 504-525-4544; www.cafedumonde.com

A farmers market for nearly two centuries, the market is home to the popular Cafe du Monde, a famous coffee stand specializing in café au lait (half coffee with chicory, half hot milk) and beignets (square-shaped doughnuts sprinkled with powdered sugar). The café never closes (except December 25), and café au lait and beignets are inexpensive. The downriver end of the French Market houses booths in which produce is sold. Daily.

FRENCH QUARTER

From Canal Street to Esplanade Avenue, and from Decatur Street on the Mississippi River to Rampart Street, 504-636-1020; www.frenchquarter.com

Whether you are in New Orleans to party, shop till you drop, soak up Creole (or voodoo) charms, sample Southern hospitality, delve into history or admire architecture, you can find what you want in the Vieux Carré. The oldest and only remaining French and Spanish settlement in the country, the Quarter offers sights, sounds, tastes and treasures to suit every interest.

FRENCH QUARTER WALKING TOURS

www.frenchquarter.com

Both the Friends of Cabildo (*1850 House Museum Store, 523 St. Ann St. on Jackson Square, 504-523-3939*) and the French Quarter Visitor Center (*419 Decatur St., -504-589-2636*) offer walking tours that cover the Quarter's history and architecture. The pace is not strenuous, but factor in the heat and humidity and dress accordingly. Licensed guides conduct the two-hour

Friends of Cibaldo tours, while interpreters from the National Park Service lead a 90-minute free tour, which is restricted to the first 25 people who show up each day. A Cibaldo tour ticket entitles you to a discount on items at the 1850 House Museum Store.
Daily.

GALLIER HOUSE
1132 Royal St., New Orleans, 504-525-5661; www.hgghh.org
For a slice of pre-Civil War life in New Orleans, check out the architect James Gallier Jr.'s home, which he designed for himself in 1857. Thoroughly modern for its time, the house boasts hot-and-cold running water and an indoor bathroom. Painstakingly restored, the house is one of New Orleans' more beautiful historic landmarks.
Monday-Friday 10 a.m.-4 p.m.

THE GARDEN DISTRICT
Magazine Street and Washington Avenue, New Orleans
Once the social center of New Orleans American (as opposed to Creole) aristocracy, the district has beautiful Greek Revival and Victorian houses with palms, magnolias and enormous live oaks on the spacious grounds in this area. Numerous celebrities have homes here in the beautiful Garden District.
A walking tour of the Garden District, conducted by a national park ranger, departs from First Street and St. Charles Avenue (by appointment).

GRAY LINE BUS TOURS
1 Toulouse St., New Orleans, 504-569-1401, 800-535-7786; www.graylineneworleans.com
View all of New Orleans' must-see sites from the comfort of an air-conditioned bus. Besides its comprehensive city tour, Gray Line offers numerous other sightseeing options, including tours of plantations, swamps and bayous, the Garden District and cemeteries. An off-the-beaten-path trek takes you to such places as the childhood neighborhood of jazz great Louis Armstrong and Faubourg Marigny, one of the earliest Creole suburbs, where the striking architecture will surely grab your attention. The company now offers a Hurricane Katrina tour, highlighting the city before, during and after the storm.

GRIFFIN FISHING CHARTERS
2629 Privateer Blvd., Lafitte, 800-741-1340; www.neworleansfishintours.com
Specializing in shallow-sea fishing for speckled trout and redfish in saltwater marshes from Lafitte down to the Gulf of Mexico, owners Raymond and Belinda Griffin can also set you up for a day of deep-sea fishing. Or combine two pursuits: Play golf in the morning and then head out to the water for some fishing. Prices include an out-of-state fishing license, rods, reels, bait, tackle, ice, po' boy sandwiches, soda, water and the cleaning and packaging of caught fish. Package plans that include lodging, meals and transportation are also available.

HARRAH'S NEW ORLEANS

8 Canal St., New Orleans, 504-533-6000, 800-847-5299; www.harrahs.com

The oldest of New Orleans's land-based casinos, Harrah's is 115,000 square feet of nonstop gambling fun. More than 100 tables offer 10 different games, including poker, craps, baccarat and roulette. You can play the slots for a penny, a dollar or up to $500. Live jazz, Creole cuisine, Mardi Gras décor and an attached hotel round out the experience. Daily.

HERMANN-GRIMA HOUSE

820 St. Louis St., New Orleans, 504-525-5661; www.hgghh.org

The Georgian design reflects the post-Louisiana Purchase American influence on traditional French and Spanish styles in the Quarter; the furnishings typify a well-to-do lifestyle during the period of 1831-1860. The restored house has elegant interiors, two landscaped courtyards, slave quarters, a stable and a working period kitchen. Speaking of the kitchen, check out Creole cooking demonstrations on the open hearth.
Monday-Friday.

HISTORIC NEW ORLEANS COLLECTION

533 Royal St., New Orleans, 504-523-4662; www.hnoc.org

Established in 1966 by local collectors General and Mrs. Kemper Williams, the Collection comprises several historic buildings that house a museum and comprehensive research center for state and local history. The main exhibition gallery presents changing displays on Louisiana's history and culture. The 1792 Merieult House features a pictorial history of New Orleans and Louisiana; the Williams Residence shows the elegant lifestyle of the Collection's founders. Changing exhibits grace several galleries. There is also a touch tour for the visually impaired.
Tuesday-Saturday 9:30 a.m.-4:30 p.m.

HOUSE OF BLUES

225 Decatur St., New Orleans, 504-310-4999; www.hob.com

Even in the eye-catching French Quarter, it is hard to miss the gaudy, neon-lit entrance to the House of Blues. Past the wildly decorated porch, you will hear live music ranging from Cajun to country and reggae to rock 'n' roll, not to mention pure, soulful blues. The Sunday Gospel brunch is justly famous and surprisingly inexpensive.

THE HOWLIN' WOLF

907 S. Peters St., New Orleans, 504-522-9653; www.howlin-wolf.com

Arguably one of New Orleans' best clubs, the Howlin' Wolf offers up live music of all sorts. Sometimes it rocks and sometimes it's got the blues, but it is always a great place to see a show. Katrina prompted the club to move just down the street from its old digs to a venue with more space. The Howlin' Wolf is popular with college students and those looking for original music and up-and-coming acts. Check out the acoustic open-mike nights on Mondays.

DEMYSTIFYING NEW ORLEANS-SPEAK

Cajun: Nickname for a Louisianan descended from the French-speaking people who began migrating to Louisiana from Nova Scotia (then Acadia) in 1755.

Creole: A person descended from early French or Spanish settlers of the U.S. Gulf states who preserves their speech and culture.

Creole: Highly seasoned food typically prepared with rice, okra, tomatoes and peppers.

Fais-do-do: When Cajuns partied in days gone by, they would bring their children along, bundle them in their blankets at bedtime, put them to sleep and party into the wee hours. Fais-do-do means "put the kids to sleep."

Faubourg: (FOE-burg) Faubourgs are neighborhoods near the French Quarter. Literally, Faubourg means "suburb."

French Quarter: The 90 square blocks that used to be the entire city of New Orleans and today encompasses 2,700 European- and Creole-style buildings.

Gris-gris: Means "X marks the spot." An X on a tomb indicates a voodoo spell, like that on the tomb of the mysterious Marie Laveau, New Orleans hairdresser-turned-legendary-voodoo-queen.

Gumbo ya-ya: Everybody talking at once.

Jazz: Louis Armstrong said, "If you gotta ask, you'll never know." With apologies to Armstrong, jazz mixes African and Creole rhythms with European styles. Irish, Germans and Italians added the brass.

Krewe: Wealthy 19th-century New Orleans citizens who bankrolled Mardi Gras balls and parades were members of carnival organizations with names like Rex (King of the Carnival). Members were called Krewe of Rex, a variation of the word crew.

Pass a good time: Live it up.

Vieux Carré: Old Square or Old Quarter, referring to the French Quarter.

Voodoo: A combination of the West African Yoruba religion and the Catholicism of French colonists in Haiti. It means "god, spirit or insight" in the Fon language of Dahomey, a former country in West Africa on the Gulf of Guinea.

Yat: A citizen. This term comes from the Ninth Ward greeting, "Where yat?"

JACKSON BREWERY

600 Decatur St., New Orleans, 504-566-7245; www.jacksonbrewery.com

This historic brewery was converted into a large retail, food and entertainment complex with 75 shops and restaurants, outdoor seating and a riverfront promenade.

Monday-Saturday 10 a.m.-8 p.m., Sunday 10 a.m.-7 p.m.

JACKSON SQUARE

615 Pere Antoine Alley, New Orleans; www.jackson-square.com

Bordered by Chartres, St. Peter, Decatur, and St. Ann streets, this area was established as a drill field in 1721 and was called the Place d'Armes until 1848, when it was renamed for Andrew Jackson, hero of the Battle of New Orleans. The statue of Jackson, the focal point of the square, was the world's first equestrian statue with more than one hoof unsupported; the American sculptor, Clark Mills, had never seen an equestrian statue and therefore did not know that the pose was thought impossible. Today, the square and surrounding plaza is one of the best places in the Quarter to catch your breath, people-watch and listen to jazz. It attracts local artists, food vendors and street performers such as mimes, magicians and musicians.

JEAN BRAGG ANTIQUES & GALLERY

600 Julia St., New Orleans, 504-895-7375; www.jeanbragg.com

The focus of this shop and gallery is on Louisianan and Southern art, especially paintings, watercolors and etchings of Louisiana and the French Quarter. Specializing in George Ohr pottery and Newcomb College pottery and craft work, the shop also offers museum-quality pieces from the late 19th and early 20th centuries. Discover vintage linens, jewelry and glassware along with Victorian furniture.

Monday-Saturday 10 a.m.-5 p.m.

JOHN JAMES AUDUBON RIVERBOAT

2 Canal St., New Orleans, 504-586-8777, 800-233-2628; www.steamboatnatchez.com

The riverboat John James Audubon provides river transportation between the Aquarium of the Americas and the Audubon Zoo seven miles upriver, round-trip or one-way; return may be made via the St. Charles Avenue Streetcar. The round-trip ticket price includes admission to both the Audubon Zoo and the Aquarium of the Americas.

LAFAYETTE SQUARE

6000 St. Charles Ave., New Orleans

The square features statues of Benjamin Franklin, Henry Clay and John Mc-Donough.

LAFITTE'S BLACKSMITH SHOP

941 Bourbon St., New Orleans

This popular bar is arguably the oldest French-style building left in the French Quarter. (After two fires in the 1700s destroyed much of the city, the Spanish style dominated rebuilding efforts.) Local lore has it that the original smithy, built sometime before 1772, served as a front for pirate Jean Lafitte's more notorious activities. The bar retains a dark, historical feel, although the local and exotic patrons lighten the atmosphere. Daily.

LAKE PONTCHARTRAIN

Lakeshore Drive, New Orleans

This is a favorite spot of locals for picnicking, fishing, running, cycling, skating or simply watching sailboats pass by. Daily.

LE CHAT NOIR

715 St. Charles Ave., New Orleans, 504-581-5812; www.cabaretlechatnoir.com

Get decked out (that is, no jeans or shorts) to check out the Cat (chat noir means "black cat") for an ever-changing schedule of cabaret, live theater and musical performances. The Bar Noir is a cozier room, perfect for a pre-show cocktail (try the house specialty, the Black Cat) or for quiet conversation with friends.

LONGUE VUE HOUSE & GARDENS

7 Bamboo Road, New Orleans, 504-488-5488; www.longuevue.com

A grand city estate furnished with original English and American antiques is on eight acres of formal and picturesque gardens. Plus there are changing exhibits in galleries and seasonal horticultural displays in the gardens. Admission: adults $10, students $5, children free. Monday-Saturday 10 a.m.-4:30 p.m., Sunday 1-5 p.m.

LOUIS ARMSTRONG PARK
800 block of N. Rampart St., New Orleans
To the left of the entrance—built to resemble a Mardi Gras float—is a stand of very old live oak trees. This area was originally known as Congo Square, where slaves were permitted to congregate on Sunday afternoons; it was also the scene of voodoo rites. After the Civil War, the square was named for General P. G. T. Beauregard. Louis Armstrong Park, which includes an extensive water garden that focuses upon a larger-than-life-size statue of Armstrong, was expanded from the original square and contains the municipal auditorium and the Theatre of the Performing Arts.

LOUISIANA STATE MUSEUM
751 Chartres St., New Orleans, 504-568-6968, 800-568-6968; lsm.crt.state.la.us
The museum comprises five properties in the French Quarter city and three sites outside of the city. Though only the residence is open to the public (a kitchen and servants' quarters complete the complex), Madame John's Legacy is a fine example of Creole architecture. Built in 1789 after the great fire of 1788, it is notable for surviving the subsequent 1795 fire. The 1850 House, named for the year it was built, holds an authentic collection of period furnishings. The Old U.S. Mint was the only mint in the country that printed currency for both the Confederacy and the U.S. government. The mint now holds state and local research materials and exhibits.
Admission: adults $6, seniors $5, children free. Tuesday-Saturday 9 a.m.-5 p.m., Sunday noon-5 p.m.

LOUISIANA SUPERDOME
Sugar Bowl Drive, New Orleans, 504-587-3663, 800-756-7074; www.superdome.com
The Dome is home field for the New Orleans Saints, Tulane University Green Wave and has hosted a variety of other sports events, including college baseball and the 2003 NCAA men's basketball Final Four. The annual Endymion Extravaganza Mardi Gras Parade and Party happens here, as well as the New Orleans Home & Garden Show, the Boat & Sport Fishing Show, the Kid's Fair & Expo and numerous concerts and other special events. In the immediate aftermath of Hurricane Katrina, the Superdome became a temporary home to thousands of people who had had to evacuate the rising floodwaters.

LOUISIANA'S CHILDREN'S MUSEUM
420 Julia St., New Orleans, 504-523-1357; www.lcm.org
Catering to toddlers and the young at heart, this museum encourages hands-on exploration. Kids can take a ride in a simulated police cruiser in the Safety First area, anchor a newscast in the Kidswatch Studio or experience bayou life in the Cajun Cottage. Other areas include Waterworks, Big City Port and Art Trek.
Children under 16 must be accompanied by an adult. Tuesday-Saturday 9:30 a.m.-4:30 p.m., Sunday noon-4:30 p.m.

LOYOLA UNIVERSITY

6363 St. Charles Ave., New Orleans, 504-865-3240, 800-465-9652; www.loyno.edu
Founded in 1912, Loyola is now home to some 3,500 students. Buildings on the 21-acre campus are Tudor Gothic in style. Daily.

M. S. RAU ANTIQUES

630 Royal St., New Orleans, 504-523-5660, 800-544-9440; www.rauantiques.com
Founded in 1912, this family-owned and family-run business is so confident of its merchandise that it offers a 125-percent guarantee on all in-store purchases. Internationally known names such as Paul Revere, Meissen, Faberg, Wedgwood, Tiffany and Chippendale are represented in the 25,000-square-foot showroom and extensive catalog. You can also pick up fabulous diamonds, jewelry, silver and objects d'art among the vast array of American and European antiques.
Monday-Saturday 9 a.m.-5:15 p.m.

MAGAZINE STREET

Magazine Street, New Orleans, 504-342-4435, 866-679-4764;
www.magazinestreet.com
Fun and funky, Magazine Street offers six miles of clothing retailers, antique establishments, gift shops, eateries and more. Most of the businesses are housed in 19th-century buildings or brick-faced cottages, which help the area maintain its other-worldly charm. You can stroll from the French Quarter through Magazine Street to the Audubon Zoo, picking up some jewelry, a piece of furniture, a book or a bite to eat along the way. Make a point to stop off at the Magazine Arcade, a mini-mall that houses eclectic shops offering antique music boxes and musical instruments, period medical equipment, dolls and their furnishings, as well as antique household items for real people.
Most shops open daily 10 a.m.-5 p.m.

MAISON LEMONNIER

640 Royal St., New Orleans
Built in 1811 and sometimes called the "Skyscraper," this was the first building in the Vieux Carré more than two stories high. This house was used as the setting of George W. Cable's novel Sieur George. Notice the YLR, for Yves LeMonnier, worked into the grillwork.

MARDI GRAS WORLD

233 Newton St., New Orleans, 504-361-7821, 800-362-8213;
www.mardigrasworld.com
For a fascinating look at where about 75 percent of Mardi Gras props and floats are made, visit this unique establishment—the world's largest of its kind. You can try on costumes; watch painters, sculptors and carpenters at work; and tour rooms filled with props and Mardi Gras paraphernalia. The Kern family's business also provides floats and props for parades across the country.
Daily 9:30 a.m.-4:30 p.m.

KINGS, KREWES, BEADS AND BALLS

Mardi Gras is both a carnival and a holiday, the day before Ash Wednesday and the Lenten season of fasting and repentance. And contrary to what you might have seen on TV or read in the news, Fat Tuesday is more than the salacious frat-boy party you might imagine. It is a bash—a huge bash—but there are plenty of different ways to celebrate in New Orleans, especially when the party is as big as Mardi Gras. The Mardi Gras season begins on Twelfth Night—January 6, a time when the festive holiday season traditionally ends. In New Orleans, Twelfth Night kicks off a season of merriment. Festivities reach fever pitch 12 days before Mardi Gras and peak on the Saturday prior to Fat Tuesday, when the city celebrates with four days of non-stop jazz, food, drink and masked balls. Perhaps most closely associated with the celebrations—aside from mayhem in the French Quarter—are the colorful parades where marchers in elaborate costumes toss plastic purple, green and gold beads to onlookers. If your visit falls during Mardi Gras, be sure to hit the highlights: On Fat Tuesday, the French Quarter is alive with visitors in mysterious, beautiful masks. Accent Annex (1420 Sams Ave.), is a good place to check out costumes, beads, doubloons and other Mardi Gras items. Be sure to taste a king cake (a large cake, plain or filled with fruit or cream cheese, coated with purple, green and gold sugar and with a tiny plastic baby hidden inside). Traditionally, whoever gets the slice with the baby provides the king cake for the next party.

At 6 p.m. on Fat Monday, the King of Rex lands at the riverfront near the French Quarter. The mayor turns over the city to him for the duration of Mardi Gras. Earlier that day, the Zulu King arrives at the riverfront and the Zulus celebrate in Woldenberg Park. The meeting of the two kings is widely celebrated.

MEMORIAL HALL—CONFEDERATE MUSEUM

929 Camp St., New Orleans, 504-523-4522; www.confederatemuseum.com

Louisiana veterans of the War Between the States founded the Hall as a repository for artifacts and memorabilia of the Confederate side of the Civil War. Opened in 1891, it is the nation's longest continuously operating museum. The museum houses flags, swords and uniforms from both officers and foot soldiers as well as an extensive collection of photographs. The widow of Confederate president Jefferson Davis donated many family items.
Monday-Saturday 10 a.m.-4 p.m.

METAIRIE CEMETERY

5100 Pontchartrain Blvd., New Orleans, 504-486-6331; www.lakelawnmetairie.com

On the former grounds of the Metairie Race Course, the largest and loveliest of New Orleans' cemeteries is home to a variety of eye-catching memorials and mausoleums. Do not miss the pyramid and sphinx Brunswig mausoleum or the former gravesite of Storyville madam Josie Arlington, whose family had her body moved when tourists flocked to the crypt. But keep your eyes open: At least one of the numerous bronze statues is said to wander the grounds, a lovely setting for a quiet stroll. You can rent a taped audio tour or choose to drive around it.
Daily 8:30 a.m.-5 p.m.

MOONWALK

615 Pere Antoine Alley, New Orleans, www.neworleansonline.com

Running the length of the French Quarter along the river levee, the Moonwalk is a pedestrian thoroughfare that connects many attractions along the river, including the Aquarium of the Americas and paddleboat cruises, as well as shops and restaurants. Or you can park yourself on a bench and watch the crowds and the river flow by. Locals and tourists make this a popular venue for an evening stroll, especially on a clear, moonlit night.

MUSÉE CONTI HISTORICAL WAX MUSEUM
917 Rue Conti, New Orleans, 504-581-1993, 800-233-5405; www.get-waxed.com
More than 150 wax figures illustrate the history of the city in this amazing—and sometimes eerie—museum. Catch Napoleon Bonaparte in his bath, Voodoo Queen Marie Laveau and her dancers and Duke Ellington playing some jazz. The figures are painstakingly constructed (even clean-shaven men have stubble) using a process that makes them seem nearly life-like, and they are set in historically accurate tableaux.
Monday, Friday 10 a.m.-4 p.m.

NATIONAL D-DAY MUSEUM
945 Magazine St., New Orleans, 504-527-6012; www.ddaymuseum.org
Opened on June 6, 2000, the 16,000 square feet of gallery space houses exhibits that trace the political and economic events leading up to the D-Day invasion in 1944. Founded by the late historian and author Stephen Ambrose, the museum offers oral histories of the men and women who participated, as well as rare film footage that helps bring World War II to life. Free lunchbox lectures on Wednesdays give insight into specific topics or personalities.
Daily 9 a.m.-5 p.m.

NEW ORLEANS BOTANICAL GARDEN
1 Palm Drive, New Orleans, 504-483-9386
This beautiful public garden lost most of its collection when Hurricane Katrina landed, but it opened again to the public in March of 2006, and flowers and plants are blooming once more.
Admission: adults $6, children $3. Tuesday-Sunday 10 a.m.-4:30 p.m.

NEW ORLEANS GHOST TOUR
625 St. Phillip St., New Orleans, 504-861-2727, 888-644-6787;
www.neworleansghosttour.com
New Orleans might never look the same after you've heard tales of her ghostly past on this walking tour. Hear about the mad butcher—who may have butchered more than beef—the sultan reportedly buried alive and other supernatural stories that will leave you with goose bumps.

NEW ORLEANS HISTORIC VOODOO MUSEUM
724 Dumaine, St., New Orleans, 504-680-0128; www.voodoomuseum.com
Marie Laveau reigned as voodoo queen of New Orleans throughout much of the 19th century. The Voodoo Museum displays her portrait and memorabilia. Although it sells the stereotypical voodoo supplies, the museum also offers serious exhibits on voodoo history and its artifacts. You can also purchase your own gris-gris bag filled with herbs, bone and charms to bring luck or love into your life.
Daily 10 a.m.-sunset.

YOU CAN'T KEEP A GOOD MAN DOWN
(BUT MAYBE YOU SHOULD)

The cemeteries of New Orleans tell a fascinating story of the city's history, geology and culture. Because the city lies below sea level, the area's earliest residents had to engineer a unique burial system. A hole dug for a six-foot grave would fill with six feet of water, causing caskets to float. Rocks placed in and on top of the coffins to weigh them down worked until a rainstorm occurred, causing the water level to rise and popping the airtight coffin right out of the ground. Eventually, large holes were drilled into the underside of the coffin so it would quickly fill with water and sink. This method, too, was abandoned, due in part to the painful sound of loved ones gurgling their way down to their final resting places.

Meanwhile, Esteban Miro, an early governor of the city, had introduced the wall vault burial system that was popular in Spain for those who wanted to be buried above ground. Economical vaults were stacked on top of one another, while wealthier families built large, ornate tombs with crypts, many of which looked like tiny mansions. Rows of tombs looked like streets, clusters of monuments looked like communities and cemeteries have thus become known as Cities of the Dead.

Several of New Orleans' 42 cemeteries offer tours. Each has its own story to tell: St. Louis Cemetery No. 1, commissioned in 1789, was the first to offer aboveground burials. Notables buried there include Homer Plessy (of Supreme Court case Plessy v. Ferguson fame) and Marie Laveau, New Orleans' mysterious voodoo queen. Lafayette Cemetery No. 1, laid out in 1833, figures prominently in Anne Rice's vampire books and was the film location for Interview with the Vampire. Metairie Cemetery has a broad range of architecture and is considered one of the most beautiful cemeteries in the world. It is the final resting place of nine Louisiana governors and notorious Storyville madam Josie Arlington.

Holt is the New Orleans oddity, a below-ground cemetery and perhaps the most touching of any cemetery in the city. A graveyard for indigents, the cemetery's graves are either unmarked or marked by a collection of poignant, handmade headstones. Buddy Bolden, the great early-20th-century jazz musician who spent the second half of his life in a mental institution, is buried here.

NEW ORLEANS HORNETS (NBA)

New Orleans Arena, 1501 Girod St., New Orleans, 504-301-4000;www.nba.com/hornets

The Hornets moved from Charlotte for the 2002-2003 NBA season to give New Orleans a National Basketball Association team for the first time since the Jazz moved to Utah in 1979. They play home games at the New Orleans Arena, where the Honeybees cheer them on and mascot Hugo the Hornet is a three-time NBA Mascot Slam Dunk Champion.

NEW ORLEANS MUSEUM OF ART

City Park, 1 Collins Diboll Circle, New Orleans, 504-658-4100; www.noma.org

Established in 1911, NOMA boasts more than 40,000 objects in its permanent collection. The strengths of the permanent collection lie in its photography and glassware exhibits, as well as notable collections of American, African, Japanese and French art, including works by Edgar Degas, who visited New Orleans in the early 1870s. World-class traveling exhibits, extensive children's programs and a sculpture garden, which opened in 2002 in the adjacent City Park, round out the attractions.

Admission: adults $8, students $7, children $4, children under 3 free.

Wednesday noon-8 p.m., Thursday-Sunday 10 a.m.-5 p.m.

NEW ORLEANS OPERA

1010 Common St., New Orleans, 504-529-2278, 800-881-4459;
www.neworleansopera.org

Operating from the Mahalia Jackson Theatre of the Performing Arts, the New Orleans Opera Association presents four operas each season, which runs from October through March. The association was founded in 1943 and stages high-quality performances of renowned operas as well as world premieres. (The 2003-2004 season opened with the world premiere of the Louisiana Purchase Opera.) English translations appear in subtitles above the stage.

NEW ORLEANS PHARMACY MUSEUM (LA PHARMACIE FRANCAISE)

514 Chartres St., New Orleans, 504-565-8027; www.pharmacymuseum.org

Louis Dufilho, the first licensed pharmacist in the U.S., operated an apothecary shop here from 1823 to 1855. The ground floor contains pharmaceutical memorabilia of the 1800s, such as apothecary jars filled with medicinal herbs and voodoo powders, surgical instruments, pharmacy fixtures and a black-and-rose Italian marble soda fountain dating back to 1855.
Admission: adults $5, seniors $4. Tuesday-Sunday 10 a.m.-5 p.m.

NEW ORLEANS SAINTS (NFL)

Louisiana Superdome, Sugar Bowl Drive, New Orleans, 504-731-1700;www.neworleanssaints.com

One of the few NFL teams that remains in its original city, the Saints joined the National Football League in 1967. The team plays home games in the Superdome, which also regularly hosts the Super Bowl, a game in which the Saints—lovingly called the "Ain'ts" by loyal but weary fans—have never played.

NEW ORLEANS SCHOOL OF COOKING & LOUISIANA GENERAL STORE

524 St. Louis St., New Orleans, 504-525-2665, 800-237-4841; www.nosoc.com

After a session at the School of Cooking, you will be a convert to Louisiana cuisine. Make a reservation for a two- or three-hour lunch class to learn the basics of Louisiana cooking and, even better, to sample the four dishes you prepare. An early 1800s-era converted molasses warehouse is home to the school and to the Louisiana General Store, where you can pick up ingredients, a cookbook and cooking utensils.

NEW ORLEANS STEAMBOAT COMPANY

2 Canal St., New Orleans, 504-586-8777, 800-233-2628; www.steamboatnatchez.com

Cruise from the heart of the French Quarter on the steamboat Natchez, the ninth steamer with that name. Launched in 1975, she's one of only six true steam-powered sternwheelers sailing on the Mississippi today. Cruises on the Natchez last two hours with an optional Creole lunch available for an additional fee. Each cruise features live narration of historical facts and highlights, jazz music in the main dining room and a calliope concert during boarding times. The Harbor/Jazz Cruises at 11:30 a.m. and 2:30 p.m. offer jazz by Duke Heitger and the Steamboat Stompers, while the 7 p.m. Dinner/Jazz Cruise features the world-renowned Dukes of Dixieland. The Dinner/Jazz Cruise offers buffet-style dining and indoor/outdoor seating. Cruises depart from the Toulouse Street Wharf.

OAK ALLEY PLANTATION
3645 Highway 18 (Great River Road), Vacherie, 225-265-2151, 800-442-5539; www.oakalleyplantation.com
This quintessential antebellum, Greek Revival 1839 plantation house has been featured in many films, including *Primary Colors* and *Interview with a Vampire*. An allée of 300-year-old live oaks leads to the mansion, which is surrounded by galleries supported by massive columns. The interior was remodeled in the 1930s with antiques and modern furnishings of the day. You have your choice of picnicking or dining at the onsite restaurant.
Admission: adult $15, students $7.50, children $4.50. Monday-Friday 10 a.m.-4 p.m., Saturday-Sunday 10 a.m.-5 p.m.

THE OLD U.S. MINT
400 Esplanade Ave., New Orleans, 504-568-6968; www.lsm.crt.state.la.us
Designed by William Strickland in 1835, the mint produced coins for both the U.S. and for the Confederate States. Today, the mint houses permanent exhibitions of jazz and the Louisiana State Museum's Historical Center, a research facility.
Tuesday-Sunday 9 a.m.-5 p.m.

PADDLE WHEELER CREOLE QUEEN AND RIVERBOAT CAJUN QUEEN
2 Canal St., New Orleans, 504-524-0814, 504-529-4567; www.creolequeen.com
The Creole Queen offers 2 1/2-hour sightseeing cruises to Chalmette National Historical Park, the site of the Battle of New Orleans, as well as three-hour dinner jazz cruises. The riverboat Cajun Queen offers harbor cruises from the Aquarium of the Americas.

PITOT HOUSE
1440 Moss St., New Orleans, 504-482-0312; www.pitothouse.org
This is one of the last remaining French colonial/West Indies-style plantation houses along Bayou St. John. Built in 1799, it was the residence of James Pitot, the first elected mayor of incorporated New Orleans. Inside the restored home you'll find antiques.
Admission: adults $7, students and children $5, children under 6 free.
Wednesday-Saturday 10 a.m.-3 p.m.

PONTALBA BUILDING
523 St. Anne St., New Orleans, 504-524-9118
Completed in 1850 and 1851 by the Baroness Pontalba to beautify the square, the building is still occupied and used as intended (with duplex apartments above ground-floor offices and shops). The buildings are now owned by the city and the Louisiana State Museum. The 1850 House is furnished in the manner of the period.
Tuesday-Sunday 9 a.m.-5 p.m.

THE PRESBYTERE

751 Chartres St., New Orleans, 504-568-6968, 800-568-6968; www.lsm.crt.state.la.us/presbex.htm

Built to house clergy serving the parish church, the Presbytere was never used for that purpose, thanks in part to a series of fires that kept it incomplete until 1813, when it was finished by the U.S. government. It is now a museum with a permanent exhibit on the history of Mardi Gras. The Presbytere, like the Cabildo, is part of the Louisiana State Museum complex. Tuesday-Sunday.

PRESERVATION HALL

726 St. Peter St., New Orleans, 504-522-2841; www.preservationhall.com

Since 1961, people have been warming the benches at this rustic music hall in the French Quarter for one reason: to hear traditional New Orleans jazz, which dates back to the early 1900s. The building is not much to look at, but do not let that deter you. You will sweat—no air-conditioning—and you will have a hard time finding a place to sit. But this place is worth it. The music here is enough to make you glad you came. Even if you're no jazzman, you will still want to nod your head to the beat at this swingin' joint. Bring the kids, too; the hall welcomes people of all ages.

Daily 8 p.m.-midnight.

RIVER CRUISES

2 Canal St., New Orleans, 504-586-8777, 800-233-2628; www.steamboatnatchez.com

Daily excursions depart from the riverfront.

RIVERFRONT STREETCAR LINE

504-248-3900; www.norta.com

Vintage streetcars follow a 1 1/2-mile route along the Mississippi riverfront from Esplanade past the French Quarter to the World Trade Center, Riverwalk, Convention Center and back.

RIVERWALK

1 Poydras St., New Orleans, 504-522-1555; www.riverwalkmarketplace.com

This 1/2-mile-long festival marketplace, converted from World's Fair pavilions, has more than 140 national and local shops, restaurants and cafés.

Monday-Saturday 10 a.m.-7 p.m., Sunday noon-6 p.m.

SAN FRANCISCO PLANTATION

2646 Highway 44 (River Road), Garyville, 985-535-2341, 888-322-1756; www.sanfranciscoplantation.org

You cannot miss this colorful mansion, a far cry from what most Americans imagine when they think of plantations. The house is a remarkable example of the "Steamboat Gothic" style with its Creole structure. Authentically restored, the interior features five decorated ceilings (two are original). The house was used as the setting of Frances Parkinson Keyes' novel Steamboat Gothic.

Daily 9:30 a.m.-4:40 p.m.

SHOPS AT CANAL PLACE

333 Canal St., New Orleans, 504-522-9200; www.theshopsatcanalplace.com

More than 50 stores, many of them high-end retailers, give this shopping center a lot of cachet. Saks Fifth Avenue anchors the mall, and Gucci, Kenneth Cole and Betsey Johnson contribute to the swanky vibe. Additional amenities include a fitness club and a post office. The Southern Repertory Theater stage is here, too.

Monday-Saturday 10 a.m.-7 p.m., Sunday noon-6 p.m.

SOUTHERN REGIONAL RESEARCH CENTER

1100 Robert E. Lee Blvd., New Orleans, 504-286-4200; www.ars.usda.gov

The center is part of the U.S. Department of Agriculture, which finds and develops new and improved uses for Southern farm crops. Guided tours are available by appointment.

Monday-Friday.

SOUTHERN REPERTORY THEATER

365 Canal St., New Orleans, 504-522-6545, 504-891-8332; www.southernrep.com

Permanently housed in The Shops at Canal Place mall since 1991, the Southern Repertory Theater (SRT) was founded in 1986 to promote Southern plays and playwrights. Plays by Southern luminaries such as Tennessee Williams, Pearl Cleage, Beth Henley and SRT founding member Rosary H. O'Neill form the basis of the theater's September-to-May season.

Days and times vary.

ST. BERNARD STATE PARK

501 St. Bernard Parkway, Braithwaite, 504-682-2101, 888-677-7823; www.lastateparks.com/stbernar

The park is approximately 358 acres near the Mississippi River, with many viewing points of the water and a network of artificial lagoons. Swimming, picnicking, a playground, trails and camping are all available. Daily.

ST. CHARLES AVENUE STREETCAR

6700 Plaza Drive, New Orleans, 504-827-7802; www.norta.com

The streetcars (never call them trolleys!) was added to the National Register of Historic Places in 1973. A ride is a quaint and relaxing way to view the varied architecture and exotic greenery of the aptly named Garden District. The 13.2-mile route can take you to tour Tulane University, drop you off at Audubon Park (where the zoo is located) and provide you with safe transport after imbibing in the French Quarter.

ST. LOUIS CATHEDRAL

615 Pere Antoine Alley, New Orleans, 504-525-9585; www.stlouiscathedral.org

The oldest continuously active cathedral in the United States, the St. Louis Cathedral is not much to look at. But its history is worth noting: it is the third church to stand on the site; the first was destroyed by a hurricane in 1722, and the second burned to the ground on Good Friday 1788. And in 2005, two large oaks fell during Hurricane Katrina and amputated a finger and a thumb of the statue of Jesus that stood near them. Stop inside for a chat with docents, who can tell you about the church's history, murals and windows (and about why the church is sinking). Daily.

TIPITINA'S

501 Napoleon Ave., New Orleans, 504-895-8477; www.tipitinas.com

Live music is what you find at Tip's—as the locals call it. The emphasis is on rock, but funk, Cajun and jazz all make the calendar. Tuesdays feature various local artists at the no-cover eighth-floor "Homegrown Nights," and Sundays often offer a $5 cover for the Cajun Fais-Do-Do.

Shows featuring nationally and locally known talent start at 10 p.m. Thursday-Sunday.

TULANE UNIVERSITY

6823 St. Charles Ave., New Orleans, 504-865-5000; www.tulane.edu

The 110-acre main Uptown campus offers art galleries and other exhibits. The Tulane University Medical Center, located downtown, includes the School of Medicine, the School of Public Health and Tropical Medicine and a 300-bed private hospital.

U.S. CUSTOM HOUSE

423 Canal St., New Orleans, Decatur and Canal Streets

Begun in 1848, interrupted by the Civil War and completed in 1881, the Greek Revival building with neo-Egyptian details was used in part as an office by Major General Benjamin "Spoons" Butler during Union occupation, and in part as a prison for Confederate soldiers. A great dome was planned but the excessive weight of the existing building caused the foundation to settle and the dome was never completed. (In 1940, the building had sunk 30 inches, while the street level had been raised three feet.) Of particular interest is the famed Marble Hall, an architectural wonder.

Monday-Friday.

WASHINGTON ARTILLERY PARK

Frenchman and Royal, New Orleans

Between the muddy Mississippi and elegant Jackson Square lies this park, named for the 141st Field Artillery, which has fought in every major conflict since the 1845 Mexican War. Broad steps serve as an amphitheater from which you can catch the escapades of the kids in the playground, the antics of the street performers, the lazy flow of the river or a great view of the French Quarter.

WHISKEY BLUE

333 Poydras St., New Orleans, 504-252-9444; www.whotels.com

Located in the nouveau-chic W Hotel, Whiskey Blue upholds the hotel's sophisticated, edgy tone with low-slung chairs, clear blue lighting and pricey (and expertly made) martinis. Smallish (it holds just 91 patrons) and intimate (there's a queen-sized bed in the middle of the place), the Blue caters to a stylish crowd taking a break from the French Quarter's free-for-all atmosphere.

Monday-Saturday 4 p.m.-4 a.m., Sunday 4 p.m.-2 a.m.

WOLDENBERG RIVERFRONT PARK

1 Canal St., New Orleans, 504-565-3033; www.auduboninstitute.org

Covering 17 acres on the riverfront, Woldenberg Park offers the city its first direct access to the river in 150 years; ships and paddle wheelers dock along the park. Visitors can choose from a variety of riverboat tours.

Sunday-Thursday 6 a.m.-10 p.m., Friday-Saturday 6 a.m.-midnight.

WORLD TRADE CENTER OF NEW ORLEANS

2 Canal St., New Orleans, 504-529-1601; www.wtcno.org

This center houses the offices of many maritime companies and foreign consulates involved in international trade. Top of the Mart, a revolving restaurant and cocktail lounge on the 33rd floor, offers fine views of the city and the Mississippi River. Daily.

SPECIAL EVENTS
BRIDGE CITY GUMBO FESTIVAL

Gumbo Festival Park on Angel Square, 1701 Bridge City Ave., New Orleans, 504-436-4712; www.hgaparish.org/gumbofestival.htm

In the Gumbo Capital of the World, festival organizers cook up more than 2,000 gallons of chicken, sausage and seafood gumbos. Jambalaya, another local specialty, is also available, along with a variety of accompaniments. You can enter a cooking contest, listen to live music, enjoy carnival rides and participate in many other activities.

Early November.

FRENCH QUARTER FESTIVAL

French Quarter, 100 Conti St., New Orleans, 504-522-5730, 800-673-5725;www.fqfi.org

Fabulous and free, the French Quarter Festival showcases local musicians on 15 stages throughout the Vieux Carré. Take in the sounds of marching bands, brass bands, jazz and Dixieland bands, Cajun, country, zydeco and anything else you can imagine. Music stages are at Jackson Square, Woldenberg Riverfront Park, Bourbon Street, Royal Street, the French Market, Le Petit Theatre at St. Peter and Chartres, and Louisiana State Museum's Old U.S. Mint at Esplanade and Decatur. Don't miss the "World's Largest Jazz Brunch"—booths can be found in Jackson Square, Woldenberg Riverfront Park and Louisiana State Museum's Old U.S. Mint.

April.

LOUISIANA SWAMPFEST

6500 Magazine St., New Orleans, 504-581-4629, 866-487-2966; www.auduboninstitute.org/swampfest

Sample fried alligator tidbits while listening to local bands play Cajun and zydeco tunes. You may want to participate in the 5K run before indulging in the food and music treats, checking out the craft village or getting some hands-on experience with live creatures in the swamp exhibit.

Early-mid November.

MARDI GRAS FESTIVAL

Main parade route travels down St. Charles Ave. and Bourbon St., 504-566-5011; www.
mardigras.com, www.mardigrasday.com

The biggest party of the year offers something for everyone. The party starts weeks before the actual date of Mardi Gras. Parades and parties are scheduled throughout the weeks leading up to Ash Wednesday and Lent. Though most of the balls are invitation-only, you pay nothing to watch the numerous parades sponsored by the secret societies that organize the festivities. And of course, Bourbon Street is open to all revelers who want to party.

Early January-late February.

NEW ORLEANS JAZZ & HERITAGE FESTIVAL

Fair Grounds Racetrack, 1751 Gentilly Blvd., New Orleans, 504-522-4786, 504-410-
4100; www.nojazzfest.com

Each year, Jazz Fest draws 500,000 visitors from around the world for an experience that sums up the best of New Orleans—music, food and culture—in one big party. The music is eclectic: the acts on any given day can include national headliners, local zydeco musicians and regional rockabilly and country bands. The main action is at the Fair Grounds, but the fun spreads to venues throughout the city. New Orleans' own Neville Brothers are always a big draw.

Late April-early May.

NOKIA SUGAR BOWL COLLEGE FOOTBALL CLASSIC

Louisiana Superdome, Sugar Bowl Drive, New Orleans, 504-525-8573;
www.nokiasugarbowl.com

Each year, two top-ranked college football teams compete in this prestigious bowl game, part of the Bowl Championship Series. From 4 p.m. to kickoff, all football lovers can party at Fan Jam, on the Gate C Bridge on the Superdome's east side. The spirited event features live music, contests, hot food and ice-cold beverages. Sugar Bowl week also includes a basketball classic and a regatta on Lake Pontchartrain.

January.

SPRING FIESTA

826 St. Ann St., New Orleans, 504-581-1367; www.springfiesta.com

For two weekends every year, New Orleans celebrates its unique heritage with this springtime festival. The fun-packed festivities include a parade of horse-drawn carriages through the French Quarter, the coronation of the festival's queen at Jackson Square, and tours of private homes and courtyards and the historic Metairie Cemetery.

Late March-April.

TENNESSEE WILLIAMS NEW ORLEANS LITERARY FESTIVAL

Le Petit Theatre du Vieux Carré, 616 St. Peter St., French Quarter, New Orleans,
504-581-1144, 800-965-4827; www.tennesseewilliams.net

Born in Mississippi, playwright Tennessee Williams adopted New Orleans as his spiritual home. The city honors him with an annual festival held around his March 26 birthday. The five days of the festival are filled with workshops on writing and publishing, a one-act play competition and a book fair, as well as performances of some of Williams' plays. You can join a literary walking tour or compete in a "Stanley and Stella" contest. Le Petit Theatre du Vieux Carré is the festival headquarters, but other venues also house activities. Late March.

WHITE LINEN NIGHT

900 Camp St., New Orleans, 504-528-3805; www.cacno.org
Catch some culture during this annual art walk and street party. August in the bayou is always hot and humid, so patrons and partiers don their coolest clothes and stroll through the Arts District, popping into galleries that stay open late, catching live dance and theater performances, and ending up at the Contemporary Arts Center for a party that goes on until the wee hours. First Saturday in August.

WHERE TO STAY

★★BEST WESTERN FRENCH QUARTER LANDMARK

920 N. Rampart St., New Orleans, 504-524-3333, 800-780-7234; www.bestwestern.com
102 rooms. Restaurant, bar. Complimentary breakfast. $61-150

★★BIENVILLE HOUSE HOTEL

320 Decatur St., New Orleans, 800-535-9603; www.bienvillehouse.com
83 rooms. Restaurant. Complimentary breakfast. Pool. $61-150

★★★CHATEAU SONESTA HOTEL

800 Iberville St., New Orleans, 504-586-0800; www.sonesta.com
Not only are the guest rooms at this elegant Sonesta extra large (with 12-foot ceilings), but most come with good views of well-landscaped courtyards or Bourbon Street, just steps away. As a bonus for business travelers, all the rooms come with high-speed Internet access. If you wake up hungry, La Chatelaine serves breakfast. For lunch or dinner, savor scrumptious seafood dishes at Ralph Brennan's Red Fish Grill. The unique-looking hotel dates all the way back to 1849, when Daniel Henry Holmes opened his D. H. Holmes Department Store, which did booming business on this very site until 1989. 251 rooms. Restaurant, bar. $251-350

★★★DAUPHINE ORLEANS HOTEL

415 Dauphine St., New Orleans, 504-586-1800, 800-521-7111;
www.dauphineorleans.com
This hotel offers guests quiet luxury and a few good stories: May Baily's Place, the hotel's bar, was once a popular 19th-century bordello in the city's red-light district. Guests and staff members claimed to have seen ghosts— perhaps the bawdy kind—lurking around here. And John James Audubon, famous naturalist and artist, painted his well-known Birds of America series from 1821-1822 in the hotel's main meeting room (which used to be a cottage). In addition to all the history, the charming boutique hotel serves guests a complimentary welcome cocktail, continental breakfast and afternoon tea. 111 rooms. Bar. Complimentary breakfast. $151-250

★★DOUBLETREE HOTEL

300 Canal St., New Orleans, 504-581-1300; www.doubletree.com

363 rooms. Restaurant, bar. Business center. Fitness center. Pool. $151-250

★★EMBASSY SUITES

315 Julia St., New Orleans, 504-525-1993, 800-362-2779;
www.embassyneworleans.com

282 suites. Restaurant, bar. Complimentary breakfast. $151-250

★★★HILTON NEW ORLEANS RIVERSIDE

Two Poydras St., New Orleans, 504-561-0500; www.neworleans.hilton.com

With its multiple levels, intimate sitting areas, soaring ceilings, long cross-walk and entrances in several different lobbies, the Hilton New Orleans Riverside lives up to its claim to be a city-within–a-city. This is not a quaint, cozy hotel. It's a busy place, frequented by families who are looking for activities to keep the kids happy and by travelers drawn to the amenities. Privileges to a nearby racquet and health club are available to guests for a small fee.
1,616 rooms. Restaurant. Business center. Fitness center. Pool. Pets accepted. $151-250

★★★HOTEL LE CIRQUE

2 Lee Circle, New Orleans, 504-962-0900; www.hilton.com

A stylish and hip crowd checks into this chic hotel, thanks to its location in the funky Arts and Warehouse District, which is home to several cutting-edge galleries, restaurants and shops. You'll feel cosmopolitan resting in one of its smart-looking guest rooms or dining in its Lee Circle Restaurant, which dishes up tasty French Creole cuisine. The hotel has one of the best locations for enjoying Mardi Gras festivities.
137 rooms. Restaurant, bar. $61-150

★★★HOTEL MONTELEONE

214 Rue Royal, New Orleans, 866-338-4684; www.hotelmonteleone.com

The French Quarter's oldest and largest hotel has been rolling out the red carpet for its guests since 1886. Katrina broke windows, so the rooms have been renovated. and though they vary in size and style, they're comfortable and well appointed. For decades, locals have favored the Monteleone's Carousel Bar, where some seats revolve around the room (hence the watering hole's name). After cocktails, take a seat inside the Hunt Room Grill for fine dining. For recreation, head up to the rooftop for a dip in the pool or a workout in the well-equipped fitness center, which offers splendid views of the French Quarter and the Mississippi River.
600 rooms. Restaurant, bar. Fitness center. Pool. $151-250

★★HOTEL PROVINCIAL

1024 Rue Chartres, New Orleans, 504-581-4995, 800-535-7922;
www.hotelprovincial.com

105 rooms. Restaurant, bar. Complimentary breakfast. $61-150

★★★HOUSE ON BAYOU ROAD

2275 Bayou Road, New Orleans, 504-945-0992, 800-882-2968;
www.houseonbayouroad.com

Experience old New Orleans at this converted plantation home, offering two acres of gardens, ponds and patios, as well as a plantation-style breakfast. 9 rooms. Children over 12 years only. Restaurant. Complimentary breakfast. $61-150

★★IBERVILLE SUITES

910 Iberville St., New Orleans, 866-229-4351, 504-523-2400; www.ibervillesuites.com

230 suites. Restaurant, bar. Complimentary breakfast. $$151-250

★★★INTERCONTINENTAL NEW ORLEANS

444 St. Charles Ave., New Orleans, 504-525-5566, 800-445-6563;
www.new-orleans.interconti.com

With translation services available, a foreign currency exchange on the premises, a global newspaper service and a staff that speaks 14 languages, the InterContinental New Orleans can't help but have a European flair. The furnishings are modern and the business accoutrements are top-notch, as are the elements that bring pleasure to travel, including a terrific health club and a restaurant that serves lavish breakfast and lunch buffets, fine traditional New Orleans cuisine and a traditional jazz Sunday brunch.

479 rooms. Restaurant, bar. Business center. Fitness center. $251-350

★★★INTERNATIONAL HOUSE

221 Camp St., New Orleans, 504-553-9550, 800-633-5770; www.ihhotel.com

At this top-rated boutique hotel, the décor is a winning blend of New Orleans style and contemporary chic. The charming folk art and handmade furniture created by Louisiana artisans serve as a pleasant reminder of Cajun country tradition, but the stainless-steel and marble accents give the intimate hotel a cosmopolitan feel. Get in touch with the spirits at Loa (the voodoo word for "deities"), a dark bar lighted only by candles.

119 rooms. Restaurant, bar.$151-250

★★★LAFAYETTE HOTEL

600 St. Charles Ave., New Orleans, 504-524-4441, 888-856-4706;
www.thelafayettehotel.com

In 1916, this small and luxurious hotel opened in the same Beaux-Arts building in which it still pampers guests. Located on Lafayette Square in the Central Business District, it often hosts executives in town on business. Its Old World-style rooms and suites are individually decorated and come well appointed; many have French doors and wrought-iron balconies, and all have English botanical prints, overstuffed easy chairs and marble bathrooms with French-milled soaps and thick terry bathrobes. Off the small but elegant lobby, guests can dine at Mike Ditka's, a gourmet steakhouse that also serves Creole and Cajun favorites.

44 rooms. Restaurant, bar. $61-150

★★★LAFITTE GUEST HOUSE

1003 Bourbon St., New Orleans, 504-581-2678, 800-331-7971;
www.lafitteguesthouse.com

Want to feel like you're visiting friends in the mid-19th century? This three-story bed and breakfast should do the trick. Each room has its own distinct Victorian flair and the Victorian ground-floor sitting room will make you want to sip a cup of afternoon tea by the crackling fireplace. Best of all, breakfast is delivered to wherever you choose: your room, your balcony or the courtyard. Most of the guest rooms have private balconies with views of Bourbon Street or the French Quarter.

14 rooms. Complimentary breakfast. $61-150

★★★LE PAVILLON HOTEL

833 Poydras St., New Orleans, 504-581-3111; www.lepavillon.com

This historic hotel has seen it all: wars, prohibition and the birth of the horse-less carriage. Through it all, it has kept its reputation as a Great Lady of New Orleans. In 1970, the Hotel Denechaud, as it was called, passed into new hands and was renamed Le Pavillon, receiving a facelift and some spectacular accoutrements: crystal chandeliers from Czechoslovakia, railings from the lobby of Paris Grand Hotel, and fine art and antiques from around the world. The Crystal Suite contains a hand-carved marble bathtub, a gift from Napoleon to a wealthy Louisiana plantation owner—just like the one in the Louvre. (But this hotel isn't too stuffy; peanut-butter-and-jelly sandwiches, milk and chocolates are offered in the lobby after hours.)

226 rooms. Restaurant, bar. $61-150

★★★LE RICHELIEU IN THE FRENCH QUARTER

1234 Chartres St., New Orleans, 504-529-2492, 800-535-9653;
www.lerichelieuhotel.com

This family-owned hotel offers an amenity you won't find at any other hotel in the French Quarter: free self-parking. As good as that sounds, many guests keep coming back to this people-pleaser for other reasons: affordable rates; comfortable, homey rooms decorated in Creole style; a cozy bar and café; and an attractive courtyard with a pool. All these pluses got the attention of ex-Beatle Paul McCartney, who checked in here for two months in the late 1970s while he was in town doing some recording work. A suite is now named after him.

86 rooms. Restaurant, bar. Pool. $61-150

★★MAISON DE VILLE AND AUDUBON COTTAGES

727 Rue Toulouse, New Orleans, 504-561-5858; www.hotelmaisondeville.com

23 rooms. Children over 12 years only. Restaurant. Complimentary breakfast. $151-250

★★MAISON DUPUY

1001 Rue Toulouse, New Orleans, 504-586-8000, 800-535-9177;
www.maisondupuy.com

200 rooms. Restaurant, bar. $151-250

★★★MELROSE MANSION

937 Esplanade Ave., New Orleans, 504-944-2255, 800-650-3323;
www.melrosemansion.com

The Melrose Mansion, overlooking the French Quarter, was built in 1884 and purchased a few years later by a New Orleans nightclub owner as a home for the girls in his conga line. Approaching the front door of a brick welcome path, you'll walk past a wrought-iron gate and ascend the grand staircase to your suite (the suites have names like Prince Edward and Miss Kitty). Descend the next morning for fresh-baked pastries and hazelnut coffee—taken in the parlor, of course.

8 rooms. Complimentary breakfast. $151-250

★★★OMNI ROYAL CRESCENT HOTEL

535 Gravier St., New Orleans, 504-527-0006, 800-578-3200;
www.omniroyalcrescent.com

The hotel lobby is an impeccable blend of modern and traditional, with shiny brass elevators, a concierge stand and colorful fresh flowers, plus refined artwork and potted palms. Unusual in New Orleans, the Omni has a restaurant serving Thai food (with American food for breakfast). The comfortable guest rooms feature touches of wood and brass.

97 rooms. Restaurant. $61-150

★★★OMNI ROYAL ORLEANS

621 St. Louis St., New Orleans, 504-529-5333; www.omniroyalorleans.com

For royal treatment in the French Quarter, settle into one of the many plush rooms at this luxury hotel, which has been pampering visitors to the city since 1960. In the comfort of your room, this chain property will spoil you with Irish linen sheets, marble baths and windows overlooking all the action in the Quarter. Dine on steak and seafood in the award-winning Rib Room, a local favorite for decades; or refresh yourself with a mint julep or two at the Touche Bar or the Esplanade Lounge. Up on the rooftop, go for a relaxing swim in the pool, work up a sweat in the fitness center or just take in the sensational views.

346 rooms. Restaurant, bar. Fitness center. Pool. $251-350

★★★THE PONTCHARTRAIN HOTEL

2031 St. Charles Ave., New Orleans, 504-524-0581; www.pontchartrainhotel.com

For more than 75 years, this grande dame has been mixing European elegance with Southern hospitality in the city's charming Garden District. In years gone by, dignitaries and celebrities frequently registered here, explaining why some of the suites bear the names of famous folks. These days, travelers like to settle into its comfortable rooms, all of which are individually decorated with antiques and original art. At breakfast, lunch or dinner, savor classic Creole and Cajun specialties at Lafitte's Restaurant. If you start your morning there, you'll likely spot local politicos and civic leaders drinking cafe au lait and biting into beignets. After the workday, local professionals often wind down in the Bayou Bar.

104 rooms. Restaurant, bar. $151-250

★★PRYTANIA PARK HOTEL

1525 Prytania St., New Orleans, 504-524-0427; www.prytaniaparkhotel.com

62 rooms. Complimentary breakfast. $61-150

★★★RENAISSANCE PERE MARQUETTE HOTEL

817 Common St., New Orleans, 504-525-1111; www.renaissancehotels.com

Though it's housed in a historic building, this hotel has a contemporary look that appeals to those who like chic décor. Given its location in the Central Business District, the Renaissance attracts business travelers, especially because every room comes with high-speed Internet access, two-line phones with data ports and work desks with lamps. But leisure travelers book rooms here, too, for its close proximity to some of the city's best shopping, restaurants and attractions, including the French Quarter. Rene Bistrot serves award-winning French cuisine at affordable prices, so you'll be vying for a table with the locals who work downtown and know where to find the best deals.

275 rooms. Restaurant, bar. $151-250

★★★THE RITZ-CARLTON, NEW ORLEANS

921 Canal St., New Orleans, 504-524-1331, 800-241-3333; www.ritzcarlton.com

The Ritz-Carlton brings its luxury brand to the edge of the French Quarter and offers the refined elegance travelers expect from the Ritz. The guest rooms have a timeless elegance topped off by feather beds and deep-soaking tubs, and the spa is renowned for its unparalleled services, delivered in a gorgeous setting. If all this relaxing makes you hungry, try the casual bistro-style FQB or Victors for its dazzling backdrop and refined cuisine. The exquisite lounge offers an unrivaled afternoon tea set to the gentle strains of a harp.

527 rooms. Restaurant, bar. Spa. $151-250

★★★ROYAL SONESTA HOTEL NEW ORLEANS

300 Bourbon St., New Orleans, 504-586-0300; www.royalsonesta-neworleans.com

Gabled windows. French doors. Wrought-iron lace balconies. Gilded mirrors. Furniture reminiscent of 18th-century France. Tranquil, beautifully landscaped courtyards. This cozy but elegant property occupies a full block right on Bourbon Street, and it looks like it belongs in this historic district. If you crave a gourmet meal, sample the contemporary French and Creole cuisine served at Begues Restaurant. For something more casual, opt for the Desire Oyster Bar, where the chefs cook up both Creole and seafood dishes. Party at the Mystick Den cocktail lounge or the Can-Can Cafe and Jazz Club. If you just want to rest and relax, lounge out by the pool on an appealing third-floor terrace.

484 rooms. Restaurant, bar. Pool. $151-250

★★★SONIAT HOUSE HOTEL

1133 Chartres St., New Orleans, 504-522-0570, 800-544-8808; www.soniathouse.com

Don't let the Soniat's location in the bustling French Quarter fool you. The quiet and intimate hotel offers an elegant respite from all the revelry outside. Its cozy rooms are housed in three Creole-style town houses dating back to the early 1800s, and are tastefully decorated with English, French and

Louisiana antiques. What the property lacks in amenities—there's no pool, restaurant or fitness center—it more than makes up for with all its charm and the superior service of its friendly, attentive staff.
33 rooms. Children over 12 years only. $151-250

★★★ST. JAMES HOTEL

330 Magazine St., New Orleans, 504-304-4000, 888-856-4485;
www.saintjameshotel.com
Even though the St. James opened just a few years ago, it has the look of a distinguished older property because it occupies a renovated building from the 1850s. The hotel looks vintage New Orleans, with wrought-iron balconies and some rooms with exposed-brick walls. Business travelers like its downtown location and the two-line phones in every room. Rooftop terraces overlook a small pool in a charming courtyard. Cuvee restaurant offers contemporary Creole cuisine and more than 500 wine choices.
90 rooms. Restaurant, bar. $151-250

★★★ST. LOUIS HOTEL

730 Rue Bienville, New Orleans, 504-581-7300, 888-535-9111; www.stlouishotel.com
All guest rooms in this French Quarter boutique hotel overlook a lovely Mediterranean courtyard lush with tropical greenery, banana trees, flowering plants and a baroque fountain. Inside, the rooms are decked out in French period reproductions, and fabulous French cuisine is featured in the Louis XVI Restaurant, a New Orleans tradition. At breakfast, the hotel serves eggs Sardou and other local favorites in its courtyard.
85 rooms. Restaurant. $151-250

★★★W NEW ORLEANS

333 Poydras St., New Orleans, 504-525-9444, 800-522-6963; www.whotels.com
This style-soaked chain is designed for savvy business travelers, but leisure guests won't mind the down comforters, Aveda products and great fitness center. Zoe Bistro offers creative French food and the lobby's Whiskey Blue bar delivers a dose of hot nightlife.
423 rooms. Restaurant, bar. Fitness center. Pool. $251-350

★★★★WINDSOR COURT HOTEL

300 Gravier St., New Orleans, 504-523-6000, 888-596-0955;
www.windsorcourthotel.com
Located in the city's business district, the Windsor Court brings a bit of the English countryside to New Orleans. The rooms feature traditional English furnishings and artwork, while bay windows provide views of the city or the Mississippi River. This full-service hotel also includes a pool, sun deck and business and fitness centers. In a city hailed for its works of culinary genius, the Windsor Court is no exception. The Grill Room is one of the hottest tables in town, while the Polo Club Lounge is ideal for cocktails.
324 rooms. Restaurant, bar. Business center. Fitness center. Pool. Pets accepted. $251-350

★★★WYNDHAM NEW ORLEANS AT CANAL PLACE

100 Rue Iberville, New Orleans, 504-566-7006; www.wyndham.com

The Wyndham's downtown location isn't the only reason business travelers give this upscale hotel a thumbs-up. They also like the oversized guest rooms and the worker-friendly amenities, including direct high-speed Internet access, ergonomic work chairs and cordless telephones. But the Wyndham's convenient location also appeals to leisure travelers. In fact, the hotel is in the Canal Place Tower, home to the Shops at Canal Place, where visitors (and locals) like to go on buying sprees in the many top-name stores, such as Saks Fifth Avenue. Everyone who beds down here appreciates the stellar views of the city from both the marble-adorned lobby (on the tower's 11th floor) and the rooms that rise above it. Hungry? The Wyndham dishes up American cuisine with a Louisiana twist in the Riverbend Grill.

438 rooms. Restaurant, bar. Pool. $251-350

★★★WYNDHAM WHITNEY HOTEL

610 Poydras St., New Orleans, 504-581-4222; www.wyndham.com

This building used to house a grand old bank, and the revived space is worth a stop, even if you're not a guest here. The lobby has beautiful plasterwork and distinguished pillars, and the private dining room used to be the bank's vault. The public dining room was the actual bank space and the hotel's impossibly thick doors, we assume, kept out robbers.

293 rooms. Restaurant, bar. $151-250

WHERE TO EAT

★★ALLEGRO BISTRO

1100 Poydras St., New Orleans, 504-582-2350

American. Lunch. Closed Saturday-Sunday. $16-35

★★ANDREW JAEGER'S HOUSE OF SEAFOOD

4250 Highway 22, Mandeville,985-624-2300; www.andrewjaegers.com

Creole, seafood. Dinner. $16-35

★★★ANTOINE'S

713 Rue St. Louis, New Orleans, 504-581-4422; www.antoines.com

Located in the French Quarter, just a short distance from Bourbon Street, Antoine's has been a fixture since 1840. And this Creole/classic French dining spot still exudes quality. The locals know which entrées are the best—the filet and any oyster dish—Rockefeller, Bienville and Foch included.

Creole. Lunch, dinner. Closed Sunday. $36-85

★★★ARNAUD'S

813 Rue Bienville, New Orleans, 504-523-5433, 866-230-8891; www.arnauds.com

In the French Quarter near Bourbon Street, this exquisite restaurant heaps refined service on diners. Partake of the trout meunière and shrimp rémoulade in a wonderful, romantic atmosphere.

French, Creole. Lunch, dinner, Sunday brunch. $36-85

★★★BACCO

310 Chartres St., New Orleans, 504-522-2426; www.bacco.com

A member of the Brennan family, located at the W Hotel in the French Quarter, this romantic Creole/Italian restaurant fuses local products with traditional Italian recipes.

Italian. Lunch, dinner. $36-85

★★★★BAYONA

430 Dauphine St., New Orleans, 504-525-4455; www.bayona.com

A little slice of the romantic Mediterranean awaits you at Bayona, a restaurant tucked into a 200-year-old Creole cottage in the heart of the French Quarter. The cozy room is often set with fresh flowers and is warmed by sunny lighting and bright colors. Chef Susan Spicer serves up her own interpretation of New Orleans cuisine, blending the ingredients of the Mediterranean with the flavors of Alsace, Asia, India and the Southwest. You'll find an outstanding waitstaff eager to guide you and answer questions about the menu. A great selection of beers, including several local brews, plus an extensive wine list round out the experience.

International. Lunch, dinner. Closed Sunday-Monday. $36-85

★★★BEGUE'S

300 Bourbon St., New Orleans, 504-553-2220; www.sonesta.com/begues

This French Quarter restaurant is in the Royal Sonesta Hotel. Meals are served in a relaxed atmosphere overlooking a tropical courtyard filled with orange trees. The specialty here is beautifully prepared Creole cuisine and an all-you-can-eat Sunday brunch that makes you wonder if there are crawfish or snapper left in any other part of the world.

Creole. Breakfast, lunch, dinner, Sunday brunch. $16-35

★★★BELLA LUNA

914 N. Peters St., New Orleans, 504-529-1583; www.bellalunarestaurant.com

Guests get a choice of two views: the French Quarter on one side and a great romantic view of the Mississippi River on the other. The cuisine is mostly American, with a spicy Creole flavor. Local favorites are the pecan-crusted pork chops, battered soft-shell crabs and the giant stuffed Gulf shrimp.

Cajun/Creole, Mediterranean. Dinner. $36-85

★★BISTRO AT MAISON DE VILLE

733 Toulouse St., New Orleans, 504-528-9206, 800-634-1600; www.maisondeville.com

Creole. Lunch, dinner. $36-85

★★BON TON CAFE

401 Magazine St., New Orleans, 504-524-3386, 888-524-5611;

Cajun. Lunch, dinner. Closed Saturday-Sunday. $16-35

★★★BRENNAN'S

417 Royal St., New Orleans, 504-525-9711; www.brennansneworleans.com

Breakfast is king at this sister restaurant to Commander's Palace in the heart of the French Quarter, but guests will enjoy the classic upscale Creole cuisine any meal of the day. Dine in the courtyard on the decadent egg dishes.

French, Creole. Breakfast, lunch, dinner, brunch. $36-85

★★★BRIGTSEN'S
723 Dante St., New Orleans, 504-861-7610; www.brigtsens.com
Frank Brigsten is the chef/owner of this delightful Uptown spot with excellent food and service to match. It is a local favorite and offers Creole dishes, with specialties of the house including blackened tuna and roasted duck.
Creole. Dinner. Closed Sunday-Monday. $16-35

★★★BROUSSARD'S
819 Conti St., New Orleans, 504-581-3866; www.broussards.com
This award-winning restaurant has been family-owned for 75 years, albeit by different families. The current owners run things with as much care and attention to detail as the Broussards did in the early 1800s. Classically French-trained chef Gunter prepares unmatched Creole fantasies; try the house-cured salmon or grilled pompano on puff pastry accompanied by shrimp, scallops and mustard-caper sauce. Wine aficionados, prepare for the 20-page wine list.
French. Dinner. $36-85

★CAFE DU MONDE
800 Decatur St., New Orleans, 504-525-4544, 800-772-2927; www.cafedumonde.com
French. Breakfast, late-night. $15 and under.

★★CAFE GIOVANNI
117 Rue Decatur, New Orleans, 504-529-2154; www.cafegiovanni.com
Creole, Italian. Dinner. Closed Sunday-Monday. $16-35

★CAFE PONTALBA
546 St. Peter St., New Orleans, 504-522-1180
Cajun, Creole. Lunch, dinner. $16-35

★★CAFE VOLAGE
720 Dublin St., New Orleans, 504-861-4227
French, Mediterranean. Lunch, dinner, Sunday brunch. $16-35

★CENTRAL GROCERY
923 Decatur St., New Orleans, 504-523-1620, 866-620-0174
Italian. Lunch. $15 and under.

★★★COMMANDER'S PALACE
1403 Washington Ave., New Orleans, 504-899-8221; www.commanderspalace.com
In the center of the Garden District stands this turquoise and white Victorian monument to Creole cuisine. The famed Brennan family has presided over the dining room since 1974, but Emile Commander originally founded it in 1880 as a fine restaurant for distinguished neighborhood families. The lush garden setting hosts live Dixieland music for the lively Saturday and Sunday jazz brunches.
Creole. Lunch, dinner, brunch. $36-85

★★CRESCENT CITY BREWHOUSE

527 Decatur St., New Orleans, 504-522-0571, 888-819-9330;
www.crescentcitybrewhouse.com
American, Cajun/Creole. Lunch, dinner. $16-35

★★★CUVEE

322 Magazine St., New Orleans, 504-587-9001; www.restaurantcuvee.com
Foodies love this restaurant for its innovative menu and excellent advice on wine and food pairings. Opened in 1999 and considered an upstart in this city of decades-old dining establishments, Cuvee has gained a reputation as one of New Orleans' finest gourmet restaurants. With just 85 seats, the intimate restaurant is housed in a landmark 1833 building whose age strangely complements its nouveau New Orleans cuisine (think sugarcane-smoked duck breast and crispy confit leg served with Hudson Valley foie gras and Roquefort-pecan risotto).
Creole. Lunch, dinner. $36-85

★★DESIRE OYSTER BAR

300 Bourbon St., New Orleans;504-586-0300; www.royalsonesta-neworleans.com/
dining.html
American, Creole, seafood. Lunch, dinner. $16-35

★★★DOMINIQUE'S

1001 Rue Toulouse St., New Orleans, 504-586-8000; www.dominiquesrestaurant.com
This French Quarter location in the beautiful Maison Dupuy Hotel features the innovative cuisine of chef Dominique Macquet. Ingredients are always the freshest available, and the breads and pastries are baked on the premises.
French. Dinner. $36-85

★★DOOKY CHASE

2301 Orleans Ave., New Orleans, 504-821-0600
Creole. Lunch, dinner. $16-35

★★★EMERIL'S RESTAURANT

800 Tchoupitoulas St., New Orleans, 504-528-9393, 800-980-8474; www.emerils.com
Emeril's is a chic and stylish hot spot in the Central Business District. With lofty ceilings, an open kitchen and a towering wooden wine wall, the restaurant is a dynamic space that suits its urban Warehouse District neighborhood. The slick food bar is a fun spot to take in the buzzing see-and-be-seen crowd. The room can get loud, but the vibe is good. The menu employs a world of herbs, spices and chilies that awaken the palate with a delicious jolt.
Cajun/Creole. Dinner. Closed Sunday. $36-85

★★FEELINGS CAFE

2600 Chartres St., New Orleans, 504-945-2222; www.feelingscafe.com
Creole. Lunch, dinner, Sunday brunch. $16-35

★★FIVE HAPPINESS

3605 S. Carrollton Ave., New Orleans, 504-482-3935; www.fivehappiness.com
Chinese. Lunch, dinner. $15 and under.

★FRENCH MARKET
1001 Decatur St., New Orleans, 504-525-7879; www.frenchmarket.org
Cajun/Creole, French. Lunch, dinner. $16-35

★★★GALATOIRE'S
209 Bourbon St., New Orleans, 504-525-2021; www.galatoires.com
Jean Galatoire, a Frenchman from the foothills of the Pyrenees, founded this landmark French Quarter restaurant in 1905. His descendants own and run it today. It's one of New Orleans' most popular restaurants (and hardest reservations) so book early.
Cajun/Creole. Lunch, dinner. Closed Monday. $36-85

★★★GAUTREAU'S
1728 Soniat St., New Orleans, 504-899-7397; www.gautreausrestaurant.com
This quintessential neighborhood bistro in Uptown is in an early 1900s-era pharmacy, with embossed tin ceilings and an antique apothecary serving as a liquor cabinet. Chef John Harris lends his classical French-trained style to a Creole-influenced menu.
American, seafood. Dinner. Closed Sunday. $36-85

★★GUMBO SHOP
630 St. Peter St., New Orleans, 504-525-1486; www.gumboshop.com
Creole, seafood. Lunch, dinner. $16-35

★★K-PAUL'S LOUISIANA KITCHEN
416 Chartres St., New Orleans, 504-596-2530; www.chefpaul.com
Cajun/Creole. Lunch, dinner. Closed Sunday. $36-85

★★LA MADELEINE
547 St. Ann St., New Orleans, 504-568-0073; www.lamadeleine.com
French. Breakfast, lunch, dinner. $15 and under.

★★★MARTINIQUE
5908 Magazine St., New Orleans, 504-891-8495; www.martiniquebistro.com
French. Dinner. $16-35

★MICHAUL'S
840 St. Charles Ave., New Orleans, 504-522-5517, 800-563-4055; www.michauls.com
Cajun. Dinner. Closed Sunday. $16-35

★MOTHER'S RESTAURANT
401 Poydras St., New Orleans, 504-523-9656; www.mothersrestaurant.net
Creole. Breakfast, lunch, dinner. $15 and under.

★★★MR. B'S BISTRO
201 Royal St., New Orleans, 504-523-2078; www.mrbsbistro.com
This famous Brennan-family institution in the French Quarter offers Creole cuisine made with local and organically grown products. It's the power lunch spot in the French Quarter and very popular for dinner.
Creole. Lunch, dinner. $36-85

★★★★THE NEW ORLEANS GRILL

300 Gravier St., New Orleans, 504-522-1994, 888-596-0955;
www.windsorcourthotel.com

Dining at The New Orleans Grill (located inside the Windsor Court Hotel) may be one of the most luxurious ways to spend an evening in the city. With a menu that changes monthly and features locally grown and organic foods whenever possible, The New Orleans Grill is known for its fabulous contemporary American cuisine. The restaurant's lounge, the Polo Room, offers live music on Friday nights.

French. Breakfast, lunch, dinner. $36-85

★★★NOLA

534 St. Louis St., New Orleans, 504-522-6652; www.emerils.com

As the most casual and accessible of Emeril's restaurants, this French Quarter location offers innovative cuisine that will please guests with dishes such as grilled pork porterhouse with brown-sugar-glazed sweet potatoes, toasted pecans and caramelized onion reduction sauce; and spicy roasted Atlantic salmon with fennel-white bean salad, pickled cherry tomatoes and lemon-herb coulis.

Creole. Lunch, dinner. $36-85

★★★PALACE CAFÉ

605 Canal St., New Orleans, 504-523-1661; www.palacecafe.com

Crabmeat cheesecake, anyone? Both contemporary and classic Creole seafood dishes are available at this upscale, lively café on historic Canal Street. Owned by Dickie Brennan of the famous restaurant family, Palace Café is revered for signature dishes such as a creamy oyster pan roast and white chocolate bread pudding. If you can't bear to leave the bread pudding, fear not: That, plus 169 other Palace Café recipes, are available in The Flavor of New Orleans Palace Café cookbook, which is available for purchase. What must be experienced in person, however, is the popular Sunday brunch with live blues music.

Cajun/Creole. Lunch, dinner, Saturday-Sunday brunch. $16-35

★★★PELICAN CLUB

312 Exchange Alley, New Orleans, 504-523-1504; www.pelicanclub.com

For fine dining in the French Quarter, look no further than this restaurant tucked away in a converted townhouse in charming Exchange Alley. Creative appetizers and sure-thing entrées, all delivered with professional service, make for an enjoyable dining experience.

International. Dinner. $36-85

★★★PERISTYLE

1041 Dumaine St., New Orleans, 504-593-9535; peristylerestaurant.com

The 19th-century French Quarter building that houses Peristyle was once a family-owned oyster house near the red-light district. Now, of course, it's home to this upscale restaurant, known for French cuisine and the large wine cellar. The menu offers dishes such as lassiette du charcutier and rosemary lamb loin chop with red onion marmalade and pine-nut-sultana red wine reduction.

French. Dinner. Closed Sunday-Monday. $36-85

★PRALINE CONNECTION
542 Frenchmen St., New Orleans, 504-943-3934; www.pralineconnection.com
Creole. Lunch, dinner. $16-35

★★RED FISH GRILL
115 Bourbon St., New Orleans, 504-598-1200; www.redfishgrill.com
Seafood. Lunch, dinner. $36-85

★★★RESTAURANT AUGUST
301 Tchoupitoulas St., New Orleans, 504-299-9777; www.rest-august.com
Step into this converted 18th-century town house and you're sure to be greeted with a hearty welcome. August's warm, exposed-brick room features vaulted ceilings and Old World antiques. Dining at August is all about being pampered, and chef John Besh, voted a Food & Wine Best New Chef in 1999, does a wonderful job of spreading the love from the kitchen with an innovative and delicious menu of dishes that marry robust ingredients from Spain and France with regional flavors. His menu changes seasonally, but two flawless signatures are the Moroccan-spiced duck with polenta and tempura dates and the BLT, made from fat, meaty fried Buster crabs, lettuce and heirloom tomatoes on a slab of brioche.
French. Lunch, dinner. Closed Sunday. $86 and up.

★SNUG HARBOR JAZZ BISTRO
626 Frenchmen St., New Orleans, 504-949-0696; www.snugjazz.com
Seafood, steak. Dinner. $16-35

★★TONY MORAN'S
240 Bourbon St., New Orleans, 504-523-4640; www.tonymorans.com
Italian. Dinner. $36-85

★★TUJAGUE'S
823 Decatur St., New Orleans, 504-525-8676; www.tujagues.com
Creole. Lunch, dinner. $16-35

★★★UPPERLINE
1413 Upperline St., New Orleans, 504-891-9822; www.upperline.com
The gracious service and excellent Creole food make this neighborhood restaurant in Uptown a local favorite. Be sure to check out the extensive collection of regional art hanging throughout the restaurant.
Cajun/Creole. Dinner. Closed Monday-Tuesday. $16-35

★★★VERANDA
444 St. Charles Ave., New Orleans, 504-525-5566; www.ichotelsgroup.com
On the second floor of the InterContinental New Orleans, opening onto the hotel's enormous faux-street, lamp-lined atrium, Veranda is an airy arena for a calming meal. Regional fare is the ticket here; Cajun, gumbo, crawfish and other New Orleans cuisine are done up in imaginative ways, but Veranda is known primarily for its lavish breakfast and lunch buffets. And the Sunday champagne jazz brunch draws both locals and visitors.
American, Creole. Breakfast, lunch, dinner, Sunday brunch. $16-35

SPA
★★★THE SPA AT THE RITZ-CARLTON, NEW ORLEANS
921 Canal St., New Orleans, 504-670-2929, 800-241-3333; www.ritzcarlton.com
Soft lighting, gleaming marble, brass chandeliers and gentle colors set a regal tone for the Spa at The Ritz-Carlton, New Orleans. This tranquil spa lets you relax and indulge like royalty—the treatment menu was inspired in part by favorite practices of French aristocrats. The Napoleon royal massage is a signature treatment that includes a heavenly citrus-scented bath prior to a lemon-verbena-scented Swedish rubdown. The body treatments are superb, and the spa's magnolia sugar scrub gently exfoliates and polishes skin while the scent of Louisiana's luscious magnolias blend with botanical extracts and aid relaxation.

OPELOUSAS
See also Lafayette
French is spoken as often as English in this charming old town, the third oldest in the state. Opelousas was a trading post from the early 1700s until 1774, when St. Landry's church was established.

WHAT TO SEE
CHICOT STATE PARK
3469 Chicot Park Road, Opelousas, 337-363-2503, 888-677-2442; www.lastateparks. com/chicot/chicot.htm
Nearly 6,000 acres of rolling woodland surround a 2,000-acre artificial lake stocked with bream, bass and crappie. Swimming, fishing, boating, hiking, picnicking, tent and trailer sites are all available. Daily.

JIM BOWIE MUSEUM
Highway 90 and Academy St., Opelousas, 337-948-6263, 800-424-5442; www.cityo-fopelousas.com
See memorabilia from the 19th-century adventurer and his famous knife, as well as local historical items in an 18th-century colonial house built by a woman named Venus. Daily.

LOUISIANA STATE ARBORETUM
Opelousas, 337-363-6289, 888-677-6100; www.crt.state.la.us/parks
The 300-acre arboretum on Lake Chicot includes more than 150 species of plant life indigenous to Louisiana. There are also nature trails. Daily.

WASHINGTON
404 N. Main St., Washington, 337-826-3627; www.washingtonla.com
Built between 1780-1835, the antebellum buildings in this historic river port include Hinckley House, House of History, Camellia Cove and De la Morandiere. Many houses are open for tours. Daily.

WHERE TO STAY
★★AMERICAN BEST VALUE INN
4165 I-49 Service Road, Opelousas, 337-948-9500
67 rooms. Restaurant, bar. Fitness center. Pool. $61-150

ST. MARTINVILLE

See also Lafayette, New Iberia

Few towns in Louisiana have a more colorful history than St. Martinville. On the winding, peaceful Bayou Teche, St. Martinville was first settled around 1760. In the years thereafter, Acadians driven out of Nova Scotia by the British drifted into St. Martinville with the hope of finding religious tolerance. The town is the setting for part of Henry Wadsworth Longfellow's Evangeline, a poem about an Acadian girl who is separated from her beloved Gabriel when the British deport the Canadians from Canada during the 18th century. Evangeline eventually settles in Philadelphia, where, as an old woman, she finds her beloved in a hospital and he dies in her arms.

Today St. Martinville is a quiet, hospitable destination for visitors who want to stop by the Evangeline Oak and Commemorative Area, sample the local cuisine or spend the night in a quiet bed and breakfast.

WHAT TO SEE
EVANGELINE OAK
On the bayou at end of Port Street

This ancient, moss-draped live oak is said to be the meeting place of the real Evangeline and her Gabriel.

LONGFELLOW-EVANGELINE STATE COMMEMORATIVE AREA
1200 N. Main St., St. Martinville, 337-394-3754; www.crt.state.la.us/parks

This 157-acre park on the banks of the Bayou Teche is a reconstruction of a typical 19th-century plantation. Begun around 1810 by Pierre Olivier du Clozel, a French Creole, the Olivier plantation employs wooden pegs; walls are made of Spanish moss-mixed bousillage and cypress; period furnishings fill the space; and there's a replica of an 1840s kitchen and a kitchen garden. Daily.

ST. MARTIN OF TOURS CATHOLIC CHURCH
133 S. Main St., St. Martinville, 337-394-7334

Established in 1765 as the mother church of the exiled Acadians, the presently restored building contains stained-glass windows; an exquisite carved baptismal font, which was a gift of Louis XVI of France; a gold and silver sanctuary light; a painting of St. Martin de Tours by Jean Francois Mouchet; and other religious artifacts. Guided tours are available by appointment only.

Behind the church's left wing is:

PETIT PARIS MUSEUM
103 S. Main St., St. Martinville, 337-394-7334

This museum contains a collection of elaborate carnival costumes, local memorabilia and a gift shop. Daily.

PRESBYTERE
133 S. Main St., St. Martinville, 337-394-7334

The priest's residence, Greek Revival in style, was constructed in 1856. By legend, it was built in such a grand manner in the hope that St. Martinville would be designated as the seat of the diocese.

SHREVEPORT

See also Bossier City

Founded in 1835 by river captain and steamboat inventor Henry Miller Shreve, Shreveport is now best known for its multiple casinos and thorough-bred racing. If you'd rather not take your chances on a slot machine, try a narrated historical tour of the Red River or tour the city's art museums, the American Rose Center or the botanical garden in RiverView Park.

WHAT TO SEE
AMERICAN ROSE CENTER
8877 Jefferson-Paige Road, Shreveport, 318-938-5402; www.ars.org
The center consists of 60 individually designed rose gardens donated by rose societies from across the U.S.
April-October, Monday-Friday 9 a.m.-5 p.m., Saturday 9 a.m.-6 p.m., Sunday 1-6 p.m.

C. BICKHAM DICKSON PARK
2283 E. Bert Kouns Loop, Shreveport; 318-673-7808
Shreveport's largest park contains a 200-acre oxbow lake with a pier. The park offers fishing, hayrides, picnicking and a playground for kids.
Daily.

LOUISIANA STATE EXHIBIT MUSEUM
3015 Greenwood Road, Shreveport; 318-632-2020; www.sos.louisiana.gov
This museum showcases remarkable dioramas and murals of the prehistory and resources of the Louisiana area. It also has exhibits of antique and modern items and a historical gallery.
Tuesday-Saturday.

R. S. BARNWELL MEMORIAL GARDEN AND ART CENTER
601 Clyde Fant Parkway, Shreveport, 318-673-7703; www.nwlagardener.org
The combination art and horticulture facility has permanent and changing exhibits. Flower displays include seasonal and native plantings of the area; the sculpture garden has a walk-through bronze statue; plus, there's a fragrance garden for the visually impaired. Daily.

R. W. NORTON ART GALLERY
4747 Creswell Ave., Shreveport, 318-865-4201; www.rwnaf.org
The art gallery specializes in American and European paintings, sculpture, decorative arts and manuscripts from the 15th to 20th centuries. It also has a large collection of Western art by Frederic Remington and Charles M. Russell.
Tuesday-Friday 10 a.m.-5 p.m., Saturday-Sunday 1-5 p.m.

WATER TOWN USA
7670 W. 70th St., Shreveport, 318-938-5475; www.watertownusa.com
This 20-acre water theme park features speed slides, adventure slides and a wave pool, plus two other pools. You can take a break at the restaurant and concessions.

SPECIAL EVENTS
LOUISIANA STATE FAIR
Fairgrounds, 3701 Hudson Ave., Shreveport, 318-635-1361;
www.statefairoflouisiana.com
One of the largest state fairs in the country, it draws more than 300,000 people annually. Entertainment includes an agriculture and livestock competition. Late October-early November.

RED RIVER REVEL ARTS FESTIVAL
Riverfront area, 101 Crockett St., Shreveport, 318-424-4000; www.redriverrevel.com
The national festival features fine arts, crafts, pottery, jewelry, music, performing arts, creative writing, poetry and ethnic foods.
Late September-early October.

WHERE TO STAY
★★BEST WESTERN CHATEAU SUITE HOTEL
201 Lake St., Shreveport, 318-222-7620, 800-845-9334; www.bestwestern.com
101 rooms. Complimentary breakfast. Restaurant, bar. Business center. Fitness center. Pool. $61-150

★★★CLARITON SHREVEPORT HOTEL
1419 E. 70th St., Shreveport, 318-797-9900; www.choicehotels.com
231 rooms. Restaurant, bar. Business center. Fitness center. $61-150

★DAYS INN
4935 W. Monkhouse Drive, Shreveport, 318-636-0080, 800-329-7466;
www.daysinn.com
148 rooms. Complimentary breakfast. Pool. Pets accepted. $61-150

★FAIRFIELD INN
6245 Westport Ave., Shreveport, 318-686-0102, 800-228-2800; www.fairfieldinn.com
105 rooms. Complimentary breakfast. $61-150

★★HOLIDAY INN
5555 Financial Plaza, Shreveport, 318-688-3000, 800-465-4329; www.holiday-inn.com
226 rooms. Restaurant, bar. Pets accepted. $61-150

WHERE TO EAT
★★DON'S SEAFOOD
207 Milam St., Shreveport, 318-865-4291; www.ulcoleman.com
Cajun, Creole. Lunch, dinner. 16-35

★SUPERIOR GRILL
6123 Line Ave., Shreveport, 318-869-3243; www.superiorgrill.com
Mexican. Lunch, dinner. $16-35

SLIDELL

See also New Orleans

Slidell offers natural attractions and scenery in southeast Louisiana. The Honey Island Swamp encompasses the parish's eastern border. Slidell's historic district, called Olde Town, is filled with antique shops and restaurants.

WHAT TO SEE

FORT PIKE STATE COMMEMORATIVE AREA

Slidell, eight miles east via Highway 190, then six miles southwest on Highway 90, 504-662-5703, 888-662-5703; www.lastateparks.com/fortpike

The fort was constructed in the 1820s to defend navigational channels leading to New Orleans. Visitors can stroll through authentic brick archways and stand overlooking the Rigolets as sentries once did. Daily.

OAK HARBOR GOLF COURSE

201 Oak Harbor Blvd., Slidell, 985-646-0110; www.oakharborgolf.com

Oak Harbor requires smart, often conservative play to score well, with water on 12 holes and challenging approaches to many greens. Designed in the style of Pete Dye, with railroad ties and bulkheads along the course, Oak Harbor is still only a touch more than 6,200 yards from the men's tees. A GPS system in each cart helps players estimate distances and speed play along one of New Orleans' newer courses, opened in 1992.

WHERE TO STAY

★LA QUINTA INN

794 E. I-10 Service Road, Slidel, 985-643-9770; www.lq.com/lq/properties

172 rooms. Bar. Complimentary breakfast. Fitness center. Pool. Pets accepted. $61-150

★★★★★ LOUISIANA

MISSISSIPPI

MISSISSIPPI IS A LAND OF GREAT AND TRAGIC STORIES. HERE, THE BLUES WERE BORN on a large cotton plantation in the early 20th century; many of the Civil War's bloodiest battles were fought; and some of the nation's most celebrated storytellers, including Tennessee Williams, William Faulkner and Eudora Welty, found their inspiration. It's no surprise that history is a part of the lore for the state's visitors, who will find beautifully preserved antebellum homes and tributes to the state's famous sons and daughters at almost every stop. Mississippians know how to celebrate their history: All year long, cities and towns host festivals when locals and visitors can hear the blues, honor Native American traditions or tour some of the South's most beautiful buildings.

Mississippi's recorded history begins when Hernando De Soto trekked across this land looking for gold 80 years before the Mayflower landed in Massachusetts. In 1699, French settlers established Mississippi's first permanent settlement near Biloxi. There was no gold to be found, but the Mississippi River had created something as valuable: immense valleys of rich soil on which cotton could be grown. Cotton plantations became common sights and eventually Mississippi joined other southern states in fighting against all attempts to abolish the plantations' primary source of labor: slavery.

The Civil War brought fierce battles to Mississippi. Many historians believe the 47-day Siege of Vicksburg sealed the South's fate. In the late 19th and early 20th centuries, the state had adopted Jim Crow laws that left Mississippi racially segregated. Nearly 100 years after the Civil War's end, the state found itself in the midst of a set of battles during the civil-rights movement, making the state a representative of the scourge of racial oppression that has stained American history.

Today the Magnolia State is still recovering from Hurricane Katrina's destructive visit in late August of 2005. Its famous Gulf Coast, a popular destination, was ravaged by the storm, and though much of the shoreline is repaired and ready for tourists, it's still a good idea to call ahead to make sure certain attractions are open.

Sandy beaches and fresh seafood aren't all Mississippi has to offer. The John C. Stennis Space Center in Gulfport is NASA's largest rocket engine test facility and offers tours and exhibits about aerospace. In Tupelo, Elvis Presley fans can visit the small white frame house in which the King was born, and travelers who stop in Oxford, home of the University of Mississippi, will find a town that worships Ole Miss football, good food and local literary greats like Faulkner, who based his Yoknapatawpa County on surrounding Lafayette County.

In short, what Mississippi provides is a powerful character, captivating settings and stories that will amaze visitors. But it ultimately offers an opportunity to see the country from a new perspective, through the stories and characters that have shaped not just this scenic land, but the nation, too.

BILOXI

See also Gulfport, Pascagoula

The oldest town in the Mississippi Valley, Biloxi has been a popular resort area since the 1840s, and after Hurricane Katrina battered its shores in August 2005, the city has worked hard to regain its place as a vacation hot spot. Many of its famed casinos have reopened and at least 60 percent of the town's hotels are back in business.

Biloxi has changed, but many of its prized possessions are still here. Fresh seafood is always available, and visitors who want to catch their own can choose from freshwater, salt water and deep-sea fishing. The beaches are open for visitors who just want to relax on the sand or swim in the surf, and spas, shops and restaurants entice visitors to indulge.

WHAT TO SEE
"BEAUVOIR"—JEFFERSON DAVIS HOME AND PRESIDENTIAL LIBRARY

2244 Beach Blvd., Biloxi, 228-388-4400; www.beauvoir.org

Hurricane Katrina damaged much of Beauvoir, but this historic estate was restored in mid-2008. Confederate President Jefferson Davis spent the last 12 years of his life here, writing The Rise and Fall of the Confederate Government and A Short History of the Confederate States of America. The adjoining museum holds artifacts from Davis and the Confederate states, and Beauvoir's staff has completed recovery and cataloguing of the artifacts that survived the storm. Here, too, is a cemetery with the Tomb of the Unknown Soldier of the Confederate States of America and a Presidential Library dedicated to Jefferson's tenure.

BILOXI CITY CEMETERY

1166 Irish Hill Drive, Biloxi; www.biloxi.ms.us

Across the rolling grass here are the burials ground of the French pioneer families of Biloxi and the Gulf Coast. John Cuevas, hero of the Cat Island War of 1812, is buried here. Daily.

HARRISON COUNTY SAND BEACH

842 Commerce St., Biloxi, 228-896-0055; www.co.harrison.ms.us

This 300-foot-wide white sand beach stretches the entire 26-mile length of the county, with a seawall separating the beach from the highway.

SMALL CRAFT HARBOR

Main Street and Highway 90, Biloxi

Visitors can view fishing boats unloading the day's catch of Gulf game fish or chart their own deep-sea fishing boat to make the big catch themselves.

SPECIAL EVENTS
BLESSING OF THE FLEET

177 First St., Biloxi, Gulf of Mexico; www.biloxiblessing.com

Hundreds of vessels manned by descendants of settlers participate in this ritual of European origin.

Last weekend in May.

MARDI GRAS
2501 Beachview Drive, Biloxi
The biggest party of the year, Mardi Gras includes a carnival and parade with colorful, festive floats.
February.

SEAFOOD FESTIVAL
Point Cadet Plaza, 120 Cadet St., Biloxi
Visitors in the early fall can catch this festival, which includes an arts and crafts show, entertainment, seafood booths and contests.
Mid-September.

WHERE TO STAY
★★★BEAU RIVAGE BY MIRAGE RESORTS
875 Beach Blvd., Biloxi, 228-386-7444, 888-567-6667; www.beaurivage.com
Las Vegas meets the French Riviera of the South at Beau Rivage. A world of its own, the resort has a 31-slip marina, a casino and other recreational and entertainment choices. The guest rooms, decorated in styles that evoke the English countryside, offer great views of the bay or ocean, and eight restaurants serve cuisine inspired by places across the globe. Sports enthusiasts charter boats for relaxing rides or sport-fishing adventures, while the spa and salon lure landlubbers with a penchant for pampering.
1,780 rooms. Restaurant, bar. Spa. $151-250

★★★GRAND CASINO HOTEL BILOXI
265 Beach Blvd., Biloxi, 228-432-2500, 800-946-2946
491 rooms. Restaurant, bar. $61-150

WHERE TO EAT
★★★MARY MAHONEY'S OLD FRENCH HOUSE
Magnolia and Water streets, Biloxi, 228-374-0163; www.marymahoneys.com
Mary Mahoney, daughter of Yugoslavian immigrants, founded this Gulf Coast landmark in 1964. The menu is full of fresh seafood dishes, such as crabmeat au gratin and fried oysters.
American. Lunch, dinner. Closed Sunday. $36-85

CLARKSDALE
Musicians in the know point to Clarksdale as the birthplace of the blues. In the early 20th century, fieldworker Henry Sloan showed Charley Patton how to play the guitar, and Patton went on to become the "Father of the Delta Blues." Muddy Waters grew up here, as did John Lee Hooker. Actor Morgan Freeman chose Clarksdale as the site of his celebrated Ground Zero blues club and his Madidi restaurant.

WHAT TO SEE
CARNEGIE PUBLIC LIBRARY
114 Delta Ave., Clarksdale, 662-624-4461; www.cplclarksdale.lib.ms.us
Located within the library is the Archaeology Museum, which has Native American pottery and other artifacts on exhibit. The library also contains a

collection of books and reports on Lower Mississippi Valley archaeology. Monday-Saturday.

DELTA BLUES MUSEUM

1 Blues Alley, Clarksdale, 662-627-6820; www.deltabluesmuseum.org
Museum highlights include video and audio recordings as well as memorabilia about blues music. There are permanent and changing exhibits and performances throughout the year as well.
March-mid-October, Monday-Saturday 9 a.m.-5 p.m.; mid-October-February, Monday-Saturday 10 a.m.-5 p.m.

NORTH DELTA MUSEUM

700 Second St., Friars Point, 662-383-2233
Archaeological and historical exhibits of early Delta life are on display, including Native American artifacts, three original log buildings and Civil War artifacts.
Tuesday-Saturday.

SPECIAL EVENTS
DELTA JUBILEE

114 Delta Ave., Clarksdale
This statewide arts and crafts festival includes the Mississippi championship pork barbecue cooking contest, a 5K run and an antique car show.
First weekend in June.

SUNFLOWER RIVER BLUES AND GOSPEL FESTIVAL

Clarksdale, www.sunflowerfest.org
For those seeking a flavor of the local music, this weekend of outdoor concerts puts on performances of the blues on Friday and Saturday, with gospel on Sunday. The food choices include local barbecue and other Southern specialties.
Early August.

WHERE TO STAY
★BEST WESTERN EXECUTIVE INN

710 S. State St., Clarksdale, 662-627-9292; www.bestwestern.com
93 rooms. Restaurant. Complimentary breakfast. $61-150

COLUMBUS

See also Starkville
Birthplace of Pulitzer Prize-winning playwright Tennessee Williams, Columbus is a mid-sized town on the Tennessee-Tombigbee Waterway. It began as a stopover on the Military Road between New Orleans and Nashville and served as a hospital town, thereby dodging Union attacks. The Columbus Female Institute, founded in 1847, later became the first state-supported school in the United States to offer education exclusively to women, the Mississippi University for Women, established in 1884.

WHAT TO SEE
BLEWETT-HARRISON-LEE MUSEUM
316 Seventh St. N., Columbus, 662-327-8888
Known also as the General Stephen D. Lee home, the museum contains articles of local history as well as Civil War exhibits. Daily.

FRIENDSHIP CEMETERY
Fourth Street S. and 13th Avenue, Columbus, 662-328-2565
The first Memorial Day—April 25, 1866—was observed here when the women of Columbus gathered to decorate graves of Union and Confederate soldiers. Daily.

LAKE LOWNDES STATE PARK
3319 Lake Lowndes, Columbus, 662-328-2110; www.mdwfp.com
This is one of the finest recreation complexes of the state parks. The grounds are approximately 600 acres with a nature trail, tennis courts, game fields, a picnicking area, children's playground, concession stands, an indoor recreation complex, cabins and campgrounds. The park also has a 150-acre lake for activities such as swimming, waterskiing, fishing and boating. Daily.

WAVERLY PLANTATION
1852 Waverley Mansion Road, Columbus, 662-494-1399
Here you'll find a classic Southern mansion with twin, circular, self-supporting stairways leading to a 65-foot-high observation cupola. The house contains original gold-leaf mirrors and Italian marble mantels. Daily.

WHERE TO STAY
★COMFORT INN
1210 Highway 45 N., Columbus, 662-329-2422, 800-228-5150; www.choicehotels.com

106 rooms. Complimentary breakfast. Business center. $61-150

★★MASTER HOST INN & SUITES
506 Highway 45 N., Columbus, 662-328-5202, 800-465-4329; www.masterhostinn.com
153 rooms. Restaurant, bar. $61-150

WHERE TO EAT
★★HARVEY'S
200 Main St., Columbus, 662-327-1639; www.eatwithus.com
Southern. Lunch, dinner. Closed Sunday. $16-35

CORINTH
See also Holly Springs
Corinth preserves and celebrates its Civil War history. The town's location as a major railroad junctions made it an important strategic site during the war. Between 1861 and 1865, as many as 300,000 soldiers from the north and the south occupied the town.

In a struggle for control of the area, 65,000 Union troops met 44,000 Confederate troops in the Battle of Shiloh; the Confederate soldiers lost and evacuated the city. Six months later, they attempted (but failed) to reclaim the city in the Battle of Corinth, the bloodiest clash of the Civil War in Mississippi.

WHAT TO SEE
BATTERY ROBINETT

102 Linden St., Corinth, 662-287-9273

This union fort was constructed on inner defense lines during the Battle of Corinth in 1862. Monuments mark the spots where Confederate soldiers died, and headstones commemorate color-bearers who fell while trying to plant a flag during battle. Daily.

CURLEE HOUSE

705 Jackson St., Corinth, 662-287-9501; www.verandahhouse.org

A restored antebellum house, this was the headquarters for Generals Bragg, Halleck and Hood during the Civil War. Daily.

JACINTO COURTHOUSE

Jacinto, 215 N. Fillmore, 662-286-8662; www.corinth.net

This is a fine example of early Federal architecture, serving first as the courthouse for old Tishomingo County. Later the site was used as both a school and a church.
Tuesday-Sunday.

GREENVILLE

See also Yazoo City

Greenville is in the Mississippi Delta on Lake Ferguson, an oxbow lake created by levees on the Mississippi River. Here visitors will find beautiful cypress groves, lively juke joints and the bright lights of casinos on the lake.

WHAT TO SEE
BIRTHPLACE OF THE FROG EXHIBIT

South Deer Creek Drive, East Leland, 662-686-2687; www.lelandms.org/kermit.html

It might not easy being green, but it is easy to celebrate the man who gave us Kermit the Frog. This exhibit, in the Washington County Tourist Center, houses Muppet memorabilia from collectors and the family of the late Jim Henson, the creator of Kermit, Miss Piggy and the rest of the Muppet gang. September-May, Monday-Saturday 10 a.m.-4 p.m., June-August, daily 10 a.m.-5 p.m.

LEROY PERCY STATE PARK

Highway 12, W., Hollandale, 662-827-5436; www.mdwfp.com

The oldest of Mississippi's state parks comprises approximately 2,400 acres of artesian springs, cypress trees and ancient oaks covered in Spanish moss. One of the four hot artesian wells provides water for an alligator pond, which can be viewed from the boardwalk. Nature trails lead through the Delta lowlands and a live alligator exhibit. Daily.

RIVER ROAD QUEEN

Highway 82, Greenville; www.steamboats.org

Built for the 1984 World's Fair, the replica of a 19th-century paddlewheel steamboat serves as the town's welcome center. Daily.

WINTERVILLE MOUNDS STATE PARK

2415 Highway 1 N., Greenville, 662-334-4684; www.ohwy.com/ms/w/winmousp.htm

One of the largest groups of Native American mounds in the Mississippi Valley, the area was a religious site and an economic and military center for thousands of Native Americans during the Mississippian era, which ended after De Soto's exploration. The park contains the Great Temple mound, which at 55 feet high is surrounded by ten smaller mounds used for a variety of purposes. Also on the grounds are picnicking shelters, a concession stand, a children's playground and a museum that houses artifacts from the mound site and adjoining territory.

Wednesday-Sunday.

SPECIAL EVENT
MISSISSIPPI DELTA BLUES AND HERITAGE FESTIVAL

Highway 1 South and Highway 454, Greenville, 601-335-3523; www.deltablues.org

The state's largest tourist attraction, this festival showcases blues musicians from across the country. More than 20,000 people arrive in Greenville to celebrate the native sounds of the Mississippi Delta, the birthplace of the blues.

September.

WHERE TO STAY
★DAYS INN

2701 Highway 82 E., Greenville, 662-334-1818; www.daysinn.com

120 rooms. Complimentary breakfast. $16-35

WHERE TO EAT
★SHERMAN'S

1400 S. Main St., Greenville, 662-332-6924

American, Italian. Lunch, dinner. Closed Sunday. $16-35

GREENWOOD

See also Grenada

Lying on both banks of the Yazoo River and surrounded by rich, black delta lands, Greenwood is in the heart of the deep South. In the town's early years, cotton boosted the local economy, and Greenwood served as an important river port in the South. After the Civil War, railroads brought more resources to the flourishing town. Today Greenwood's historic downtown district is undergoing a revival. Dozens of buildings have been restored, and unique shops, restaurants and galleries are popping up in the district.

WHAT TO SEE
COTTONLANDIA MUSEUM

1608 Highway 82 W., Greenwood, 662-453-0925; www.cottonlandia.org
Exhibits highlight the history of the Mississippi Delta, its people and its land from 10,000 B.C. to the present. There is also an exhibit focused on the work of Mississippi artists, a verdent garden and a gift shop.
Monday-Friday 9 a.m.-5 p.m., Saturday-Sunday 2-5 p.m.

WHERE TO STAY
★BEST WESTERN GREENWOOD

635 Highway 82 W., Greenwood, 662-455-5777, 888-455-5770; www.bestwestern.com
100 rooms. Complimentary breakfast. Pool. $61-150

★COMFORT INN

401 W Highway 82, Greenwood, 662-453-5974, 800-228-5150; www.choicehotels.com
60 rooms. Complimentary breakfast. $61-150

WHERE TO EAT
★★CRYSTAL GRILL

423 Carrollton Ave., Greenwood, 662-453-6530
Seafood, steak. Lunch, dinner. Closed Monday. $16-35

GRENADA

See also Greenwood
Home to Grenada Lake, the town in north-central Mississippi has plenty of opportunities to play outdoors. The lake attracts fishermen, boaters and campers who want to relax on its shores, while a newly-constructed 18-hole lakeside golf course gives duffers a chance to get in on the action as well.

WHAT TO SEE
GRENADA LAKE

2088 Scenic Loop 333, Grenada, 662-226-5911
Covering approximately 35,000 acres, with 200 miles of shoreline, the lake features swimming, water sports, fishing, hunting, boating, archery, tennis, camping and picnicking. Daily.

HUGH WHITE STATE PARK

3170 Hugh White State Park Road, Grenada, 662-226-4934; www.mdwfp.com
Located on Grenada Lake, the 1,581-acre park includes a swimming beach, a pool, a boat ramp and rentals, nature and bicycle trails, campgrounds, a picnicking shelter and a lodge. Daily.

SPECIAL EVENT
THUNDER ON WATER FESTIVAL

Grenada Lake, 800-373-2571
A parade, children's fishing rodeo, antique car show, boat light parade and several speed boat races are just part of what makes up this summer festival. Second weekend in June.

WHERE TO STAY
★★AMERICA'S BEST VALUE INN
1750 Sunset Drive, Grenada, 662-226-7816, 800-880-8866;
www.americasbestvalueinn.com
61 rooms. Complimentary breakfast. Restaurant. $61-150

★COMFORT INN
1552 Sunset Drive, Grenada, 662-226-1683, 800-228-5150; www.choicehotels.com
64 rooms. Complimentary breakfast. $61-150

GULFPORT
See also Biloxi, Ocean Springs
Gulfport's greatest asset—its prime spot near the Gulf of Mexico—became a liability in August of 2005, when Hurricane Katrina damaged much of the Gulf Coast, including many of Gulfport's buildings. The city is rebuilding, and this resort town is open for business. The same beaches that attracted visitors in the 1920s await sunbathers today, and Gulfport's proximity to lakes, rivers, bays and bayous make it an angler's paradise. The city has boutique shops, colorful casinos and several 18-hole golf courses open to the public.

WHAT TO SEE
JOHN C. STENNIS SPACE CENTER
NASA Space Center, 38 miles west via I-10, Gulfport, 228-688-2370; www.ssc.nasa.gov
In the 1960s and 1970s, locals would quip, "If you want to go to the moon, you have to go through Hancock County, Mississippi," part of the Gulfport-Biloxi metro area and home to the Stennis Space Center. NASA's largest rocket engine test facility, the Stennis Space Center was the testing site for Saturn V and for the first and second stages of the Apollo manned lunar program, which landed the first men on the moon in 1969. The Stennis Space Center hosts NASA and 18 federal and state agencies involved in oceanographic, environmental and national defense programs. There is a visitor center with a 90-foot Space Tower, films, demonstrations, indoor and outdoor exhibits and guided tours. Daily.

PORT OF GULFPORT
Mississippi Technical Center, 200 E Main St., Starkville, 662-324-7776;
www.starkville.org
The 1,320-foot-wide harbor separates the port's two parallel piers, which includes one of the largest banana import facilities in the U.S. Daily.

SHIP ISLAND EXCURSIONS
Gulfport Yacht Harbor, Highway 90, Gulfport, 228-864-1014; www.msshipisland.com
Come here to catch a passenger ferry that leaves from the Gulfport Yacht Harbor for a one-hour trip to Ship Island, 12 miles off the coast. You can spend as much time on the island as you like, as long as you catch the last ferry of the day, at either 2:30 or 5 p.m. depending on the day and time of year.

SPECIAL EVENT
MISSISSIPPI DEEP-SEA FISHING RODEO
Small Craft Harbor, Highways 49 and 90, Gulfport, 228-388-2271;
www.mississippideepseafishingrodeo.com
The "rodeo" attracts fishermen from the U.S., Canada and Latin America, who compete in this deep-sea and freshwater fishing classic. Children can compete, too, in the junior division. The festivities include a carnival, food and fireworks.
Early July.

WHERE TO EAT
★★VRAZEL'S
3206 W. Beach Blvd., Gulfport, 228-863-2229; www.vrazels.com
American. Lunch, dinner. Closed Sunday. $36-85

HATTIESBURG
See also Laurel
Hattiesburg's founder, William Hardy, named the town after his wife, Hattie. When railroads were routed through Hattiesburg during the late 19th century, the town began to thrive. Today, Hattiesburg boasts a booming arts scene and one of the largest historic districts in southeast Mississippi. The buildings reflect architectural styles from 1884 to 1930. Hattiesburg is also home to the University of Southern Mississippi; residents and visitors can enjoy the university's cultural and athletic events.

WHAT TO SEE
DE SOTO NATIONAL FOREST
654 W. Frontage Road, Chickasaw Ranger District, Wiggins, 601-965-4391, 601-528-6160; www.fs.fed.us/r8/mississippi
At approximately 500,000 acres, the park includes the Black Creek Float Trip, which offers 50 miles of scenic streams, and the Black Creek Trail, which has 41 miles of woodland paths, 10 of which go through 5,000 acres of Black Creek Wilderness. Activities include swimming, fishing, hiking, horse riding, picnicking and primitive camping. Daily.

PAUL B. JOHNSON STATE PARK
319 Geiger Lake Road, Hattiesburg, 601-582-7721; www.mdwfp.com
The park contains more than 805 acres of pine forest and a spring-fed lake that provides excellent facilities for water sports. Waterskiing is a popular activity here. Daily.

UNIVERSITY OF SOUTHERN MISSISSIPPI
2700 Hardy St., Hattiesburg, 601-266-4491; www.usm.edu
The University's library houses a large collection of original illustrations and manuscripts for children's books by authors and artists from here and abroad. The American Rose Society looks after a garden that blooms from spring to mid-December. Daily.

WHERE TO STAY
★★RAMADA INN
6595 Highway 49 N., Hattiesburg, 601-599-2001, 800-228-5150; www.ramada.com
119 rooms. Restaurant, bar. Complimentary breakfast. $61-150

★★HOLIDAY INN
6563 Highway 49 N., Hattiesburg, 601-268-2850, 800-465-4329; www.holiday-inn.com
128 rooms. Restaurant, bar. $61-150

WHERE TO EAT
★★CHESTERFIELD'S
2507 Hardy St., Hattiesburg, 601-582-2778; www.hattiesburg.org
Seafood, steak. Lunch, dinner. $16-35

★★CRESCENT CITY GRILL
3810 Hardy St., Hattiesburg, 601-264-0657; www.nsrg.com
Creole, French. Lunch, dinner. $16-35

HOLLY SPRINGS
See also Memphis, TN
Holly Springs crowns the ridge along which a Native American trail once led from the Mississippi to the tribal home of the Chickasaw Nation. Holly Springs has a reputation for preserving its historical buildings, including the antebellum homes that rose during a prosperous era in the 19th century. But perhaps its most remarkable attraction is Graceland, a museum full of Elvis memorabilia, open 24 hours a day.

WHAT TO SEE
HOLLY SPRINGS NATIONAL FOREST
1000 Front St., Oxford, 662-965-4391; www.fs.fed.us/r8/mississippi
Intensive erosion control measures are carried out within this 152,200-acre area. Activities include fishing, large and small game hunting and boating at Puskus, Chewalla and Tillatoba lakes. Daily.

KATE MAN CLARK ART GALLERY
300 E. College Ave., Holly Springs
Endowed by the artist to house her works permanently, the gallery contains more than 1,000 paintings done while Clark studied under William Merritt Chase in New York in the early 1900s. Clark returned to her native Holly Springs in 1923 and stored her work here until her death 40 years later. Also on site are three canvasses by Chase and one by Rockwell Kent.

MARSHALL COUNTY HISTORICAL MUSEUM
220 E. College Ave., Holly Springs, 662-252-3669; www.marshallcountyms.org
The museum houses local historical artifacts, a Civil War room, as well as quilts, dolls, toys, antique clothing and wildlife exhibits.
Monday-Saturday.

RUST COLLEGE

150 Rust Ave., Holly Springs, 662-252-8000; www.rustcollege.edu

This historically black liberal arts college rests on the site of a campground for General Grant's troops. On campus is Leontyne Price Library, home to the Roy Wilkins Collection on civil rights.
Daily.

JACKSON

See also Mendenhall, Yazoo City

Jackson sits on the bluffs above the Pearl River, a site chosen by French Canadian pioneer Louis LeFleur for its proximity to navigable water, a necessary resource for a new settlement's economic future. Named for Major General Andrew Jackson, the hero of the South who would become the seventh president of the United States, the growing town became the capital of Mississippi in 1821. During the Civil War, the town was burned by Union troops, and Jackson earned the unfortunate nickname "Chimneyville."

In 1868, the "Black and Tan" convention that met in Jackson was the first political organization in Mississippi with black representation. Its attendees framed a state constitution that gave black citizens the right to vote and enabled a few to attain high political office.

Not surprisingly, in the early to mid-20th century, Jackson was not immune from the increased racial tensions that plagued the nation and especially the South. During the civil-rights movement, clashes between white supremacists and black activists came to a head here, when Ku Klux Klan member Byron de la Beckwith murdered civil-rights leader Medgar Evers in 1963. More than 30 years later, Beckwith was convicted of the crime.

In the second half of the 20th century, Jackson's population grew steadily and the city established itself as a main metropolis of the South. With the influx of residents came more recreational and cultural activities. Today, art galleries, museums, historic homes, theaters and blues and jazz clubs line city streets.

Jackson is Mississippi's most populated city with more than 400,000 residents, but it feels smaller because the population is relatively spread out. Most of the city's cultural offerings are downtown, but visitors trek to Jackson's different neighborhoods to get a real feel for the city. Ridgeland, a few miles from the city center, is a hotbed of restaurants, hotels and shops that range from chain stores to locally owned boutiques. Farish Street, west of downtown, was a center of African-American culture, politics and business after the Civil War. Once a vibrant community, Farish Street is now economically depressed but full of fascinating sites and stories. And Mid North, a comfortable residential area, is home to Millsaps College.

WHAT TO SEE
ARCHIVES AND LIBRARY DIVISION

Jackson, 601-359-6876, 601-576-6876; www.mdah.state.ms.us

Here you'll find the state archives, history collections and a research library.
Daily.

BATTLEFIELD PARK
Porter Street and Langley Avenue, Jackson
The site of a Civil War battle, the park contains an original cannon and trenches.

CONFEDERATE MONUMENT
East end of Capitol Street at State Street, Jackson
This monument was built with money raised by the women of Mississippi and by legislative appropriations. Daily.

GOVERNOR'S MANSION
300 E. Capitol St., Jackson, 601-359-6421; www.mdah.state.ms.us
Restored to its original Greek revival style, the mansion houses antiques and period furnishings. The grounds occupy an entire block and features gardens and gazebos.
Tours: Tuesday-Friday mornings.

JACKSON ZOOLOGICAL PARK
2918 W. Capitol St., Jackson, 601-352-2580; www.jacksonzoo.com
More than 400 mammals, birds and reptiles are housed here in naturalized habitats.
Daily 8 a.m.-4 p.m.

MANSHIP HOUSE
420 E. Fortification St., Jackson, 601-961-4724; www.mdah.state.ms.us
This restored Gothic revival cottage circa 1855 was the residence of Charles Henry Manship, mayor of Jackson during the Civil War. Here you'll find period furnishings as well as fine examples of wood graining and marbling.
Tuesday-Friday 9 a.m.-4 p.m., Saturday 10 a.m.-4 p.m.

MISSISSIPPI AGRICULTURE & FORESTRY MUSEUM AND NATIONAL AGRICULTURAL AVIATION MUSEUM
1150 Lakeland Drive, Jackson, 601-713-3365, 800-844-8687; www.mdac.state.ms.us
This complex, covering 39 acres, includes a museum exhibit center, forest trail, a 1920s living history town and farm.
Monday-Saturday 9 a.m.-5 p.m.

MISSISSIPPI MUSEUM OF ART
380 South Lamar St., Jackson, 601-960-1515; www.msmuseumart.org
Exhibitions of 19th- and 20th-century works by local, regional, national and international artists are on display here. The museum's collection also includes African-American folk art, photographs, a sculpture garden, a hands-on children's gallery and a restaurant.
Tuesday-Saturday 10 a.m.-6 p.m., Sunday noon-6 p.m.

MISSISSIPPI PETRIFIED FOREST
124 Forest Park Road, Flora, 601-879-8189; www.mspetrifiedforest.com
Surface erosion has exposed giant trees up to six feet in diameter. Onsite are petrified logs that were deposited in the Mississippi area as driftwood by a

prehistoric river, a self-guided nature trail and a museum at the visitor center that has a gift shops and dioramas as well as wood, gem, mineral and fossil displays. Daily.

MISSISSIPPI SPORTS HALL OF FAME AND MUSEUM

1152 Lakeland Drive, Jackson, 601-982-8264, 800-280-3263; www.msfame.com

The museum celebrates great athletes who hail from Mississippi, including Walter Payton, Archie Manning and George "Boomer" Scott. Touch-screen television kiosks play archival sports footage. Through interactive technology, visitors can play championship golf courses, kick soccer balls into "goals" and throw a baseball into a "field."

Monday-Saturday 10 a.m.-4 p.m.

MUNICIPAL ART GALLERY

839 N. State St., Jackson, 601-960-1582;www.jacksonms.gov

The gallery features changing exhibits in a variety of media displayed in an antebellum house.

Admission: free. Tuesday-Saturday 9 a.m.-5 p.m. Sunday 2-5 p,m.

MUSEUM OF NATURAL SCIENCE

2148 Riverside Drive, Jackson, 601-354-7303; www.mdwfp.com/museum

Collections, designed for research and education, cover Mississippi's vertebrates, invertebrates, plants and fossils. Exhibits and aquariums depict the ecological story of the region, and educational programs and workshops are offered for all ages.

Monday-Friday 8 a.m.-5 p.m., Saturday 9 a.m.-5 p.m., Sunday 1-5 p.m.

MYNELLE GARDENS

4736 Clinton Blvd., Jackson, 601-960-1894

This 5-acre display garden has thousands of azaleas, camellias, daylilies, flowering trees and other perennials, reflecting pools, a statuary, an Oriental garden and an all-white garden. The turn-of-the-century Westbrook House is open for viewing. Daily.

OLD CAPITOL

100 S. State St., Jackson, 601-576-6920; www.mdah.state.ms.us/museum

The State Historical Museum here traces state history in a restored Greek revival building that was the state capitol from 1839 to 1903. Onsite is also a collection of Jefferson Davis memorabilia.

Monday-Friday 8 a.m.-5 p.m., Saturday 9:30 a.m.-4:30 p.m., Sunday 12:30-4:30 p.m.

ROSS R. BARNETT RESERVOIR

115 Madison Landing Circle, Ridgeland, 601-354-3448, 601-856-6574;www.rossbar-nettreservoir.org

This reservoir is 43 miles long and was created by damming the Pearl River. Activities include swimming, fishing, boating, and facilities include a playground and picnicking shelters. Daily.

SMITH ROBERTSON MUSEUM

528 Bloom St., Jackson, 601-960-1457; www.city.jackson.ms.us

This museum highlights the history and culture of African-American Mississippians from pre-slavery times to the present. Onsite is a large collection of photos, books, documents, arts and crafts.

Monday-Friday 9 a.m.-5 p.m., Saturday 10 a.m.-1 p.m., Sunday 2-5 p.m.

STATE CAPITOL

400 High St., Jackson, 601-359-3114

Impeccably restored in 1979, the lavish, Beaux-Arts-style capitol building was patterned after the national capitol in Washington. When the legislature is in session, visitors can take a seat in the chamber of the state House or Senate to watch some political wrangling. On the first floor, the Hall of Governors holds portraits of the state's governors since Mississippi Territory was created in 1798.

Tours can be arranged by appointment only.

THE OAKS HOUSE MUSEUM

823 N Jefferson St., Jackson, 601-353-9339; www.theoakshousemuseum.org

This Greek revival cottage, built of hand-hewn timber by James H. Boyd, former mayor of Jackson, was occupied by General Sherman during the siege of 1863. The house contains period furniture.

Tuesday-Saturday 10 a.m.-3 p.m.

SPECIAL EVENTS
DIXIE NATIONAL LIVESTOCK SHOW AND RODEO

Mississippi Coliseum, 1207 Mississippi St., Jackson, 601-961-4000;
www.mdac.state.ms.us

World Championship cowboys compete in a thrilling rodeo, complete with rodeo clowns, barrel racers and ropers. When you're not watching bull riders hold on for dear life, enjoy the parade, pageant and Dixie National Rodeo Dance.

Late January-mid-February; rodeo second week in February.

NATIONAL CUTTING HORSE ASSOCIATION SHOW*Mississippi Coliseum,*

1207 Mississippi St., Jackson, 601-961-4000; www.dixienational.org

Challengers from across the U.S. participate in amateur and professional rider competitions. Late March.

WHERE TO STAY
★★EDISON WALTHALL HOTEL

225 E. Capitol St., Jackson, 601-948-6161, 800-932-6161;
www.edisonwalthallhotel.com

208 rooms. Restaurant, bar. Fitness center. Pool. $61-150

★★★HILTON JACKSON

1001 E. County Line Road, Jackson, 601-957-2800, 888-263-0524; www.hilton.com

The hotel offers a full-service restaurant, a courtyard pool, a poolside fitness center, a complimentary airport shuttle and more. The property is near many of the local area attractions.

276 rooms. Restaurant, bar. Business center. Fitness room. Pool. $61-150

★LA QUINTA INN
616 Briarwood Drive, Jackson, 601-957-1741, 800-687-6667; www.laquinta.com
144 rooms. Complimentary breakfast. Fitness center. Pool. Pets accepted.
$61-150

WHERE TO EAT
★COCK OF THE WALK
141 Madison Landing, Jackson, 601-856-5500; www.cockofthewalk.biz
American. Dinner. $15 and under.

★★DENNERY'S
330 Greymont Ave., Jackson, 601-354-2527
American. Lunch, dinner. Closed Sunday. $16-35

★★NICK'S
1501 Lakeland Drive, Jackson, 601-981-8017; www.nicksrestaurant.com
Seafood. Dinner. Closed Sunday. $16-35

LAUREL
See also Hattiesburg
Built by two sawmill men in the piney woods of southeastern Mississippi after reconstruction, Laurel is a charming southern town with oak-lined streets and historic homes.

WHAT TO SEE
LANDRUM'S HOMESTEAD
1356 Highway 15 S., Laurel, 601-649-2546; www.landrums.com
This recreation of a late 1800s settlement Includes a blacksmith shop, a grist mill, a display of gem mining and a general store.
Monday-Saturday 9 a.m.-5 p.m.

LAUREN ROGERS MUSEUM OF ART
565 N. Fifth Ave., Laurel, 601-649-6374; www.lrma.org
The museum features 19th- and 20th-century American and European paintings, 18th-century Japanese woodblock prints, English Georgian silver and Native American baskets.
Tuesday-Saturday 10 a.m.-4:45 p.m., Sunday 1-4 p.m.

WHERE TO STAY
★★RAMADA
1105 Sawmill Rd., Laurel, 601-649-9100, 800-272-6232; www.ramada.com
207 rooms. Restaurant, bar. $61-150

MENDENHALL

See also Jackson

Fish, fish and more fish is one reason to visit this small city, home to lakes and 178,000 acres of forest.

WHAT TO SEE
BIENVILLE NATIONAL FOREST

3473 Highway 35 S., 601-469-3811; www.fs.fed.us/r8/mississippi/bienville

Fish-filled lakes, beautiful pine woods and well-maintained campsites make Bienville an ideal place to play outdoors. The forest's 178,000 acres attract hunters, fishermen, hikers, mountain bikers and anyone who just needs to find peace, quiet and a beautiful setting. Activities include swimming, boating, hiking, horse back riding, picnicking and camping.

D'LO WATER PARK

27 miles south via Highway 49, Mendenhall, 601-847-4310; www.dlowaterpark.com

This park is spread out over 85 acres. Activities include swimming, canoeing and fishing, while facilities include a playground, playing fields, a snack bar, picnicking shelters, boat ramps and rentals, campgrounds and cabins. Daily.

MERIDIAN

See also Hattiesburg, Jackson

Founded at the junction of two railroads, Meridian was Mississippi's golden city during the turn of the 20th century. Today the city has nine distinct historic districts and more downtown historic buildings than any city in the state.

WHAT TO SEE
BIENVILLE NATIONAL FOREST

3473 Highway 35, 601-469-3811; www.fs.fed.us/r8/mississippi/bienville

Fish-filled lakes, beautiful pine woods and well-maintained campsites make Bienville an ideal place to play outdoors. The forest's 178,000 acres attract hunters, fishermen, hikers, mountain bikers and anyone who just needs to find peace, quiet and a beautiful setting. Daily.

FRANK W. WILLIAMS HOUSE

905 Martin Luther King, Jr. Memorial Drive, Meridian, 601-483-8439

This Victorian home, circa 1886, features stained glass, oak paneling, parquet floors and detailed gingerbread. There are special Christmas tours. Monday-Saturday.

JIMMIE RODGERS MUSEUM

1725 Jimmie Rodgers Drive, Meridian, 601-485-1808; www.jimmierodgers.com

Fashioned after an old train depot, the museum houses souvenirs and memorabilia of the "Father of Country Music," including a rare Martin 00045 guitar.
Daily.

MERIDIAN MUSEUM OF ART

628 25th Ave., Meridian, 601-693-1501; www.meridianmuseum.org
Permanent and changing exhibits include paintings, graphics, photographs, sculpture and crafts by regional artists.
Tuesday-Sunday.

MERREHOPE

905 Martin Luther King Jr. Memorial Drive, Meridian, 601-483-8439;
www.merrehope.com
The stately 20-room mansion, first built in 1859, features unusual wood-work, handsome columns, mantels and stairway. There are special Christmas tours.
Monday-Saturday.

SPECIAL EVENT
JIMMIE RODGERS MEMORIAL FESTIVAL

Meridian, 601-482-8001; www.jimmierodgers.com/festival.html
Boot-scoot to Meridian for this festival, which celebrates country and western music with performances by big-name headliners and local talent, a barbecue cook-off and car show. May.

WHERE TO STAY
★BEST WESTERN OF MERIDIAN

2219 S. Frontage Road, Meridian, 601-693-3210, 800-528-1234;
www.bestwestern.com
122 rooms. Pool. $61-150

NATCHEZ

See also Woodville
Natchez delivers the enchantment of the Old South, with a plantation atmosphere where everything seems beautiful and romantic. Greek revival mansions, manicured gardens and lawns, tree-shaded streets and southern hospitality abound in this museum of the antebellum South.
Named for a Native American tribe, Natchez has seen French, Spanish, English, Confederate and U.S. flags fly over the city, one of the oldest in the Mississippi Valley. Vestiges of the Spanish influence can still be seen along South Wall Street, near Washington Street, a charming neighborhood once restricted to the Spanish dons.

WHAT TO SEE
CANAL STREET DEPOT

Canal and State streets, Natchez
Located one block from the Mississippi River, the Depot houses the Natchez Pilgrimage Tour and Tourist Headquarters, a children's factory outlet and old-fashioned shops. Also available is information on historic Natchez and the surrounding area as well as carriage tours through the Natchez Historic District, presented with a 35-minute overview of the town's antebellum history along with tours of Victorian townhouses and churches. Daily.

EMERALD MOUND

2680 Natchez Trace Parkway, Natchez, 601-442-2658; www.cr.nps.gov

One of the largest mounds in North America, Emerald Mound was a ceremonial center for ancestors of the Natchez Indians between A.D. 1250 and 1600. Daily.

GRAND VILLAGE OF THE NATCHEZ

400 Jefferson Davis Blvd., Natchez, 601-446-6502; www.mdah.state.ms.us

Here you'll find a museum, an archaeological site, nature trails, a picnic area and a gift shop.

Monday-Saturday 9 a.m.-5p.m., Sunday 1:30-5 p.m.

HISTORIC JEFFERSON COLLEGE

16 Old North St., Washington, 601-442-2901; www.mdah.state.ms.us

The Jefferson College campus was the site, in 1817, of the first state Constitutional Convention. Jefferson Davis was among the famous Mississippians who attended the school. No longer used as a college, it is now listed on the National Register of Historic places. A museum interprets the early history of the territory. The site includes nature trails and an area for picnicking.

Monday-Saturday 9 a.m.-5 p.m., Sunday 1-5 p.m.

HISTORIC SPRINGFIELD PLANTATION

Natchez, Highway 553 Fayette Mississippi, 601-786-3802

Believed to be the first mansion erected in Mississippi, the main house remains nearly intact with little remodeling over the years. Built for Thomas Marston Green Jr. a wealthy planter from Virginia, and the site of Andrew Jackson's wedding, the mansion displays original hand-carved woodwork, Civil War equipment, railroad memorabilia and a narrow-gauge locomotive. Daily.

HOMOCHITTO NATIONAL FOREST

Natchez, northeast and southeast via Highway 84, 98, 33, 601-965-4391, 601-384-5876; www.fs.fed.us/r8/mississippi/homochitto

This 189,000-acre forest was the first of Mississippi's six national forests, established in 1936. Camp in any of the three recreation areas, and hike through the eastern half of the park, renowned among hikers for its irregular terrain and excellent trail system.

Activities include swimming, fishing, hunting, picnicking and camping.

THE HOUSE ON ELLICOTT HILL

211 N. Canal St., Natchez, 601-442-2011

This is the site where, in 1797, Andrew Ellicott raised the first American flag in the lower Mississippi Valley. Built in 1798, the house overlooks both the Mississippi and the terminus of the Natchez Trace. The house is fully restored and authentically furnished. Daily.

LONGWOOD

140 Lower Woodville Road, Natchez, 601-442-5193

This enormous, Italianate-detailed "octagon house" is crowned with an onion dome. Because the house was under construction at the start of the Civil War, its interiors were never completed above first floor. Containing 1840 furnishings, Longwood is owned and operated by the Pilgrimage Garden Club. Daily.

MAGNOLIA HALL

South Pearl and Washington, Natchez, 601-442-6847; www.natchezgardenclub.com
The last great mansion to be erected in the city before the outbreak of the Civil War, Magnolia Hall is an outstanding example of Greek revival architecture. The mansion contains period antiques and a costume museum. Daily.

MELROSE ESTATE HOME

1 Melrose Ave., off Highway 61, Natchez, 601-446-5790; www.nps.gov/natc
The National Park Service oversees this historic mansion and grounds and tells the plantation story from a national perspective. The house is open for guided tours only, with self-guided tours available for the slave quarters. Daily.

MONMOUTH

36 Melrose Ave., Natchez, 601-442-5852; www.monmouthplantation.com
Registered as a National Historic Landmark, the monumental Greek revival house and auxiliary buildings, once owned by Mexican War hero General John Anthony Quitman, have been completely restored, with antique furnishings and extensive gardens. Monmouth also has guest rooms and tours available. Daily.

MOUNT LOCUST

2680 Natchez Trace Parkway, Natchez, 601-445-4211
One of Mississippi's oldest structures, Mount Locust was built in the 1780s and used as an inn on the Natchez Trail.

NATCHEZ STATE PARK

230B Wickliff Road, Natchez, 601-442-2658; www.mdwfp.com
The park's horse trails are believed to be abandoned plantation roads that lead to Brandon Hall, home of the first native Mississippi governor, Gerard Brandon, who served 1826-1831. Activities here include fishing, boating, picnicking and camping. Daily.

NATCHEZ VISITOR CENTER

640 S. Canal, Natchez, 800-647-6742; www.cityofnatchez.com
This spacious visitor center on the bluff above the Mississippi River offers tourist services, including a film on the city's history and heritage. Daily.

ROSALIE

100 Orleans St., Natchez, 601-445-4555; www.rosaliemansion.com
This red brick Georgian mansion with a Greek revival portico served as the headquarters for the Union Army during occupation of Natchez. The original furnishings date from 1857, and the grounds contain gardens overlooking the

SIGHTSEEING IN THE HISTORIC DISTRICT

Visit Natchez for a glimpse of the antebellum South. Built on a high bluff overlooking the Mississippi River, the town has a compact downtown area that history buffs will want to explore. Many of the historic buildings now house museums, where visitors can learn more about the town's fascinating history, and there are plenty of restaurants, cafés and shops to break up a day of sightseeing. Start upriver and work your way back down. The oldest house in town, built in 1799, is the small two-story House on Ellicott Hill (North Canal at Jefferson, 601-442-2011). Settler Andrew Elliott raised the American flag here in defiance of Spain, which claimed the broad plain along the Gulf to the Mississippi River as Spanish West Florida.

Walk away from the river down Jefferson, then up Pearl Street a block to Stanton Hall (601-442-6282). A stately mansion built in 1857, Stanton Hall fits the classic image of opulent antebellum architecture. Find fine dining and theater in the cottage house. Keeping strolling down Pearl Street toward the commercial district.

Two blocks down, carriage tours depart from the entranceway of the Natchez Eola Hotel. Around the corner on Main Street, in the old Post Office building, the Museum of Afro-American History and Culture (601-445-0728), provides an important reminder of the other side of the town's antebellum history.

Two blocks farther south along Pearl, Magnolia Hall (215 S. Pearl St., 601-442-6672), a Greek revival mansion, built in 1858, is now a house museum. A block west toward the river is the Governor Holmes House (207 S. Wall St., 601-442-2366). Home of the last governor of the Mississippi Territory, Holmes became the first state governor when Mississippi joined the Union in 1817. Like many of the historic houses in town, it also operates as an inn.

At Wall Street and Washington, get a bite to eat at one of the cafés or a great area bookshop. Cross Canal Street and skip down a block to visit Rosalie, on the bluff at South Broadway, a lovely brick mansion that served as Union Army headquarters during the Civil War.

Walk upriver a couple of blocks until you see the steep road leading down the bluff. This leads to Natchez Under-the-Hill, once the neighborhood that catered to the seedier side of the steamboat trade. Today it is harmless, though it retains the look and spirit of the Old West frontier. There are several family restaurants and a tavern called the Saloon, all with great river views. Down at the water, the Lady Luck riverboat casino operates around the clock. If you've parked at the visitor center, your car is right up the hill from here.

Mississippi River.
Daily 9:30 a.m.-4:30 p.m.

STANTON HALL
401 High St., Natchez, 601-446-6631
This elaborate antebellum mansion is surrounded by giant oaks and contains original chandeliers, marble mantels, Sheffield hardware and French mirrors.
Daily 9 a.m.-4:30 p.m.

SPECIAL EVENTS
GREAT MISSISSIPPI RIVER BALLOON RACE WEEKEND
640 S. Canal St., Natchez; www.natchezballoonrace.com
As many as 100 hot-air balloons fly at once during this fall festival, which also offers musical entertainment and food.
Third weekend in October.

NATCHEZ OPERA FESTIVAL

64 Homochitto St., Natchez; www.alcorn.edu/opera

At the Margaret Martin Performing Arts Center on the Mississippi River, the festival draws performers from different parts of the country to Natchez's fine stage in the spring.

April-May.

WHERE TO STAY
★★★DUNLEITH PLANTATION

84 Homochitto St., Natchez, 601-446-8500, 800-433-2445; www.dunleith.com

This luxurious home has recently been restored to its pre-Civil War style.

9 rooms. Children over 14 years only. Complimentary breakfast. $151-250

★★ISLE OF CAPRI CASINO & HOTEL

645 S. Canal St., Natchez, 601-445-0605, 800-722-5825; www.isleofcapricasino.com

147 rooms. Restaurant. $61-150

★★★MONMOUTH PLANTATION

36 Melrose Ave., Natchez, 601-442-5852, 800-828-4531;
www.monmouthplantation.com

Visitors might expect to see Scarlet O'Hara herself gliding through the vast courtyards of this beautiful plantation home. During the day, stroll or take a carriage ride through the historic site; in the evening, enjoy a five-course dinner served in the elegant dining room.

30 rooms. Children over 14 years only. Complimentary breakfast. $151-250

★★NATCHEZ EOLA HOTEL

110 Pearl St., Natchez, 601-445-6000; www.natchezeola.com

131 rooms. Restaurant, bar. Business center. Fitness center. $61-150

WHERE TO EAT
★★CARRIAGE HOUSE

401 High St., Natchez, 601-445-5153; www.stantonhall.com

American. Lunch. $16-35

★COCK OF THE WALK

200 N. Broadway, Natchez, 601-446-8920

American. Dinner. $16-35

OCEAN SPRINGS

See also Biloxi, Gulfport, Pascagoula

Across the bay from Biloxi, Ocean Springs was severely damaged by Hurricane Katrina in August 2005. The popular Ocean Springs Yacht Club is gone, as are several of the area's historic buildings. The bridge that connected Ocean Springs and Biloxi was destroyed, but a new bridge was completed in 2008. Despite Katrina's wallop, Ocean Springs is still a beautiful destination. It has a thriving arts community and a secluded downtown area with galleries, unique restaurants and diverse architecture.

WHAT TO SEE
GULF COAST RESEARCH LAB/J. L. SCOTT MARINE EDUCATION CENTER & AQUARIUM

703 E. Beach Drive, Ocean Springs, 228-374-5550; www.usm.edu/gcrl
The J.L. Scott Marine Education Center in Biloxi was destroyed by Hurricane Katrina in August 2005. Employees of the aquarium recovered many of the animals, and facilities in the Southeast have adopted the animals until the aquarium is rebuilt. The research lab still hosts professional events and programs for locals, such as a children's sea camp.

WHERE TO EAT
★★JOCELYN'S

Highway 90 E., Ocean Springs, 228-875-1925
French, Creole. Dinner. Closed Sunday-Monday. $16-35

OXFORD

See also Grenada
Oxford was named for the English university city in an effort to lure the University of Mississippi to the site. It worked. In 1848 the university opened. Today, "Ole Miss," with its forested, hilly campus, dominates the area, and Oxford relishes its role as a college town.

Locals also relish Oxford's reputation as a jewel of the South, complete with an historic town square, eclectic restaurants, stylish boutiques and tree-lined neighborhoods. Stick around long enough and you'll hear a local mantra: "We may never win every game, but we aren't never lost a party."

The city knows how to have a good time, but it also has a certain appeal for writers. William Faulkner, Nobel Prize-winning author, lived near the university at "Rowan Oak," and many landmarks of his fictional Yoknapatawpha County can be found in surrounding Lafayette County. John Grisham keeps a house here, too.

WHAT TO SEE
UNIVERSITY ARCHIVES

University Library, Oxford, 662-232-7408
Here you'll find the historical and literary works by and about Mississippians. The Faulkner collection includes translations of his writings in 35 languages; exhibit of his awards, including the Nobel Prize; manuscripts and first editions.
Monday-Friday 8 a.m.-5 p.m.

UNIVERSITY MUSEUMS

University Avenue and Fifth Street, Oxford, 662-232-7073
Housed in two adjoining buildings, the collections include Greek and Roman antiquities, antique scientific instruments as well as African-American, Caribbean and Southern folk art.
Tuesday-Saturday 9:30 a.m.-4:30 p.m., Sunday 1-4 p.m.

UNIVERSITY OF MISSISSIPPI

University Avenue, Oxford, 662-915-7431; www.olemiss.edu

Football is religion here, and the Rebels' fans take it very seriously. If you're here on game day, you'd better root for the right team. If you miss the game, Ole Miss still has plenty of offerings for visitors.

WHERE TO STAY
★DOWNTOWN OXFORD INN & SUITES

400 N. Lamar Blvd., Oxford, 662-234-3031, 800-780-7234; www.downtownoxfordinn.com

123 rooms. $61-150

★DAYS INN

1101 Frontage Road, Oxford, 662-234-9500; www.daysinn.com

100 rooms. Restaurant. Pool. Pets accepted. $61-150

★SUPER 8

2201 Jackson Ave. W., Oxford, 662-234-7013; www.super8.com

116 rooms. Complimentary breakfast. Pool. Pets accepted. $61-150

WHERE TO EAT
★★DOWNTOWN GRILL

110 Courthouse Square, Oxford, 662-234-2659; www.downtowngrill.net

American. Breakfast, lunch, dinner. Closed Sunday. $16-35

PASCAGOULA

See also Biloxi, Ocean Springs; Mobile, AL

Hurricane Katrina heavily damaged Pascagoula during her rampage of the Gulf Coast in August 2005. Still, this resort town, which is also Mississippi's busiest port, is rebuilding and welcomes visitors who want to smell the salt air, play a little golf or try their luck with a fishing pole.

The town gets its name from the Pascagoula Native Americans, who lived here before European settlers arrived. Local legend says that a young chieftain wooed and won the heart of a princess in the neighboring Biloxi tribe, even though she was betrothed. The Biloxi chief, enraged, attacked the Pascagoula tribe. Realizing they would not win, the Pascagoula joined hands and walked, singing, into the river that bears their name. To this day, the legend says, you'll hear their singing from the Pascagoula River.

WHAT TO SEE
MISSISSIPPI SANDHILL CRANE NATIONAL WILDLIFE REFUGE

7200 Gautier Vancleave Road, Pascagoula, 228-497-6322; www.fws.gov/mississippisandhillcrane/

Established to protect endangered cranes, the refuge has three units that total 18,000 acres. Also here is a three-quarter-mile wildlife trail mile with interpretive panels, an outdoor exhibit and areas for bird-watching. The visitor center has slide programs by request, a wildlife exhibit, paintings and maps. Monday-Friday 8 a.m.-4 p.m.

OLD SPANISH FORT AND MUSEUM

4602 Fort St., Pascagoula, 228-769-1505

Built by the French, later captured by the Spanish, the fort has walls of massive cypress timbers cemented with oyster shells, mud and moss that are 18 inches thick. Said to be the oldest structure in the Mississippi Valley, the site contains a museum with Native American relics as part of its collection. Daily.

SCRANTON NATURE CENTER

IG Levy Park at Pascagoula River, Pascagoula, 228-938-6612;
www.cityofpascagoula.com

The Center has marine and wetlands exhibits housed in a restored shrimping boat.
Tuesday-Saturday.

SINGING RIVER

Pascagoula River, Pascagoula

There is indeed a singing sound from the river, which is best heard on late summer and autumn nights. The sound seems to get louder, coming nearer until it seems to be underfoot. Scientists have made several guesses about the sound's source: It could be made by fish, sand scraping the hard slate bottom, natural gas escaping from the sand bed or a current sucked past a hidden cave. But no one has ever confirmed the exact source.

WHERE TO STAY

★★LA FONT INN

2703 Denny Ave., Pascagoula, 228-762-7111, 800-647-6077; www.lafontinn.com

192 rooms. Restaurant, bar. Fitness center. $61-150

PASS CHRISTIAN

See also Biloxi, Gulfport

Hurricane Katrina almost completely destroyed this little town in August 2005, but Pass Christian is rebuilding, hoping to regain its status as a scenic resort town, a reputation it first earned before the Civil War. Pass Christian was the site of the South's first yacht club, and it has hosted six vacationing U.S. presidents: Jackson, Taylor, Grant, Theodore Roosevelt, Wilson and Truman. And as if that's not enough, the world's largest oyster reef is offshore.

WHAT TO SEE

THE FRIENDSHIP OAK

University of Southern Mississippi's Gulf Park campus, Pass Christian, 228-865-4500;
www.usm.edu

The Oak has become a symbol of the Gulf Coast's strength in the wake of Hurricane Katrina. It has been standing since 1487, five years before Columbus arrived in the new world. The oak has a 16-foot trunk, limbs larger than 5 feet in diameter and a root system that held fast enough to keep the tree standing through the storm. Legend says that people who stand together in the tree's shadow will remain friends forever.

WHERE TO STAY
★★CASINO MAGIC BAY TOWER HOTEL
711 Hollywood Blvd., Bay St. Louis, 228-467-9257, 800-562-4425;
www.casinomagic.com
201 rooms. Restaurant, bar. $61-150

PORT GIBSON
See also Vicksburg
Port Gibson is where the Blues Highway and the Natchez Trace meet, which makes it a good place to begin an adventure in western Mississippi. Many antebellum houses and buildings remain in Port Gibson, lending support to the story that during the Civil War, Union General Grant spared the town on his march to Vicksburg with the words, "It's too beautiful to burn."

WHAT TO SEE
ENERGY CENTRAL
Grand Gulf Road, Port Gibson, 601-437-6393
Here you'll find exhibits and hands-on displays about nuclear energy and electricity.
Monday-Friday.

FIRST PRESBYTERIAN CHURCH
Church and Walnut streets, Port Gibson, www.fpcportgibson.com
The church features a gold-leaf hand with a finger pointing skyward that tops its steeple. The interior includes an old slave gallery and chandeliers taken from the steamboat Robert E. Lee.

GRAND GULF MILITARY PARK
Grand Gulf Road, Port Gibson, 601-437-5911; www.grandgulfpark.state.ms.us
This site marks the former town of Grand Gulf, which lost 55 of 75 city blocks to Mississippi floods between 1855 and 1860. During the Civil War, the town's population was waning when Confederate troops and Union forces clashed here, first in the spring of 1862 and again in the spring of 1863. The park today includes fortifications, an observation tower, a cemetery, sawmill, dog-trot house, memorial chapel, water wheel and grist mill, a carriage house with vehicles used by the Confederates, a four-room cottage reconstructed from the early days of Grand Gulf and several other pre-Civil War buildings. A museum in the visitor center displays Civil War, Native American and prehistoric artifacts.
Daily 8 a.m.-5 p.m.

OAK SQUARE
1207 Church St., Port Gibson, 601-437-4350
This restored 30-room mansion has six fluted, Corinthian columns, each standing 22 feet tall, as well as antique furnishings from the 18th and 19th centuries. There are extensive grounds, a courtyard and a gazebo. Guest rooms are available and tours can be made by appointment.

ROSSWOOD PLANTATION
Highway 552, Lorman, 800-533-5889; www.rosswood.net
This classic Greek revival mansion designed by David Shroder, architect of Windsor, features columned galleries, 10 fireplaces, 15-foot ceilings, a winding stairway and slave quarters in the basement. The first owner's diary has survived and offers details of antebellum life on a cotton plantation. The 14 rooms are furnished with antiques. Guest rooms are available.

THE RUINS OF WINDSOR
Old Rodney Road, Port Gibson, 601-437-4351; home.olemiss.edu
These 23 stately columns are all that is left of a four-story mansion built in 1860 at a cost of $175,000 and destroyed by fire in 1890. Its proximity to the river and size made it a natural marker for Mississippi River pilots, including Samuel Clemens (better known as Mark Twain).

SARDIS
See also Oxford
From antebellum architecture to thousands of acres of parks, Sardis is a bit of the South that's just waiting to be explored.

WHAT TO SEE
GEORGE PAYNE COSSAR STATE PARK
165 County Road 170, Oakland, 662-623-7356
The park, covering 900 acres, is situated on a peninsula jutting into Enid Lake. Activities include swimming, camping, waterskiing and fishing, and facilities include a boating ramp, nature and bicycle trails, a miniature golf area, picnicking shelters, a playground, a concession stand, a restaurant (year-round, Wednesday-Sunday), a lodge and cabins.

HEFLIN HOUSE MUSEUM
304 S. Main, Sardis, 662-487-3451
One of the few remaining antebellum structures in Sardis and Panola County, this house features exhibits on the history of Panola County from the pre-Columbus period to 1900.
Monday-Friday by appointment.

SARDIS LAKE AND DAM
Nine miles east off I-55, Sardis, 662-563-4531; www.sardislake.com
This lake, with a 260-mile shoreline formed by damming the Little Tallahatchie River, is part of the Yazoo Basin flood control project, and is noted for its natural white sand beaches. Activities include swimming, and facilities include a playground, playing fields, a snack bar, picnicking shelters, boat ramps and rentals, campgrounds and cabins.

STARKVILLE
See also Columbus
Mississippi State University makes its home here and drives the local economy. Starkville got a piece of the country music spotlight when Johnny Cash sang about the town in a song called "Starkville County Jail."

WHAT TO SEE
MISSISSIPPI STATE UNIVERSITY
One mile east on University Drive, Starkville, 662-325-2323; www.msstate.edu
Originally Mississippi Agricultural and Mechanical College, the college became a state university in 1958. The Bulldogs' campus is approximately 750 acres, and visitors are welcome to tour many of the university's buildings and collections. A few to consider: the Arboretum; the Charles H. Templeton, Sr. Music Museum, with more than 200 self-playing instruments; Dunn Seiler Museum, home to geological pieces including a triceratops skull and saber-toothed tiger head; University Art Gallery; and the Chapel of Memories.

NATIONAL WILDLIFE REFUGE
Starkville, 662-323-5548; www.fws.gov/noxubee
This 48,000-acre refuge, which includes 1,200-acre Bluff Lake, offers space for more than 200 species of birds, including waterfowl, wild turkey, the endangered bald eagle and red-cockaded woodpecker, as well as alligators and deer. Daily.

OKTIBBEHA COUNTY HERITAGE MUSEUM
206 Fellowship St., Starkville, Fellowship and Russell Streets, 662-323-0211;
www.cityofstarkville.org
Artifacts from the county's past are housed in the former GM&O railroad station.
Tuesday-Thursday.

WHERE TO STAY
★RAMADA
403 Highway 12 E., Starkville, 662-323-6161; www.ramada.com
173 rooms. Bar. $61-150

WHERE TO EAT
★★HARVEY'S
406 Highway 12 E., Starkville, 662-323-6062; www.eatwithus.com
Seafood, steak. Lunch, dinner. Closed Sunday. $16-35

TUPELO
See also Oxford
Tupelo was once home to "rock 'n' roll" royalty: Elvis Presley was born in a two-room house here in 1935. Not surprisingly, tourism gives a big economic boost to this mid-sized town in northeast Mississippi. Visitors are also drawn by the Natchez Trace Parkway, a scenic route from Natchez, Miss., to Nashville, Tenn., which commemorates a route taken by Native Americans and early pioneers.

WHAT TO SEE
ELVIS PRESLEY PARK AND MUSEUM
306 Elvis Presley Drive, Tupelo, 662-841-1245; www.elvispresleybirthplace.com
More than 50,000 die-hard Elvis fans make a pilgrimage to the small white frame house where the King lived for the first three years of his life. The mu-

seum houses a collection of Elvis memorabilia as well as a chapel. Monday-Saturday 9 a.m.-5 p.m., Sunday 1-5 p.m.

NATCHEZ TRACE PARKWAY VISITOR CENTER

300 W. Main St., Tupelo; www.nps.gov/natr

The 444-mile parkway commemorates the route, used by Native Americans and early settlers, that connected the Mississippi River to central Tennessee.

OREN DUNN MUSEUM OF TUPELO

689 Rutherford Drive, Tupelo, 662-841-6438; www.orendunnmuseum.org

Displays include NASA space equipment used in Apollo missions; Elvis Presley room; reproductions of Western Union office, general store, train station, log cabin; as well as Civil War and Chickasaw items. Daily.

TOMBIGBEE NATIONAL FOREST

Tupelo, 20 miles south, off Natchez Trace Parkway, 601-965-4391; www.fs.fed.us/r8/tombigbee

This section of the forest, along with a tract to the south on Highway 15 near Louisville, totals 66,341 acres. Davis Lake provides swimming, fishing, picnicking, and camping, with electric hookups and a dump station available. Daily.

TOMBIGBEE STATE PARK

264 Cabin Drive, Tupelo, 662-842-7669; www.mdwfp.com

This is a 702-acre park with a spring-fed lake. Activities include swimming, archery and fishing. Facilities include a playground, playing fields, a snack bar, picnicking shelters, boat ramps and rentals, campgrounds and cabins.

TRACE STATE PARK

2139 Faulkner Road, Belden, 662-489-2958

On 2,500 acres with a 600-acre lake, you can find activities that include swimming, canoeing, and fishing and facilities such as a playground, a boat ramp, a horse riding trail, a golf course, a snack bar, picnicking shelters, boat ramps and rentals, campgrounds and cabins. Daily.

TUPELO NATIONAL BATTLEFIELD

2680 Natchez Trace Parkway, Tupelo, 601-680-4025; www.nps.gov/tupe
This is a one-acre tract near the area where the Confederate line was formed to attack the Union position. You'll find a marker with texts and maps that explain the battle. Daily.

WHERE TO STAY
★HOLIDAY INN EXPRESS

1612 McClure Cove, Tupelo, 662-620-8184, 800-465-4329; www.hiexpress.com
124 rooms. Complimentary breakfast. $61-150

★RAMADA

854 N. Gloster St., Tupelo, 662-844-4111, 800-272-6232; www.ramada.com
230 rooms. Restaurant, bar. $61-150

WHERE TO EAT
★JEFFERSON PLACE

823 Jefferson St., Tupelo, 662-844-8696; www.jeffersonplacetupelo.com
American. Lunch, dinner. Closed Sunday. $16-35

★MALONE'S FISH & STEAK HOUSE

1349 Highway 41, Tupelo, 662-842-2747
Steak. Dinner. Closed Sunday-Monday. $15 and under.

★★PAPA VANELLI'S

1302 N. Gloster, Tupelo, 662-844-4410; www.vanellis.com/papavanelli.html
Greek, Italian. Lunch, dinner. $16-35

VICKSBURG

See also Port Gibson

Originally an important river port, Vicksburg has a fascinating riverfront along the Mississippi River and the Yazoo Canal. Part of the town sits on a high bluff overlooking the river, a location that led to what is perhaps Vicksburg's biggest role in America history: the Civil War's Siege of Vicksburg.

By June 1862, the Union controlled the Mississippi River with the exception of Vicksburg, which was in Confederate hands. The town's location made it impossible for Union leaders to move traffic up or down the river without subjecting the boats to withering fire from strong Confederate batteries. This position made it possible to maintain communication lines with Louisiana, which were vital to the Confederacy.

The soldiers in Vicksburg fought off Union advances several times before General Grant's army surrounded the city and laid siege. For 47 days, Grant's army pounded Vicksburg with mortar and cannon fire, and the local citizens, hiding in caves, nearly starved. Eventually, on July 4, 1863, the Confederates agreed to surrender the city, a move that gave the North strategic power and led to its victory. Because the city fell on July 4, the citizens of Vicksburg did not celebrate Independence Day until World War II.

Modern Vicksburg is nearly surrounded by the Vicksburg National Military Park, which is as much a part of the town as the streets and antebellum houses. The downtown district has art galleries, shops, restaurants, museums and antique stores, and Vicksburg's natural beauty makes it a haven for visitors who want to spend time outdoors.

WHAT TO SEE
ANCHUCA HISTORIC MANSION AND INN
1010 First East St., Vicksburg, 601-661-0111, 888-686-0111;
www.anchucamansion.com
This restored Greek revival mansion is furnished with period antiques and gas-burning lanterns. The site also includes guest rooms, landscaped gardens and a brick courtyard. Daily.

BIEDENHARN MUSEUM OF COCA-COLA MEMORABILIA
1107 Washington St., Vicksburg, 601-638-6514; www.biedenharncoca-colamuseum.
com
This is the building in which Coca-Cola was first bottled in 1894. The museum includes a restored candy store, an old-fashioned soda fountain and a collection of Coca-Cola advertising and memorabilia. Daily.

CEDAR GROVE
2200 Oak St., Vicksburg, 601-636-1000, 800-862-1300; www.cedargroveinn.com
This mansion was shelled by Union gunboats during the Civil War. Though it's restored, a cannonball is still lodged in the parlor wall. The site includes a roof garden with view of the Mississippi and Yazoo rivers, a tea room, many original furnishings, more than 4 acres of formal gardens, courtyards, fountains, guest rooms and gazebos. Daily.

DUFF GREEN
1114 First East St., Vicksburg, 601-636-6968, 800-992-0037;
www.duffgreenmansion.com
This mansion features Palladian architecture. Shelled by Union forces during the Civil War, the site was then used as a hospital for Confederate and Union troops. The house is now restored with antique furnishings. Guided tours, guest rooms and high tea are available by reservation. Daily.

MARTHA VICK HOUSE
1300 Grove St., Vicksburg, 601-638-7036; www.marthavickhouse.com
Built by the daughter of the founder of Vicksburg, Newit Vick, the house features a Greek revival façade, a restored interior furnished with 18th- and 19th-century antiques and an outstanding art collection. Daily.

MCRAVEN HOME
1445 Harrison St., Vicksburg, 601-636-1663; www.mcraventourhome.com
This home was the heaviest-shelled house during the Siege of Vicksburg. Visitors can take a view of the architectural record of Vicksburg history, from frontier cottage 1797 to Empire 1836 and finally to elegant Greek revival townhouse 1849, as well as many original furnishings. Original brick walks surround the house, and outside is a garden of live oaks, boxwood, magnolia and many plants. Daily.

OLD COURT HOUSE MUSEUM

1008 Cherry St., Vicksburg, 601-636-0741; www.oldcourthouse.org

Built with slave labor, this building offers a view of the Yazoo Canal from its hilltop position. Here, Grant raised the U.S. flag on July 4, 1863, signifying the end of fighting after 47 days. The courthouse now houses an extensive display of Americana. The Confederate room contains weapons and documents on the siege of Vicksburg. There is also a pioneer room, a furniture room as well as Native American displays and objets d'art.

Monday-Saturday 8:30 a.m.-4:30 p.m., Sunday 1:30-4:30 p.m.

VICKSBURG NATIONAL MILITARY PARK & CEMETERY

3201 Clay St., Vicksburg, 601-636-0583; www.nps.gov/vick

This historic park, the site of Union siege lines and a hardened Confederate defense, borders the eastern and northern sections of the city. A visitor center is at the park entrance, on Clay Street at I-20. The site also contains a museum with exhibits and audiovisual aids. Take a self-guided 16-minute tour. Daily 8 a.m.-5 p.m.

WHERE TO STAY

★★★ANCHUCA

1010 First E. St., Vicksburg, 888-686-0111, 800-469-2597; www.anchucamansion.com

Climb the narrow, greenery-lined steps to this pre-Civil War mansion offering guest rooms with private baths, a full breakfast and afternoon tea. Built around 1830 in Greek revival style, the common rooms are furnished with period antiques and romantic, gas-burning chandeliers.

7 rooms. Complimentary breakfast. $61-150

★★BATTLEFIELD INN

4137 I-20 N Frontage Road, Vicksburg, 601-638-5811, 800-359-9363; www.battlefieldinn.org

117 rooms. Complimentary breakfast. Restaurant, bar. $61-150

★BEST INN

2390 S. Frontage Road, Vicksburg, 601-634-8607, 800-237-8466; www.bestinn.com

70 rooms. Pets accepted. $61-150

★★★CEDAR GROVE MANSION INN

2200 Oak St., Vicksburg, 601-636-1000, 800-862-1300; www.cedargroveinn.com

This 5-acre, garden-like property includes guest rooms, cottages and suites. All accommodations include a full breakfast, afternoon tea and evening sherry and chocolates. The inn's chef, Andre Flowers, turns out New Orleans cuisine at Andre's Restaurant.

34 rooms. Restaurant. Complimentary breakfast. $61-150

★★★DUFF GREEN MANSION

1114 First East St., Vicksburg, 601-638-6662, 800-992-0037; www.duffgreenmansion.com

This large 1856 Palladian mansion was used as a hospital for both Confederate and Union soldiers during the Siege of Vicksburg. Each of the bedrooms has a

fireplace and porch and are furnished in period antiques and reproductions.
7 rooms. Complimentary breakfast. Business center. $61-150

★MOTEL 6
4127 N. Frontage Road, Vicksburg, 601-638-5077, 800-466-8356; www.motel6.com
62 rooms. Pets accepted. $61-150

WHERE TO EAT
★★CEDAR GROVE
2200 Oak St., Vicksburg, 601-636-1000; www.cedargroveinn.com
American. Dinner. Closed Monday. $16-35

★★EDDIE MONSOUR'S
127 Country Club Drive, Vicksburg, 601-638-1571
American. Lunch, dinner. Closed Sunday. $16-35

★WALNUT HILLS ROUND TABLES
1214 Adams St., Vicksburg, 601-638-4910; www.walnuthillsms.net
American. Lunch, dinner. Closed Saturday. $16-35

WOODVILLE
See also Natchez
First settled in the 18th century, Woodville is the home of The Woodville
Republican, the oldest newspaper and the oldest business institution in Mis-
sissippi. The town still has many beautiful 19th-century houses and some of
the state's first churches. These include Woodville Baptist, 1809; Woodville
Methodist, 1824; and St. Paul's Episcopal 1823, which has an Erben organ
from 1837.

WHAT TO SEE
ROSEMONT PLANTATION
Main Street, Woodville, 601-888-6809; www.rosemontplantation1810.com
This was home of Jefferson Davis and his family. His parents, Samuel and
Jane Davis, moved to Woodville and built the house when the boy was 2 years
old. The Confederate president grew up here and returned to visit his family
throughout his life. Many family furnishings remain, including a spinning
wheel that belonged to Jane. Five generations of the Davis family are buried
on this 300-acre plantation.
Tuesday-Saturday 10 a.m.-5 p.m.

WILKINSON COUNTY MUSEUM
Bank Street, Woodville, 601-888-3998; www.historicwoodville.org
Housed in a Greek revival-style building, the museum features changing ex-
hibits and period room settings.
Monday-Saturday.

YAZOO CITY

See also Jackson

Railroad aficionados, you're in for a treat. Yazoo City is home to the Casey Jones Railroad Museum, site of the 1900 train wreck.

WHAT TO SEE
CASEY JONES RAILROAD MUSEUM

10901 Vaughan Road, Vaughan, 662-673-9864; www.trainweb.org
Site of the famous 1900 Casey Jones train wreck, the state-owned museum covers the story of the crash, local railroad history and folklore. Artifacts, including a 1923 steam locomotive, are on display.
Monday-Saturday.

DELTA NATIONAL FOREST

Ranger's Office, Rolling Fork, 601-873-6256; www.fs.fed.us/r8/mississippi/delta
Here you'll find numerous small lakes, streams and green tree reservoirs contained on 59,500 acres. Activities include primitive camping, fishing and hunting for squirrel, raccoon, turkey, waterfowl, rabbit, woodcock and deer. There is also the Blue Lake picnic area and walking trail as well as the Sweetgum, Overcup Oak and Green Ash natural areas.

YAZOO HISTORICAL MUSEUM

Triangle Cultural Center, 332 N. Main St., Yazoo City, 662-746-2273
Exhibits cover the history of Yazoo County from prehistoric times to the present, with Civil War artifacts and fossils.
Admission: free. Daily.

TENNESSEE

TENNESSEE IS A PLACE OF CONTRASTS. IT'S HEARING THE BLUES ON MEMPHIS' FAMOUS
Beale Street and paying homage to the King of Rock 'n' Roll at Graceland.
It's hiking through the Great Smoky Mountains and cruising along the Mississippi River. It's strolling through historic Civil War battlefields and learning about the power of the atomic bomb at Oak Ridge National Laboratory.

Tennessee's landscape is no less diverse. The eastern part of the state is characterized by mountains, including the picturesque Great Smokies. West of the mountains, the land stretches into valleys surrounded by wooded ridges. Here visitors find Knoxville, a short drive from Great Smoky Mountains National Park. Knoxville is home of the University of Tennessee—which inspires great devotion among locals—and a blossoming music scene. Further west and south, Chattanooga is an outdoor enthusiast's dream, thanks to its spot in the Appalachian Mountains near the Cumberland Plateau. On a clear day, visitors can see Tennessee, Georgia, North and South Carolina and Alabama from the top of Lookout Mountain.

The center of the state is dominated by the Cumberland Plateau's flat-topped mountains and further west, the Highland Rim, an elevated plain surrounding the Nashville Basin. Here, the center of the country music universe doubles as the state's capital. Nashville is home to the Grand Ole Opry, the country's longest continuously running live radio show, and The District, a lively downtown neighborhood where visitors will find music stars and starry-eyed hopefuls singing their hearts out after hours. Beyond its country music mayhem, the state capital is also a sophisticated city of museums, universities, historical sites and first-class dining.

West Tennessee flattens into the Gulf Coastal Plain. Most of the region has rolling hills, but near the Mississippi River on the western edge of the state, the land flattens out. Memphis is the urban hub here, and a recent renaissance in the downtown core has given Memphis a new vibe. No longer second fiddle to Nashville's music scene, Memphis celebrates its reputation as the home of the blues and the birthplace of rock 'n' roll.

Of course, these cities are separated by Tennessee's many small and mid-sized towns, each of which has a unique story to tell. Tennessee has been inspired and molded by some of America's greatest legends—Davy Crockett, Daniel Boone, W.C. Handy, B.B. King, Elvis Presley, Alex Haley and three American presidents among them—and numerous historic landmarks chronicle the state's movers and shakers.

Tennessee's tourism bureau has a motto: "the stage is set for you." It's true. So pick your scene and your role, and grab your share of Tennessee's limelight.

CHATTANOOGA
See also Chatsworth, Chickamauga
Walled in on three sides by the Appalachian Mountains and the Cumberland Plateau, Chattanooga has one of the South's most beautiful natural settings, which makes it a popular destination with outdoor enthusiasts. But its urban

cultural offerings are also a draw: Here visitors find one of the world's largest freshwater aquariums, several noted art museums and theaters and even a museum dedicated to car towing. Chattanooga is the birthplace of miniature golf, the site of the first Coca-Cola bottling plant and has the steepest passenger incline railway in the country.

It's a city celebrated in song and heralded in history. The Cherokees called it "Tsatanugi" ("rock coming to a point"), describing Lookout Mountain, which stands like a sentinel over the city. They called the creek here "Chickamauga" ("river of blood").

Cherokee Chief John Ross founded the city. It was a starting point for the "Trail of Tears," when Native Americans from three states were herded by federal troops and forced to march to Oklahoma in the winter of 1838. Chattanooga also had a front-row seat to one of the Civil War's fateful battles: The Battle of Chickamauga in the fall of 1863 was one of the turning points of the Civil War. It ended when Union forces overpowered entrenched Confederate forces on Missionary Ridge; more than 34,500 men died. General Sherman's march to the sea began immediately thereafter.

Chattanooga emerged as an important industrial city at the end of the Civil War, when soldiers from both sides returned to stake their futures in this commercially strategic city. In 1878, Adolph S. Ochs moved to Chattanooga from Knoxville, purchased the *Chattanooga Times* and made it one of the state's most influential newspapers. Although he later went on to publish the *New York Times*, Ochs retained control of the Chattanooga journal until his death in 1935.

Sparked by the Tennessee Valley Authority, the city's greatest period of growth began in the 1930s. In the past few years, millions of dollars have been spent along Chattanooga's riverfront, making it a popular visitor destination.

WHAT TO SEE
BATTLES FOR CHATTANOOGA MUSEUM

1110 E. Brow Road, Lookout Mountain, 423-821-2812;

www.battlesforchattanooga.com

An automated, 3-D display re-creates the Civil War Battles of Chattanooga using 5,000 miniature soldiers, flashing lights, smoking cannons and crackling rifles. Also here are dioramas of area history prior to the Civil War.

June-August, daily 9 a.m.-5 p.m.; September-May, daily 10 a.m.-5 p.m.

CHATTANOOGA AFRICAN-AMERICAN MUSEUM

200 E. Martin Luther King Blvd., Chattanooga, 423-266-8658; www.caamhistory.com

This educational institution highlights African-American contributions to the growth of Chattanooga and the nation.

Monday-Friday 10 a.m.-5 p.m., Saturday noon-4 p.m.

CHATTANOOGA CHOO-CHOO

Terminal Station, 1400 Market St., Chattanooga, 423-266-5000, 800-872-2529;

www.choochoo.com

The song made it famous, but the Chattanooga Choo-Choo began chugging through the South and Midwest in the 1880s. The converted 1909 train station contains a hotel and restaurants. It also boasts formal gardens, fountains, pools, turn-of-the-century shops and a model railroad museum. Daily 8 a.m.-10 p.m.

CHATTANOOGA NATURE CENTER AT REFLECTION RIDING
400 Garden Road, Chattanooga, 423-821-9582; www.reflectionriding.org
This park meant for leisurely driving offers winding three-mile trips with vistas: historic sites, trees, wildflowers, shrubs, reflecting pools. It's also a wetland walkway, with a nature center, hiking trails and outdoorsy programs. Monday-Saturday.

CRAVENS HOUSE
Chattanooga, 423-821-7786
The house is the oldest-surviving structure on the mountain, restored with period furnishings. The original house, which was the center of the "Battle Above the Clouds," was destroyed; the present structure was erected on the original foundations in 1866.
Mid-June-mid-August, daily.

CREATIVE DISCOVERY MUSEUM
321 Chestnut St., Chattanooga, 423-756-2738; www.cdmfun.org
The museum encourages children to learn about the world by playing instruments, climbing through a replica of a riverboat and creating art, among other hands-on activities. Exhibit areas include the Artist's Studio, Inventor's Clubhouse, Musician's Studio and Excavation Station.
Daily 10 a.m.-5 p.m.

INTERNATIONAL TOWING & RECOVERY HALL OF FAME & MUSEUM
3315 Broad St., Chattanooga, 423-267-3132; www.internationaltowingmuseum.org
The museum spotlights the people and vehicles that are reliable as soon as your car decides that it isn't. Dedicated in the autumn of 1995, this museum is just a block away from where the Ernest Holmes Company made the very first automobile wrecker. The museum has a large collection of antique toy trucks and towing and wrecking equipment, as well as a hall of fame.
Admission: adults $8, children $4, children under 5 free. Monday-Saturday 10 a.m.-4:30 p.m., Sunday 11 a.m.-5 p.m.

HOUSTON MUSEUM OF DECORATIVE ARTS
201 High St., Chattanooga, 423-267-7176; www.thehoustonmuseum.com
The museum features glass, porcelain, pottery, music boxes, dolls, a collection of pitchers and country-style furniture.
Monday-Friday 9:30 a.m.-4 p.m.

HUNTER MUSEUM OF AMERICAN ART
10 Bluff View, Chattanooga, 423-267-0968; www.huntermuseum.org
Built on a bluff overlooking the Tennessee River, the museum has an outdoor beauty that's rivaled only by its art collection. The offerings include paintings, sculpture, glass, drawings, a permanent collection of major American artists and changing exhibits.
Tuesday-Saturday 9:30 a.m.-5 p.m., Sunday noon-5 p.m.

LOOKOUT MOUNTAIN

Chattanooga, south of town via Ochs Highway and Scenic Highway, 800-825-8366;
www.lookoutmountain.com

The mountain towers more than 2,120 feet above the city, offering clear-day views of Tennessee, Georgia, North Carolina, South Carolina and Alabama. During the Civil War, the "Battle Above the Clouds" was fought on the slope.

LOOKOUT MOUNTAIN INCLINE RAILWAY

3917 St. Elmo Ave., Chattanooga, Lower Station, 423-821-4224;
www.lookoutmountain.com

The world's steepest passenger incline railway climbs Lookout Mountain to 2,100-feet altitude. Near the top, the grade reaches a 72.7 degree angle; passengers ride glass-roofed cars to witness the steepness. The Smoky Mountains can be seen from Upper Station observation deck. Daily.

NICKAJACK DAM AND LAKE

3490 TVA Road, Jasper

The Tennessee Valley Authority dam impounds the lake with 192 miles of shoreline and 10,370 acres of water surface. Fishing and a boat launch are available. Daily.

POINT PARK

110 Point Park Road., Lookout Mountain, 423-821-7786

Get a view of Chattanooga and Moccasin Bend from the observatory. Monuments, plaques and a museum tell the story of battle. There's also a visitor center for the park, which is part of Chickamauga and Chattanooga National Military Park. Daily.

RACCOON MOUNTAIN CAVERNS AND CAMPGROUND

319 W. Hills Drive, Chattanooga, 423-821-9403, 800-823-2267;
www.raccoonmountain.com

More than 5 1/2 miles of underground passageways offer views of beautiful rock formations. Opt for the Crystal Palace Tour for an overview of the cave's history and geology, or get a little dirty on one of the "wild" cave expeditions that give visitors a chance to examine undeveloped parts of the caverns. Several of these expeditions offer overnight stays in the cave. It's also a full-facility campground. Daily.

ROCK CITY GARDENS

1400 Pattern Road, Lookout Mountain, 706-820-2531; www.seerockcity.com

Among these 14 acres of mountaintop trails and vistas, visitors will find unique rock formations (including one called Fat Man's Squeeze), a 180-foot "swing-a-long" bridge and a critter classroom, where visitors learn about the creatures that live on or near Lookout Mountain. Daily.

RUBY FALLS-LOOKOUT MOUNTAIN CAVERNS

1720 S. Scenic Highway, Chattanooga, 423-821-2544; www.rubyfalls.com

Under the battlefield are twin caves with onyx formations, giant stalactites

THE COPPER BASIN

For a look at some of Tennessee's most beautiful landscapes, take a drive along Highway 64 east of Chattanooga. You'll cruise through the scenic Cherokee National Forest, alongside the churning Ocoee River and through the badlands of the Copper Basin.

From Chattanooga, take I-75 north toward Cleveland and then take Highway 64 east to the Georgia border (take the bypass around Cleveland). From outside the town of Ocoee, Highway 64 runs east through 24 miles of the Cherokee National Forest alongside the Ocoee River.

The river, which hosted the 1996 Olympic Whitewater Competition, lures daring paddlers to one of the premier white-water runs in the country. A series of Class III and IV rapids with nicknames like "Broken Nose," "Diamond Splitter," "Tablesaw" and "Hell Hole" hints at the river's reputation as one of the Southeast's greatest white-water runs. The acclaimed white water lies between two dams built and managed by the Tennessee Valley Authority (TVA) for hydroelectric power. The TVA can dry up or "turn on" the white water as easily as turning a spigot. Two dozen outfitters around Ocoee lead guided rafting expeditions downriver for half-day or full-day excursions; try Nantahala Outdoor Center (800-232-7238), Ocoee Outdoors (800-533-7767) or Southeastern Expeditions (800-868-7238).Connect with the outdoors in a more laid-back fashion at the Parksville Lake Recreation Area, 11 miles from Ocoee off Highway 64. The park offers a nice spot for picnics, boating or camping in stands of pine and dogwood trees. Enjoy a few leisurely hours here before continuing on to the Copper Basin.

Between Ducktown and Copperhill at the Georgia border, the Copper Basin gets its name from the copper mines that flourished here in the 1800s. Unfortunately, the industry clear-cut the forest and generated copper sulfide fumes that devastated what was then left of the local environment, creating a stark desert out of the once-lush forested terrain. In the 1930s, the Civilian Conservation Corps was sent in to restore the area, and after five forgiving decades and active land reclamation, the Copper Basin is beginning to recover. The Ducktown Basin Museum, 1/4 mile north of Highway 64 on Highway 68 (423-496-5778), tells the story of the copper industry. The remains of the town's first copper mine are nearby, as are the towns of Copperhill, Tennessee, and McCaysville, Georgia, both of which have historic districts worth a visit. From downtown Copperhill, the Blue Ridge Scenic Railway (800-934-1898), an antique locomotive with a red caboose, takes passengers to Blue Ridge, Georgia. There are several restaurants and cafés right across the street from the depot.

and stalagmites of various hues; at 1,120 feet below the surface, Ruby Falls is a 145-foot waterfall inside Lookout Mountain Caverns. Get a view of the city from the tower above the entrance building. Guided tours are available. Daily.

SIGNAL POINT ON SIGNAL MOUNTAIN

Chattanooga, nine miles north on Ridgeway Avenue; www.sigmtn.com

The mountain was used for signaling by Cherokees and later by Confederates. By looking almost straight down to the Tennessee River from Signal Point Military Park (off St. James Boulevard), visitors get a glimpse of the "Grand Canyon of Tennessee."

TENNESSEE AQUARIUM

1 Broad St., Chattanooga, 423-265-0695, 800-262-0695; www.tnaqua.org

The aquarium was the first major freshwater life center in the country, fo-

cusing primarily on the natural habitats and wildlife of the Tennessee River and related ecosystems. Within this 130,000-square-foot complex are more than 9,000 animals in their natural habitats. The aquarium recreates riverine habitats in seven major freshwater tanks and two terrestrial environments and is organized into five major galleries: Appalachian Cove Forest; Tennessee River Gallery; Discovery Falls; Mississippi Delta; and Rivers of the World. The highlight of the aquarium is the 60-foot-high central canyon, designed to give visitors a sense of immersion into the river.
Daily 9:30 a.m.-6 p.m.

TENNESSEE VALLEY RAILROAD
4119 Cromwell Road, Chattanooga, 423-894-8028; www.tvrail.com
The South's largest operating historic railroad has steam locomotives, diesels and passenger coaches of various types. Trains take passengers on a six-mile ride, including through a tunnel. There's an audiovisual show and displays.
June-August, daily; September-May, Monday-Friday.

SPECIAL EVENT
RIVERBEND FESTIVAL
180 Hamm Road, Chattanooga, 423-756-2211; www.riverbendfestival.com
More than 100 musicians perform during the nine-day festival along the Tennessee River. The fest also offers sporting events, children's activities and a fireworks display.
Mid-June.

WHERE TO STAY
★★★CHATTANOOGA MARRIOTT AT THE CONVENTION CENTER
2 Carter Plaza, Chattanooga, 423-756-0002, 800-228-9290; www.marriott.com
This high-rise hotel is in the heart of downtown, next to the convention center and near shopping, restaurants and great nightlife. Guest rooms feature contemporary furnishings and décor. Great downtown views can be seen from the third-floor outdoor pool area.
342 rooms. Restaurant, bar. Pool. $61-150

★★CLARION HOTEL
407 Chestnut St., Chattanooga, 423-756-5150; chattanooga.doubletree.com
186 rooms. Restaurant, bar. Business center. Pets accepted. $61-150

★HAMPTON INN CHATTANOOGA
7013 Shallowford Road, Chattanooga, 423-855-0095, 800-426-7866;
www.hamptoninn.com
167 rooms. Complimentary breakfast. $61-150

★★HOLIDAY INN CHATTANOOGA-CHOO CHOO
1400 Market St., Chattanooga, 423-266-5000, 800-872-2529; www.choochoo.com
363 rooms. Restaurants, bar. Fitness center. Pool. $61-150

WHERE TO EAT
★★★212 MARKET
212 Market St., Chattanooga, 423-265-1212; www.212market.com
Local produce and meats are used in the frequently changing menu at 212 Market, a family-owned and operated restaurant in the heart of downtown Chattanooga. The brick exterior is set off with striped awnings and flower boxes, and the interior features contemporary Southwest décor, set off by colorful dinnerware, oak tables and chairs, local artwork and live plants. Guests can dine upstairs on the outdoor balcony, where there is seating at wrought-iron umbrella tables. A pianist performs every Friday evening, and a jazz band performs every third Sunday of the month.
Contemporary American. Lunch, dinner. $16-35

★COUNTRY PLACE
7320 Shallowford Road, Chattanooga, 423-855-1392;
www.countryplacerestaurant.com
Southern. Breakfast, lunch, dinner, brunch. $15 and under.

★★MOUNT VERNON RESTAURANT
3535 Broad St., Chattanooga, 423-266-6591; www.mymtvernon.com
American, Southern. Lunch, dinner. Closed Sunday. $16-35

CHEROKEE NATIONAL FOREST
This 630,000-acre forest, cut by river gorges and creased by rugged mountains, lies in two separate strips along the Tennessee-North Carolina boundary, northeast and southwest of Great Smoky Mountains National Park. A region of thick forests, streams and waterfalls, the forest takes its name from the Native American tribe. There are more than 700 miles of hiking trails, including part of the Appalachian Trail. The forest's 30 campgrounds, 30 picnic areas, eight swimming sites, 13 boating sites and seven white-water rivers practically guarantee that visitors will find outdoor adventure and scenic beauty on this expanse of land. Hunting for game, including wild boar, deer and turkey, is permitted under Tennessee game regulations. Fees may be charged at recreation sites

---

CLARKSVILLE
See also Nashville
Many of Clarksville's first settlers were American Revolutionary War veterans who received land here when the government couldn't afford to pay them for their services. Today it is one of Tennessee's fastest-growing areas. The town's attractions are diverse. The Downtown Artists' Co-op supports the city's visual arts community, while the performing arts center attracts national headliners and international legends to its stage. Nearby parks preserve the natural beauty and historic significance of Clarksville and its surroundings.

WHAT TO SEE
BEACHHAVEN VINEYARD & WINERY
1100 Dunlop Lane, Clarksville, 931-645-8867; www.beachavenwinery.com
Tour the vineyard and winery and then hit the tasting room. There is also a picnic area on the grounds. Daily.

CUSTOMS HOUSE MUSEUM

200 S. Second St., Clarksville, 931-648-5780; www.customshousemuseum.org
Built in 1898 as a U.S. Post Office and Customs House, the museum houses changing history, science and art exhibits.
Tuesday-Saturday 10 a.m.-5 p.m., Sunday 1-5 p.m.

DUNBAR CAVE STATE NATURAL AREA

Clarksville, five miles southeast via Highway 79, 931-648-5526; www.tennessee.gov
This 110-acre park with a small scenic lake was once a fashionable resort; the cave itself housed big-band dances. The old bathhouse has been refurbished to serve as a museum and visitor center. Daily.

PORT ROYAL STATE HISTORIC AREA

Five miles east via Highway 76, near Adams, 931-358-9696; www.state.tn.us
At the confluence of Sulphur Fork Creek and the Red River, Port Royal was one of the state's earliest communities and trading centers. A 300-foot covered bridge spans the river. Daily 8 a.m.-sunset.

WHERE TO STAY
★COUNTRY INN & SUITES BY CARLSON CLARKSVILLE

3075 Wilma Rudolph Blvd., Clarksville, 931-645-1400, 800-531-1900; www.country-inns.com
125 rooms. Complimentary breakfast. Fitness center. Pool. $61-150

★HAMPTON INN

190 Holiday Road, Clarksville, 931-552-2255; www.hamptoninn.com
77 rooms. Complimentary breakfast. $61-150

★QUALITY INN

803 N. Second St., Clarksville, 931-645-9084; www.qualityinn.com
130 rooms. Bar. Complimentary breakfast. $61-150

★★RIVERVIEW INN

50 College St., Clarksville, 931-552-3331, 877-487-4837; www.theriverviewinn.com
154 rooms. Restaurant, bar. Pool. $61-150

COLUMBIA

See also Franklin, Lewisburg
James K. Polk, 11th president of the United States, spent his boyhood in Columbia and returned here to open his first law office. The town attracts visitors who want to see Polk's ancestral home, tour the town's many antebellum houses or celebrate mules, which Columbia does with great fanfare one week each April.

WHAT TO SEE
ANCESTRAL HOME OF JAMES K. POLK

301 W. Seventh St., Columbia, 931-388-2354; www.jameskpolk.com
Built by Samuel Polk, father of the president, the federal-style house is fur-

nished with family possessions, including furniture and portraits used at the White House. Gardens link the house to an adjacent 1818 building owned by the president's sisters. There's also a visitor center.

April-October, Monday-Saturday 9 a.m.-5 p.m., Sunday 1-5 p.m.; November-March, Monday-Saturday 9 a.m.-4 p.m., Sunday 1-5 p.m.

THE ATHENAEUM
808 Athenaeum St., Columbia, 931-381-4822; www.athenaeumrectory.com
These Moorish buildings were used as a girls' school after 1852. During the Civil War, the rectory became headquarters of Union Generals Negeley and Schofield.

February-December, Tuesday-Sunday.

SPECIAL EVENT
MULE DAY
Mule Day Office, 1018 Maury County Park Drive, Columbia, 931-381-9557; www.muleday.com
To honor the role mules played in the town's history—providing important labor for farms—Columbia celebrates with activities including a liar's contest, an auction, a parade, a mule pull, a square dance, bluegrass night, a pioneer craft festival and a knife and coin show.

First weekend in April.

WHERE TO STAY
★DAYS INN
1504 Nashville Highway, Columbia, 931-381-3297; www.daysinn.com
54 rooms. Complimentary breakfast. Pool. Pets accepted.$61-150

WHERE TO EAT
★★THE OLE LAMPLIGHTER
1000 Riverside Drive, Columbia, 931-381-3837
Seafood, steak. Dinner. $36-85

COOKEVILLE
See also Crossville
Cookeville is part of the state's upper Cumberland region, an area rich with public lands and waterways. Visitors trek to this region for outdoor recreation, including hiking, white-water rafting, golf, fishing and camping. For folks who don't want to be quite so close to Mother Nature, there are several historic museums, a couple of wineries and plenty of shops that sell antiques, arts and crafts in this part of Tennessee.

WHAT TO SEE
APPALACHIAN CENTER FOR CRAFTS
1560 Craft Center Drive, Smithville, 615-597-6801; www.tntech.edu/craftcenter
The center is on 600 acres overlooking Center Hill Lake. Operated by Tennessee Technological University, it has teaching programs in fiber, metal, wood, glass and clay. There are also exhibition galleries.

Daily 9 a.m.-5 p.m.

BURGESS FALLS STATE NATURAL AREA
4000 Burgess Falls Drive, Sparta, 931-432-5312;
www.state.tn.us/environment/parks/BurgessFalls
The scenic riverside trail leads to an overlook of a 130-foot waterfall, considered one of the most beautiful in the state, in a gorge on the Falling Water River.
Daily 8 a.m.-sunset.

CENTER HILL DAM AND LAKE
158 Resource Lane, Lancaster, 931-858-3125; www.smithvilletn.com
This 250-foot-tall dam controls the flood waters of the Caney Fork River and provides electric power. The lake has a 415-mile shoreline. It provides ample opportunities for swimming, waterskiing, fishing, boating, hunting, picnicking at six recreation areas around the reservoir and camping. Daily.

WHERE TO STAY
★BEST WESTERN THUNDERBIRD MOTEL
900 S. Jefferson Ave., Cookeville, 931-526-7115, 800-528-1234;
www.bestwestern.com
76 rooms. Complimentary breakfast. Fitness center. Pool. Pets accepted. $61-150

★★HOLIDAY INN COOKEVILLE
970 S. Jefferson Ave., Cookeville, 931-526-7125, 800-465-4329; www.clarionhotel.com
198 rooms. Restaurant, bar. Complimentary breakfast. $61-150

WHERE TO EAT
★★NICK'S
895 S. Jefferson Ave., Cookeville, 931-528-1434
Seafood, steak. Lunch, dinner, brunch. Closed Monday. $16-35

CROSSVILLE
See also Cookeville
More than 36,000 tons of multicolored quartzite are quarried in the Crossville area each year and sold for construction projects throughout the country. But visitors come here for something else: golf. The self-titled "Golf Capital of Tennessee," Crossville has a dozen courses, including Tennessee's highest elevation course at Renegade Mountain. The area offers more than 200 holes, enough to keep even the most avid golfer busy for a while.

WHAT TO SEE
CUMBERLAND MOUNTAIN STATE PARK
24 Office Drive, Crossville, 931-484-6138; www.state.tn.us
This park, along the Cumberland Plateau, is 1,820 feet above sea level. It stands on the largest remaining timberland plateau in America and has a 35-acre lake. The park also provides a pool, a bathhouse, fishing, boating (rentals), nature trails and programs, tennis, picnicking, a playground, a snack bar, a dining room, camping, tent and trailer sites and cabins.
Daily 7 a.m.-10 p.m.

HOMESTEADS TOWER MUSEUM
96 Highway 68, Crossville, 931-456-9663
The tower was built in 1937-1938 to house administrative offices of the Cumberland Homesteads, a New Deal-era project. A winding stairway leads to a lookout platform at the top of the octagonal stone tower. At the base of the tower is a museum with photos, documents and artifacts from the 1930s and 1940s. March-December daily.

WHERE TO STAY
★LA QUINTA INN CROSSVILLE
4038 Highway 127 N., Crossville, 931-456-9338, 800-531-5900; www.laquinta.com
60 rooms. Complimentary breakfast. Business center. Pool. Pets accepted. $61-150

FORT DONELSON NATIONAL BATTLEFIELD AND CEMETERY

The site of the Union's first major victory during the Civil War, Fort Donelson is famous for General Ulysses S. Grant's demand for "unconditional and immediate surrender" when Confederate General Simon B. Bucker proposed a truce. Nothing helped Grant so much during this four-day battle as weak generalship on the part of Confederate commanders John B. Floyd and Gideon J. Pillow. Although the Confederates repelled an attack by federal ironclad gunboats, bad decisions by the Confederate leaders left them with no choice but to surrender. Thanks to Grant's victory at Fort Donelson, coupled with the fall of Fort Henry 10 days earlier, the Union had passageways to the heart of the South: the Tennessee and Cumberland rivers. In Grant, northerners had a new hero. His terse surrender message stirred their imaginations, and he was quickly dubbed "Unconditional Surrender" Grant.

Today the fort walls, outer defenses and river batteries still remain and are well-marked to give the story of the battle. A visitor center features a 10-minute slide program, a museum and touch exhibits. A six-mile, self-guided auto tour includes a visit to the fort, the cemetery and the Dover Hotel, where Buckner surrendered. The park is open year-round, dawn to dusk.

FRANKLIN
See also Columbia, Nashville
Franklin is a favorite of Civil War buffs, who come to retrace the Battle of Franklin, a decisive clash that took place November 30, 1864. General John B. Hood, attempting to prevent two Union armies from uniting, outflanked the troops of General John Schofield. Late that afternoon, Hood discovered the Union troops, dug-in around the Carter House. For five hours the battle raged. In the morning Hood found that the Schofield troops had escaped across the river to join forces with the Union army at Nashville. The Confederates suffered 6,252 casualties, including the loss of five generals at Carnton Plantation and a sixth general 10 days after the battle. The North suffered 2,326 casualties.

WHAT TO SEE
CARTER HOUSE
1140 Columbia Ave., Franklin, 615-791-1861; www.carterhouse1864.com
The house served as the command post for the Union forces during the Bat-

tle of Franklin. It now houses a Confederate museum with documents, uniforms, flags, guns, maps and Civil War prints. Go on a guided tour of house and grounds and see a video presentation.
Monday-Saturday 9 a.m.-5 p.m., Sunday 1-5 p.m.

HERITAGE TRAIL
Franklin, north and south on Highway 31
The trail provides a scenic drive along the highway from Brentwood through Franklin to Spring Hill, an area that was plantation country in the mid-1800s. Southern culture is reflected in the drive's many antebellum and Victorian houses; Williamson County was one of the richest areas in Tennessee when the Civil War broke out.

HISTORIC CARNTON AND MCGAVOCK CONFEDERATE CEMETERY
1345 Carnton Lane, Franklin, 615-794-0903; www.carnton.org
This federal-type house was modified in the 1840s to reflect Greek Revival style. Built by an early mayor of Nashville, the house was a social and political center. At the end of the Battle of Franklin, which was fought nearby, four Confederate generals lay dead on the back porch. The nation's largest private Confederate cemetery is adjacent. Daily.

HISTORIC DISTRICT
First Avenue and North Margin Street surrounding the Town Square and the Confederate Monument, Franklin
See the earliest buildings of Franklin, dating back to 1800; those along Main Street are exceptional in their architectural designs and are part of a historic preservation project.

WHERE TO STAY
★BEST WESTERN FRANKLIN INN
1308 Murfreesboro Road, Franklin, 615-790-0570; www.bestwestern.com
142 rooms. Complimentary breakfast. Pool. $61-150

GALLATIN
See also Nashville
About 25 miles from Nashville, Gallatin still has an air of the antebellum South, thanks to its historic town square. Visitors come to this area for outdoor recreation, a dose of American history and an opportunity to find antiques.

WHAT TO SEE
CRAGFONT
200 Cragfont Road, Castalian Springs, 615-452-7070;www.tennesseeanytime.org
This late Georgian-style house was built for General James Winchester, Revolutionary War hero, by masons and carpenters brought from Maryland. It is named for the rocky bluff on which it stands. It has a galleried ballroom, weaving room, wine cellar and federal-period furnishings. There are also restored gardens.
Mid-April-November, Tuesday-Saturday 10 a.m.-5 p.m., Sunday 1 p.m.-5 p.m.

TROUSDALE PLACE

183 W. Main St., Gallatin, 615-452-5648;

The two-story brick house built in the early 1800s was the residence of Governor William Trousdale. Inside is period furniture and a military history library.

WYNNEWOOD

210 Old Highway 25, Castalian Springs, 615-452-5463;www.sumnercountytourism.com

Considered the oldest and largest log structure ever built in Tennessee, this log inn was originally constructed as a stagecoach stop and mineral springs resort. President Andrew Jackson visited here many times.

April-October, daily; November-March, Monday-Saturday.

WHERE TO STAY
★GUESTHOUSE INN GALLATIN

221 W. Main St., Gallatin, 615-452-5433, 800-214-8378; www.guesthouseintl.com

86 rooms. $61-150

★HOLIDAY INN EXPRESS

615 E. Main St., Hendersonville, 615-824-0022; www.holiday-inn.com

93 rooms. Complimentary breakfast. Pool. $61-150

GATLINBURG

See also Pigeon Forge, Sevierville, Townsend

Gatlinburg has retained most of its mountain charm while tapping into the stream of tourists that flows through the town en route to Great Smoky Mountains National Park, the country's most visited national park. Home to only about 3,500 people, the city has accommodations for 40,000 guests, who stop here to experience the town's mountain heritage. Visitors can wander through local shops, many of which sell mountain handicrafts. For folks looking for a quieter stroll, visitors might choose the river walk along Little Pigeon River. The area offers outdoor activities year-round, including downhill skiing, horseback riding, golf and hiking.

WHAT TO SEE
GATLINBURG SPACE NEEDLE

115 Historic Nature Trail, Gatlinburg, 865-436-4629; www.gatlinburgspaceneedle.com

A glass-enclosed elevator takes you to a 342-foot-high observation deck for a view of the Smoky Mountains. Daily.

SKY LIFT

765 Parkway, Gatlinburg, 865-436-4307; www.gatlinburgskylift.com

The double-chairlift ride up to Crockett Mountain is 2,300 feet. Get a view of the Smoky Mountains en route and from observation deck at the summit. A snack bar and gift shop are available.

Daily, weather permitting.

SPECIAL EVENTS
SCOTTISH FESTIVAL AND GAMES
Gatlinburg; www.gsfg.org
Sample Scottish heritage with bagpipe marching bands, highland dancing and sheep dog demonstrations.
Third weekend in May.

SMOKY MOUNTAIN LIGHTS & WINTERFEST
107 Park Headquarters Road, Gatlinburg, 865-453-6411;
www.smokymountainwinterfest.com
The citywide winter celebration includes Yule log burnings, more than 2 million lights and other special events.
Late November-February.

SPRING WILDFLOWER PILGRIMAGE
Gatlinburg Chamber of Commerce, 888-898-9102; www.springwildflowerpilgrimage.org
This event offers numerous wildflower, fauna and natural history walks, seminars, art classes and a variety of other programs. It is held outdoors at the Great Smoky Mountains National Park, as well as in a variety of indoor venues around Gatlinburg.
Late April.

WHERE TO STAY
★★BUCKHORN INN
2140 Tudor Mountain Road, Gatlinburg, 865-436-4668, 866-941-0460;
www.buckhorninn.com
16 rooms. Restaurant. Complimentary breakfast. $151-250

★★★CHRISTOPHER PLACE, AN INTIMATE RESORT
1500 Pinnacles Way, Newport, 423-623-6555, 800-595-9441;
www.christopherplace.com
Tucked away in the scenic Smoky Mountains of Tennessee, this antebellum inn is restored to its original splendor. Enjoy the romantic ambience of the Mountain View dining room while savoring four courses selected daily by the chef.
8 rooms. Children over 13 years only. Complimentary breakfast. $151-250

★★EDGEWATER HOTEL-GATLINBURG
402 River Road, Gatlinburg, 865-436-4151, 800-423-9582; www.edgewater-hotel.com
205 rooms. Bar. Complimentary breakfast. Business center. Fitness center. Pool. $61-150

★★★EIGHT GABLES INN
219 N. Mountain Trail, Gatlinburg, 865-430-3344, 800-279-5716; www.eightgables.com
In a wooded setting that inspires tranquility, this country inn is perfect for a romantic getaway. Explore nearby attractions such as fly fishing, golf and white-water rafting, or opt to spend the afternoon on the porch, admiring the grounds. Guest rooms are furnished with feather-top beds; suites have fireplaces and two-person whirlpool tubs. In addition to a five-course breakfast,

GREAT SMOKY MOUNTAINS NATIONAL PARK

The park straddles the Tennessee-North Carolina border amid the lofty peaks of the Appalachian Mountains. The most visited of the national parks, it attracts more than 9 million visitors a year, who come to play in one of the East's best destinations for outdoor recreation. The park's reputation as a haven for wildlife and a variety of plant life—including fields of colorful wildflowers—does not hurt, either.

More than 900 miles of trails snake through the park, giving hikers intimate views of the mountain ridges wrapped in "smoky" fog. Seventy miles of the Appalachian Trail follow the state line along the high ridge of the park. For a less traveled trek, head toward Buckhorn Gap or Ramsey Cascade to wander through the quiet old-growth forests, home to a variety of giant trees. If you are in search of good photo ops, hike to any one of the park's many waterfalls, fueled by the area's 85 inches of annual rainfall. Among the most popular are Abrams, Grotto, Hen Wallow, Juney Whank, Laurel and Rainbow falls, though most of the rivers and streams in the park have waterfalls.

The park is not just for outdoor enthusiasts. History buffs too will find adventures, thanks to nearly 80 preserved historic structures, including houses, barns, churches and grist mills. Cades Cove is an outdoor museum reflecting the life of the original mountain settlers. Visitors will also see remnants of the Cherokee Indian Nation throughout the park. The Cherokee occupied these mountains before European settlers arrived, but in the winter of 1838-1839, the Cherokee were forced to travel the "Trail of Tears" to Oklahoma.

At the start of your visit to Great Smoky Mountains National Park, stop at one of the three visitor centers: Oconaluftee in North Carolina, two miles north of Cherokee on Highway 441; Sugarlands in Tennessee, two miles south of Gatlinburg; and Cades Cove in Tennessee, 10 miles southwest of Townsend. All have exhibits and information about the park.

Park naturalists conduct campfire programs and hikes during summer. There are also self-guided nature trails. LeConte Lodge, accessible only on foot or horseback, is a concession within the park (late March to mid-November). Fishing is permitted with a Tennessee or North Carolina state fishing license.

the room rate includes nightly dessert and access to the inn's pantry. The inn serves candlelight dinners of regional Southern cuisine three days a week. 19 rooms. Children over 10 years only. Complimentary breakfast. Restaurant. Spa. $151-250

★GREYSTONE LODGE AT THE AQUARIUM

559 Parkway, Gatlinburg, 865-436-5621, 800-451-9202; www.greystonelodgetn.com
257 rooms. Complimentary breakfast. $61-150

★★HOLIDAY INN SUNSPREE RESORT GATLINBURG

520 Historic Nature Trail, Gatlinburg, 865-436-9201, 800-435-9201; www.4lodging.com
400 rooms. Restaurant, bar. Fitness center. Pool. $61-150

★★PARK VISTA HOTEL & CONVENTION CENTER

705 Cherokee Orchard Road, Gatlinburg, 865-436-9211, 800-421-7275;
www.parkvista.com
312 rooms. Restaurant, bar. Business center. Fitness center. Pool. $61-150

WHERE TO EAT
★BRASS LANTERN
710 Parkway, Gatlinburg, 865-436-4168; www.brasslantern-gatlinburg.com
American. Lunch, dinner. $16-35

★★MAXWELL'S STEAK AND SEAFOOD
1103 Parkway, Gatlinburg, 865-436-3738; www.maxwellssteakandseafood.com
American. Dinner. $16-35

★★PARK GRILL
110 Parkway, Gatlinburg, 865-436-2300; www.parkgrillgatlinburg.com
American. Dinner. $16-35

★★THE PEDDLER RESTAURANT
820 River Road, Gatlinburg, 865-436-5794; www.peddlerparkgrill.com
Steak. Dinner. $16-35

GREENEVILLE
See also Limestone
Some of Tennessee's most rugged heroes come from Greeneville: Davy Crockett was born a few miles outside of town in 1786, and President Andrew Johnson lived here and became the town's alderman. Eventually, he climbed the political ladder to the White House, where he served as Lincoln's vice president and then, after Lincoln's assassination, the president of the United States.

WHAT TO SEE
DAVY CROCKETT BIRTHPLACE STATE PARK
1245 Davy Crockett Park Road, Limestone, 423-257-2167;www.state.tn.us
The 100-acre site overlooking the Nolichuckey River serves as a memorial to Crockett—humorist, bear hunter, congressman and hero of the Alamo. A small monument marks Crockett's birthplace; nearby is a replica of the log cabin in which he was born in 1786. The park also has a swimming pool, picnicking, camping, a museum and visitors center. Daily.

ANDREW JOHNSON NATIONAL HISTORIC SITE
See the tailor shop, two houses and the burial place of the 17th president of the United States. Apprenticed to a tailor during his youth, Andrew Johnson came to Greeneville, Tenn., from his native Raleigh, N. C. in 1826. After years of service in local, state and federal governments, Senator Johnson remained loyal to the Union when Tennessee seceded. After serving as military governor of Tennessee, Johnson was elected vice president in 1864. On April 15, 1865, he became president following the assassination of Abraham Lincoln. Continued opposition to the radical program of Reconstruction led to his impeachment in 1868. Acquitted by the Senate, he continued to serve as president until 1869. In 1875, Johnson became the only former president to be elected to the U.S. Senate.

WHERE TO STAY
★★CHARRAY INN
121 Serral Drive, Greeneville, 423-638-1331, 800-852-4682; www.charrayinn.com
36 rooms. Restaurant. Complimentary breakfast. $61-150

★COMFORT INN
1790 E. Andrew Johnson Highway, Greeneville, 423-639-4185, 888-557-5007; www.choicehotels.com
90 rooms. Restaurant, bar. Complimentary breakfast. Pets accepted. $61-150

HURRICANE MILLS
See also Dickson
This Tennessee town is best known for being the site of country singer Loretta Lynn's ranch.

WHAT TO SEE
LORETTA LYNN'S RANCH
44 Hurricane Mills Road, Hurricane Mills, 931-296-7700; www.lorettalynn.com
Tours take guests through the country music star's house, a museum, Mooney's Ranch Office, the Butcher Holler Home and a simulated coal mine. Plus, they'll get a peek at Western and general stores and Loretta Lynn's Record Shop. The ranch also offers swimming, fishing, hiking, tennis and camping. April-October, daily.

NOLAN HOUSE
375 Highway 13 N., Waverly, 931-296-2511
This restored 12-room Victorian house offers period furnishings, a redoubt trail, a dog-trot and a family graveyard. Overnight stays are available. Tours: Monday-Saturday.

WHERE TO STAY
★★BEST WESTERN OF HURRICANE MILLS
15542 Highway 13 S., Hurricane Mills, 931-296-4251; www.bestwestern.com
89 rooms. Restaurant. Complimentary breakfast. Pool. Pets accepted. $61-150

★DAYS INN
15415 Highway 13 S., Hurricane Mills, 931-296-7647; www.daysinn.com
78 rooms. Restaurant. Pool. Pets accepted. $61-150

JACKSON
See also Memphis
Located between Memphis and Nashville in western Tennessee, Jackson is named for President Andrew Jackson; many of the president's soldiers and his wife's relatives settled here. The city's other famous son, John Luther "Casey" Jones, a railroad engineer, died in 1900 trying to stop his train from hitting a stopped freight train in Mississippi. Jones was the only one to die in the crash, making him a hero immortalized in ballads and legends.

WHAT TO SEE
BROOKS SHAW & SON OLD COUNTRY STORE
56 Casey Jones Lane, Jackson, 731-668-1223; www.caseyjonesvillage.com
This turn-of-the-century general store, located in Casey Jones Village, keeps more than 15,000 antiques on display. If you get hungry, there's also a restaurant, an ice-cream parlor and a confectionery shop. Daily.

CASEY JONES HOME AND RAILROAD MUSEUM
30 Casey Jones Lane, Jackson, 731-668-1222; www.caseyjones.com
See the original house of the high-rolling engineer who, on April 30, 1900, climbed into the cab of "Old 382" on the Illinois Central Railroad and took his "farewell trip to that promised land"—and a place in American folklore. On display are Jones' personal and railroad memorabilia, including railroad passes, timetables, bells and steam whistles; also check out the type of steam locomotive that was driven by Jones and restored 1890s coach cars. Daily.

CASEY JONES VILLAGE
56 Casey Jones Lane, Jackson, 731-668-1223; www.caseyjones.com
This complex of turn-of-the-century shops and buildings focuses on the life of one of America's most famous railroad heroes.
Daily 6:30 a.m.-9 p.m.

CHICKASAW STATE RUSTIC PARK
20 Cabin Lake, Henderson, 731-989-5141, 800-458-1752; www.state.tn.us
The park covers 11,215 acres features two lakes. Swimming, fishing, boating (rentals), horseback riding, picnicking, a playground, a recreation lodge, tent and trailer sites and cabins are all available.
Daily 6 a.m.-10 p.m.

CYPRESS GROVE NATURE PARK
866 Highway 70 W., Jackson, 731-425-8316; www.jacksonrecandparks.com
A boardwalk winds through a 165-acre cypress forest. There's also an observation tower, a nature center and a picnic shelter. Daily.

PINSON MOUNDS STATE ARCHAEOLOGICAL AREA
460 Ozier Road, Pinson, 731-988-5614; www.state.tn.us
The area contains the remains of ancient mounds of the Middle Woodland Mound period and more than 10 ceremonial and burial mounds of various sizes, including Sauls. There's also a nature trail, picnicking and a museum.
Monday-Saturday 8 a.m.-4:30 p.m., Sunday 1-5 p.m.

WHERE TO STAY
★AMERICA'S BEST VALUE INN
21045 Highway 22 N., Wildersville, 731-968-2532; www.bestvalueinn.com
40 rooms. Complimentary breakfast. Pool. Pets accepted. $61-150

★★HOLIDAY INN
541 Carriage House Drive, Jackson, 731-668-6000, 800-222-3297; www.holiday-inn.com
136 rooms. Restaurant, bar. Business center. Fitness center. Pool. $61-150

★★THE OLD ENGLISH INN
2267 N. Highland Ave., Jackson, 731-668-1571
80 rooms. Complimentary breakfast. $61-150

WHERE TO EAT
★OLD COUNTRY STORE
56 Casey Jones Lane, Jackson, 731-668-1223; www.caseyjonesvillage.com
American. Breakfast, lunch, dinner. $15 and under.

JAMESTOWN
See also Cookeville
Once a hunting ground for Davy Crockett and later Sergeant Alvin C. York, Jamestown was also the home of Cordell Hull, FDR's secretary of state.

WHAT TO SEE
HISTORIC RUGBY
Highway 5517, Rugby, 423-628-2441, 888-214-3400; www.historicrugby.org
Social reformer Thomas Hughes founded this English colony in the 1880s in hopes of creating a utopian society founded on cooperative enterprise and Christian values. Residents enjoyed natural parks, recreation and cultural activities such as literary societies. Financial problems, a typhoid epidemic and unusually severe winters contributed to the community's demise, but much as been preserved for visitors' pleasure today. Of 17 original Victorian buildings remaining, four are open to the public. Hughes Public Library, unchanged since opening in 1882, contains a unique 7,000-volume collection from the Victorian era. A visitor center is in Rugby Schoolhouse; guided walking tours are available. There is also picnicking and hiking in surrounding river gorges on trails built by original colonists.
Monday-Saturday 9:30 a.m.-5:30 p.m., Sunday noon-5:30 p.m.

PICKETT STATE RUSTIC PARK
4605 Pickett Park Highway, Jamestown, 931-879-5821; www.state.tn.us
The park covers 14,000 acres in Cumberland Mountains. It offers unusual rock formations, caves and natural bridges. There's much to do: a sand beach, swimming, fishing, boating, nature trails, backpacking, picnicking, concessions, a recreation lodge, camping and cabins.
Daily 7:30 a.m.-sunset.

JOHNSON CITY
See also Elizabethton, Kingsport
A favorite of lists ranking the nation's best small cities, Johnson City mixes a metropolitan style with mountain air, affordable living and some of Tennessee's wildest history. (Legend has it that the city was one of Al Capone's alcohol distribution points during Prohibition.)

WHAT TO SEE
APPALACHIAN CAVERNS
420 Cave Hill Road, Blountville, 423-323-2337; www.appalachiancaverns.com
When it is hot, caving will cool you off. These giant underground chambers—made colorful by deposits of manganese, copper, calcium and other elements—served Native Americans in need of shelter, hid soldiers during the Civil War and protected moon shiners during Prohibition.
Monday-Saturday 9 a.m.-6 p.m., Sunday 1-6 p.m.

HANDS ON! REGIONAL MUSEUM
315 E. Main St., Johnson City, 423-434-4263; www.handsonmuseum.org
The museum showcases more than 20 hands-on exhibits designed for children of all ages. Traveling shows also stop by.
Monday-Friday 9 a.m.-5 p.m., Saturday 10 a.m. -5 p.m., Sunday 1-5 p.m.

HISTORIC DISTRICT
Visitors Center, 117 Boone St., Jonesborough, 423-753-5961
This four-by-six-block area through the heart of town reflects 200 years of history. See private residences; commercial and public buildings of federal, Greek Revival and Victorian styles; brick sidewalks; and old-style lampposts.

JONESBOROUGH
Jonesborough, six miles west off Highway 11 E., 423-753-1030;
www.jonesboroughtn.org
It's the oldest town in Tennessee and the first capital of the state of Franklin (prior to Tennessee obtaining statehood).

JONESBOROUGH HISTORY MUSEUM
117 Boone St., Johnson City, 423-753-1015; www.jonesboroughtn.org
Exhibits highlight the history of Jonesborough from pioneer days to the early 20th century. Daily.

ROCKY MOUNT HISTORIC SITE & OVERMOUNTAIN MUSEUM
200 Hyder Hill Road, Piney Flats, 423-538-7396; www.rockymountmuseum.com
The log house, territorial capitol under Governor William Blount from 1790 to 1792, is restored to original simplicity with 18th-century furniture, a log kitchen, a slave cabin, a barn, a blacksmith shop and a smokehouse. Costumed interpreters reenact a day in the life of a typical pioneer family; the 1 ½-hour tour includes Cobb-Massengill house, the kitchen and slave cabin, as well as a self-guided tour through the adjacent Museum of Overmountain History.
Monday-Saturday.

TIPTON-HAYNES HISTORIC SITE
2620 S. Roan St., Johnson City, 423-926-3631; www.tipton-haynes.org
This was the site of the 1788 Battle of the Lost State of Franklin. Six original buildings and four reconstructions span American history from pre-colonial days through the Civil War.

WATAUGA DAM AND LAKE

Hampton, about 20 miles east of Johnson City off Highway 321

Surrounded by the Cherokee National Forest and flanked by the Appalachian Mountains, Watauga Reservoir is arguably one of the most beautiful in the world and boasts excellent fishing. Below Watauga Dam is a wildlife observation area, where visitors can view waterfowl. The Appalachian Trail passes nearby.

WHITEWATER RAFTING

Cherokee Adventures, 2000 Jonesborough Road, Erwin, 423-743-7733, 800-445-7238;
www.cherokeeadventures.com

A variety of guided white-water rafting trips blast through the Nolichucky Canyon and some of the deepest gorges east of the Mississippi River and along the Watauga and Russell Fork rivers.
March-November.

SPECIAL EVENT
NATIONAL STORYTELLING FESTIVAL

116 W. Main St., Jonesborough, Johnson City, 423-753-2171;
www.storytellingcenter.com

Johnson City calls itself the storytelling capital of the world, and this festival is lauded as one of the finest sources of entertainment in the country. During this three-day gathering, story lovers come to hear tales told by some of the country's best storytellers.
First weekend in October.

WHERE TO STAY
★★BEST WESTERN JOHNSON CITY HOTEL & CONFERENCE CENTER

2406 N. Roan St., Johnson City, 423-282-2161, 877-504-1007;
www.bwjohnsoncity.com

180 rooms. Restaurant, bar. Complimentary breakfast. $61-150

★★DOUBLETREE HOTEL JOHNSON CITY

211 Mockingbird Lane, Johnson City, 423-929-2000, 800-222-8733;
www.doubletreejohnsoncity.com

184 rooms. Restaurant, bar. Fitness center. Pool. $61-150

★HAMPTON INN

508 N. State of Franklin Road, Johnson City, 423-929-8000, 800-426-7866;
www.hamptoninn.com

77 rooms. Complimentary breakfast. Pool. $61-150

WHERE TO EAT
★FIREHOUSE

627 W. Walnut St., Johnson City, 423-929-7377; www.thefirehouse.com

American. Lunch, dinner. Closed Sunday. $15 and under.

★★PEERLESS
2531 N. Roan St., Johnson City, 423-282-2351; www.thepeerlessinc.com
American. Dinner. Closed Sunday. $16-35

KINGSPORT
See also Johnson City
In the northeast corner of the state, Kingsport was one of the first stops for 18th-century pioneers heading west. The Great Indian Warrior & Trader Path cut through this area, as did Island Road, the first road built in Tennessee. Kingsport has come a long way from its days as a pioneer outpost. Today it is a popular destination for golfers and outdoor enthusiasts.

WHAT TO SEE
BAYS MOUNTAIN PLANETARIUM
853 Bays Mountain Park Road, Kingsport, 423-229-9447; www.baysmountain.com
The plant and animal sanctuary covers 3,000 acres, offers 25 miles of trails. On the grounds you'll also find a nature interpretive center; an aviary; a deer pen; otter, bobcat and wolf habitats; nature programs; an ocean pool; a planetarium; an exhibition gallery and library. Stop by the observation tower and the19th-century farmstead museum and take a barge ride on the 44-acre lake. Daily.

BOATYARD PARK
151 E. Main St., Kingsport, 423-246-2010; www.kingsportparksandrecreation.org
On the banks of the north and south forks of the Holston River, the park offers the Netherland Inn museum, picnic areas, playgrounds, boating, fishing and footpaths along the river.

EXCHANGE PLACE
4812 Orebank Road, Kingsport, 423-288-6071; www.exchangeplace.info
The restored 19th-century farm once served as a facility for exchanging horses and Virginia currency for Tennessee currency. There's also a crafts center onsite.
May-October, weekends or by appointment.

NETHERLAND INN
2144 Netherland Inn Road, Kingsport, 423-335-5552; www.netherlandinn.com
The large frame and stone structure on the site of King's Boat Yard was a celebrated stop on the Great Stage Road and was operated for more than 150 years as an inn and the town's entertainment center. U.S. presidents Andrew Jackson, Andrew Johnson and James K. Polk visited the inn during its heyday, between 1818 and 1841. Now a museum with 18th- and 19th-century furnishings, the complex includes a well house, flatboat, garden, log cabin, children's museum and museum shop.
May-September, Saturday-Monday; April, October, Saturday-Sunday.

WARRIORS' PATH STATE PARK
490 Hemlock Road, Kingsport, 423-239-8531; www.state.tn.us
A swimming pool, a water slide, a bathhouse, fishing and boating, nature

bridle trails, 18-hole golf, a driving range, disc golf, a playground and concessions keep this park busy. The campground is on the shores of Patrick Henry Reservoir on the Holston River. The first-come, first-served wooded sites have picnic tables and grills. But plan ahead—the sites are usually full by Tuesday of race week.

SPECIAL EVENT
KINGSPORT FUN FEST
151 E. Main St., Kingsport, 423-392-8800; www.funfest.net
The citywide fest has more than 100 events, including hot-air balloon races, sports and entertainment.
Late July.

WHERE TO STAY
★★DAYS INN
805 Lynn Garden Drive, Kingsport, 423-246-7126, 800-329-7466; www.daysinn.com
65 rooms. Complimentary breakfast. Pool. $61-150

★★★MARRIOTT MEADOWVIEW RESORT
1901 Meadowview Parkway, Kingsport, 423-578-6600, 800-228-9290; www.meadowviewresort.com
Whether you decide to stick around the beautiful grounds of this vast resort or catch the excitement of a race at Bristol, the amenities and atmosphere here will not -disappoint. For sporty types, the resort offers tennis, basketball, golf, mountain biking, freshwater fishing and volleyball; for those looking to relax, a dip in the outdoor pool.
195 rooms. Restaurant, bar. Pool. Tennis. Golf. $61-150

KNOXVILLE
See also Maryville
The first capital of Tennessee, Knoxville began as a frontier outpost on the edge of the Cherokee nation, the last stop for 18th-century pioneers on their way west. It was known for whisky and wild times, but as it grew up, Knoxville became a commercial leader, leveraging its prime spot on the Tennessee River to boost its economy. During the Civil War, east Tennessee had many Union sympathizers, and though Confederate troops seized the city initially, it eventually fell to Union forces.

The 20th century brought growth and prosperity to Knoxville, and this growth has continued into the 21st century. This is the land of bluegrass and country music, but Knoxville also knows how to rock. Visitors will find a booming music scene and several citywide festivals that highlight the region's talent and celebrate its culture and history. Old City, the restored warehouse district near the river, was Knoxville's black eye at the turn of the 20th century, but today, it's the lively geographic heart of the city, full of coffee shops, art galleries, jazz clubs and boutiques.

Part of the city's culture is its allegiance to the University of Tennessee, located in Knoxville. Football fans, wearing (and sometimes painted) orange flood the stadium in the fall to cheer on the Volunteers, and in the off-season, the town enjoys the cultural benefits of the local university.

WHAT TO SEE
BECK CULTURAL EXCHANGE CENTER-MUSEUM OF BLACK HISTORY AND CULTURE

1927 Dandridge Ave., Knoxville, 865-524-8461; www.discoveret.org/beckcec
The center preserves the achievements of Knoxville's African-American citizens from the early 1800s. The gallery features changing exhibits of local and regional artists.
Tuesday-Saturday.

CONFEDERATE MEMORIAL HALL

3148 Kingston Pike S.W., Knoxville, 865-522-2371; www.knoxvillecmh.org
The antebellum mansion with Mediterranean-style gardens served as headquarters of Confederate General. James Longstreet during the siege of Knoxville. Maintained as a Confederate memorial, the 15-room house is furnished with museum pieces, a collection of Southern and Civil War relics and a library of Southern literature.
Tuesday, Thursday-Friday.

CRESCENT BEND (ARMSTRONG-LOCKETT HOUSE) AND W. PERRY TOMS MEMORIAL GARDENS

2728 Kingston Pike, Knoxville, 865-637-3163
Here you'll find collections of American and English furniture, English silver and extensive terraced gardens.
March-December, Tuesday-Sunday.

EAST TENNESSEE DISCOVERY CENTER & AKIMA PLANETARIUM

516 N. Beaman St., Knoxville, Chilhowee Park, 865-594-1494; www.etdiscovery.org
Much more fun than high school biology, this museum has interactive exhibits that kids and adults will find fascinating. Exhibits include a live honey bee colony, an arthropod exhibit with giant Madagascar missing cockroaches, a series that teach about energy and a space shuttle with interactive control panels.
Monday-Saturday.

GOV. WILLIAM BLOUNT MANSION

200 W. Hill Ave., Knoxville, 865-525-2375; www.blountmansion.org
The house of William Blount, governor of the Southwest Territory and signer of the U.S. Constitution, was the center of political and social activity in the territory. It's been restored to its condition of late 1700s with period furnishings, Blount memorabilia and an 18th-century garden. Tennessee's first state constitution was drafted in the governor's office behind the mansion.
April-mid-December, Monday-Saturday 9:30 a.m.-5 p.m.; January-March, Monday-Friday 9:30 a.m.-5 p.m.

JAMES WHITE'S FORT

205 E. Hill Ave., Knoxville, 865-525-6514; www.discoveret.org
The original pioneer house was built by the founder and first settler of Knoxville. Restored buildings include the smokehouse, blacksmith shop and museum.
March-mid-December, Monday-Saturday; January-February, Monday-Friday.

KNOXVILLE MUSEUM OF ART

1050 World's Fair Park, Knoxville, 865-525-6101; www.knoxart.org

The museum holds four galleries, gardens, a great hall and the ARTcade. See the impressive collection of graphics on display.

Tuesday-Saturday 10 a.m.-5 p.m., Sunday 1-5 p.m.

KNOXVILLE ZOO

3500 Knoxville Zoo Drive, Knoxville, 865-637-5331; www.knoxville-zoo.org

The zoo is home to more than 1,000 animals, including red pandas (which the zoo has had much success breeding), snow leopards, gorillas, elephants and about 100 species of reptiles. The African elephants Mamie, Jana, Edie and Tonka paint with their trunks, and their artwork has sold for as much as $1,350. Kids will enjoy the petting zoo. Daily.

MARBLE SPRINGS

1220 W. Gov. John Sevier Highway, 865-573-5508; www.discoveret.org/jsma

This is the restored house of John Sevier, the state's first governor. The original cabin and other restored buildings rest on 36 acres.

Tuesday-Sunday 10 a.m.-5 p.m.

MCCLUNG HISTORICAL COLLECTION

East Tennessee Historical Center, 500 W. Church Ave., 865-544-5744

More than 38,000 volumes of history and genealogy covering Tennessee and Southeastern U.S. are housed in the center. Daily.

RAMSEY HOUSE (SWAN POND)

2614 Thorngrove Pike, Knoxville, 865-546-0745; www.ramseyhouse.org

The first stone house in Knox County, built for Col. Francis A. Ramsey, was a social, religious and political center of early Tennessee. The restored gabled house with an attached kitchen features ornamental cornices, keystone arches and period furnishings. Picnicking is available.

April-October, Tuesday-Sunday; November-March, by appointment.

TENNESSEE VALLEY AUTHORITY

400 W. Summit Hill Drive, Knoxville, 865-632-2101; www.tva.gov

One of the South's largest projects is the Tennessee Valley Authority, an independent corporate agency owned by the federal government created by an Act of Congress on May 18, 1933. Designed to lift the South out of a long-term economic slump, the TVA was the brainchild of President Franklin D. Roosevelt. The TVA produces power, controls navigation and prevents floods and erosion for most of Tennessee; areas of Alabama, Mississippi and Kentucky; and small sections of Virginia, Georgia and North Carolina. A lot of the TVA's work goes on behind the scenes, but the most visible benefit for visitors (aside from electricity, of course) is the 600,000 surface acres of water and 11,000 miles of shoreline created by the TVA dams. The lakes provide excellent fishing for bass, walleye, crappie and other fish, with no closed season, and public parks line the lakes. In the 1960s, the TVA developed a 40-mile-long recreational and environmental education area in western Kentucky and Tennessee called Land Between the Lakes.

SPECIAL EVENTS
DOGWOOD ARTS FESTIVAL
106 W. Summit Hill Drive, Knoxville, 865-637-4561; www.dogwoodarts.com
The fest offers more than 150 events and activities throughout the community, including arts and crafts exhibits and shows; more than 80 public and private gardens on display; musical entertainment; parades; sporting events; more than 60 miles of marked dogwood trails for auto or free bus tours; special children's and senior citizen activities.
Mid-late April.

TENNESSEE VALLEY FAIR
Chilhowee Park, 3301 E. Magnolia Ave., Knoxville, 865-637-5840, 865-215-1471; www.tnvalleyfair.org
At the fair, get some entertainment, take a spin on the carnival rides, see livestock and agricultural shows, enter contests and view exhibits and fireworks.
September.

WHERE TO STAY
★★COURTYARD KNOVILLE CEDAR BLUFF
216 Langley Place, Knoxville, 865-539-0600; www.courtyard.com
78 rooms. Restaurant. $61-150

★★★CROWNE PLAZA KNOXVILLE
401 Summit Hill Drive, Knoxville, 865-522-2600; www.crowneplaza.com
Located in the heart of downtown Knoxville, this hotel is convenient to many attractions, including the historic shopping district and the Old City.
197 rooms. Restaurant, bar. Fitness center. $61-150

★★HOLIDAY INN SELECT-KNOXVILLE
525 Henley St., Knoxville, 865-522-2800; www.holiday-inn.com
293 rooms. Restaurant, bar. Pool. $61-150

★★★HILTON KNOXVILLE
501 W. Church Ave., Knoxville, 865-523-2300; www.hilton.com
Located in downtown Knoxville and near the Tennessee River, this hotel offers great views from the upper floors. The University of Tennessee Conference Center is across the street, and many attractions and restaurants are nearby. The décor and furnishings are contemporary, and the lobby features a large granite fireplace with bookshelves on either side.
317 rooms. Restaurant, bar. Fitness center. Pool. $61-150

WHERE TO EAT
★APPLE CAKE TEA ROOM
11312 Station W. Drive, Knoxville, 865-966-7848
American. Lunch. Closed Sunday. $16-35

★BUTCHER SHOP
806 World Fair Park Drive, Knoxville, 865-637-0204; www.thebutchershop.com
Steak. Dinner. $16-35

★★CALHOUN'S
10020 Kingston Pike, Knoxville, 865-673-3444; www.calhouns.com
American. Lunch, dinner. $16-35

★★CHESAPEAKE'S
500 N. Henley St., Knoxville, 865-673-3433; www.chesapeakes.com
Seafood. Lunch, dinner. $16-35

★★COPPER CELLAR
1807 Cumberland Ave., Knoxville, 865-673-3411; www.coppercellar.com
American. Dinner. Closed Sunday. $$

★★LITTON'S
2803 Essary Road, Knoxville, 865-687-8788; www.littonburgers.com
American. Lunch, dinner. Closed Sunday. $16-35

★★NAPLES
5500 Kingston Pike, Knoxville, 865-584-5033; www.naplesitalianrestaurant.net
Italian. Lunch, dinner. $16-35

★★★THE ORANGERY
5412 Kingston Pike, Knoxville, 865-588-2964; www.theorangeryrestaurant.com
A beautiful winding staircase is the first thing diners notice when they enter this elegant restaurant. Its interior is decorated with French provincial furnishings, chandeliers and antiques. A piano player entertains diners in the lounge, and large windows provide natural light and wonderful views of the beautiful gardens in the courtyard. The continental menu features specialties such as veal porterhouse, prime New York strip steak, buffalo with caramelized shallots, and elk chop with vegetable purée. Diners are sure to find perfect pairings for their meals on the restaurant's extensive wine list.
Continental. Lunch, dinner. Closed Sunday. $36-85

★★★REGAS
318 N. Gay St., Knoxville, 865-637-3427; www.connorconcepts.com
First opened as a stool-and-counter joint in 1919, Regas has since become one of Knoxville's most popular restaurants. The décor has a rich, Old World elegance with a cozy fireplace, beamed ceilings and brick-and-wood walls. The hearty lunch and dinner menus feature classic American cuisine, including steaks, chops, seafood and chicken. Save room for Regas' famous red velvet cake.
American. Lunch, dinner. Closed Sunday. $16-35

MANCHESTER
See also Monteagle
Manchester is a vibrant community with plenty to see and do. The annual Bonnaroo Music and Arts Festival is held here on a 700-acre farm, which draws music lovers here each summer.

WHAT TO SEE
JACK DANIEL'S DISTILLERY
280 Lynchburg Highway, Lynchburg, 931-759-4221; www.jackdaniels.com
This is the nation's oldest registered distillery. Eighty-minute guided tours include a look at the rustic grounds, limestone spring cave and old office. Daily 9 a.m.-4:30 p.m.

NORMANDY LAKE
Manchester, eight miles west, two miles upstream from Normandy; www.tva.gov
Completed in 1976, the dam that impounds the lake is 2,734 feet high. Controlled releases provide a scenic float way (28 miles) below the dam with public access points along the way. During the summer, the pool is open; in the spring and fall, there's excellent fishing. Picnicking and camping are available as well. Daily.

OLD STONE FORT STATE ARCHAEOLOGICAL PARK
732 Stone Fort Drive, Manchester, 931-723-5073; www.state.tn.us/environment
The 600-acre park surrounds the earthen remains of a more than 2,000-year-old walled structure built along the bluffs of the Duck River. Fishing, picnicking, a playground and camping are available.
Daily 8 a.m.-sunset.

SPECIAL EVENT
BONNAROO MUSIC & ARTS FESTIVAL
Manchester; www.bonnaroo.com
This four day camping festival draws music lovers to a 700-acre farm to see live music performances, along with comedy performances, film, art and more. Past performers have includes Bruce Springsteen and the E Street Band, Phish, Wilco, Beastie Boys, Yeah Yeah Yeahs and Al Green.
June.

WHERE TO STAY
★★AMBASSADOR INN AND LUXURY SUITES
925 Interstate Drive, Manchester, 931-728-2200, 800-237-9228;
www.ambassadorinn.com
105 rooms. Complimentary breakfast. Fitness center. $61-150

WHERE TO EAT
★OAK
947 Interstate Drive, Manchester, 931-728-5777
American. Lunch, dinner, brunch. Closed Monday. $15 and under.

MARYVILLE
See also Knoxville, Townsend
Maryville and its twin city, Alcoa, provide a scenic gateway to the Great Smoky Mountains National Park. Maryville was once the home of Sam Houston, the only man in U.S. history to serve as governor of two states. In 1807 he moved to this area from Virginia with his widowed mother and eight brothers.

WHAT TO SEE
MARYVILLE COLLEGE
502 E. Lamar Alexander Parkway, Maryville, 865-981-8000; www.maryvillecollege.edu
This liberal arts college has 20 buildings that represent architectural trends from 1869-1922. The Fine Arts Center has plays, concerts and exhibits. Tours of the campus leave Fayerweather Hall from the admissions office twice daily Monday through Friday.

SAM HOUSTON SCHOOLHOUSE
3650 Old Sam Houston School Road, Maryville, 865-983-1550
The restored log building was where Sam Houston taught in 1812 at a tuition rate of $8 per term. There's a museum of Houston memorabilia in the nearby visitor center.
Tuesday-Saturday 10 a.m.-5 p.m., Sunday 1-5 p.m.

WHERE TO STAY
★★★★BLACKBERRY FARM
1471 W. Millers Cove Road, Walland, 37886, 865-984-8166; www.blackberryfarm.com
On a 4,200-acre estate in the foothills of Tennessee's Great Smoky Mountains, Blackberry is one of the South's most celebrated country inns. Those in the know commend its exquisite location, first-rate service and delicious food—the inn produces its own cheese, eggs, honey, vegetables and fruit for its guests. The property's two ponds and stream beckon anglers who travel here solely for the Orvis-endorsed fly-fishing; other diversions include horseback riding, swimming, hiking and tennis. Epicureans savor the regionally inspired haute cuisine. Housed in a charming 1870s farmhouse, the Aveda Concept Spa offers signature treatments using local blackberries to soothe and rejuvenate the body.
44 rooms. Children over 10 years only. Restaurant. $251-350

WHERE TO EAT
★★★★THE BARN AT BLACKBERRY FARM
1471 W. Millers Cove Road, Walland, 800-648-4252; www.blackberryfarm.com
Designed in the same country-meets-luxury style that Blackberry Farm exhibits in its rooms, the visually stunning Barn restaurant allows guests to sample regionally inspired dishes on a nightly basis. Chef Adam Cooke uses the freshest ingredients from Blackberry Farm's onsite heirloom garden and its housemade cheese, eggs and honey, and incorporates these ingredients into his unique Smoky Mountain "Foothills Cuisine." Diners choose from three menus: A chef's tasting menu, an à la carte menu or a garden tasting, featuring items such as seared foie gras with blackberries, frisee and toast. American. Dinner. $36-85

MEMPHIS
See also Covington, KY
Old South meets modern metropolis in Memphis, thanks in part to a recent revival of the downtown area. This rebirth has given Memphis a shiny new face to go with its epic musical legacy and prime location on the banks of the Mississippi River.

Named after the Egyptian city, Memphis means "place of good abode," a translation that rings true for Elvis fans, who make Graceland the second most-visited home in the U.S. (Only the White House attracts more visitors each year.) But if you have no interest in searching for the King's ghost, Memphis is still a hot destination, especially for music lovers.

Don't let Nashville fool you: American music owes a lot of its success to Memphis. "Father of the Blues" W.C. Handy scribbled the first written blues music here, Elvis made his first recording here and on Beale Street, legends such as B.B. King and Muddy Waters gave life to the blues. Rock 'n' roll grew up here, too, when Sam Phillips of Sun Studio recorded musicians who fused country music and blues into rockabilly, the precursor to rock 'n' roll.

Memphis offers more than music history (though that's the prime attraction). It is home to more than a dozen institutions of higher learning, including the University of Memphis and Rhodes College. A civic ballet, a symphony orchestra, an opera company, a repertory theater and art galleries help create the city's rich cultural life.

WHAT TO SEE
BEALE STREET
203 Beale St., Memphis, 901-526-0110; www.bealestreet.com
This is part of a seven-block entertainment district stretching east from the Mississippi River bluffs with restaurants, shops, parks and theaters. There's a statue of W. C. Handy in Handy Park (Third and Beale streets).

THE CHILDREN'S MUSEUM OF MEMPHIS
2525 Central Ave., Memphis, 901-458-2678; www.cmom.com
This hands-on discovery museum has created an interactive "kid-sized city," including a bank, grocery store and skyscraper, among others. Other exhibits include Art Smart, where kids sculpt, paint and draw; Going Places, where children "fly" a real airplane and watch a hot-air balloon ride. Save time to explore other special workshops and exhibits.
Monday-Saturday 9 a.m.-5 p.m., Sunday noon-5 p.m.

CHUCALISSA ARCHAEOLOGICAL MUSEUM
1987 Indian Village Drive, Memphis, 901-785-3160; www.cas.memphis.edu
The archaeological project of the University of Memphis sits at the site of a Native American village founded about A.D. 900 and abandoned circa 1500. Native houses and temple have been reconstructed; archaeological exhibits are on display. The museum showcases artifacts and dioramas and there's a 15-minute slide program.
Tuesday-Sunday.

CRYSTAL SHRINE GROTTO
5668 Poplar Ave., Memphis, 901-767-8930
This crystal cave made of natural rock, quartz, crystal and semiprecious stones was carved out of a hillside by naturalistic artist Dionicio Rodriguez in the late 1930s. There are also scenes by the artist depicting the life of Jesus and biblical characters. Daily.

W. C. HANDY'S HOME

352 Beale St., Memphis, 901-522-1556

W. C. Handy wrote "Memphis Blues," "St. Louis Blues" and other classic tunes here. It also houses a collection of Handy memorabilia.
Tuesday-Saturday 11 a.m.-4 p.m.

DIXON GALLERY AND GARDENS

4339 Park Ave., Memphis, 901-761-5250; www.dixon.org

Hugo Norton Dixon and Margaret Oates Dixon, philanthropists and community leaders, left their home, grounds and a large portion of their estate to fund this museum and garden complex for the enjoyment and education of Memphis residents and visitors. The museum is surrounded by 17 acres of formal gardens with a camellia house and garden statuary. The exhibition galleries display American and French Impressionist and post-Impressionist art, British portraits and landscapes and 18th-century German porcelain.
Tuesday-Friday 10 a.m.-4 p.m., Saturday 10 a.m.-5 p.m.

GRACELAND

3734 Elvis Presley Blvd., Memphis, 901-332-3322, 800-238-2000; www.elvis.com

No visit to Memphis is complete without a stop at Graceland to pay homage to the King of Rock 'n' Roll. The main attraction is the 60- to 90-minute tour of the home, where visitors swoon over the King's living room, dining room, music room, jungle room and kitchen, among other spaces. You'll also see the trophy room, where Elvis' gold records and awards are kept, and the Meditation Garden, where Elvis' own eternal flame blazes. Here, too, see Elvis' gravesite, likely covered in flowers and mementos from devoted fans. You can take separate tours of the Automobile Museum, which features Elvis' collection of Cadillacs—including the famous 1955 pink Cadillac—and other cars and motorcycles; his custom jets, the Lisa Marie and the Hound Dog II; and Sincerely Elvis, a small museum of fan-related items. Don't miss the nearby gift shops for an amazing assortment of Elvis-related kitsch.
March-October, Monday-Saturday 9 a.m.-5 p.m., Sunday 10 a.m.-4 p.m.; November-February, Monday, Wednesday-Sunday 10 a.m.-4 p.m.

LICHTERMAN NATURE CENTER

5992 Quince Road, Memphis, 901-767-7322; www.memphismuseums.org

The 65-acre wildlife sanctuary includes a 12-acre lake, greenhouse and hospital for wild animals. There are also three miles of hiking trails and places for picnicking.
Tuesday-Sunday.

MEEMAN-SHELBY FOREST STATE PARK

910 Riddick Road, Millington, 901-876-5215, 800-471-5293; www.state.tn.us

This 13,467-acre pristine state park features two lakes, a campground, fishing, boating and a swimming pool and is a beautiful setting for a leisurely hike or walk. Meeman-Shelby Forest State Park has more than 20 miles of hiking trails. However, since some of the trails are in the Mississippi River bottom, they are off limits during managed hunts.
Daily 7 a.m.-10 p.m.

MEMPHIS BOTANIC GARDEN

750 Cherry Road, Memphis, 901-576-4100; www.memphisbotanicgarden.com

The garden encompasses 96 acres; 20 formal gardens here include the Japanese Garden of Tranquility, the Rose Garden and the Wildflower Garden. A special Sensory Garden stimulates all five senses.

Days and times vary.

MEMPHIS BELLE

Jim Webb Restoration Center, 8101 Hornet Ave., Millington, 901-412-8071, 800-507-6507

Named for the pilot's wartime sweetheart, this B-17 bomber and her crew were the first to complete 25 missions over Nazi targets and return to the U.S. during WWII without losing any crew members or incurring any major injuries. The Memphis Belle shot down eight enemy fighters, most likely destroyed five others and damaged at least a dozen more. The famous plane is undergoing restoration at Millington Municipal Airport, after which she will be moved to a new museum. The public may visit the "Belle" at hangar N7 while she is under restoration.

Tuesday-Friday 10 a.m.-3 p.m.; Monday, Saturday by appointment.

MEMPHIS BROOKS MUSEUM OF ART

1934 Poplar Ave., Memphis, 901-544-6200; www.brooksmuseum.org

The largest art museum in Tennessee has more than 7,000 pieces in its permanent collection, including drawings, paintings, sculpture, prints, photographs and decorative arts such as glass and textiles. Its collections contain three centuries' worth of works from Africa, Asia, Europe and North and South America, with an emphasis on European and American art of the 18th through 20th centuries. Highlights include paintings by Andrew Wyeth, Winslow Homer and Georgia O'Keeffe; sculptures by Auguste Rodin; and prints by Thomas Hart Benton. The museum's Brushmark Restaurant, with terrific views of Overton Park through the floor-to-ceiling windows or on the outdoor terrace, serves lunch.

Tuesday-Friday 10 a.m.-4 p.m., Thursday 10 a.m.-8 p.m., Saturday 10 a.m.-5 p.m., Sunday 11:30 a.m.-5 p.m.

MEMPHIS PINK PALACE MUSEUM AND PLANETARIUM

3050 Central Ave., Memphis, 901-320-6320; www.memphismuseums.org

Exhibits at this recently expanded and remodeled museum focus on the natural and cultural history of the Mid-South. Visitors might enjoy the full-scale reproduction of an original Piggly Wiggly grocery store and a replica of an old-fashioned pharmacy with a soda fountain. The themes of the exhibits reflect the area's diversity: insects, birds, mammals, geology, pioneer life, medical history and the Civil War. The museum also has a planetarium and an IMAX Theater.

Monday-Thursday 9 a.m.-4 p.m., Friday-Saturday 9 a.m.-9 p.m., Sunday noon-6 p.m.

MEMPHIS QUEEN LINE RIVERBOATS

45 Riverside Drive, Memphis, 901-527-5694; www.memphisqueen.com

Troll the river on one of the sightseeing or evening music cruises aboard a Mississippi riverboat.

Sightseeing: March-November, daily. Evening cruises: April-October, Friday-Saturday.

MEMPHIS ROCK 'N' SOUL MUSEUM

FedExForum, 191 Beale St., Memphis, 901-205-2533; www.memphisrocknsoul.org

Showcasing Memphis as the crossroads of blues, rock 'n' roll and country music, this museum features exhibits such as B. B. King's first "Lucille" guitar and Dick Clark's podium from American Bandstand.

Daily 10 a.m.-7 p.m.

MEMPHIS ZOO

2000 Galloway Ave., Memphis, 901-333-6500, 800-290-6041; www.memphiszoo.org

The Memphis Zoo houses more than 3,500 animals in naturalistic habitats with names such as Cat Country, Primate Canyon, Animals of the Night, China and Once Upon a Farm. Two of the most popular animals at the zoo are Ya Ya and Le Le, the giant pandas from China—do not miss them. The zoo is large, but it's easy to get around, especially if you board the tram and cruise around the park. Take a break from viewing the animals to go for a ride on the carousel or get a bite to eat at the café.

March-October, daily 9 a.m.-6 p.m.; November-February, daily 9 a.m.-5 p.m.

MUD ISLAND RIVER PARK

125 N. Front St., Memphis, 901-576-7241, 800-507-6507; www.mudisland.com

This 52-acre island, accessible by monorail or pedestrian walkway, is a unique park designed to showcase the character of the river. The River Walk is a five-block-long scale model of the lower Mississippi River from Cairo, Ill., to the Gulf of Mexico (guided tours are available). The River Museum features 18 galleries that chronicle the development of river music, art, lore and history. Also here are films, a playground, riverboat excursions, shops, restaurants and a 5,400-seat amphitheater. Daily.

NATIONAL CIVIL RIGHTS MUSEUM

450 Mulberry St., Memphis, 901-521-9699; www.civilrightsmuseum.org

Opened in 1991, this is the nation's first civil-rights museum. It honors the American civil-rights movement and the people behind it, from colonial to present times. The museum is at the former Lorraine Motel, where Dr. Martin Luther King Jr. was assassinated in 1968. Exhibits include sound and light displays, audiovisual presentations and visitor participation programs. There is also an auditorium, a gift shop and a courtyard.

June-August, Monday, Wednesday-Saturday 9 a.m.-6 p.m., Sunday 1-6 p.m.; September-May, Monday, Wednesday-Saturday 9 a.m.-5 p.m., Sunday 1-5 p.m.

PYRAMID ARENA
1 Auction Ave., Memphis, 901-521-9675
This 32-story, 22,500-seat stainless-steel and concrete pyramid, which over-looks the Mississippi River, is fashioned after the ancient Egyptian Great Pyramid of Cheops. It's used as a multi-sports and entertainment arena. The NBA's Memphis Grizzlies left the Pyramid for the FedEx Forum in the 2006-2007 season. Tours are not available.

RACE-ON DRIVING EXPERIENCE
3638 Fite Road Millington, Memphis, 901-527-6174, 866-472-2366; www.4raceon.com
If you are jealous of watching the pros have all the fun, test your skills behind the wheel of a NASCAR vehicle around the 3/4-mile paved tri-oval track at Memphis Motorsports Park (on non-race days, of course). The season runs from March to November, but times and dates vary, so call for a schedule.

STAX MUSEUM OF AMERICAN SOUL MUSIC
926 E. McLemore Ave., Memphis, 901-946-2535; www.soulsvilleusa.com
This museum is built on the original site of Stax Records, the Memphis-based record label that launched the careers of Otis Redding, Isaac Hayes, Sam and Dave and other stars of the 1960s and 1970s. Featured here are more than 2,000 exhibits, including Hayes' gold-trimmed, peacock-blue "Super-fly" Cadillac.
March-October, Monday-Saturday 9 a.m.-4 p.m., Sunday 1-4 p.m.; November-February, Monday-Saturday 10 a.m.-4 p.m., Sunday 1-4 p.m.

SUN STUDIO
706 Union Ave., Memphis, 901-521-0664, 800-441-6249; www.sunstudio.com
Music legends such as Elvis Presley, Jerry Lee Lewis, Johnny Cash, B. B. King, Roy Orbison and Carl Perkins made their first recordings in this small studio. The 45-minute tour is worth the stop, and you can even make your own custom recording.
Daily 10 a.m.-6 p.m.

T. O. FULLER STATE PARK
1500 Mitchell Road, Memphis, 901-543-7581
This 384-acre park is where Spanish explorer Hernando De Soto is believed to have crossed the Mississippi. It has a swimming pool, a bathhouse, golf, picnicking and campsites.
Daily 8 a.m.-sunset.

VICTORIAN VILLAGE
600 Adams Ave., Memphis
These 18 landmark buildings, either preserved or restored, range in style from Gothic Revival to neo-classical. Daily.

SPECIAL EVENTS
BEALE STREET MUSIC FESTIVAL
Memphis; www.memphisinmay.org
One of the country's best blues events, the festival happens in what blues

buffs consider the center of the universe. Musicians from around the world come to Memphis for this musical family reunion, part of the "Memphis in May" festivities.
Early May.

ELVIS PRESLEY INTERNATIONAL TRIBUTE WEEK
3734 Elvis Presley Blvd., Memphis, 901-332-3322, 800-238-2000; www.elvis.com
Thousands of people come to Memphis from all around the world for this event-packed week to celebrate and remember the King of Rock 'n' Roll. More than 30 events—including concerts, tours, street parties, fan forums and even an Elvis fashion show—take place.
Mid-August.

MEMPHIS IN MAY INTERNATIONAL FESTIVAL
88 Union Ave., Memphis, 901-525-4611; www.memphisinmay.org
The month-long community-wide celebration focuses on the cultural and artistic heritage of Memphis while featuring a different nation each year. Major events occur weekends, but activities are held daily. It includes the Beale Street Music Festival, World Championship Barbecue Cooking Contest and Sunset Symphony.
May.

ZYDECO FESTIVAL
Beale Street, Memphis
Cajun-Creole and zydeco blues bands entertain in Beale Street clubs.
Early February.

WHERE TO STAY

★★COURTYARD MEMPHIS EAST
6015 Park Ave., Memphis, 901-761-0330, 800-321-2211; www.memphisparkavecourt-yard.com
146 rooms. Restaurant. $61-150

★★DOUBLETREE HOTEL
5069 Sanderlin Ave., Memphis, 901-767-6666; www.doubletree.com
265 rooms. Restaurant, bar. Fitness center. Pool. $61-150

★★DOUBLETREE HOTEL MEMPHIS DOWNTOWN
185 Union Ave., Memphis, 901-528-1800, 800-222-8733; www.doubletree.com
280 rooms. Restaurant, bar. Fitness center. Pool. $61-150

★★EMBASSY SUITES
1022 S. Shady Grove Road, Memphis, 901-684-1777, 800-362-2779; www.embassysuites.com
125 suites. Restaurant, bar. Complimentary breakfast. Fitness center. Pool. $61-150

★★HOLIDAY INN
160 Union Ave., Memphis, 901-525-5491, 888-300-5491;
www.hisdowntownmemphis.com
192 rooms. Restaurant, bar. $151-250

★★★HILTON MEMPHIS
939 Ridge Lake Blvd., Memphis, 901-684-6664, 800-445-8667; www.hilton.com
Towering 27 stories above the Memphis area, this hotel looks ultramodern on
the outside but is bright and roomy on the inside. The hotel is in the entertainment and business district, just minutes from downtown Memphis.
405 rooms. Restaurant, bar. Fitness center. Pool. $151-250

★★★MADISON HOTEL
79 Madison Ave., Memphis, 901-333-1200; www.madisonhotelmemphis.com
The jazzy spirit of Memphis is brought to life at the Madison Hotel. This
boutique hotel dazzles the senses with its striking interiors, which employs
bold colors, geometric patterns and modern furnishings. The Madison is located in the heart of the city's business and entertainment districts and is
within walking distance to the famed Beale Street and Orpheum Theatre.
Guest rooms are fitted with state-of-the-art technology for those traveling
on business, while luxurious Italian bed linens, duvets and whirlpool baths
appeal to all visitors.
110 rooms. Complimentary breakfast. Restaurant, bar. Business center. Fitness center. Pool. $251-350

★★★MARRIOTT MEMPHIS
2625 Thousand Oaks Blvd., Memphis, 901-362-6200, 800-627-3587;
www.marriott.com
Near this property are attractions such as Graceland and the Mall of Memphis. Rooms are spacious and include modern amenities for a comfortable
stay.
320 rooms. Restaurant, bar. $61-150

★★★MARRIOTT MEMPHIS DOWNTOWN
250 N. Main St., Memphis, 901-527-7300, 888-557-8740;
www.memphismarriottdowntown.com
This hotel, offering spacious guest rooms, is 20 minutes from the Memphis
International Airport and near shopping, museums, the world-famous Beale
Street and Mud Island.
600 rooms. Restaurant, bar. $151-250

★★★★THE PEABODY MEMPHIS
149 Union Ave., Memphis, 901-529-4000, 800-732-2639; www.peabodymemphis.com
The Peabody is a Memphis landmark. Perhaps best known for its signature
ducks that march twice daily to splash in the hotel's fountain, this grand
hotel is also a shopping destination (it's the home of Lansky's, Elvis' favorite
clothing store). The hotel's impressive array of amenities include a comprehensive health club, an indoor pool and Gould's Day Spa and Salon. The
hotel's popular Capriccio Restaurant, Bar and Café serves delicious Italian

dishes, while Chez Philippe adds a little twist to traditional French cuisine. 464 rooms. Restaurant, bar. Fitness center. Pool. Spa. $251-350

★★★SHERATON CASINO AND HOTEL
1107 Casino Center Drive, Robinsonville,800-391-3777; www.harrahs.com
Try your luck at blackjack, roulette, craps, Caribbean stud poker or slots at this hotel's 92,000-square-foot casino. The Tudor-style mansion houses 40 table games and 1,300 slot and video poker machines, an adjoining hotel, a restaurant, a spa and live entertainment seven days a week.
134 rooms. Restaurant, bar. Spa. $151-250

WHERE TO EAT
★ALFRED'S
197 Beale St., Memphis, 901-525-3711, 888-433-3711; www.alfredsonbeale.com
American. Lunch, dinner, late-night. $16-35

★BUCKLEY'S FINE FILET GRILL
5355 Poplar Ave., Memphis, 901-683-4538; www.buckleysgrill.com
Italian, steak. Dinner. $16-35

★CHARLIE VERGOS RENDEZVOUS
52 S. Second St., Memphis, 901-523-2746, 888-464-7359; www.hogsfly.com
Barbecue. Lunch, dinner. Closed Sunday-Monday. $15 and under.

★★AUTOMATIC SLIM'S TONGA CLUB
83 S. Second St., Memphis, 901-525-7948
Caribbean. Lunch, dinner, late-night. Closed Sunday. $16-35

★★CAFÉ 61
85 S. Second St., Memphis, 901-523-9351; www.cafe61memphis.com
Cajun, Southern, Asian. Lunch, dinner, late-night, brunch. $16-35

★★★★CHEZ PHILIPPE
149 Union Ave., Memphis, 901-529-4000, 800-732-2639; www.peabodymemphis.com
For more than a decade, this sexy, sophisticated restaurant in the historic Peabody Memphis hotel has been a favorite of foodies, movie stars, celebrity chefs and well-heeled locals. Like clockwork, the crowds show up every evening, filling Chez Philippe's stunning dining room for the opportunity to feast on the culinary artwork on display. The service is efficient and unobtrusive, and the atmosphere is hushed, elegant and refined. Chef Reinaldo Alfonso applies simple, seasonal ingredients to the delicate dishes of French and Asian origin, occasionally accented with regional flair. Leave room for dessert: Chez Philippe is known for its soufflés.
French. Dinner. Closed Sunday-Monday. $36-85

★THE CUPBOARD
1400 Union Ave., Memphis, 901-276-8015
American. Lunch, dinner. $15 and under.

★★★ERLING JENSEN
1044 S. Yates Road, Memphis, 901-763-3700; www.ejensen.com
This cutting-edge restaurant is one of the most popular in Memphis. Savor the shrimp and lobster terrine trimmed with mesclun greens and champagne vinaigrette, the quail and red cabbage, or the rich creamy bisques and foie gras preparations.
International. Dinner. $36-85

★★★GRILL 83
83 Madison Ave., Memphis, 901-333-1224; www.grill83.com
Uniquely decorated, this chic restaurant is a good choice for a romantic evening or a special occasion. All the mouth-watering steak selections are accompanied with cabernet reduction, maitre d' butter and tobacco onions. Enticing nonsteak options, such as pan-seared Tasmanian salmon and pan-roasted breast of Ashley Farms chicken, are also offered. Conveniently located in the heart of downtown Memphis, Grill 83 is close to historic Beale Street, entertainment and the Mississippi River.
Steak. Breakfast, lunch, dinner. $36-85

★INDIA PALACE
1720 Poplar Ave., Memphis, 38104, 901-278-1199
Indian. Lunch, dinner. $16-35

★★PAULETTE'S
2110 Madison Ave., Memphis, 901-726-5128; www.paulettes.net
French. Lunch, dinner, brunch. $16-35

★★★RONALDO GRISANTI AND SONS
2855 Poplar Ave., Memphis, 901-323-0007
Everything is freshly prepared at this restaurant, which is in a small strip mall east of downtown. Specialties of the northern Italian menu include gorgonzola-stuffed filets, fresh sea bass and pasta la elfo with shrimp, garlic and mushrooms.
Italian. Dinner. Closed Sunday. $36-85

MURFREESBORO
See also Nashville
Thanks to Murfreesboro's location in the center of Tennessee, it was almost named the state capital. The legislature met here from 1819 to 1826, but it never returned after convening in Nashville. The area is rich in Civil War history and is known for its antique shops.

WHAT TO SEE
OAKLANDS
900 N. Maney Ave., Murfreesboro, 615-893-0022; www.oaklandsmuseum.org
This 19th-century mansion, an architectural blend of four different periods, was a social center before the Civil War and was the command headquarters for Union Colonel W. W. Duffield, who surrendered Murfreesboro to Confederate General Nathan Bedford Forrest at the house. Rooms are restored and furnished with items appropriate to the Civil War period. Grounds are

landscaped in period style.
Tuesday-Saturday 10 a.m.- 4 p.m., Sunday 1-4 p.m.

WHERE TO STAY
★★DOUBLETREE HOTEL MURFREESBORO
1850 Old Fort Parkway, Murfreesboro, 615-895-5555, 800-222-8733; www.doubletree. com
168 rooms. Restaurant, bar. Complimentary breakfast. Fitness center. Pool. Pets accepted. $61-150

★ BAYMONT INN AND SUITES MURFREESBORO
2230 Armory Drive, Murfreesboro, 615-896-1172, 800-426-7866; www.baymontinns. com
114 rooms. Complimentary breakfast. Business center. Fitness center. Pool. Pets accepted. $61-150

★★CLARION INN & SUITES
2227 Old Fort Parkway, Murfreesboro, 615-896-2420, 800-465-4329; www.clarionhotel. com
179 rooms. Restaurant, bar. $61-150

★SUPER 8
1414 Princeton Place, Hermitage, 615-871-4545; www.super8.com
65 rooms. Complimentary breakfast. $61-150

WHERE TO EAT
★★PARTHENON MEDITERRANEAN
1935 S. Church St., Murfreesboro, 615-895-2665; www.parthenondining.com
Mediterranean. Lunch, dinner, late-night. $16-35

★SANTA FE STEAK CO
1824 Old Fort Parkway, Murfreesboro, 615-890-3030; www.santafecattle.com
American. Lunch, dinner, late-night. $16-35

NASHVILLE
See also Franklin, Gallatin, Murfreesboro
Nashville's role as the capital of Tennessee gets overshadowed by its reputation as Music City, center of the country music universe. But Nashville is more than a town crawling with country music stars and starry-eyed hopefuls. It's a sophisticated city with impressive museums, eclectic restaurants, more than one major-league sports team and a lively downtown district.

Of course, for most visitors, great restaurants and world-class museums are just icing on the country music cake: They come here to feel the rhythm of a city where unknowns sing their hearts out in hopes of a shot at stardom and where country music gods and goddesses record albums, cut deals and sometimes even perform in some of the city's most intimate clubs.

One of the best places to feel this rhythm is downtown, a historic neighborhood that was recently revitalized. The offerings here vary from big-name nightclubs, including B. B. King Blues Club & Grill and the famous Wildhorse Saloon, to dive bars where musicians play day and night in hopes of a big break. In between the clubs and bars are restaurants, shops and historic landmarks.

No visit to Nashville would be complete without a stop by the Grand Old Opry in the Music Valley area. The Opry began as a weekly radio show in 1925, and crowds flocked to the studio to see performers as they sang on air, prompting the show to move several times into larger and larger facilities. The show airs every weekend from its updated digs at the Grand Ole Opry House and draws some of country music's hottest stars and living legends.

Often called the "Athens of the South" for its rich cultural and intellectual life, Nashville is home to 16 colleges and universities, several major religious publishing firms and about 750 churches. And to top it all off, the city's Parthenon is the world's only full-size replica of the Athenian architectural masterpiece.

If you don't know George Straight from George Jones, you'll have fun in Nashville, but if you're a true fan of country music, a visit to Nashville will be pure heaven.

WHAT TO SEE
ADVENTURE SCIENCE MUSEUM
800 Fort Negley Blvd., Nashville, 615-862-5160; www.adventuresci.com
Kids will love this hands-on science museum. There are six main areas to explore here: Earth Science, Creativity and Invention, Sound and Light, Air and Space, Health and Energy. You can find all of these concepts represented on the Adventure Tower, a 75-foot-tall structure with seven levels of activities. Other exhibits include Construction Junction, Mission Impossible and Dino Rumble.
Tuesday-Sunday.

BELLE MEADE PLANTATION
5025 Harding Road, Nashville, 615-356-0501, 800-270-3991; www.bellemeadeplantation.com
The antebellum mansion and outbuildings were once part of a 5,300-acre working plantation. At the turn of the 20th century, John Harding's Belle Meade was considered the greatest thoroughbred breeding farm in the country. Visitors will get a glimpse of the elegance of late-19th-century Southern aristocrats in this 14-room Greek Revival mansion, which contains Empire and Victorian furnishings and an heirloom showcase with racing trophies and mementos. Also on the grounds are the Dunham Station log cabin and Carriage House, containing one of the South's largest carriage collections.
Monday-Saturday 9 a.m.-5 p.m., Sunday 11 a.m.-5 p.m.

BELMONT MANSION
1900 Belmont Blvd., Nashville, 615-460-5459; www.belmontmansion.com
Built in the 1850s in the style of an Italian villa, this mansion, once considered one of the finest private residences in the U.S., has original marble statues, Venetian glass, gasoliers, mirrors and paintings in the 15 rooms open to the public; gardens feature a large collection of 19th-century ornaments and cast-iron gazebos. Monthly garden tours are also available.
Monday-Saturday 10 a.m.-4 p.m., Sunday 1-4 p.m.

BEALE STREET

Ever since W. C. Handy set up shop in the early 1900s, Beale Street has been known around the world as the home of the blues and the inspiration for rock 'n' roll. Blues legends such as B. B. King, Furry Lewis and Rufus Thomas got their starts here, and the street still attracts budding musicians to its nightclubs. Beale Street was a thriving commercial center for Memphis's African-American community for much of the 20th century and today, it is the city's prime entertainment district. Some say the strip lost its character in the transition from a gritty no-man's-land, but the folks dancing on the sidewalks to street musicians' tunes don't seem to mind a bit.

From the top of the hill at Second Street you can look down on all the action. Here you'll find B. B. King's club and Elvis Presley's, both upscale supper clubs with name entertainment—sometimes even the King of the Blues himself. Stay on the lookout for the ghost of Elvis.

At Third Street and Beale, a statue of W. C. Handy stands in front of an amphitheater that is the venue for many local music festivals, concerts and other events. Down the street, the Orpheum Theatre hosts Broadway shows, and the New Daisy Theatre welcomes up-and-comers (and occasionally, artists who are their way back down).

CENTENNIAL SPORTSPLEX

222 25th Ave. N., Nashville, 615-862-8480; www.nashville.org/sportsplex

This 17-acre fitness and recreation facility is mainly for middle Tennessee residents, but visitors can purchase passes in blocks of ten visits. The complex includes an aquatic center, a fitness center, a tennis center and two ice rinks that are open to the public. Its also home to the Nashville Predators, the area's NHL team.

CHEEKWOOD BOTANICAL GARDEN AND MUSEUM OF ART

1200 Forrest Park Drive, Nashville, 615-356-8000; www.cheekwood.org

This one is for art lovers and garden fanatics. Cheekwood, once the private home and estate of the Cheek family, is now a cultural center set on 55 acres. The site, which was opened to the public in 1960, includes a museum with a permanent collection of 19th- and 20th-century American art; a Botanic Hall with an atrium of tropical flora and changing plant exhibits; public greenhouses; and five major gardens specializing in dogwood, wildflowers, herbs, daffodils, roses and tulips.

Tuesday-Saturday 9:30 a.m.-4:30 p.m., Sunday 11 a.m.-4:30 p.m.

COUNTRY MUSIC HALL OF FAME AND MUSEUM

222 Fifth Ave. S. Nashville, 615-416-2001, 800-852-6437;
www.countrymusichalloffame.com

A tribute to all things country music, this museum will give fans goose bumps, and even folks who aren't interested in the tunes will appreciate the history and American pop culture on display here. Elvis's gold-leafed Cadillac is parked here, and visitors can gawk at a lyric sheet scribbled with Bob Dylan's signature. This $37 million complex includes displays with costumes and instruments donated by country music legends from Minnie Pearl to George Jones. You can also check out the restored Historic RCA Studio B, where more than 1,000 top 10 hits from Elvis Presley, Willie Nelson and other stars were recorded.

Daily 9 a.m.-5 p.m.

ELLINGTON AGRICULTURAL CENTER

440 Hogan Road, Nashville, 615-837-5197;www.state.tn.us

This former horse barn sits on a historic estate. It's the oldest Agricultural Hall of Fame in the U.S. In it, you'll find farm tools, equipment and household items of the 19th century.

Monday-Friday.

ERNEST TUBB RECORD SHOP

417 Broadway, Nashville, 615-255-7503; www.etrecordshop.com

When Ernest Tubb and the Texas Troubadours weren't out touring in a big silver bus, the country music star was tending to his other love, the Ernest Tubb Record Shop. The original E.T. died in 1984, but the store continues to sell nothing but country music releases. Offerings range from hard-to-find treasures to the newest smash hits. The store on Music Valley Drive (*2416 Music Valley Drive, 615-889-2474*) also features the Texas Troubadour Theatre, home of the Midnight Jamboree every Saturday.

FISK UNIVERSITY

1000 17th Ave. N., Nashville, 615-329-8500; www.fisk.edu

The university is a National Historic District with Jubilee Hall deemed a historic landmark. The Carl Van Vechten Art Gallery houses the Stieglitz Collection of modern art. The Aaron Douglas Gallery holds a collection of African art.

FORT NASHBOROUGH

170 First Ave. N., Nashville, 615-862-8400; www.nashville.gov

Patterned after the pioneer fort established several blocks from this site in 1779, the replica is smaller and has fewer cabins. There are stockaded walls and exhibits of pioneer implements.

Tuesday-Sunday.

GENERAL JACKSON SHOWBOAT

Opry Mills, Opry Mills Drive, Nashville, 615-458-3900; www.generaljackson.com

Named after the first steamboat working the Cumberland River as far back as 1817, this 300-foot paddlewheel riverboat—the world's largest showboat these days—offers lunch cruises (a buffet plus a country music show) and elegant dinner cruises (includes a Broadway-style show).

GRAND OLE OPRY

2802 Opryland Drive, Nashville, 615-871-5043; www.opry.com

You haven't made it in Music City USA as a country star until you've graced the stage of the world's longest-running radio show. Every weekend, the Opry showcases the best of bluegrass, country, gospel, swing and Cajun. Part of the thrill for the audience is never knowing which stars will make surprise appearances.

Friday 7:30 p.m., Saturday 6:30 p.m. and 9:30 p.m.; also Tuesday in summer, 7 p.m.

GRAND OLE OPRY TOURS

2800 Opryland Drive, Nashville, 615-883-2211; www.gaylordhotels.com

One-hour, three-hour and all-day bus tours take visitors to houses of country music stars, Music Row, recording studios and on a backstage visit to the Grand Ole Opry House.

THE HERMITAGE

4580 Rachel's Lane, Nashville, 615-889-2941; www.thehermitage.com

Rebuilt after a fire in 1834, this Greek Revival residence of President Andrew Jackson is furnished almost entirely with original family pieces, many of which were associated with Jackson's military career and years in the White House. The mansion has been completely restored to its appearance from 1837 to 1845, Jackson's retirement years. Tours of the 660-acre estate are narrated by historically costumed interpreters. The tour includes a museum; the Tulip Grove Mansion; the Hermitage Church; a garden with graves of Jackson and his wife, Rachel; two log cabins; a visitor center; and a biographical film on Jackson.

April-October, daily 8:30 a.m.-5 p.m.; November-March, daily 9 a.m.-4:30 p.m.

NASHVILLE ZOO

3777 Nolensville Road, Nashville, 615-833-1534; www.nashvillezoo.org

At the Nashville Zoo, designers have gone to great lengths to make it seem as if you're simply walking through the woods and stumbling upon otters, cheetahs, apes, macaws and other animals. The zoo recently added an African elephant savannah exhibit.

April-October, daily 9 a.m.-6 p.m.; November-March, daily 9 a.m.-4 p.m.

OLD HICKORY LAKE

Nashville, six miles northeast of Nashville on the Cumberland River, 615-822-4846; www.lrn.usace.army.mil

This 22,000-acre lake has 440 miles of shoreline, eight marinas and an abundance of water fowl and wading birds—a perfect place to spend a lazy day on the water. The lake is shared by pleasure boats, sailboats, personal watercraft, fishing boats and commercial barges. Daily.

OPRY MILLS

433 Opry Mills Drive, Nashville, 615-514-1000, 800-746-7386; www.oprymills.com

There's something for just about everyone at this 1.2 million-square-foot shopping, dining and entertainment complex. The mall's unique combination of manufacturers' outlets and specialty stores provides shoppers with everything from clothing bargains to high-end sporting and outdoor goods. Noteworthy stores include Banana Republic Factory Store; Off 5th; and Barnes & Noble. Keep in mind the whopping 9.25 percent sales tax when making your purchasing decisions. When you're ready for a break from shopping, have a bite at Rainforest Café, enjoy a sundae at Ghirardelli Chocolate Shop, or take in a movie on one of 20 screens or at the IMAX theater.

Monday-Saturday 10 a.m.-9 p.m., Sunday 11 a.m.-6 p.m.

THE PARTHENON

2600 W. End Ave., Nashville, 615-862-8431; www.nashville.gov/parthenon

The replica of the Parthenon of Pericles' time was built in plaster for the Tennessee Centennial of 1897 and later reconstructed in concrete aggregate. As in the original, there is not a straight horizontal or vertical line, and no two columns are placed the same distance apart. A 42-foot-tall statue of the goddess Athena stands inside; she is the tallest indoor statue in the country. It also houses 19th- and 20th-century artworks, changing art exhibits and replicas of Elgin Marbles.

October-March, Tuesday-Saturday 9 a.m.-4:30 p.m.; April-September, Tuesday-Saturday 9 a.m.-4:30 p.m., Sunday 12:30-4:30 p.m.

RADNOR LAKE STATE NATURAL AREA

1160 Otter Creek Road, Nashville, 615-373-3467; www.state.tn.us

Located just south of Nashville, this 1,100-acre environmental preserve features an 85-acre lake and some of the highest hills in the Nashville Basin. The area provides scenic, biological and geological areas for hiking, observation, photography and nature study. Daily.

RYMAN AUDITORIUM & MUSEUM

116 Fifth Ave. N., Nashville, 615-458-8700; www.ryman.com

The Mother Church of Country Music underwent an $8.5 million facelift in the 1990s. Now this National Historic Landmark hosts concerts and a museum that tells its story. (Don't leave without buying a box of GooGoos in the museum gift shop.) A tour of the auditorium is available.

Daily 9 a.m.-4 p.m.; evening show times vary.

SAM DAVIS HOME

1399 Sam Davis Road, Nashville, 615-459-2341; www.samdavishome.org

Described as "the most beautiful shrine to a private soldier in the U.S.," this stately house and 168-acre working farm have been preserved as a memorial to Sam Davis, a Confederate scout caught behind Union lines and tried as a spy. Offered his life if he revealed the name of his informer, Davis chose to die on the gallows. His boyhood home is restored and furnished with many original pieces; the grounds include a kitchen, a smokehouse, slave cabins and a family cemetery where Davis is buried.

June-August, Monday-Saturday 9 a.m.-5 p.m., Sunday 1-5 p.m.; September-May, Monday-Saturday 10 a.m.-4 p.m., Sunday 1-4 p.m.

STATE CAPITOL

600 Charlotte Ave., Nashville, 615-741-2692; www.state.tn.us

The capitol building is a distinguished reminder that Nashville is not just the capital of the country music world. Construction of the capitol began in 1845 and lasted until 1859, and it is built of local Tennessee limestone and marble quarried and cut by slaves and convicts. The architect, William Strickland, died before the building was completed, and his body was entombed within the building's northeast wall. The Greek Revival structure has an 80-foot tower that rises above the city, and columns grace the ends and sides. The building houses the governor's offices, the chambers of the state Senate and

the House of Representatives. During Union occupation of Nashville from 1862 to 1865, the capitol was used as Fortress Andrew Johnson.
Monday-Friday.

TENNESSEE STATE MUSEUM
Polk Cultural Center, 505 Deaderick St., Nashville, 615-741-2692, 800-407-4324; www.tnmuseum.org
This museum is one of the largest in the nation, with 60,000 square feet of exhibition space. It houses an awesome Civil War collection. The permanent exhibits illustrating life in Tennessee focus on the prehistoric, Frontier, Age of Jackson, Antebellum, Civil War and Reconstruction periods. Artifacts on display include Andrew Jackson's 1829 inaugural hat, an 1850s-style parlor, a steatite shaman's medicine tube and a hand-drawn map of the Shiloh battlefield prepared for Confederate General Beauregard. After visiting the main museum, walk across the street to check out the Military Museum in the War Memorial Building.
Tuesday-Saturday 10 a.m.-5 p.m., Sunday 1-5 p.m.

TENNESSEE TITANS (NFL)
The Coliseum, 1 Titans Way, Nashville, 615-565-4200; www.titansonline.com
Tennesseans have enthusiastically embraced their NFL team, the Titans (formerly the Houston Oilers). The 68,000-seat Coliseum, an outdoor stadium set on the Cumberland River with a great view of downtown Nashville, regularly fills with rabid fans. If you stay downtown, the stadium is just a short walk across the river. Tickets can be tough to come by, so make sure to call well in advance.

TRAVELLERS REST PLANTATION AND MUSEUM
636 Farrell Parkway, Nashville, 615-832-8197; www.travellersrestplantation.org
This restored federal-style house belonged to Judge John Overton. Maintained as a historical museum with period furniture, records and letters, the building reflects the history and development of early Tennessee. The 11-acre grounds have formal gardens, a weaving house and a smokehouse.
Monday-Saturday 10 a.m.-4 p.m., Sunday 1-4 p.m.

THE UPPER ROOM CHAPEL AND MUSEUM
1908 Grand Ave., Nashville, 615-340-7200; www.upperroom.org
The chapel has a polychrome wood carving of Leonardo da Vinci's The Last Supper, said to be the largest of its kind in the world. The museum contains various religious artifacts, including seasonal displays of 100 Nativity scenes and Ukrainian Easter eggs.
Monday-Friday.

VANDERBILT UNIVERSITY
W. End Avenue and 21st Avenue S., Nashville, 615-322-7311; www.vanderbilt.edu
The 330-acre campus features 19th- and 20th-century architectural styles. The Fine Arts Gallery has a permanent collection supplemented by traveling exhibits. The Blair School of Music offers regular concerts.

WILDHORSE SALOON
120 Second Ave. N., Nashville, 615-902-8200; www.wildhorsesaloon.com

Welcome to boot-scootin' paradise. The Wildhorse Saloon is the place to go line dancing in Nashville, and even if you have two left feet, you should go for the live music and celebrity sightings. Set in a three-level historic warehouse on Nashville's Music Row, the club features live country acts Tuesday through Saturday nights. A DJ supplements the acts, and the saloon offers free dance lessons for folks who aren't too shy to shake their hips with the experts. If all that dancing makes you hungry, the restaurant serves award-winning Southern barbecue from 11 a.m. to midnight. Children younger than 18 are allowed with parents.

Restaurant: daily 11 a.m.-midnight; nightclub: until 2 a.m.

WHERE TO STAY
★AMERISUITES
202 Summit View Drive, Brentwood, 615-661-9477; www.amerisuites.com

126 suites. Complimentary breakfast. Fitness center. Pool. $61-150

★★COURTYARD VANDERBILT/WEST END
1901 W. End Ave., Nashville, 615-327-9900, 800-245-1959; www.courtyard.com

223 rooms. Restaurant. Fitness center. Pool. $61-150

★★DOUBLETREE HOTEL
315 Fourth Ave. N., Nashville 615-244-8200, 800-222-8733;
www.nashville.doubletree.com

337 rooms. Restaurant, bar. Business center. Fitness center. Pool. $151-250

★★EMBASSY SUITES HOTEL NASHVILLE-AIRPORT
10 Century Blvd., Nashville, 615-871-0033, 800-362-2779; www.nashvilleairport.
embassysuites.com

296 suites. Complimentary breakfast. Restaurant, bar. Business center. Fitness center. Pool. $61-150

★FAIRFIELD INN BY MARRIOTT NASHVILLE OPRYLAND
211 Music City Circle, Nashville, 615-882-9133; www.marriott.com

109 rooms. Complimentary breakfast. Business center. Fitness center. $61-150

★★★GAYLORD OPRYLAND RESORT AND CONVENTION CENTER
2800 Opryland Drive, Nashville, 615-889-1000, 888-777-6779; www.gaylordhotels.com

Adjacent to the Grand Ole Opry, this resort is a natural choice for music fans, but with championship golf, outlet mall shopping, and plenty of other activities nearby, this resort has something for everyone. Nine acres of tropical gardens and flowing rivers are tucked inside climate-controlled glass atriums, allowing guests to enjoy the "outdoors" year-round. Guests can even take a ride aboard the hotel's Delta Flatboats without ever going outside. For those who do want to venture out, two outdoor pools beckon sunbathers and swimmers. Variety is the spice of life here, with an endless supply of dining and recreational choices.

2,881 rooms. Restaurant, bars. Pool. Spa. $251-350

★★★★★THE HERMITAGE HOTEL
231 Sixth Ave. N., Nashville, 615-244-3121, 888-888-9414;
www.thehermitagehotel.com

The Hermitage Hotel is the Grand Dame of Nashville's hotels. Opened in 1910 and renovated in 2003, this glorious downtown hotel offers white-glove service and plenty of opportunities to indulge. Its lobby is magnificent, with vaulted ceilings of stained glass, arches decorated with frescoes and intricate stonework. The spacious guest rooms are filled with elegant traditional furnishings, creating a warm and welcoming atmosphere. On the lower level, you will find the Capitol Grille, one of Nashville's best restaurants. The adjacent Oak Bar, with its emerald-green club chairs and dark wood paneling, is a top spot for relaxing before or after dinner.

122 rooms. Restaurant, bar. Business center. Fitness center. Spa. Pets accepted. $251-350

★★HOLIDAY INN
2613 W. End Ave., Nashville, 615-327-4707, 800-465-4329; www.holiday-inn.com

300 rooms. Restaurant, bar. Pool. $61-150

★★★HOTEL PRESTON
733 Briley Parkway, Nashville, 615-361-5900, 877-361-5500; www.hotelpreston.com

This stylish spot is more city chic than cowboy country, though Opryland and all of the city's famous places are within easy reach. The guestrooms and suites blend sophistication with a bit of whimsy—you can get everything from a lava lamp to a pet fish, an art kit and even a rubber ducky upon check-in. Café Isabella whips up Italian favorites with a dash of Southern spirit (think baked ziti and chicken pot pie), while the trendy Pink Slip bar provides libations and live, local music.

190 rooms. Restaurant, bar. $251-350

★★★HUTTON HOTEL
1808 W. End Ave., Nashville, 615-340-9333; www.huttonhotel.com

The newest hotel to inhabit the trendy West End neighborhood, Hutton Hotel brings a contemporary style to Music City. The lobby is chic and cool with minimalist seating areas and wood-paneled walls. Amenities include a state-of-the-art fitness center, 24-hour business center and a complimentary coffee bar in the lobby. Guest rooms are outfitted in a modern décor with flat-screen TVs and granite baths. If that's not enough, the hotel is one of the most environmentally-friendly hotels in the city, boasting eco-friendly elevators and air-conditioning units, LED lights and a green recycling program.

248 rooms. Restaurant, bar. Business center. Fitness center. $151-250

★★★LOEWS VANDERBILT HOTEL NASHVILLE
2100 W. End Ave., Nashville, 615-320-1700, 800-336-3335; www.loewshotels.com

This upscale property is conveniently in the heart of the Vanderbilt district, between Vanderbilt University and downtown. The exterior is nicely landscaped, featuring a fountain in the front and patio seating. Comfortable guest rooms, which offer views of either the campus or city, feature quality-bedding, mini-bars, plush robes and Bloom toiletries. The works of Harold

Kraus, a renowned Nashville artist, are featured onsite at the Kraus Gallery. 340 rooms. Restaurant, bar. Business center. Fitness center. Spa. $151-250

★★★MILLENNIUM MAXWELL HOUSE NASHVILLE

2025 Metro Center Blvd., Nashville, 615-259-4343, 866-866-8086; www.millenniumhotels.com

This modern hotel offers personalized service and excellent accommodations. Just five minutes north of downtown Nashville and 15 minutes from the Grand Ole Opry, the hotel is a perfect base for all travelers. Guests can enjoy views of the city from the upper floors.

287 rooms. Restaurant, bar. $151-250

★★★RENAISSANCE NASHVILLE HOTEL

611 Commerce St., Nashville, 615-255-8400, 800-327-6618; www.renaissancehotels.com/bnash

Located between the business district and the city's tourist area, this hotel is near fine dining, great shopping and plenty of attractions.

673 rooms. Restaurant, bar. Business center. Fitness center. Pool. $151-250

★★★SHERATON MUSIC CITY

777 McGavok Pike, Nashville, 615-885-2200, 800-325-3535; www.sheratonmusiccity.com

This property resembles a mansion in the Deep South. It is convenient to Nashville proper—three miles from the airport, five miles from Opry Mills and seven miles from downtown.

410 rooms. Restaurant, bar. Complimentary breakfast. Business center. Pool. Spa. $151-250

★★★SHERATON NASHVILLE DOWNTOWN HOTEL

623 Union St., Nashville, 615-259-2000, 800-447-9825; www.sheraton-nashville.com

This contemporary hotel is in the heart of downtown Nashville near the capitol building, a location that makes it popular with business travelers and legislators. Guests are offered a host of amenities and services, including room service, turndown service, plush robes and Sheraton's signature beds. The concierge provides carefree planning regardless of whether you are in Nashville for business, pleasure or a little of both.

474 rooms. Restaurant, bar. Fitness center. $151-250

★★★WYNDHAM UNION STATION HOTEL

1001 Broadway, Nashville, 615-726-1001; www.unionstationhotelnashville.com

Housed in a historic 1897 train station, the Wyndham Union Station is a National Historic Landmark. The lobby has marble floors, a vaulted ceiling of Tiffany stained glass and ornate carved woodwork. Business services and concierge service help make each guest's stay pleasant and carefree, and complimentary wine and cheese is offered to guests in the evening. With its downtown location only a few blocks from Second Avenue and Music Row, the Wyndham is close to much of the entertainment, dining and nightlife that Nashville has to offer, with complimentary shuttle service to nearby attractions.

137 rooms. Restaurant, bar. Business center. $151-250

WHERE TO EAT

★BOSCOS PIZZA KITCHEN AND BREWERY
1805 21st Ave. S., Nashville, 615-385-0050; www.boscosbeer.com
Italian, pizza. Lunch, dinner, late-night, Sunday brunch. $16-35

★★BOUND'RY
911 20th Ave. S., Nashville, 615-321-3043; www.pansouth.net
International. Dinner, late-night. $36-85

★★★★CAPITOL GRILLE
231 Sixth Ave. N., Nashville, 615-345-7116; www.thehermitagehotel.com
Located in the elegant Hermitage Hotel, the Capitol Grille offers an equally posh dining experience. Near the state capitol, the Grille hosts many a power lunch, but it's also a popular spot for theatergoers who want to enjoy a fine meal before a show at the nearby Tennessee Performing Arts Center. Executive chef Tyler Brown oversees creative Southern cuisine; the menu is full of such dishes as Niman Ranch pork with sweet potato juice and veal loin with root vegetables. Truffle mac and cheese and spicy fried green tomato with spicy pepper relish are just a few of the restaurant's irresistible side dishes, and desserts like flourless chocolate ganache torte end the evening on a perfect note. Located downstairs in the historic Hermitage Hotel, this Southern-influenced restaurant offers a different menu each week.
American, Southern. Breakfast, lunch, dinner, late-night, Sunday brunch. $36-85

★★DARFONS RESTAURANT & LOUNGE
2810 Elm Hill Pike, Nashville, 615-889-3032; www.darfonsrestaurant.com
American. Lunch, dinner. Closed Sunday. $16-35

★★★F. SCOTT'S
2210 Crestmoor Road, Nashville, 615-269-5861; www.fscotts.com
This large restaurant gives off a friendly, elegant vibe, thanks to several small dining rooms. Popular jazz musicians play nightly, and chef Will Uhlhorn's menu features contemporary American dishes such as seared New York strip with spicy pecan sweet potato hash, squash casserole and thyme chive Barnaise, and spicy cornmeal-dusted pan-fried trout.
American. Dinner. Bar. $36-85

★★GERMANTOWN CAFÉ
1200 Fifth Ave. N., Nashville, 615-242-3226; www.germantowncafe.com
American. Lunch, dinner, Sunday brunch. $16-35

★★LOVELESS CAFÉ
8400 Highway 100, Nashville, 615-646-9700; www.lovelesscafe.com
American, Southern. Breakfast, lunch, dinner. $15 and under.

★★MAD PLATTER
1239 Sixth Ave. North, Nashville, 615-242-2563;
American, International. Lunch, dinner. $16-35

★★MARGOT CAFÉ

1017 Woodland St., Nashville, 615-227-4668; www.margotcafe.com
Mediterranean. Dinner, Sunday brunch. Closed Monday. $16-35

★★MERCHANTS

401 Broadway, Nashville, 615-254-1892; www.merchantsrestaurant.com
American. Lunch, dinner. $36-85

★★MIDTOWN CAFÉ

102 19th Ave. S., Nashville, 615-320-7176; www.midtowncafe.com
Southern. Lunch, dinner. $36-85

★MONELL'S

1235 Sixth Ave. N., Nashville, 615-248-4747
Southern. Breakfast, lunch, dinner. $15 and under.

★★★THE OLD HICKORY STEAKHOUSE

2800 Opryland Drive, Nashville, 615-871-6848; www.gaylordopryland.com
Located in the Opryland Hotel, this special-occasion steakhouse offers refined dining in an atmosphere of dark wooden furniture and dimly lit rooms.
Designed as an elegant plantation-style house, the restaurant offers wrap-
around porch seating. Elegant table settings and beautiful gardens complete
the setting. The restaurant also offers a cigar lounge and special-event wine
tastings. In addition, there is an artisanal cheese cart with 25 varieties of
cheeses and a large wine selection.
Steak. Dinner. $86 and up.

★★★THE PALM

140 Fifth Ave. S., Nashville, 615-742-7256; www.thepalm.com
A great spot for star-gazing—not the celestial kind—and beef-eating, The
Palm is one of Nashville's most popular scenes. Serious-sized steaks, chops
and seafood dishes grace the menu at this legendary steakhouse. Also found
among the meaty menu selections are Italian-tinged dishes like linguine and
clams, spaghetti marinara and tomato capri salad. Going strong since 1926,
The Palm has expanded its empire to 25 cities across the country, including
Philadelphia, Las Vegas and Dallas.
Steak. Lunch, dinner. $36-85

★★★RUTH'S CHRIS STEAK HOUSE

2100 W. End Ave., Nashville, 615-320-0163; www.ruthschris.com
Born from a single New Orleans restaurant that Ruth Fertel bought in 1965
for $22,000, the Ruth's Chris Steak House chain has made it to the top of
every steak lover's list. Aged prime Midwestern beef is broiled to your liking
and served on a heated plate, sizzling in butter, a staple ingredient used gen-
erously in most entrees. Sides like creamed spinach and fresh asparagus with
hollandaise are not to be missed, and seven different potato preparations,
from a one-pound baked potato with everything to au gratin potatoes with
cream sauce and cheese are offered. The rich, dark wood walls and dim lighting give the dining room a cozy feel, making it perfect for special dinners.
Steak. Dinner. $36-85

★SITAR INDIAN RESTAURANT
116 21st Ave. N., Nashville, 615-321-8889; www.sitarnashville.com
Indian. Lunch, dinner. $15 and under.

★★SPERRY'S
5109 Harding Road, Nashville, 615-353-0809; www.sperrys.com
Seafood, steak. Dinner. $36-85

★★STOCK-YARD
901 Second Ave. N., Nashville, 615-255-6464; www.stock-yardrestaurant.com
Steak. Dinner. $36-85

★★SUNSET GRILL
2001 Belcourt Ave., Nashville, 615-386-3663, 866-496-3663; www.sunsetgrill.com
International. Lunch, dinner, late-night. $16-35

★★TAYST
2100 21st Ave. S., Nashville, 615-383-1953; www.taystrestaurant.com
American, Mediterranean. Dinner. Closed Sunday-Monday. $16-35

★★TIN ANGEL
3201 W. End Ave., Nashville, 615-298-3444; www.tinangel.net
International. Lunch, dinner, Sunday brunch. $16-35

★★★VALENTINO'S
1907 W. End Ave., Nashville, 615-327-0148; www.valentinosnashville.com
A popular spot for romantic dinners, Valentino's is set in a charming old house with several dining areas that feature beautiful Old World décor. The menu features rustic Italian fare such as vegetable ravioli, farfalle with salmon and chicken Marsala.
Italian. Lunch, dinner. Closed Sunday. $36-85

★★ZOLA
3001 W. End Ave., Nashville, 615-320-7778; www.restaurantzola.com
Mediterranean. Dinner. $36-85

NATCHEZ TRACE STATE RESORT PARK
Named for the pioneer trail that connected Nashville and Natchez, Miss., this 48,000-acre park is the largest recreation area in western Tennessee. If the near limitless outdoor recreation is not enough to attract you, the park is also home to a pecan tree that is said to be the world's third largest. Four lakes provide swimming, fishing, boating (launch, rentals), nature trails, backpacking, picnicking, a playground and a recreation lodge. Tent and trailer sites, cabins and an inn are also at the park.

WHERE TO STAY
★COUNTRY HEARTH INN & SUITES
21045 Highway 22 N., Wildersville, 731-968-2532, 800-780-7234;
www.countryhearth.com
40 rooms. Complimentary breakfast. $61-150

★PIN OAK LODGE
567 Pin Oak Lodge Lane, Wildersville, 731-968-8176, 800-250-8616; www.tnstateparks.com
47 rooms. Restaurant. Complimentary breakfast. Pool. $61-150

OAK RIDGE
See also Knoxville
Oak Ridge was built during World War II to house Manhattan Project workers involved in the production of uranium 235 (the first atomic bomb's explosive element). Once one of the most secret places in the United States, Oak Ridge is now host to thousands who come each year, drawn by the mysteries of nuclear energy. Built by the U.S. government, Oak Ridge is known for scientific research and development. Although many of the installations are still classified, the city has not been restricted since March 1949.

WHAT TO SEE
AMERICAN MUSEUM OF SCIENCE AND ENERGY
300 S. Tulane Ave., Oak Ridge, 865-576-3200; www.amse.org
Much cooler than physics class, this museum is one of the world's largest energy exhibitions. Here you'll learn about fossil fuels, energy alternatives, resources and research through hands-on exhibits, displays, models, films, games and live demonstrations.
Monday-Saturday 9 a.m.-5 p.m., Sunday 1-5 p.m.

CHILDREN'S MUSEUM OF OAK RIDGE
461 W. Outer Drive, Oak Ridge, 865-482-1074; www.childrensmuseumofoakridge.org
Hands-on exhibits and displays include the International Gallery, Discovery Lab, Playscape, Nature Walk, Pioneer Living and Oak Ridge history. Performances, exhibits, seminars, workshops are also on offer.
September-May, Tuesday-Friday 9 a.m.-5 p.m., Saturday 10 a.m.-4 p.m., Sunday 1-4 p.m.; June-August, Monday-Friday 9 a.m.-5 p.m., Saturday 10 a.m.-4 p.m., Sunday 1-4 p.m.

FROZEN HEAD STATE PARK
964 Flat Fork Road, Wartburg, 37887, 423-346-3318; www.state.tn.us
The park takes up more than 12,000 acres in Cumberland Mountains. It offers trout fishing, hiking trails, picnicking, a playground, primitive camping and a visitor center.
Daily 8 a.m.-sunset.

INTERNATIONAL FRIENDSHIP BELL
Badger Avenue, Oak Ridge
A symbol of everlasting peace, the bell was designed to celebrate the dedication of Manhattan Project workers. Daily.

OAK RIDGE ART CENTER
201 Badger Ave., Oak Ridge, 865-482-1441; www.oakridgeartcenter.org
The center holds a permanent collection of original paintings, drawings and prints.
Tuesday-Friday 9 a.m.-5 p.m., Saturday-Monday 1-4 p.m.

UNIVERSITY OF TENNESSEE ARBORETUM

901 S. Illinois Ave., Oak Ridge, 865-483-3571; www.forestry.tennessee.edu
This arboretum is part of the University of Tennessee Forestry Experimental Station. More than 1,000 species of trees, shrubs and flowering plants thrive on 250 acres. Self-guided tours and a visitor center are available.
Monday-Friday 8 a.m.-noon, 1-5 p.m.

WHERE TO STAY
★DAYS INN

206 S. Illinois Ave., Oak Ridge, 865-483-5615, 800-329-7466; www.daysinn.com
80 rooms. Complimentary breakfast. Pool. Pets accepted. $61-150

★★DOUBLETREE HOTEL

215 S. Illinois Ave., Oak Ridge, 865-481-2468; www.doubletree.com
167 rooms. Restaurant, bar. Business center. Fitness center. Pool. Pets accepted. $61-150

★HAMPTON INN

208 S. Illinois Ave., Oak Ridge, 865-482-7889, 800-426-7866; www.hamptoninn.com
60 rooms. Complimentary breakfast. Business center. Pool. $61-150

PARIS

See also Jackson
Do not let the 60-foot replica of the Eiffel Tower fool you: Paris, Tenn., is a long way from its namesake. But this small town near Kentucky Lake is a great place for outdoor recreation and a quiet stroll down the downtown streets. If you are in town in late April, you will enjoy the self-titled "World's Biggest Fish Fry," when revelers consume about 12,500 pounds of catfish.

WHAT TO SEE
NATHAN BEDFORD FORREST STATE PARK

1825 Pilot Knob Road, Eva, 731-584-6356; www.state.tn.us
On the west bank of Kentucky Lake, a monument marks the spot where, in 1864, Confederate General Forrest set up artillery. Undetected by Union forces, the hidden batteries destroyed both the Union base on the opposite shore and its protective warships on the Tennessee River. The area is now an 800-acre park offering fishing and canoe access to the lake. Nature trails and programs, backpacking, picnicking, a playground, camping and a group lodge are available. Trace Creek Annex, located across Kentucky Lake, interprets a portion of the military history of the area.
Daily 7 a.m.-10 p.m.

SPECIAL EVENT
WORLD'S BIGGEST FISH FRY

Henry County Fairgrounds, Paris; www.paristnchamber.com
Yes, partygoers consume about 12,500 pounds of catfish at this festival. When they are not eating, they enjoy a rodeo, a square dance and contests (including a catfish race).
Last week in April.

WHERE TO STAY
★ECONO LODGE PARIS
1297 E. Wood St., Paris, 731-642-8881;
98 rooms. Complimentary breakfast. Pool. $61-150

PIGEON FORGE
See also Gatlinburg, Sevierville
Located in the shadow of the Smokies, this resort town is a popular destination for vacationing families. The town has everything from outlet malls and the Dollywood theme park to theaters and go-cart tracks.

WHAT TO SEE
THE COMEDY BARN
2775 Parkway, Pigeon Forge, 865-428-5222; www.comedybarn.com
This family comedy variety show has magicians, jugglers, comedians and live music.
March-December, daily.

DOLLYWOOD
1020 Dollywood Lane, Pigeon Forge, 865-428-9488; www.dollywood.com
Dolly Parton's entertainment park provides more than 40 musical shows daily. It also has more than 30 rides and attractions and 70 shops and restaurants. Daily.

FLYAWAY INDOOR SKYDIVING
3106 Parkway, Pigeon Forge, 877-293-0639; www.flyawayindoorskydiving.com
A vertical wind tunnel simulates skydiving. The instructor assists participants in the flight chamber and explains how to maneuver the body to soar, turn and descend. There's also an observation gallery.
March-November, daily.

MEMORIES THEATRE
2141 Parkway, Pigeon Forge, 865-428-7852, 800-325-3078;
www.memoriestheatre.com
Each show is a tribute to musical legends of the past and present, such as Tom Jones, Cher, Elvis Presley, Kenny Rogers and Buddy Holly.
Monday-Saturday 8 p.m.

THE OLD MILL
2944 Middle Creek Road, Pigeon Forge, 865-453-4628; www.old-mill.com
This water-powered mill has been in continuous operation since 1830, grinding cornmeal, grits, whole wheat, rye and buckwheat flours. The dam falls are illuminated at night.
April-November, Monday-Saturday.

SMOKY MOUNTAIN CAR MUSEUM
2970 Parkway, Pigeon Forge, 865-453-3433
Cloud nine for car lovers, this museum houses more than 30 gas, electric and steam autos, including Hank Williams Jr.'s "Silver Dollar" car, James

Bond's "007" Aston Martin, Al Capone's bulletproof Cadillac, the patrol car of Sheriff Buford Pusser from the movie *Walking Tall* and Elvis Presley's Mercedes.

May-October, daily.

WHERE TO STAY
★BEST WESTERN PLAZA INN
3755 Parkway, Pigeon Forge, 865-453-5538, 800-232-5656; www.bwplazainn.com
201 rooms. Complimentary breakfast. $61-150

★★HOLIDAY INN
3230 Parkway, Pigeon Forge, 865-428-2700, 800-782-3119; www.4lodging.com
210 rooms. Restaurant. Fitness center. Pool. Pets accepted. $61-150

★HOTEL PIGEON FORGE INN & SUITES
2179 Parkway, Pigeon Forge, 865-428-7305, 866-896-2950;
www.hotel-pigeonforge.com
123 rooms. Complimentary breakfast. $61-150

★QUALITY INN
3756 Parkway, Pigeon Forge, 865-453-3490, 800-925-4443;
www.qualityinnpigeonforge.com
127 rooms. Complimentary breakfast. Restaurant. Pool. $61-150

WHERE TO EAT
★OLD MILL
164 Old Mill Ave., Pigeon Forge, 865-429-3463; www.old-mill.com
American. Breakfast, lunch, dinner. $16-35

SEVIERVILLE
See also Gatlinburg, Pigeon Forge
Founded as part of the independent state of Franklin, the town and surrounding county were named for John Sevier, who later became the first governor of Tennessee. Minutes from the Great Smoky Mountain National Park, the town is a good base for people who want to enjoy some of Tennessee's most scenic land.

WHAT TO SEE
DOUGLAS DAM AND LAKE
Sevierville, 11 miles northeast off Highway 66, 865-453-3889; www.tva.gov/
This Tennessee Valley Authority dam on the French Broad River was built on a 24-hour work schedule during World War II to furnish power for national defense. It impounds a lake that's 43 miles long with 555 miles of shoreline. At Douglas, you can go swimming, fishing, boating and camping. Daily.

FORBIDDEN CAVERNS
455 Blowing Cave Road, Sevierville, 865-453-5972; www.forbiddencavern.com
Tennessee has more caves than any other state, and the tour through the Forbidden Caverns is a spectacular show, even if it does get a little help from

manmade additions, like lights and stereophonic sound presentation.
April-November, daily 10 a.m.-6 p.m.

NASCAR SPEEDPARK

1545 Parkway, Sevierville, 865-908-5500; www.nascarspeedpark.com
Raring for some time on the racetrack? You can get into the action—and into the cars—at NASCAR SpeedPark. Eight tracks offer levels ranging from the quarter-mile Smoky Mountain Speedway for drivers 16 and older, down to the Baby Bristol, a 200-foot starter track for kids. Or climb into a mock stock car and experience centrifugal forces, turns and crash impacts as you "drive" a full-motion NASCAR Silicon Motor Speedway simulator. Other attractions include a state-of-the-art arcade, kiddie rides, an indoor climbing wall, miniature golf and bumper boats.

SMOKY MOUNTAIN DEER FARM

478 Happy Hollow Lane, Sevierville, 865-428-3337; www.deerfarmzoo.com
The petting zoo includes deer, zebra, pygmy goats and llamas. There are also pony rides and horseback riding.
Daily 10 a.m.-5:30 p.m.

WHERE TO STAY
★QUALITY INN MOUNTAIN RIVER SUITES

860 Winfield Dunn Parkway, Sevierville, 865-428-5519, 800-441-0311;
www.qualityinn.com
97 rooms. Complimentary breakfast. Pool. Pets accepted. $61-150

★RAMADA

4010 Parkway, Sevierville, 865-453-1823, 800-272-6232; www.ramada.com
134 rooms. Complimentary breakfast. Pool. Pets accepted. $61-150

WHERE TO EAT
★APPLEWOOD FARM HOUSE

240 Apple Valley Road, Sevierville, 865-428-1222
American. Breakfast, lunch, dinner. $15 and under.

SHILOH NATIONAL MILITARY PARK

Bitter, bloody Shiloh was the first major Civil War battle in the West and one of the fiercest in history. In two days, April 6 and 7, 1862, nearly 24,000 men were killed, wounded or missing. The South's failure to destroy General Grant's army opened the way for the attack on and siege of Vicksburg, Miss., but it was also a costly battle for the North.

Grant's Army of the Tennessee, numbering almost 40,000, was camped near Pittsburg Landing and Shiloh Church, waiting for the Army of the Ohio under General Don Carlos Buell to attack the Confederates who, they thought, were near Corinth, Mississippi, 20 miles south. But the brilliant Southern General Albert Sidney Johnston surprised Grant with an attack at dawn on April 6.

Although Johnston was mortally wounded on the first day, the Southerners successfully pushed the Union Army back and nearly captured their supply base at Pittsburg Landing. On the second day, however, the Northerners, reinforced by the 17,918-man Army of the Ohio, counterattacked and forced the Confederates to retreat toward Corinth.

At Shiloh, one of the first tent field hospitals ever established helped save the lives of many Union and Confederate soldiers. Among the men who fought this dreadful battle were John Wesley Powell, who lost an arm but later went down the Colorado River by boat and became head of the U.S. Geological Survey; James A. Garfield, 20th president of the United States; Ambrose Bierce, famous satirist and short-story writer; and Henry Morton Stanley, who later uttered the famous phrase, "Dr. Livingstone, I presume."

WHAT TO SEE
NATIONAL CEMETERY
Savannah
The cemetery sits on 10 acres on a bluff overlooking Pittsburg Landing and the Tennessee River. Buried here are about 3,800 soldiers, two-thirds of whom are unidentified. Daily.

TOWNSEND
See also Gatlinburg, Maryville

WHAT TO SEE
TUCKALEECHEE CAVERNS
825 Caverns Road, Townsend, 865-448-2274; www.tuckaleecheecaverns.com
This cathedral-like main chamber is the largest cavern room in the eastern U.S. There are drapery formations, a walkway over subterranean streams and flowstone falls.
Daily 9 a.m.-6 p.m.

WHERE TO STAY
★★★RICHMONT INN B&B
220 Winterberry Lane, Townsend, 865-448-6751, 866-267-7086; www.richmontinn.com
Just 10 minutes from the entrance to Great Smoky Mountains National Park, this charming inn affords an elegant escape. The comfort and coziness of the rustic accents, such as wide-planked and slate floors, high exposed-beam ceilings and country furniture, are enhanced by the formal, attentive service.
14 rooms. Children over 12 years only. Restaurant. Complimentary breakfast. $61-150

★VALLEY VIEW LODGE
Highway 321, Townsend, 865-448-2237, 800-292-4844; www.valleyviewlodge.com
138 rooms. Complimentary breakfast. Pool. Pets accepted. $61-150

INDEX

★★★★★ INDEX

305

M

★★★★★ INDEX

319

N

O

★★★★★ INDEX

327

ALABAMA

ARKANSAS

KENTUCKY

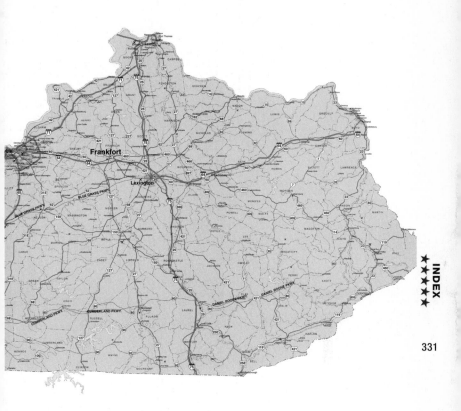

LOUISIANA

TENNESSEE

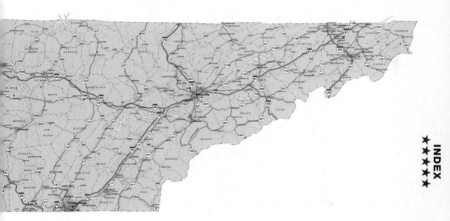

MISSISSIPPI

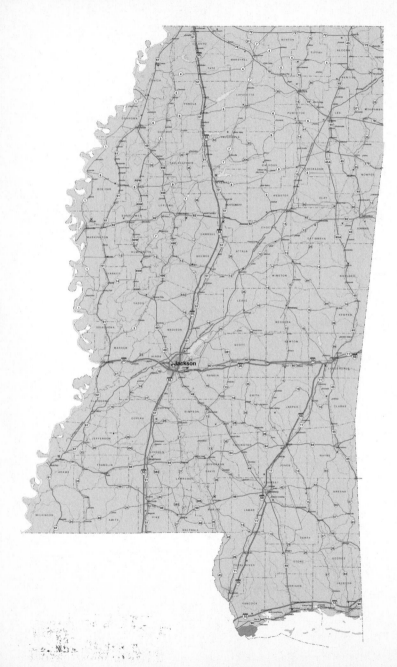